The Girls' History and Culture Reader
The Nineteenth Century

The Girls' History and Culture Reader

The Nineteenth Century

EDITED BY

Miriam Forman-Brunell and Leslie Paris

UNIVERSITY OF ILLINOIS PRESS

Urbana, Chicago, and Springfield

Library of Congress Cataloging-in-Publication Data
The girls' history and culture reader : the nineteenth century /
edited by Miriam Forman-Brunell and Leslie Paris.
p.   cm.
Includes bibliographical references and index.
ISBN 978-0-252-03574-6 (cloth : alk. paper)
ISBN 978-0-252-07765-4 (pbk. : alk. paper)
1. Girls—United States—History—19th century.
2. Girls—United States—Social conditions.
3. United States—Social life and customs—19th century.
I. Forman-Brunell, Miriam, 1955– II. Paris, Leslie.
HQ777.G576   2011
305.23082'097309034—dc22   2010020847

For our children,
Miriam and Noah Paris and
Zoë and Perry Brunell,
who have brought so much joy
into our lives.

Contents

Credits

The Girls' History and Culture Reader

The Nineteenth Century

In the older times it was seldom said to little
girls, as it always has been said to boys, that they
ought to have some definite plan, while they were
children, what to be and do when they were grown
up. [. .] But girls, as well as boys, must often have
been conscious of their own peculiar capabilities—
must have desired to cultivate and make use of their
individual powers. When I was growing up, they
had already begun to be encouraged to do so.
—*Lucy Larcom, 1824–1893, recalling her girlhood.*[1]

Introduction

As a young child in the small coastal town of Beverly, Massachusetts,
Lucy Larcom attended public school, was a prolific reader, and had free time
to play. Her father was a retired merchant and sea captain; her mother took
charge of raising ten children, of whom Lucy was next to youngest. But when
Lucy's father died, her life took a dramatic turn. Her widowed mother, unable
adequately to support the remaining children at home, moved the family to
the new mill town of Lowell, Massachusetts, to run a boardinghouse. At the
age of eleven, to help support her family, Lucy left school to become a factory
worker at a textile mill.[2]

In the nineteenth century, girlhood took many forms, reflecting the nation's diversity, its divisions, and the particular circumstances of individual girls'
lives. The experiences of native-born rural white girls, of African American
girls living as slaves in the South prior to the Civil War, of immigrant girls in
the growing cities, and of Native American girls living on the (shifting) western
frontier were appreciably different. Girls' varied lives and expectations reflected
their particular racial, class, ethnic, and regional backgrounds; their divergent

legal statuses; generational cohorts; and individual family circumstances. Had Lucy's father survived her childhood, or had her mother been more successful in her business venture, Lucy would undoubtedly have enjoyed some of the new opportunities available to middle-class daughters. Middle-class girls had increasing leisure time and extended formal educations, sometimes through high school and even college; these signs of refinement enhanced their families' class status. However, the great majority of nineteenth-century American girls made far more direct contributions to their families' well-being.

Across many variations, nineteenth-century girls shared certain commonalities. As females and as children they were at once marginal and central to American political and social life. Girls had little access to power, and even the most elite girls did not expect to attain the same citizenship rights at adulthood (such as voting rights) as did boys of their class. Yet during a century in which adult women carved out new roles for themselves as reformers, writers, spiritual advocates, and industrial workers, girls found inspiration in new models for female activism at home and in the public sphere. Girls were also the focus of significant public attention. Parents worked to socialize their daughters toward their future roles as good wives, mothers, and workers. Reformers, who represented girls as bellwethers of the health of the nation, vacillated between describing them as innocents in need of protection in an increasingly predatory world, and expressing anxiety about girls' independence and their sexual curiosity. And as Larcom suggests, over the course of the century increasing numbers of girls were also encouraged "to cultivate and make use of their individual powers," and—within limits—to follow their own interests. While middle-class girls benefited most from a new ideal of protected childhood, girls of all kinds worked to find their own voices in varied circumstances.

Girls were at once protected and exploited, restrained and adventurous, relatively unseen and highly exposed, complex realities that are illuminated in *The Girls' History and Culture Reader*. Bringing together influential scholarship that places girls at the center of historical analysis and that offers critical insights into the historical experiences of girls, the essays in the chapters that follow showcase the diverse ways in which age and gender intersected in the lives of nineteenth-century girls; explore thematic concerns that have shaped historical research on American girlhood; and illustrate a range of methodological approaches to girls' history. Collectively, these chapters trace a number of pivotal issues: girls' patterns of socialization and education; their historical experiences of work and play; their practices of consumption and production; the relation between girls' lived realities and various discursive representations of girlhood; girls' efforts to balance adults' expectations with their own quests for personal autonomy; girls' negotiation of their bodies and sexual identities (which were also the subject of particular adult anxiety and fascination); and their sense of themselves both as girls and as members of broader communities.

Girlhood is never merely a biological stage. Rather, as these essays collectively make clear, it is a period of life whose meaning and endpoint have been made in particular historical contexts. The term encompasses both cultural constructions of girlhood and girls' own lived experiences in particular historical circumstances. The parameters of girlhood have been defined as much by legal designations, social practices, girls' degree of biological maturation, and broader ideological and political forces as by actual age. As Jane Hunter has argued, the very term *girl* shifted significantly in meaning in the nineteenth century; in the early years of the century, a girl was a female inferior of age and status, but by the end of the century the term had acquired far more positive connotations, so much so that middle-class older adolescents and young women chose to see themselves as adventurous "girls" instead of virtuous "young ladies."[3] While many long-standing adult ideas about girlhood persisted, these ideas were continually challenged and reinterpreted, both by adults and by girls themselves. The *Reader* aims to deepen our understanding of these varied processes in shaping girlhood, as well as the import of generation as a historical force in American culture.

Girls' History Scholarship

The field of girls' history is itself relatively young. It owes its most significant scholarly debt to women's history and gender history, connected fields that have since the 1960s made gender a central category of historical analysis, and that have made possible remarkable access to women's lives in varied historical contexts. However, gender historians have traditionally privileged the adult years of the life span without reflecting extensively on the significance of age. Girls sometimes appear in passing in book chapters on women's early education or socialization, but more often as preface to rather than as the focal point of scholarly work. While in monographs girls appear as the subjects of first book chapters meant to anchor the historical experiences of grown women, in women's history textbooks girls are usually only supporting characters: the objects of women's reform efforts, for instance, or older adolescents entering courtships.

The complexity of the relation between girlhood and womanhood calls for more concerted scholarly attention. What did girlhood mean, for instance, to the native-born "Lowell Mill girls" who were some of the first industrial workers of the 1820s and 1830s? "Mill girls" tended to be young, and some were as young as eleven-year-old Lucy Larcom, but most were older adolescents and unmarried young women workers, ages sixteen to twenty-five, who often called themselves girls or were known as girls. These "girl" identities denoted their inferior roles, represented their supposedly protected status in relation to ostensibly patriarchal employers, and protected their respectability as unmarried workers living away from home. Yet to speak of this cohort as "girls" may risk obscuring the histories of younger girls who also labored in the new industrial economy, but who have remained marginal figures in labor history and women's and gender history.

The essays in the *Reader*, by speculating on what is particular to girls' experience of gender and age, demonstrate how dynamically these categories have operated to shape female experience. Issues that might seem of greater relevance to adult women than girls—such as sexuality, work, community relations, and politics—also resonated centrally in the lives of girls, but age significantly shaped girls' perspectives and their relative access to power and opportunity. For example, new ideas about girlhood and womanhood emerged during various waves of reform-minded social activism, but while girls identified with their mothers' quests for self-definition in certain respects, the two generations were sometimes at odds concerning their respective roles and aspirations. Standard periodizations of women's history (and American history more broadly) have tended to be less informative about these specific generational distinctions.

Nonetheless, the field of girls' history owes a significant debt to women's history scholarship, and to feminist scholarship more generally. Most historians of the "new" women's history initially focused on adults, but some pioneering historians examined the early years in women's lives. During the 1970s, for example, Ann D. Gordon and Carroll Smith-Rosenberg investigated the socialization and education of middle-class northeastern girls of the late eighteenth and nineteenth centuries.[4] At the same time, feminist scholars in other fields were pursuing similar research agendas and speaking across disciplines. For instance, the work of sociologist and psychoanalytic theorist Nancy Chodorow, which focused on the importance of the mother-daughter bond, provided an analytic frame for Nancy M. Theriot's historical exploration of nineteenth-century girls' socialization by (and in relation to) their mothers. While psychologist Carol Gilligan pursued questions about American girls' moral development in a study published in the 1980s, Joan Jacobs Brumberg historicized anorexia nervosa in her examination of girls' refusal to eat.[5]

Anne Scott MacLeod's 1984 study of preadolescent girls' defiance of adults' gendered prescriptions presaged a number of other important studies of the early 1990s onward exploring the ways in which girlhood itself was socially and culturally constructed. Karen Calvert's material culture analysis of childhood from the colonial era through the nineteenth century contributed to this endeavor by making gender a central category of analysis. Miriam Forman-Brunell's history of dolls and their uses brought to light the struggles that ensued between girls and adults over the meanings of girlhood in nineteenth- and early-twentieth-century America. Other scholars blurred the boundaries between history and literature in their research on girls' peer cultures, their play, and their participation in popular culture. Jane Hunter and Barbara Sicherman both explored middle-class Victorian girls' self-definition through reading and writing, and literary scholar Lynne Vallone described nineteenth-century "girls' culture" as a central space of female definition. Expanding on Vallone's theme, Sherrie Inness argued influentially that the new interdisciplinary field of "girls' culture" studies offered a means of understanding gender and society more broadly.[6]

Similar concerns energized other feminist scholars who began to pursue specifically girl-focused research agendas. Much "girls' studies" research developed in fields that were more contemporary in their orientation, such as cultural studies, media studies, and sociology. Communications studies scholars in particular were influenced by cultural studies scholar Angela McRobbie, who had conducted ethnographic research on British girls' youth cultures of the 1970s, and by British cultural studies scholar Carolyn Steedman, whose 1987 memoir of her own working-class girlhood was simultaneously theoretical and autobiographical.[7] Whether in history, literature, or media studies, scholars of girls explored themes (such as girls' friendship networks and popular culture) that more conventional scholars traditionally considered frivolous or unserious. Through their individual scholarship and in recent encyclopedic works such as *Girlhood in America* (2001) and *Girl Culture* (2007), these new scholars showed how such research offered a unique lens through which to assess girls' political identity and cultural agency.[8]

Over the past two decades, historical work on girls has also been strengthened by the new children's history, which has focused extensively on age as a category of historical analysis and, to varying degrees, has considered children's gendered socialization. This literature initially focused primarily upon boys, but has expanded dramatically since the 1990s, allowing girls' history scholars to make use of many new synthetic histories of nineteenth-century childhood and youth. As this scholarship makes clear, childhood provides a unique vantage point from which to reflect upon broader nineteenth-century movements, including the growth of cities, the emergent industrial economy, immigrant experience, the rising importance of formal education, the economic insecurity that pervaded even middle-class life, and shifting racial and gender relations.[9]

The Girls' History and Culture Reader aims to set the strengths of these various modes of inquiry into conversation with one another: demonstrating how age matters as a category of analysis for gender history, offering interdisciplinary approaches to girlhood, and providing material for more historically grounded girls' studies scholarship in associated fields. The essays that follow share an interest in questions of individual and collective agency and the structures within which girls are raised. They seek to broaden understandings of what constitutes the political, what is entailed by work and play, how sexualities are formed and experienced, the importance of peers, and how sites of socialization such as education and consumer culture function at once as tools of adult-led socialization and as vehicles for girls' own sense of power.

The scholars whose work appears in this volume provide a range of approaches to the particular methodological challenges confronting girl-centered historical research. Put simply, most historical archives do not specifically collect materials on girls. This is a reflection both of girls' marginalization as subjects of historical research and of the paucity of information on girls in traditional forms of historical documentation. Nineteenth-century girls generally had little access to public platforms such as newspapers or speeches, very few were polled, relatively few wrote about their experiences, and fewer still had those writings preserved. Those who did garner attention or leave a historical record tended to be from a small, well-educated elite, or, alternatively, were the working-class subjects of middle-class reformers' efforts at charity or reform. To uncover girls' worlds and the institutions through which they were socialized, the authors of the essays collected in the *Reader* have culled a wide range of sources. These include court records; the institutional records of organizations that oversaw girls; girls' personal diaries and women's oral history reflections on their youth; the cultural realm of novels, music, magazines, toys, and school publications. Girls' history scholars also interpret such behaviors as play and resistance to authority as primary sources that elucidate girls' unique historical position and practices.

It is our hope that the *Reader* will help to facilitate the movement of girls as historical subjects from the margins to the mainstream. At present, little of this scholarship has permeated standard historical frameworks. In history college texts that introduce fields and characterize canons, girls still remain largely outside the scope of defining historiographic essays and authoritative Americanist anthologies. When nineteenth-century girls appear in standard surveys of the United States, they generally do so only in passing. Yet girls are in some ways particularly representative of nineteenth-century Americans. In 1800, when the average age of the population was 16, the nation was demographically as well as imaginatively youthful. A century later, forty percent of the population was under the age of eighteen.[10] A deeper consideration of childhood and adolescence, and a greater acknowledgment of generation as a historical force in American culture and society, can help to propel girls out of a room of their own and into standard historiographic essays, master narratives, and authoritative anthologies as a necessary element, not simply as an optional and charmingly girlish addition to the canon.

Major Themes of The Reader

The essays that follow consider varied possibilities and enduring constraints in the lives of nineteenth-century girls. Covering almost thirty years of scholarship, *The Girls' History and Culture Reader* brings together classic early work and newer scholarship in the field. Several of the chapters in the *Reader* were originally published in volumes focused primarily upon women; Carroll Smith-Rosenberg, Deborah Gray White, and Christine Stansell, for example, are all better known as scholars of grown women. The *Reader* pairs these selections with a number of more recent essays specifically by girls' history scholars. This mix seeks to recenter more canonical, ostensibly women-centered works, to situate the newer, explicitly girl-centered ones historiographically, and to address how girls' experiences overlap with and differ from those of adult women.

The historical literature on girls from which the *Reader* draws has tended to overrepresent white, middle-class, northeastern girls. To some extent, this volume reflects the field's biases, but it aims to illuminate a more diverse cross section in order to demonstrate similarities and differences among girls. Girls' age, race, ethnicity, sexual identities, religious and regional backgrounds, as well as their individual personalities, were significant factors in shaping their experiences and marking their horizons. A few of the essays included in this collection briefly consider boys as well, in order to more clearly demonstrate the gendered dimensions of the historical categories of childhood and adolescence. These various comparisons help us to rethink both the broader historical terms of girlhood and the particularities of smaller groups of girls in particular circumstances, casting light on the experiences of millions of young Americans who have tended to appear in the historical record only at the margins.

The roughly chronologically organized essays address several major themes essential to the study of girls. First is the significance of age itself: how various stages of girlhood were culturally demarcated, and how these stages mattered to girls. How did the transitions of girlhood (for example, from childhood into adolescence) vary by region, race, ethnicity, or generation? How did puberty serve to delineate girls' social position, or even to mark the end of girlhood? As the following essays suggest, girlhood is a series of stages in the life cycle, not a single stage, and it has spanned important developmental and physical divides. The age at which girls could work, were freed or pressured to be sexually active or to marry, and attended formal schools varied over time and from place to place, so the demarcation of the end of girlhood and the beginning of womanhood was never consistent.

Puberty represented a critical juncture in all girls' lives. As Deborah Gray White argues in "The Life Cycle of the Female Slave," the social realms of enslaved African American girls and boys were not differentiated by sex until puberty. At adolescence, a strict sex role separation ensued. Enslaved female adolescents entered a sex-segregated "female world" within which, White demonstrates, their productive and reproductive labor was shaped by the economic and sexual imperatives of the planters who owned them. Anne Scott MacLeod's "The *Caddie Woodlawn* Syndrome: American Girlhood in the Nineteenth Century" also draws an important distinction between the lives of younger girls and adolescents. MacLeod argues that girls had significant personal freedom prior to adolescence. Drawing on fiction and white girls' autobiographies, MacLeod notes that these girls keenly felt the loss of autonomy as their horizons were increasingly restricted in adolescence.

As a number of the essays in this collection suggest, middle-class girls experienced a gradual lengthening of girlhood, especially its final stage. Their parents increasingly emphasized companionate parenting practices, characterized by longer periods of financial support and more emphasis on emotional connection. Carroll Smith-Rosenberg's "The Female World of Love and Ritual: Relations Between Women in Nineteenth-Century America" argues that while girls experienced significant restrictions on their relations with older boys and men as they grew older, their lives were also characterized by intimate emotional bonds among girls and women, both in their extended families and at school. As Smith-Rosenberg suggests, middle-class adolescent girls' friendships were marked by a high degree of freedom of expression, both emotionally and physically.

Schooling and literacy represent a second critical theme for scholars of nineteenth-century girls. In the early nineteenth century, most American girls were educated at home. The meaning of that education varied considerably. Most free girls learned to read, and all girls acquired the domestic skills they would need to run households as adults. But by the 1830s, a small number of northeastern girls also attended private girls' seminaries and coeducational "common schools." By the second half of the century, a small but growing number of girls attending the nation's expanding public high schools went on to enroll at women's colleges and coeducational public universities. By the end of the century, twice as many girls as boys attended public high schools.[11]

These shifts speak to the rising importance and availability of formal (and extended) education, especially for middle-class girls; education not only offered exciting new opportunities to such girls, it signaled their class status as girls at a remove from paid (or forcible) employment. As Anya Jabour explains in "'Grown Girls, Highly Cultivated': Female Education in an Antebellum Southern Family," education was part of southern upper-class white families' strategies for preparing their daughters for womanhood. Drawing on the history of one such family, Jabour demonstrates that elite southern parents valued some degree of formal education up to adolescence as part of their daughters' training in social, religious, and personal improvement. But as enthusiasm for educating republican women declined in the 1820s and 1830s, the curriculum shifted; the education of the family's youngest daughters emphasized domestic instruction and community benevolence over the scholastic training that had been the focus of the eldest sister.

For many girls from disadvantaged backgrounds, education represented an important means of bettering their circumstances. After the Civil War, for instance, northern educators traveled to the South to teach former slaves of all ages, seeing in literacy a route to emancipation. For some girls, however, formal schooling represented a form of social coercion. Carol Devens's "'If We Get the Girls, We Get the Race': Missionary Education Of Native American Girls" explores white missionaries' interest in schooling Native American girls as a means of encouraging religious conversions and enticing girls to reject traditional ways. In the second half of the nineteenth century, Devens argues, mission schools began to focus specifically on girls, responding to the belief that educated women raised more virtuous male citizens. However, many Native American families tried particularly to keep their girls out of these institutions, noting the demoralizing and disorienting effects of such schools on their girls and on traditional mother-daughter relationships.

Girls' education extended well beyond the classroom. As Jane Hunter argues in "Inscribing the Self in the Heart of the Family: Diaries and Girlhood in Late-Victorian America," the practice of keeping a diary was a means of self-discovery and self-determination for literate middle-class girls. A number of the adolescents who would become social reformers by the turn of the century wrote diary entries that blended Victorian ideals of "true womanhood" with private reflection on (and release from) parental domination. In the pages of their supposedly private diaries, Hunter shows how girls could imagine roles for themselves not entirely in line with middle-class feminine ideals.

A third area of significant scholarship concerns girls' diverse experiences of their bodies. Rural girls were often engaged in strenuous labor by early adolescence. In contrast, elite girls were taught that physical exertion was not ladylike until, very late in the century, a new athletically emancipated ideal came into being. Few girls were instructed explicitly about sex or sexual enjoyment. Some girls, however, found in their bodies a means to express sensuality and pleasure. Susan McCully's "'Oh I Love Mother, I Love Her Power': Shaker Spirit Possession and the Performance of Desire" examines the phenomenon of spirit possession by young girls in a Shaker community in upstate New York during the 1830s and 1840s. As McCully explains, girls' religious possession represented the attempt of social subordinates to gain personal power, while their rituals of polymorphic eroticism expressed a range of repressed sexual desires.

Girls' emotional turmoil often took more hazardous bodily expressions. Nancy M. Theriot's "Psychosomatic Illness in History: The 'Green Sickness' among Nineteenth-Century Adolescent Girls" explores the historical phenomenon known as chlorosis, a psychosomatic illness characterized by a loss of appetite and a disturbed mental state. The term chlorosis—what we today would identify as anorexia—was used specifically for adolescent girls of the mid-to-late century. Where Smith-Rosenberg celebrates a loving female sphere, Theriot suggests one more fraught with intergenerational tension; for Theriot, the diagnosis of chlorosis reflected the result of stress between mothers and their daughters at a time of changing social conditions.

Sexual maturation has long been a key marker of girls' physical and developmental trajectory toward womanhood. This maturation has taken place in diverse cultural contexts; notions of "appropriate" sexualities, and girls' age at puberty, degree of sexual experimentation outside of marriage, and courtship histories have all varied. While female modesty (and girls' innocence more particularly) was enshrined as a virtue in nineteenth-century American culture, a significant minority of unmarried girls were sexually active, sometimes but not always by choice. By midcentury, numerous reformers organized around the figure of the innocent but corruptible girl. As Christine Stansell argues in "Women on the Town: Sexual Exchange and Prostitution," the visibility of adolescent prostitutes in midcentury New York City brought the sex trade to greater public attention. But reformers were concerned about more than prostitution; they were also fearful about working-class adolescent girls' and young women's apparent emancipation from patriarchal regulation more generally.

Adolescent black girls in slavery were particularly likely to be sexually exploited. As Mary Niall Mitchell argues in "'Rosebloom and Pure White,' Or So It Seemed," abolitionist campaigns skillfully employed disturbing and titillating images of very light-skinned, enslaved southern girls in order to stir northern abolitionist audiences. The girls' bodies appeared to offer "proof" of the indignity of slavery, revealing that many young girls who appeared white were actually the progeny of interracial coercive unions; the images further implied that the peculiar institution could expand to include the enslavement of whites. However horrifying their implications to contemporaries, the photographs appealed to new sentimental ideas about white childhood, as well as voyeuristic interest in girls who appeared likely to meet the same fate as their enslaved mothers, becoming the objects of their masters' sexual appetites.

A fourth theme of significant interest to girls' history scholars concerns girls' socialization through recreation and consumer culture. By the second half of the century, a new and expanding consumer industry offered girls age-specific fashions, toys, reading material, and spaces of play, thereby teaching girls important lessons in gender roles, sexual mores, and even national belonging. Yet even the most prescriptive fiction was not entirely straightforward. As Barbara Sicherman's "Reading *Little Women*: The Many Lives of a Text" suggests, Louisa May Alcott's 1868 *Little Women* was a cultural phenomenon that performed "cultural work" for diverse communities of girl readers. While Sicherman uses the novel to showcase the rise of a girls' literary market in the United States, she illustrates the specificity of readers' experiences of the novel within that broader market.

By the end of the nineteenth century, women's relative emancipation was mirrored in girls' lives. More girls had extended educations, participated in sports, and found in consumer culture important opportunities for youthful self-definition. However, girls' growing independence, whether as consumers, wage earners, students, or participants in popular culture, remained the source of ongoing intergenerational debate, and as a group girls continued to experience less personal freedom than boys. Girls' own play reflected the interplay of adult efforts to shape their horizons and girls' own creative pursuit of autonomy. Miriam Forman-Brunell's "The Politics of Dollhood in Nineteenth-Century America" uses the material culture of play as evidence of the complexity and contested nature of girls' socialization. As Forman-Brunell explains, adults believed that dolls were useful vehicles of girls' feminine socialization, but girls themselves sometimes appropriated dolls for other, often more subversive purposes. Through doll play, girls challenged parental authority, social customs and gender roles, thereby working to determine their own girls' culture.

Collectively, these essays represent some of the most influential scholarship in the field over the past thirty years. In our selections, we have aimed to balance regions and diverse kinds of girlhoods, essays focused on ideologies of girlhood and those texts that emphasize girls' own experiences, and older and newer scholarship.[12] Much research remains. We know far more about middle-class girls' reading habits, for example, than about working-class girls' experiences of paid labor. We know more about girls from the perspective of the adults who tried to educate, reform, or punish them than we do about their own strategies and aspirations. The literature on urban girls of the northeast is far larger than that on southern, western, and rural girls. We know more about white girls of all classes than we do about girls of other races, particularly nineteenth-century Latina, Asian-American, and Native American girls. We know little about girls' sexual interests. More scholars have focused on adolescents, about whom historical records are often stronger, than on younger girls. We hope this volume will spur scholars to pursue further research on girlhood, both as a category that has been defined, contested, and employed in various historical and cultural contexts, and as an identity that girls have used to understand their lives.

We are deeply thankful to the many individuals and institutions who contributed to the creation of *The Girls' History and Culture Reader*. We owe a great debt to our editor, Kendra Boileau, for seeing promise in this project and for making it a reality. For their lively reviews and excellent suggestions we enthusiastically thank historians Eileen Boris and Elizabeth Pleck. The University of Missouri Research Board generously provided the book subvention grant that paid for the permissions and production. A Standard Research Grant from the Social Sciences and Humanities Research Council of Canada funded some of the final editorial work. The complicated process of scanning, formatting, proofreading, and permission-getting required the assistance of many—Jennifer Clark, Breanne Ertmer, Adrienne Qualis, Matt Blankenship, Emily Purdue, Sarah Crossley, Mary McMurray, Zoë Brunell and Perry Brunell, Amy Brost, and Gail Green. In addition to this capable crew, we thank the many scholars whose work is featured in the *Reader* as well the broader community of scholars in women's history, girls' studies, gender history, and children's history whose pathbreaking work on the history of girls forged this new and vibrant field of study. And finally, to John Pitcher and Claude Brunell: thank you both from the bottom of our hearts.

Notes

1. Lucy Larcom, *A New England Girlhood, Outlined from Memory* (Lenox, Mass.: Hard Press, 2006 [orig. ed. 1889]), 77.
2. On Lowell's "mill girls," see Thomas Dublin, *Women at Work: The Transformation of Work and Community in Lowell, Massachusetts, 1826–1860* (New York: Columbia U. Press, 1979).
3. Jane H. Hunter, *How Young Girls Became Ladies: The Victorian Origins of American Girlhood* (New Haven: Yale U. Press, 2002).
4. Carroll Smith-Rosenberg, "The Female World of Love and Ritual: Relations Between Women in Nineteenth-Century America," *Signs* 1, no. 1 (1975): 1–29; Ann D. Gordon, "The Young Ladies' Academy of Philadelphia," in Carol Berkin and Mary Beth Norton, eds., *Women of America: A History* (Boston: Houghton Mifflin, 1979), 68–91.
5. Nancy Chodorow, *The Reproduction of Mothering: Psychoanalysis and the Sociology of Gender* (Berkeley: U. of California Press, 1978); Nancy M. Theriot, *Mothers and Daughters in Nineteenth-Century America: The Biosocial Construction of Femininity* (Lexington: U. Press of Kentucky, 1996); Carol Gilligan, *In a Different Voice: Psychological Theory and Women's Development* (Cambridge: Harvard University Press, 1982); Joan Jacobs Brumberg, *Fasting Girls: The Emergence of Anorexia Nervosa as a Modern Disease* (Cambridge: Harvard U. Press, 1988).

6. Anne Scott MacLeod, "The *Caddie Woodlawn* Syndrome: American Girlhood in the Nineteenth Century," in Mary Lynn Stevens Heininger, Karin Calvert, Barbara Finkelstein and Kathy Vandell, Anne Scott MacLeod, and Harvey Green, *A Century of Childhood 1820–1920* (Rochester, N.Y.: Margaret Woodbury Strong Museum, 1984), 97–119; Karen Calvert, *Children in the House: The Material Culture of Early Childhood, 1600–1900* (Boston: Northeastern University Press, 1992); Miriam Formanek-Brunell, *Made to Play House: Dolls and the Commercialization of American Girlhood, 1830–1930* (New Haven: Yale U. Press, 1993); Jane Hunter, "Inscribing the Self in the Heart of the Family: Diaries and Girlhood in Late-Victorian America," *American Quarterly* 44, no. 1 (March 1992), 51–81; Barbara Sicherman, "Reading *Little Women*: The Many Lives of a Text," in Linda K. Kerber, Alice Kessler-Harris, and Kathryn Kish Sklar, eds., *U.S. History as Women's History: New Feminist Essays* (Chapel Hill: University of North Carolina Press, 1995), 245–266; Lynne Vallone and Claudia Nelson, *The Girls' Own: Cultural Histories of the Anglo-American Girl* (Athens: University of Georgia Press, 1994); Lynne Vallone, *Disciplines of Virtue: Girls' Culture in the Eighteenth and Nineteenth Centuries* (New Haven: Yale U. Press, 1995); Sherrie A. Inness, *Delinquents and Debutantes: Twentieth-Century Girls' Cultures* (New York: New York U. Press, 1998), 4.

7. Angela McRobbie and Jenny Garber, "Girls and Subcultures," in Stuart Hall and Tony Jefferson, *Resistance through Ritual* (London: Hutchinson, 1976); Angela McRobbie, *Feminism and Youth Culture from Jackie to Just Seventeen* (London: MacMillan Publishing Co., 1991); Carolyn Steedman, *Landscape for a Good Woman: A Story* (New Brunswick, N.J.: Rutgers U. Press, 1987).

8. Miriam Forman-Brunell, ed., *Girlhood in America: An Encyclopedia* (Santa Barbara, Calif.: ABC-CLIO, 2001) and Claudia Mitchell and Jacqueline Reid-Mitchell, eds., *Girl Culture, An Encyclopedia* (Westport, Conn.: Greenwood Press, 2007).

9. The literature on nineteenth-century childhood includes Viviana A. Zeliger, *Pricing the Priceless Child: The Changing Social Value of Children* (New York: Basic Books, 1985); N. Ray Hiner and Joseph M. Hawes, eds., *Growing Up in America: Children in Historical Perspective* (Urbana: University of Illinois Press, 1985); Elliott West, *Growing Up with the Country: Childhood on the Far Western Frontier* (Albuquerque: University of New Mexico Press, 1989); Elliot West and Paula Petrik, eds., *Small Worlds: Children and Adolescents in America, 1850–1950* (Lawrence: University of Kansas Press, 1992); Harvey J. Graff, *Conflicting Paths: Growing Up in America* (Cambridge: Harvard University Press, 1995); Wilma King, *Stolen Childhood: Slave Youth in Nineteenth-Century America* (Bloomington: Indiana University Press, 1995); Jacqueline S. Reinier, *From Virtue to Character: American Childhood, 1775–1850* (New York: Twayne Publishers, 1996); Priscilla Ferguson Clement, *Growing Pains: Children in the Industrial Age, 1850–1890* (New York: Twayne Publishers, 1997); James Marten, *The Children's Civil War* (Chapel Hill: University of North Carolina Press, 1998); Marie Jenkins Schwartz, *Born in Bondage: Growing Up Enslaved in the Antebellum South* (Cambridge: Harvard U. Press, 2000); Joseph Illick, *American Childhoods* (Philadelphia: University of Pennsylvania Press, 2002); Steven Mintz, *Huck's Raft: A History of American Childhood* (Cambridge: Belknap Press of Harvard University Press, 2004); Karen Sanchez-Eppler, *Dependent States: The Child's Part in Nineteenth-Century American Culture* (Chicago: U. of Chicago Press, 2005).

10. Michael R. Haines and Richard Hall Steckel, *A Population History of North America* (New York: Cambridge U. Press, 2000), 683; Reynolds Farley and John Haaga, *The American People: Census 2000* (New York: Russell Sage Foundation, 2005), 208.

11. See Jean Ferguson Carr, "Nineteenth-Century Girls and Literacy," in Jane Greer, *Girls and Literacy in America: Historical Perspectives to the Present* (Santa Barbara, Calif.: ABC-CLIO, 2003), 51–77.

12. Nineteenth-century girls' history includes the work of numerous excellent scholars whose research, for reasons of space, is not represented in this volume. See, for example, Anne M. Boylan, "Growing Up Female in Young America, 1800–1860," in Joseph M. Hawes and N. Ray Hiner, *American Childhood* (Westport, Conn.: Greenwood Press, 1985), 153–184; Kimberly A. Smith, "'The First Effort of an Infant Hand': An Introduction to Virginia Schoolgirl Embroideries, 1742–1850," *Journal of Early Southern Decorative Arts* 16, no. 2 (1990): 30–101; Devon A. Mihesuah, "Too Dark to Be Angels: The Class System among the Cherokees at the Female Seminary," *American Indian Culture and Research Journal* 15, no. 1 (1991): 29–52; Ramon Gutierrez, "Honor and Marriage," in *When Jesus Came, the Corn Mothers Went Away: Marriage, Sexuality, and Power in New Mexico, 1500–1846* (Stanford: Stanford University Press, 1991), 227–240; Victoria Bissell Brown, "Golden Girls: Female Socialization among the Middle Class of Los Angeles, 1880–1910," in Elliott West and Paula Petrik, eds., *Small Worlds: Children & Adolescents in America, 1850–1950* (Lawrence: University Press of Kansas, 1992), 232–254; Paula Korus, "Mui Tsai: Chinese Slave Girls in the Inland Northwest," *Pacific Northwest Forum* 6, no. 1 (1992): 38–43; Peter N. Stearns, "Girls, Boys, and Emotions: Redefinitions and Historical Change," *Journal of American History* 80, no. 1 (1993): 36–74; Kathryn Kish Sklar, "The Schooling of Girls and Changing Community Values in Massachusetts Towns, 1750–1820," *History of Education Quarterly* 33, no. 4 (Winter 1993): 511–542; Karen Sanchez-Eppler, "Temperance in the Bed of a Child: Incest and Social Order in Nineteenth-Century America," *American Quarterly* 47, no. 1 (March 1995): 1–33; Melanie Dawson, "The Miniaturizing of Girlhood: Nineteenth-Century Playtime and Gendered Theories of Development," in Caroline E. Levander and Carol J. Singley, eds., *The American Child: A Cultural Studies Reader* (New Brunswick, N.J.: Rutgers University Press, 2003), 63–84; Melissa Klapper, *Jewish Girls Coming of Age in America, 1860–1920* (New York: New York University Press, 2005); Nell Painter, "Soul Murder and Slavery: Toward a Fully Loaded Cost Accounting," in Linda K. Kerber, Alice Kessler-Harris, and Kathryn Kish Sklar, eds., *U.S. History as Women's History: New Feminist Essays* (Chapel Hill: University of North Carolina Press, 1995), 125–146; Peter W. Bardaglio, "Sex Crimes, Sexuality, and the Courts," in *Reconstructing the Household: Families, Sex, and the Law in the Nineteenth-Century South* (Chapel Hill: University of North Carolina Press, 1995), 37–78; Crista DeLuzio, *Female Adolescence in American Scientific Thought, 1830–1930* (Baltimore: Johns Hopkins U. Press, 2007); Lynn Ann Sacco, *Unspeakable: Father-Daughter Incest in American History* (Baltimore: Johns Hopkins University Press, 2009); Martha Saxton, "French and American Childhoods: St. Louis in the Early Republic," in James Marten, ed., *Children and Youth in a New Nation* (New York: New York U. Press, 2009), 69–90.

"Us colored women had to
go through a plenty."[1]

CHAPTER 1

The Life Cycle of the Female Slave

Deborah Gray White

The life of an individual in any society is a series of passages from one stage to another and from one occupation to another.[2] Yet, although each stage in a person's life may be very different from that which preceded it, an individual is not always aware that one period of his or her life has ended and a new one begun. For women, the beginning and cessation of the menses help define life's transitions, as does the beginning of motherhood. For the antebellum slave woman, biology combined with the demands made on her for plantation labor to delineate the series of passages that marked her life. The experiences of slave women from one plantation to the next, from one region of the South to the next, from the cotton, to the sugar, to the rice plantation were obviously different, but there was a pattern that defined the general contours of life for average bondwomen. This general pattern is the subject of this chapter.

For slave girls childhood was neither carefree nor burdensome. For the most part children lived in an age-segregated world so that with the exception of the elderly slaves whose responsibility it was to supervise the young, girls and boys had little contact with adult slaves who were away in the fields most of the day.[3]

But the children's world was by no means segregated by sex. Boys and girls were constant companions and it seems that neither work nor play was strictly differentiated on the basis of sex. There was almost no activity engaged in by girls that was not, at some time or another, also engaged in by boys. For instance, while girls were used as nurses, the term used by antebellum whites and blacks to describe someone who supervised infants and toddlers, so too were boys. Nelson Birdson of Alabama indicated that the first work he remembered doing was "nussing a baby boy."[4] Similarly, an Arkansas slave claimed that until he was old enough to chop cotton, all he did was "nurse babies."[5] That boys as well as girls were used as babysitters was also recorded by Frances Kemble, the English wife of a Georgia rice planter. She was incensed to find that girls and boys "from eight to twelve and older" did little more than "tend baby" while sickly women were forced to do field work.[6] Both sexes performed a variety of other kinds of work, such as "toting" water to thirsty field hands, collecting the mail, and tending livestock.

Similarly, play was not strictly differentiated or categorized as "masculine" or "feminine." Millie Evans explained that along with jump rope she busied herself "running, jumping, skipping and just everything."[7] Tag, or "You Can Catch Me," was another one of her favorite games. A Tennessee woman remembered that as a child she played a game called "Smut," which was just like cards except that it was played with grains of corn. Marbles was another game she played, but her biggest amusement was "running through the woods, climbing trees, hunting grapes and berries."[8] Joseph Holmes's recollections of his sister's childhood in slavery also indicates that play for little girls was not restricted to certain spheres: "If I jumped in de ribber tuh swim, she did hit too; if I clum' a tree or went th'ough a briar patch, she don hit right behin' me." His sister was also his companion in hunting rabbits, coons, and turtles.[9]

The memories of these former slaves suggest that girls were not kept close to home in the exclusive company of women and were not socialized at an early age to assume culturally defined feminine roles. Black girls on the plantation spent most of their time in a sexually integrated atmosphere. Even the experience of the young female domestic offers little evidence of early differential socialization since boys were just as likely as girls to be found doing kitchen and housekeeping chores. This easy integration of boys and girls is perhaps understandable in the context of their future plantation roles. Since both girls and boys were expected to become field hands, and they often found themselves doing similar work in later life, it is not surprising that as children they did the same chores and played the same games. This does not mean that parents did not relate to girls and boys differently—there is no way of knowing if they did or did not. It does seem, however, that parents were more concerned that children, regardless of sex, learn to walk the tightrope between the demands of the whites and expectations of the blacks without falling too far in either direction. It was probably more important for nine-year-old girls to learn that conversations among blacks in the slave quarters were not for white consumption, than it was for them to learn that cooking was a "feminine" activity. Sometimes girls, as well as boys, found that satisfying both masters and mistresses and fathers and mothers could be difficult. Linda Brent, for instance, learned at a young age just how hard it could be when she heard her father chastise her brother for running to his mistress when his father had summoned him at the same time. "You are *my* child," said Brent's father, "and when I call you, you should come immediately, if you have to pass through fire and water."[10] If their activities of work and play are any indication of the degree of sex role differentiation that existed before age ten or twelve, then young girls probably grew up minimizing the difference between the sexes while learning far more about the differences between the races.

During the teen years, however, as girls were integrated into the work force, more strict role separation became the rule. In childhood, girls and boys had dressed much the same, in simple smock-like shirts or slips. But at some point in preadolescence, girls turned in their homespun shirts for dresses, and boys were supplied with pants.[11] While boys and girls, about twelve to sixteen, still performed the same kind of work, they were now more likely to be included in a work gang, which was sometimes called the "trash gang." The trash gang was assigned such tasks as raking stubble, pulling weeds, or doing light hoeing. At harvest time on cotton plantations they usually picked cotton.[12] Joining the trash gang had to be a more significant turning point for girls than for boys since this work gang, made up of pregnant women, women with nursing infants, young teenagers, and old slaves, was predominantly female. This was the first time that girls found themselves in an overwhelmingly female world. The importance of this step is underscored by recent evidence that pinpoints the peak growth spurt for slave girls, measured by height and weight, at around thirteen, and menarche approximately two years later.[13] Slave girls experienced these critical physiological changes at a time when their social milieu was shifting to include women who were about to become mothers, women who were nursing mothers, and elderly women, who, although past their childbearing years, had firsthand knowledge of the particulars of motherhood. Slave sources reveal little about the interaction of the members of this work gang, but its role in the socialization of adolescent girls was probably significant. At the very least it can reasonably be assumed that girls who worked and ate with childbearing and mature women daily developed some sense of what was expected of them in their future role of mother. It could very well be that the three-generational trash gang played a major role in teaching girls about life under slavery, as well as particulars regarding men, marriage, and sex.

Although the early teenage years brought hard work and a painful awareness of what it meant to be a slave, these years were also marked by puberty and a budding interest in boys. When girls traded their homespun shirts for calico dresses they usually dyed one dress a bright color for Sunday and special occasions.[14] If a young lady had attracted the eye of some young man, she was very likely to receive a hoop made out of a grapevine to wear under that dress. Gus Feaster of South Carolina observed that this was the age when young women stopped eating and claimed they had no appetite. Apparently, it was not "stylish" for "courtin' gals" to "eat much in public."[15] Instead of running and jumping and hunting 'coons, young adults "went to walk an' hunted chestnuts." The chestnuts were not for eating, however. According to Alabama born Lucindy Lawrence Jordon, "us would string dem an' put 'em 'round our necks an' smile at our fellers."[16]

If it was a transitional period for young ladies, it was also a period of apprehension for parents, especially mothers. The mother of slaves is very watchful, explained Linda Brent. "After they have entered their teens, she lives in daily expectation of trouble. This leads to many questions. If a girl is of a sensitive nature, timidity keeps her from answering truthfully and this well-meant course has a tendency to drive her from maternal counsels."[17] A slave mother's anxiety stemmed partly from her fear that her young daughters would fall prey to the licentious black and white men on the plantation. On Southern plantations mothers often schooled their daughters on avoiding the sexual overtures of these men. When one woman saw the overseer sneering at her daughter, she told her "not to let any of 'em go with her," and when Lucy McCullough's mother saw Lucy coming across the field with her dress rising too far, she promptly tore the hem out in the sight of everyone.[18]

In the long run, however, a mother could do little but hope that her daughter made it through adolescence and young womanhood unscathed by sexual abuse. In this respect homeliness could be a great asset, for antebellum sources seem to support Brent's statement regarding female slaves: "If God has bestowed beauty upon her it will prove her greatest curse," because "that which commands admiration in the white woman, only hastens the degradation of the female slave."[19]

A slave mother's uneasiness during her daughter's adolescence also grew out of her desire to protect her daughter from the responsibilities of adulthood. Mothers seemed to want girls to grow up slowly, and so they tried to limit their daughters' contact with members of the opposite sex. "Courtin' wasn't fast," noted one ex-slave.[20] W. M. Green complained that "girls acted like de old folks and dey did not carry on."[21] The vigilance of some mothers equaled that of a

North Carolina woman who never let her daughter out of her sight when the latter was with her beau. It was one year before she allowed her daughter to walk with her future son-in-law and then she made sure that she was "setting dere on de porch lookin.'"[22]

Some slave mothers apparently tried to shelter their daughters from the adult world by withholding knowledge of the mechanics of childbirth. For instance, Mississippian Frances Fluker claimed: "I come a woman 'for I knowed what it was . . . They didn't tell me nothin.'"[23] Another woman noted that at age twelve or thirteen, she and an older girl went around to parsley beds and hollow logs looking for newborn babies. "They didn't tell you a thing," she said. At age twenty she was still ignorant about reproduction: "I didn't know how long I had to carry my baby. We never saw nothing when we were children."[24] Minnie Fulkes, a Virginia woman, had a similar story. She married at the uncommon age of fourteen but knew nothing about sex: "I slept in bed, he on his side an' I on mine for three months."[25] Still others testified that their mothers told them that doctors brought babies, and that "people was very particular in them days. They wouldn't let children know anything."[26]

Try as they might, mothers could not forever shelter their daughters from the complex considerations that courtship involved. Despite the preferences of their mothers, teenage slave girls seem to have had a degree of sexual freedom unknown to Southern white girls. In a conscious comparison of the mores that bound white women to sexual prudery with those that afforded black women the opportunity to experiment with sex, Mary Boykin Chesnut, with a hint of envy, wrote: "These negro women have a chance here that women have nowhere else. They can redeem themselves—the impropers can. They can marry decently and nothing is remembered agains these colored ladies."[27] A plantation owner told Frederick Olmsted that slave men and women seldom married without "trying each other out . . . for two or three weeks, to see how they are going to like each other."[28] Black testimony also reveals premarital sexual contact between the sexes. Of his relationship with young single women, Oklahoma-born John White said: "I favor them with something extra from the kitchen. Then they favors me—at night."[29] Another male former slave recalled that boys sang a "vulgar" song to girls inviting them to "come out tonight."[30]

"Marriage" patterns and the way slave children were spaced also suggest that slave girls started sexual activities relatively early and were free to change their minds during the mate selection process. Usually female slaves had their first child in their nineteenth year (about two years earlier than Southern white women), waited a few years before having their second child, and then beginning with the second child had subsequent children at two and a half year intervals.[31] Most bonded women married the father of their first child but many established a more enduring relationship with someone other than their first child's father and went on to marry and have the rest of their children with him.

If it is difficult for the historian to reconcile the contradictions between the vigilance of slave mothers and the reality of permissive sex, the problem only gets more complex when planter demands are considered. Slave women in their late teens and early twenties were not free to consider their future without considering that their childbearing ability was of economic consequence to their owners. Since some masters figured that at least 5 to 6 percent of their profit would accrue from natural increase, this period in the bondwoman's life was beset with pressures that free women did not experience.[32] On one front there were norms and rites dictated by the slave's culture, those designed to usher females out of the asexual world of childhood, through puberty, and into the sexual world of marriage and motherhood. The slow pace of courtship dictated by anxious mothers is a good example of a standard set not by the whites, but by black slaves. On another front there was the white master whose sometimes subtle and sometimes not so subtle manipulation of the slave woman and her environment was aimed at maximizing the number of children born to his slaves. Into these crosscurrents stepped a very naive young woman who, along with the young men in her life, had her own ideas about sex and courtship.

However she felt about the mores her mother tried to inculcate, the young slave woman could not ignore her master's wishes, which, in one way or another, were made quite clear. Slave masters wanted adolescent girls to have children, and to this end they practiced a passive, though insidious, kind of breeding. Thus, while it was not unheard of for a planter to slap a male and female together and demand that they "replenish the earth," it was more likely that he would use his authority to encourage young slaves to make binding and permanent the relationships they themselves had initiated. Some did this by granting visitation privileges to a young man of a neighboring plantation who had taken an interest in a particular young woman. If the man and woman married, these visitations continued throughout the marriage. Occasionally, arrangements were made whereby a slave owner purchased a slave so that a man and woman could marry and live together.[33]

The typical plantation manual should arrest any thoughts that the attention masters paid to getting young slave women attached stemmed from unselfish benevolence. On the contrary, marriage was thought to add "to the comfort, happiness and health of those entering upon it, besides ensuring greater increase."[34] Indeed, on the morning after her wedding, Mammy Harriet of the Burleigh estate in Georgia was greeted by her mistress singing: "Good morning, Mrs. Bride. I wish you joy, and every year a son or daughter."[35] Malinda Bibb's master was a little less tactful. Henry Bibb recalled that when he asked

Malinda's master for her hand in marriage, "his answer was in the affirmative with but one condition, which I considered to be too vulgar to be written."[36] Too often, when two people declared their intention to marry, as on a North Carolina plantation, all the master said was "don't forget to bring me a little one or two for next year."[37]

Beyond the verbal prodding used to encourage young women to reproduce were the more subtle practices that were built into the plantation system. For instance, pregnant women usually did less work and received more attention and rations than nonpregnant women.[38] This policy was meticulously outlined to overseers and managers. Richard Corbin of Virginia told his manager that "breeding wenches more particularly you must instruct the Overseers to be Kind and Indulgent to, and not force them when with child upon any service or hardship that will be injurious to him."[39] While this practice was designed to ensure the continued good health of mother and fetus alike, it also doubled as an incentive for overworked slave women to have children. As previously noted, the trash gang, to which women were assigned in the latter stages of pregnancy, did relatively lighter work than that done by other hands. On plantations where the workload was exhausting and backbreaking, a lighter work assignment could easily have proved incentive to get pregnant as often as possible, and according to Francis Kemble it did just that. Writing about the women on her husband's Georgia and South Carolina rice plantations she noted: "On the birth of a child certain additions of clothing and an additional weekly ration are bestowed on the family, and these matters, as small as they may seem, act as powerful inducements." There can be little doubt that the women in the Georgia settlements were conscious of their owner's stress on natural increase. On one trip through the slave quarters, Kemble visited women who held their babies out for her inspection proclaiming: "Missus, tho' we no able to work, we make little niggers for massa."[40]

As part of their manipulation of reproduction some slave owners adopted the practice of rewarding prolific women. Every time a baby was born on one of Major Wallon's plantations, the mother was given a calico dress and a "bright, shiny silver dollar."[41] B. Talbert, a Virginia planter, took this policy to its extreme. In 1792 he bought a woman named Jenny and promised her that when she had a child for every one of his five children he would set her free. In the space of eleven years Jenny had six children, and in 1803, she and her youngest child were emancipated by Talbert.[42] Though only a few slaveholders were so "charitable," many adhered to the instructions in Plowden C. J. Weston's *Plantation Manual*. Weston advised that "women with six children alive at any one time are allowed all Saturday to themselves."[43]

If these inducements were not sufficient to secure the cooperation of the slave of childbearing age, the master always had recourse to punitive measures, such as the sale of women incapable of having children. Since much of a young woman's worth was in her unborn children, nonchildbearing women were less valuable to slaveholders than childbearing women. Both masters and slave traders were often unscrupulous in their methods of disposing of such women. In 1852 an Alabama master bought three women only to find that one of them had syphilis, another had gonorrhea, and the third suffered from the effects of an umbilical hernia, all of which rendered them, in the opinion of the buyer, "scarcely valuable as breeders." A Georgia farmer was likewise cheated out of the nine hundred dollars he had paid for a young woman. Less than a week after the sale, the woman was found to be suffering from a uterine infection. So common were such misrepresentations that judges and juries established a policy for dealing with such cases. If a buyer took possession of a woman who had been certified as fit to bear children by the seller, and it could be demonstrated that the seller knew the woman was incapable of having children, the sale was voided and the proceeds were refunded. These two planters got their money back, but some did not.[44]

Infertile women could, therefore, expect to be treated like barren sows and be passed from one unsuspecting buyer to the next. This was confirmed by a slaveholder who confessed to Northerner Frederick Olmsted that he had known a great many slave women to be sold off because they did not have children.[45] Berry Clay confirmed that "a barren woman was separated from her husband and usually sold."[46] Planter interest in a slave woman's offspring was long-range and often conflicted with that of a slave couple. For instance, Mary Reynold's husband wanted to buy her from her master, but her master refused because he was "never one to sell any but old niggers who was past working in the fields and past their breeding time."[47] John Tayloe of Virginia was similar in this respect, except he sold females both before and after their childbearing years. Of the twenty-nine females he sold off his Mount Airy plantation between 1809 and 1828, four were small children, sixteen were girls aged nine to seventeen, and the remaining nine were mature women. No childbearing women were sold. An ex-slave summed it up: If a woman was a good breeder, "they was proud of her;" if not, they got rid of her.[48]

If the subtle manipulations of slaveholders failed in their aim, and if a young bondwoman cared so little about her own security as to refuse to have children, then masters could and sometimes did resort to outright force. The story of Texan Rose Williams is a case in point. According to Williams she had been at Master Hawkins' place for about a year when Hawkins approached her and told her she was changing accommodations: "You gwine live with Rufus in that cabin over yonder. Go fix it for living." Rose attributed her naïveté to her youth (she was only about sixteen) for she assumed that she was only "to tend cabin for Rufus and some other niggers." She soon learned otherwise and promptly rebelled: "We-uns has supper, then I goes here and there talking till I's ready for sleep, and then I gits in the bunk. After I's in, that nigger come crawl in the bunk with me." Rose put her foot against him and shoved him on to the floor. An infuriated Rufus reported the incident to Hawkins who forthwith informed Rose of her duty to "bring forth portly children." Reinforcing his point, he told Rose that he had paid "big money" for her "cause I wants you to raise me childrens." She complied with his wishes only under his threats of a beating. But Rose Williams was influenced by more than fear of physical abuse. Her inclination to resist was tempered by the fact that Hawkins had bought her whole family off the auction block: "I thinks 'bout Massa buying me offen the block and saving me from being sepa-rated from my folks and 'bout being whipped at the stake. There it am. What am I's to do? . . . I yields." She gave in, but, as Williams herself revealed, the incident was shattering: "I never marries, 'cause one 'sperience am 'nough for this nigger. After what I does for the massa, I's never wants no truck with any man. The lord forgive this colored woman, but he have to 'scuse me and look for some other for to 'plenish the earth."[49]

The pressures on the female slave in young womanhood were not always laid to rest after marriage and childbirth. The birth of children bought some security for a married couple, but the vagaries of the market economy and a slave owner's death or peculiar whims were unpredictable factors that could result in the sale or permanent separation of a husband and wife. A young woman's search for another spouse with whom to have more children for her owner was expected to begin immediately. Not long after separation, both husband and wife would either find or be given a new spouse. When William Wells Brown asked Sally why she had married so soon after the sale of her husband, Ben, her earnest reply was that the master made her do it. So too, when Lavinia, another of Brown's acquaintances, was separated from her loved one, her master compelled her, on pain of the lash, to choose another. When she absolutely refused, she got a whipping.[50] Deacon Whitefield, one of Henry Bibb's masters, "graciously" provided one of his slave women with a slave named Steven, whom she quickly rejected. But the driver's lash made her think twice, and she reluctantly accepted him.[51]

If the evidence of the slaveholder's efforts to cajole and coerce slave women to have children in the cause of profit speaks for itself, the precise psychological and physiological effects of slave owner manipulation on young black women are more difficult to gauge. The ex-slaves' sensitivity on the subject suggests that bondwomen knew they were cogs in the plantation regime's reproductive machine. In all probability, slave owner manipulation was responsible for the two-year difference between the beginning of childbearing years in slave women and in Southern white women.[52] Although plantation owners succeeded in hastening the onset of the bonded woman's childbearing years, it appears that plantation blacks may have managed to deprive them of total victory. This conclusion is implicit in a study done by economists James Trussell and Richard Steckel, who have estimated the mean age of slave women at first birth to be 20.6 years. By using height and weight data obtained from the manifests of slave ships they also put the age of menarche at fifteen. Since a period of about 2.6 years of sterility usually follows menarche, the average female slave *delayed childbearing for at least two years* after attaining reproductive capacity.[53] Therefore, although slaveholders tried to get slave women to have as many children as physically possible, owners fell short of their aim.

Why? It could be that what owners perceived as better treatment and lighter work was not enough. Adolescent girls who did not get enough to eat, who suffered from any number of vitamin deficiencies, and who spent long days in the crop might have been unable to have children any earlier than they did. Moreover, regardless of how good the treatment, how light the work, or how sufficient the diet, if planter policies made for a shortage of males, then bonded women would have to compete for mates. There was a good chance that the woman who did not experience courtship during adolescence would begin childbearing later than her counterpart who had an adolescent courtship or might never have children at all. For instance, on some of the Ball plantations in antebellum South Carolina, Cheryll Cody found a direct correlation between the number of women who never bore children and an unbalanced sex ratio. On those plantations where women outnumbered men, there was also a significant number of women who never had children. The descendants of John Ball indirectly influenced female slave decisions on mate selection and childbearing through their sale, purchase, and dispersal policies.[54] Owners could also influence these decisions by prohibiting "abroad" relationships, those relationships between bonded men and women of different plantations. All these are possible explanations for why the average young slave woman did not begin childbearing two years earlier than she did.

We must not, however, lose sight of the kind of pressure the blacks of the quarters exerted on young slave women. As Herbert Gutman has demonstrated, the slave family was remarkably stable, and served as a transmitter of culture. The care taken by slaves to obey the Seventh Commandment, the solemnity of the marriage ceremony, whether the bond was sealed in the Big House parlor or sand-covered yard, revealed that African Americans understood their family to be a haven in a heartless Southland. It was within the slave family that a man, humiliated by the overseer's commands or lash, received respect. There, too, the overworked or brutally punished bondwoman received compassion.[55] We have noted how mothers agonized over their daughter's initial encounters with the opposite sex, how mothers tried to make courtship proceed at a slow

Deborah Gray White

pace, and how there seems to have been a virtual conspiracy against revealing the particulars of the mechanics of childbirth. If these slave mores were at odds with the slave owner's desire to turn every young black woman into a "brood mare," they were also at odds with the slave owner's stereotypical notion of slave women as Jezebels. Young adults in the slave community, eager to impress the opposite sex, and experiencing for the first time the excitement of courtship, might have resisted these mores. However, most older and more mature slaves knew that the unions that Southern whites could cavalierly dismiss as promiscuous and inconsequential were often buffers against slave owner callousness and insensitivity. Given the important place that the slave family occupied in the community of the quarters, slave parents had every reason in the world to caution young courting girls to proceed slowly.

Their attitude about motherhood supplied additional reason. For the bondwoman who adhered to the prevailing mores of the quarters, marriage sanctioned motherhood, not sexual intercourse. Prenuptial intercourse was not considered evil, nor was it, as too many Southern whites mistakenly assumed, evidence of promiscuity. Slaves rejected guilt-laden white sexual attitudes.[56] The African American slave, like the Melanesian, the West African, the Bantu, the North American Indian, and the nineteenth-century Englishman living in Britain's agricultural districts, dissociated the two sides of procreation, and believed that marriage licensed parenthood rather than sexual intercourse.[57] If teenage girls were not bound to chastity by puritanical ideas that made it a sin to be anything but true to the traditional white worn on the wedding day, they were circumscribed by mothers who were intent on protecting their daughters against the premature assumption of maternal responsibility.

Many slave mothers adhered to mores that made motherhood almost sacred, mores rooted in the black woman's African past. In traditional West Africa, mothers, by virtue of their having and nurturing children, ensured the survival of the lineage, the consanguineal corporate group that controlled and dictated the use and inheritance of property, provided access to various political and/or religious offices, regulated marriages, and performed political and economic functions.[58] In matrilineal societies it was through the mother that affiliation to the lineage was established. Mothers were the genetically significant link between successive generations. Her line determined her children's succession, inheritance, rights, obligations, and citizenship. Though most political offices were held by men, political status was conferred by women.[59] In the more common patrilineal societies, fathers were the kinship link, yet mothers were still important. It was through a man's wife that his ancestral line was perpetuated. She gave him heirs through whom he passed on his property and status. In all African societies having children meant having wealth, since their work translated into material gain.[60]

In traditional West Africa the most important responsibility of each individual was to have children. Thus women, as child bearers and nurturers, were absolutely central to African family and tribal life. In many societies a marriage was not considered consummated until after the birth of the first child. The birth of this child signaled a rite of passage for both partners, for they were no longer considered adolescents but adults. For some men it meant being able to set up an independent household away from their father's control. For women, having a child was the most important rite of passage in their life. It was after the birth of the first child that most African women left their family of origin to take up residence in their husband's compound, among the members of his lineage. African women were valued for their work, which contributed to the economic success of the family, but their greatest asset was their fecundity.[61]

West African women both respected and enjoyed their status as mothers. With their children, especially their daughters, they had their most enduring and cherished relationships.[62] Because mothers lived with and nurtured their children in a hut separate from their husbands, the mother-child relationship usually had more depth and emotional content than either the father-child or the husband-wife relationship.[63] At some point, often at puberty but sometimes earlier, sons left their mother's hut to join the men of the lineage segment, but they never severed the mother-son emotional bond. If they were members of a polygynous unit their attachment to their mothers was exceptionally strong since they shared her only with other blood siblings, while they shared their fathers both with blood siblings and the children of his other wives. In such a setting the African mother became the watchdog for her children, protecting their claim to inherit their father's property.[64]

[. . .] At no stage in her life cycle was the plantation slave woman immune to the brutality of the system. And yet, most women enjoyed the love and companionship of other slaves throughout their lifetime, most knew the excitement of courtship and the joys of motherhood. In addition, most slave girls grew up believing that boys and girls were equal. Had they been white and free, they would have learned the contemporary wisdom of nineteenth-century America, that women were the maidservants of men, that women were feeble and delicate, intellectually unfit for all but the most rudimentary education. As it was, because they were black and slave they learned that black women had to be the maidservants of whites, but not necessarily of men. They learned, too, from both the whites of the Big House and the blacks of the quarters that becoming a mother was the most important of life's transitions for slave women and that caring for young children would always be an important female responsibility.

Notes

1. George Rawick, ed., *The American Slave, a Composite Autobiography*, 19 vols. (Westport, Conn.: Greenwood, 1972): Va., 16:2. (Hereafter cited with the foregoing construction.)
2. Arnold van Gennep, *The Rites of Passage* (Chicago: University of Chicago Press, 1960), pp. 2–3.
3. For more information on the life of children and the age-segregated world they lived in see Eugene Genovese, *Roll, Jordan, Roll, The World the Slaves Made* (New York: Vintage, 1974), pp. 508–509.
4. Ala., 6:33.
5. Ark., 10 (5): 155.
6. Frances Anne Kemble, *Journal of a Residence on a Georgian Plantation*, John A. Scott, ed. (New York: Knopf, 1961), p. 156. See also Beth G. Crabtree and James W. Patton, eds., *"Journal of a Secesh Lady" The Diary of Catherine Devereux Edmondston 1860–1866* (Raleigh, N.C.: Division of Archives and History, 1979), p. 45.
7. B. A. Botkin, ed., *Lay My Burden Down: A Folk History of Slavery* (Chicago: University of Chicago Press, 1945), p. 62.
8. Ophelia S. Egypt, J. Masuoka, and Charles S. Johnson, eds., *Unwritten History of Slavery, Autobiographical Accounts of Negro Ex-Slaves* (Nashville, Tenn.: Fisk University Press, 1945), p. 15.
9. Ala., 6:197.
10. Linda Brent, *Incidents in the Life of a Slave Girl*, Lydia Maria Child, ed. (New York: Harcourt Brace Jovanovich, 1973 [1861]), p. 7.
11. Botkin, ed., *Lay My Burden Down*, pp. 63, 90, 141–142; Frederick Olmstead, *The Cotton Kingdom*, David Freeman Hawke, ed. (New York: Bobbs-Merrill, 1971), p. 152; William Howard Russell, *My Diary North and South (Canada, Its Defenses, Condition, and Resources)*, 3 vols. (London: Bradbury and Evans, 1863), 1:387.
12. Ga., 13(3):160; Louis Hughes, *Thirty Years a Slave* (Milwaukee: South Side, 1897), p. 41; Mo., 10(7):255; Frederick Olmstead, *A Journey in the Seaboard Slave States* (New York: Dix and Edwards, 1856), p. 430; *Plantation Manual*, Southern Historical Collection, University of North Carolina at Chapel Hill, Chapel Hill, North Carolina. (Hereafter cited as SHC.); Olmstead, *Cotton Kingdom*, pp. 78, 175; Kemble, *Journal of a Residence on a Georgian Plantation*, pp. 87, 197; Hughes, *Thirty Years a Slave*, pp. 22, 41; Benjamin Drew, *The Refugee: A North-Side View of Slavery, in Four Fugitive Slave Narratives* (Reading, Mass.: Addison, Wesley, 1969), p. 128; Adwon Adams Davis, *Plantation Life in the Florida Parishes of Louisiana 1836–1846 as Reflected in the Diary of Bennet H. Barrow* (New York: Columbia University Press, 1943), p. 127; Crabtree and Patton, eds., *"Journal of a Secesh Lady,"* p. 46.
13. James Trussel and Richard Steckel, "The Age of Slaves and Menarche and Their First Birth," *Journal of Interdisciplinary History* (Winter 1978), 8:504.
14. Miss., 7(2):44; Olmstead, *Seaboard Slave States*, pp. 27–28, 112; S.C., 2(2):47; Botkin, ed., *Lay My Burden Down*, p. 80, 113.
15. S.C., 2(2):47; Botkin, ed., *Lay My Burden Down*, p. 145.
16. Ala., 6:243.
17. Brent, *Incidents in the Life of a Slave Girl*, p. 57.

18. Ga., 12(4):292; Ga., 13(3):69.

19. Brent, *Incidents in the Life of a Slave Girl*, p. 17.

20. Egypt, ed., *Unwritten History*, pp. 68.

21. Ibid., p. 167; see also S.C., 2:201.

22. Norman Yetman, *Voices From Slavery* (New York: Holt, Rhinehart and Winston, 1970), p. 102.

23. Ark., 8(2):319.

24. Fisk University, *Unwritten History*, p. 10.

25. Va., 16:15.

26. Fisk University, *Unwritten History*, p. 8; Va., 16:25.

27. C. Vann Woodward, ed., *Mary Chesnut's Civil War* (New Haven: Yale University Press, 1981), p. 307.

28. Olmstead, *Back Country*, p. 169.

29. Okla., 6:280.

30. S.C., 2(2):51–52.

31. Although historian Robert Fogel and Stanley Engerman cite the slave woman's age at first birth at 22.5, other historians, including Herbert Gutman and Richard Dunn, have found the age to be substantially lower. Dunn found the average age at first birth on the Mount Airy Virginia Plantation to be 19.22 years. Gutman found the range to be from 17–19. Economists James Trussell and Richard Steckel have found the age to be 20.6 years. See Robert Fogel and Stanley Engerman, *Time on the Cross, The Economics of American Negro Slavery* (Boston: Little, Brown, 1974), pp. 137–138; Richard Dunn, "The Tale of Two Plantations: Slave Life at Mesopotamia in Jamaica and Mount Airy in Virginia, 1799–1828," *William and Mary Quarterly* (January 1977), 34:58; Herbert Gutman, *The Black Family in Slavery and Freedom, 1750–1925* (New York: Pantheon Books, 1976), pp. 50, 75, 124, 171; James Trussell and Richard Steckel, "Age of Slaves at Menarche and First Birth," p. 504; the term *marriage* is used in this text with the understanding that legal marriage among slaves was prohibited.

32. *Industrial Resources of the Southern and Western States* 3 vols. (Washington, D.C.: Government Printing Office, 1854), 1:163.

33. Mo., 10(7):310; Fisk University, *Unwritten History*, 61–62; Ga., 13(3): 79, 262; Ark., 10(7):14; Letter, Richard J. Arnold to Mr. Swanson, May 22, 1937, in Arnold Screven Family Papers, Series B, 1811–1869, SHC; Frederick Olmstead, *A Journey in the Back Country 1853–1854* (New York: Putnam's Sons, 1907), p. 154.

34. *Plantation Manual*, SHC.

35. Susan Dabney Smedes, *Memorials of a Southern Planter*, Fletcher M. Green, ed. (New York: Knopf, 1965), p. 42.

36. Henry Bibb, "Narrative of the Life and Adventures of Henry Bibb, an American Slave," in *Puttin' on Ole Massa*, Gilbert Osofsky, ed. (New York: Harper and Row, 1969), p. 79.

37. N.C., 2:32. See also Ga., 12(1):165.

38. John Spencer Basset, ed., *The Southern Plantation Overseer as Revealed in His Letters* (Northampton, Mass.: Southworth, 1925), pp. 31, 139, 141; Ulrich Bonnell Phillips, ed., *Plantation and Frontier Documents, 1649–1863*, 2 vols. (Cleveland: Arthur H. Clarke, 1909), 1:312; Kemble, *Journal of a Residence on a Georgian Plantation*, p. 179.

39. Phillips, ed., *Plantation and Frontier Documents*, 1:109.

40. Kemble, *Journal of a Residence on a Georgian Plantation*, pp. 95, 127.

41. Ga., 13(4):8.

42. Helen T. Caterall, ed., *Judicial Cases Concerning American Slavery and the Negro*, 5 vols. (Washington, D.C.: Carnegie Institute of Washington, 1936), 2:151–152.

43. Bassett, *Plantation Overseer*, p. 32. See also Raymond and Alice Bauer, "Day-to-Day Resistance to Slavery," *Journal of Negro History* (October 1942), 27:415.

44. Catterall, ed., *Judicial Cases*, 3:65, 204. See also ibid., 69, 79, 164, 195, 213, 523, 541; ibid., 2:214, 392.

45. Olmsted, *Seaboard Slave States*, p. 55.

46. Ga., 12(1):191.

47. Botkin, ed., *Lay My Burden Down*, p. 119.

48. Dunn, "Two Plantations," p. 58; Mo., 10(7):253.

49. Botkin, ed., *Lay My Burden Down*, pp. 160–162.

50. William Wells Brown, "Narrative of William Wells Brown, a Fugitive Slave," in Osofsky, ed., *Ole Massa*, p. 214.

51. Bibb in Osofsky, ed., *Ole Massa*, p. 119. See also Mo., 10(7):135. See also Harriet Martineau, *Society in America*, 3 vols. (London: Saunders and Otley, 1837), 2:156; Fla., 17:168; Miss., 6:114; Va., 16:11.

52. Trussell and Steckel. "The Age of Slaves at Menarche and First Birth," p. 492.

53. Ibid.

54. Cheryll Ann Cody, "Slave Demography and Family Formation. A Community Study of the Ball Family Plantations, 1720–1896," (Ph.D. dissertation, University of Minnesota, 1982), pp. 59. 155, 156.

55. See, for example, what historian Leslie Howard Owens says about the slave family: Leslie Howard Owens, *This Species of Property, Slave Life and Culture in the Old South* (Oxford: Oxford University Press, 1976), pp. 200–202; see also Genovese, *Roll, Jordan, Roll*, pp. 450–458.

56. Gutman, *The Black Family*, pp. 14, 17, 31–33, 67.

57. Niara Sudarkasa, "Female Employment and Family Organization in West Africa," in Filomina Chioma Steady, *The Black Woman Cross-Culturally* (Cambridge, Mass.: Schenkman, 1981), p. 53.

58. Agnes Akousua Aidoo, "Ashante Queen Mothers in Government and Politics in the Nineteenth Century," in Steady, *The Black Woman Cross-Culturally*, p. 65. See also Monique Gessain, "Coniagui Women," in Denise Paulme, ed., *Women of Tropical Africa* (Berkeley: University of California Press, 1963), p. 17.

59. Paulme, ed., *Women of Tropical Africa*, pp. 11–12. Gessain, "Coniagui Women," p. 17. Melville Herskovits, *The Myth of the Negro Past* (Boston: Beacon, 1978 [1941]), p. 186–187.

60. Gessain, "Coniagui Women," p. 28; Marguerite Dupire, "The Position of Women in a Pastoral Society (The Fulani Wo Daa Be, Nomads of the Niger)," in Paulme, ed., *Women of Tropical Africa*, p. 58, 62.

61. Gessain, "Coniagui Women," p. 42; Dupire, "The Position of Women in a Pastoral Society," pp. 56, 72.

62. Niara *Sudarkasa*, "Interpreting the African Heritage in Afro-American Family Organization," in Harriete Pipes McAdoo, ed., *Black Families* (Beverly Hills, Calif.: Sage, 1981), p. 42–43.

63. Ibid.; Nancy Tanner, "Matrifocality in Indonesia and Africa and among Black Americans," in Michelle Zimbalist Rosaldo and Louise Lamphere, eds., *Women, Culture and Society* (Stanford: Stanford University Press, 1974), p. 147; Sylvia Leith-Ross, *African Women: A Study of the Ibo in Nigeria* (London: Routledge and Kegan Paul, 1939), p. 127; Herskovitz, *Myth of the Negro Past*, p. 64.

64. Gessain, "Coniagui Women," p. 43; Dupire, "The Position of Women in a Pastoral Society," p. 73.

CHAPTER 2

"Grown Girls, Highly Cultivated"

Female Education in an Antebellum Southern Family

Anya Jabour

In 1824 Elizabeth Wirt received a letter from William H. Cabell, her brother-in-law, suggesting that she turn the supervision of her Washington, D.C., household over to her two oldest daughters, Laura and Elizabeth G. ("Liz"), in order to visit her relatives in Richmond, Virginia. This was a visit of "duty" that Elizabeth had been deferring with the excuse that neither young woman was prepared for the responsibility of running the Wirt house. Cabell was scandalized that Laura, at twenty-one, and Liz, at fifteen, were unacquainted with even the rudiments of household management. "Two *grown* girls, & *highly cultivated* girls, who cannot be trusted with the care of the house and of the children for ten days," he charged, were surely a sign that Elizabeth had been remiss in training her daughters. Elizabeth, Cabell maintained, had devoted too much attention to her daughters' intellectual development and too little to their practical learning in housewifery. He recommended a decisive shift in Elizabeth's parenting strategy. "Altho they have not heretofore attended much to your domestic matters, I am sure it is because they have not thought it necessary—make it necessary," Cabell urged, "and they will attend to them as carefully as you would do or could do[.]"[1]

Elizabeth Wirt easily could have dismissed her brother-in-law's letter as the rantings of a meddlesome relative. William Cabell showed little appreciation for the growing interest in women's education in the early national South that had led the Wirts to raise "highly cultivated" daughters. Furthermore, he overlooked the important role that Elizabeth's husband, U.S. Attorney General William Wirt, played in the education of the Wirts' children. But Cabell's letter, coming as it did at a critical juncture in the Wirts' lives and in a broader dialogue on women's proper role in the South and the nation, marked an important turning point for Elizabeth and William Wirt and their six daughters: Laura, Liz, Catharine, Ellen, Rosa, and Agnes. During the 1820s the Wirts shifted the responsibility for their daughters' education from their father to their mother and changed the emphasis from the classics to more feminine pursuits. Although the Wirts finally committed themselves to a seemingly more restrictive approach to the cultivation of their "grown girls" and to an apparently limited role for women in the Old South, the revolutionary potential of their earlier experiments with advanced education for women was modified and incorporated into the training in "domestic matters" that the Wirts provided for their youngest daughters. The Wirts pioneered a new model of female education that, although intended to accommodate women's prescribed roles, actually redefined what it meant to be a "grown girl, highly cultivated" in the antebellum South. By the 1830s, the Wirts had established a plan for female education that laid the groundwork for women's organizations in the South even as it accepted limited intellectual horizons.

The Wirt family's correspondence in these years illuminates a critical era in which attitudes toward female education and women's proper roles in antebellum America and in the U.S. South were undergoing profound changes. Linda K. Kerber and others have demonstrated that educational reformers in revolutionary and early national America favored higher education for women. Such education was valuable, proponents argued, because it prepared women for their important duties as virtuous wives and "republican mothers."[2] Catherine Clinton's study of women in the seaboard South between 1780 and 1835 likewise suggests that elite southern families valued their daughters' education highly. However, Clinton notes a pattern of decline in southern women's education toward the end of that period. The classics were replaced by embroidery. Not until the 1850s did higher education for southern women regain its former popularity.[3]

The education of the Wirts' daughters both reflected and resisted a regional pattern of academic retrenchment that was itself shaped by a broader national concern with making women's education useful. Attitudes toward what Anne

Firor Scott has labeled the "ambiguous reform" of women's education were linked to perceptions of a woman's proper role in society. As the enthusiasm for educating republican women waned in the 1820s and 1830s, families and educators sought new justifications for female education.[4] This search took on a distinctive regional dimension. While northeasterners perceived classical education and domestic training as compatible and even complementary, several studies suggest that southerners in the 1830s had little faith in the efficacy of educating women.[5]

In the hiatus between the enthusiasm for educating republican women in the opening decades of the nineteenth century and the push to provide a "Southron" education for "southern belles" in the 1850s and early 1860s, southern families struggled to justify female education.[6] During this period, the Wirts searched for a suitable educational strategy for their daughters. Although Elizabeth and William Wirt hoped to provide their younger daughters with training that would complement, rather than challenge, their designated role as southern wives, they also helped to create a basis for distinctive southern female communities that emphasized women's relationships with each other, their responsibilities to society, and the importance of lifelong self-cultivation. By the 1830s the Wirts had established a pattern for women's education that would become the standard for women's academies, seminaries, and finally colleges in the antebellum South.

The Wirts were well-to-do, white southerners. Elizabeth Gamble Wirt was the second daughter of Colonel Robert Gamble, a veteran of the American Revolution and a respected Richmond merchant. William Wirt, the orphaned son of immigrant tavern keepers, was an ambitious man linked by marriage to some of the leading families of Virginia and Maryland. Following their marriage in 1802, Elizabeth and William Wirt lived in Williamsburg, Norfolk, and Richmond, Virginia; Washington, D.C.; and Baltimore, Maryland. Although the Wirts were wealthy enough to maintain a household that included five to ten slaves and, on occasion, free servants, they were not members of the South's planter elite. During their married life, Elizabeth and William Wirt never owned or lived on a plantation; their livelihood came from investments and from William's career as a lawyer. By 1817, when he was appointed U.S. attorney general, William Wirt's legal services were much sought after. Throughout his twelve-year tenure as attorney general, he represented his own clients in court in Virginia, Maryland, and, less frequently, Pennsylvania and Massachusetts in addition to fulfilling official duties in the nation's capital.[7]

Female education was a priority for the Wirts. During the early national period, both Elizabeth and William Wirt were caught up in the enthusiasm for women's learning. Elizabeth herself had benefited from the drive for women's education. She had attended a private female seminary in Richmond under the direction of a family friend and clergyman, John D. Blair. Blair demanded high achievement in French and arithmetic, and he may have anticipated the curriculum of the Richmond Female Academy, established in 1807, which included Latin, Greek, mathematics, history, geography, and natural philosophy or physics. In the book on flowers that she published in 1829, Elizabeth demonstrated easy familiarity with Latin and Greek terms as well as with English and American literature.[8] William began to contemplate women's abilities in an 1804 essay, "On the Condition of Women." He expanded his thoughts in the essays published under the pseudonym "Old Bachelor" first in the Richmond newspapers and later as a book. William followed the lead of distinguished educator and physician Benjamin Rush when he advocated women's education in the latter collection. William appealed to the logic of republican womanhood, writing that "my purpose is to court the fair; nay, if I can, to draw them into a conspiracy to bring about a revolution in this country, which I am sensible that I can never effect without their aid. . . . *The virtues of this country are with our women, and the only remaining hope of the resurrection of the genius and character of the nation rests with them*," he wrote in eloquent italics. Women would best guide the nation to virtue, William continued, "if to their virtues and their personal graces, they would superadd that additional culture of the mind which would fit them for this noble task" of uplifting the moral character of their sons and husbands.[9]

The Wirts made it their mission to provide such "culture of the mind" starting with their eldest child, Laura, born in 1803. William designed an ambitious plan of education for the Wirts' first daughter. "I have a notion of making my daughter a classical scholar," he confided to his friend Dabney Carr. "She is quick and has a genius—her person will not be unpleasing," noted William, but more significantly, "her *mind, may* be made a *beauty*." Laura's "course of education" might delay her debut until the age of seventeen, William noted, "but, I think, so much the better; for I would not wish her to be married under twenty. . . ."[10]

William's plan to make Laura "a classical scholar" required her to study a broad range of subjects under her parents' combined guidance. In many elite southern families, a daughter's advanced education demanded the close attention of her father, who was in charge of designing the curriculum and choosing secondary schools. The "course of education" that William resolved upon for six-year-old Laura included Latin, French, Italian, Spanish, and English grammar, as well as dancing, painting, and playing the piano. Laura's liberal arts curriculum and her lawyer-father's supervision made her early training very similar to that of northern girls whose professional fathers insisted that their daughters—especially their firstborn ones—apply themselves rigorously to every subject.[11]

While William directed Laura's curriculum from afar, Elizabeth was in charge of her early studies. In 1809 William wrote to Elizabeth to express his hope that Laura would, with her mother's assistance, "set to learning in earnest." He fondly daydreamed that in a few years Laura would outshine "all the girls in town put together." The Wirts worked together closely to achieve this objective. At Elizabeth's request, in 1810 William ordered a "large Atlas," a telescope, field glasses, an orrery, and "Arrowsmiths map of the world" for Laura's home schooling. Elizabeth's enthusiastic participation in the couple's first ambitious experiments with their oldest daughter's education set the Wirts apart from northern families like Abigail and Bronson Alcott and Margarett and Timothy Fuller, in which the mothers stayed on the sidelines of home education and expressed alienation from their precocious daughters and single-minded husbands.[12]

As Laura advanced in her studies, her father took on the chief responsibility for her instruction in advanced subjects such as Latin. Day schools and visiting instructors supplemented Laura's home instruction during the Wirts' years in Virginia. The specialized instructors and schoolteachers were men who were expected to report to both Elizabeth and William on Laura's progress in the classics. However, perhaps reflecting the schoolmasters' own assumptions or a shift in the Wirts' division of responsibility, the male tutors directed their letters to William, although Elizabeth frequently commented on Laura's teachers and made decisions about Laura's schooling both independently and in consultation with her husband. As Laura advanced in her lessons with promising speed, William took primary responsibility for directing her studies. His hope, he confided to Laura when she was seven years old, was that "every body will say by & bye that you are the most sensible and fine girl in Virginia."[13]

Despite their eager attempts to improve Laura's mind, the Wirts demonstrated remarkably little concern about her future. William did not seem to doubt that Laura would debut at seventeen and marry within three years. Occasionally he expressed concern that advanced schooling might harm his daughter's future marital prospects. "I want her to be something better than common," he confided to Elizabeth, "not a bold unblushing lady of fashion, nor a loquacious & disgusting pedant: but an happy union of female gentleness and delicacy, with masculine learning & genius—simple yet elegant— soft and timid, yet dignified & commanding." For the most part, however, William seems to have been swayed by the arguments of turn-of-the-century advocates of female education like Mary Wollstonecraft, Benjamin Rush, and Judith Sargent Murray, who maintained that women could attain both the full complement of intellectual advantages and womanly modesty and charm. Advances in female education would not threaten women's femininity, reformers assured post-Revolutionary Americans, and would prepare women to be better wives and mothers. William demonstrated his confidence in the compatibility of girlhood schooling and a woman's duty to marry in his comments in 1809. Suiting a woman's education to her future, he thought, was as simple as beginning her education early enough to allow her to complete her schooling prior to her debut. Reconciling himself to the impossibility of educating the Wirts' precocious six-year-old daughter together with her younger (and less intelligent) brother Robert, he noted that "he has a great . . . more time" for learning. By contrast, "Laura ought to have her education by the time she is sixteen," he planned. "That is little enough for all the acquirements I wish her to possess."[14]

Elizabeth's thoughts on her husband's long-term plans for Laura were not recorded, but she seems to have been satisfied with his reasoning. Like Abigail Alcott, she seems to have fully accepted her husband's ideas about child rearing during their early years as parents. Elizabeth's letters to her husband were filled with bright accounts of Laura's progress, requests for teaching supplies, and reminders that William should write letters to Laura in order to inspire her to further study.[15]

The Wirts' early approach to female education made few special accommodations for a southern woman's future as a wife and mother. In 1815, when the Wirts considered hiring a private tutor for Laura, then twelve years old, and Robert, age ten, the "system of study" that William devised was ambitious. "Natural philosophy—astronomy—chemistry—botany—form a part of the system," he explained. In addition, William expected both Laura and her brother to study Latin, English, French, history, philosophy, literature, grammar, and arithmetic. William designed several drafts of a daily schedule that extended from 5:30 A.M. to 10 P.M., marking off hours for sleep, dressing, exercise, music, meals, and conversation as well as formal subjects. Unlike Thomas Jefferson's otherwise similar programs for his two daughters, William Wirt's schemes were not marked with names and, therefore, did not differentiate by sex.[16]

As Laura began to undertake more advanced subjects, she looked more and more to her father for direction. By the time his daughter was eight years old, William boasted to casual acquaintances that she easily outpaced boys' academic achievements. "Tell Laura," he wrote in a letter home in 1812, "there was a gentleman here to-day with a pretty little boy nine years old who was only learning to read english and tell her how proud I felt to be able to boast that I had a daughter not yet nine years old, that was reading Erasmus." Laura admired her father and wrote to him frequently about her studies and to request his assistance with difficult passages in "my Caesar." In late 1817, when William accepted the position of U.S. attorney general, fourteen-year-old Laura was eager to continue her studies in the Wirts' new home. "I am determined to study very hard after I get to Washington," she promised her father.[17]

Although William had become Laura's chief tutor, Elizabeth had been a willing ally in the "system of study" that he had designed for Laura. By the time the Wirts moved to Washington, D.C., their family included nine children, ranging in age from under one year to fourteen years old, with another (and final) child on the way. Elizabeth was preoccupied with the care and home education of the younger children as well as with extensive household production in the Wirts' Richmond establishment—which included five to ten slaves, occasionally a hired servant, and a variety of outbuildings—and seems to have been happy to leave her oldest daughter's education to her husband. Although she felt herself inadequate to the task of instructing Laura in the classics, she encouraged her husband to continue in the path that the Wirts had marked out for their oldest daughter.[18]

Following the move to Washington in 1817, the Wirts began to change their approach to female education. Writing to his kinsman Peachey Gilmer, William admitted to a "prejudice in favor of keeping daughters under their own mother's eye" and praised the benefits of "domestic education," in which children were "under the direction of their mother." Like their older sister, Liz and Catharine Wirt had been introduced to classical subjects through a combination of home schooling, visiting instructors, and day schools. During the Wirts' first year in Washington, all three girls attended a local female seminary chosen by their father. By 1818 William had become convinced that the seminary was "not well systematized" and "the children are left rather too much to themselves, to learn or not as they please." Like the parents in Jane Turner Censer's study of North Carolina planter families, the Wirts wished to develop their daughters' personal qualities as well as their minds. Dissatisfaction with the girls' mental and moral development spurred William to withdraw them from the academy. A "domestic education," William hoped, would enable the girls to acquire the "daily examples and habitudes" that were essential to the process of "slow & gradual growth."[19]

The Wirts' behavior toward their oldest daughter as she entered adolescence hinted at changes to come in their approach to the education of Laura's younger sisters. While her father continued to direct her studies, women teachers and Laura's female kin—her mother and aunt—assumed primary responsibility for setting Laura's daily schedule. Laura briefly attended a female academy in the city, then continued her lessons, including Latin, at home. After a bout of scarlet fever in 1819, Laura went to the plantation of her aunt, Elizabeth's sister Nancy, in Buckingham County, Virginia, for the summer. Nancy's husband, William H. Cabell, promised to "keep her to her books following the course [her father] shall prescribe" alongside her cousin, Louisa

Elizabeth Cabell. Although Laura's uncle was in charge of her studies, Laura's stay in the countryside was part of a common planter practice of "aunt adoption," in which young women learned to look to their female kin as guides in domestic matters. When Laura returned home to Washington, her formal schooling ended. William, concerned for his daughter's excessively intellectual bent, withdrew from parenting, prompting her to charge him with "neglect." Elizabeth took charge of her daughter, supervising her lessons in sewing and baking and preparing for her debut.[20]

The shift from school to home and from paternal to maternal direction was common for teenage girls in nineteenth-century America.[21] In Laura's case, the Wirts' concern for keeping her "under the direction of [her] mother" was probably related to her imminent debut. In 1817, as Elizabeth and William planned for the move to Washington, fourteen-year-old Laura "received a ticket to the Cotillion . . . parties for the whole Season." Although both William and Elizabeth considered her too young for courtship, they were already making plans for that eventuality. William planned to purchase "a pair of large elegant horses" and a new carriage for the day when "Miss Laura comes forward," and Elizabeth hoped to build two more rooms onto the house to accommodate her oldest daughter's debut into society. Like Margarett and Timothy Fuller, the Wirts may have begun to view their daughter differently as she entered adolescence and began to show signs of physical maturity. For young Margaret Fuller, the informal socialization that preceded a woman's entry into the marriage market prompted her parents to lay new emphasis on feminine propriety. Similarly, preparation for their oldest daughter's debut and prospective marriage provoked Elizabeth and William Wirt to reevaluate their roles in all of their daughters' lives and to question the usefulness of female education.[22]

As they laid plans for Laura's debut, the Wirts shifted more responsibility for her upbringing to Elizabeth and downplayed academic pursuits. Although this division of responsibility was not uncommon for nineteenth-century families, the parent who initiated the shift varied. In some northern families that produced future writers, thinkers, and reformers, fathers, such as Timothy Fuller, took primary responsibility for girls' education, but when their daughters became adolescents they yielded control to their more domestic-minded wives. In other families, mothers encouraged their tomboy daughters to continue their education and helped them to resist their more conservative fathers' antiacademic stance.[23] In the Old South, young planter-class women commonly received their principal direction from other women, especially their own mothers, who socialized them into their role as southern women. As Elizabeth Fox-Genovese has suggested, women from the slaveholding class received their most important direction from their mothers. Because only other women could provide young women with role models for adulthood within the context of antebellum southern society, maternal direction quickly overshadowed the lessons that girls had learned from their fathers, tutors, or schoolteachers.[24]

In the Wirt family, Elizabeth and William seem to have shared the decision to redirect the supervision of Laura's education from her father to her mother and to change her curriculum from a classical education to domestic activities. William may well have initiated the shift. Letters from Elizabeth to William in 1818 reveal that he was primarily responsible for Laura's education and that her studies fared poorly during his extended absences to attend courts in Virginia and Maryland. Elizabeth encouraged her husband to return home and resume his responsibilities as the family tutor, but he did not. Instead, as his legal responsibilities increased, William began to consider the possible disadvantages of continued education for his oldest daughter. For William, concern for Laura's debut inspired a new concern for the compatibility of education and femininity. In December 1818 he advised Laura in his usual style to "estimate properly the value of youthful study . . . and apply it to yourself[.]" By 1820, however, William had begun to worry that his parenting had been overly concerned with academic achievement. An intelligent woman "may be admired," William wrote to Laura, "but she will never be beloved." William reminded Laura that "to make yourself pleasing" was "the sweetest charm" of "your sex." William's letter to his daughter indicated the shift in his thinking from the previous decade, when he had confidently anticipated that Laura could achieve a union of feminine grace and masculine genius. He had by 1820 begun to anticipate the fears of a new generation of Americans: femininity and intellect were incompatible, and learned women were unattractive—and all-too-often unmarriageable—bluestockings.[25]

Although amenable to Laura's continued studies at home, Elizabeth also expressed new concern for Laura as a candidate for marriage. She left to William's discretion whether or not to continue Laura's home studies; meanwhile, Elizabeth directed her daughter in domestic skills and the art of pleasing others. During Laura's visit to her aunt's plantation in the summer of 1820, Elizabeth's letters to her were peppered with comments designed to prepare Laura for courtship and marriage. Laura's personal grooming and appearance became matters of immense importance. "[T]ell me . . . every thing about yourself," Elizabeth urged. "[A]t what hour you arose in the morning—how you arrayed yourself for the day—who helped you to make up your ruffs, &c &c?" Elizabeth also worried that Laura had not been properly trained for the housekeeping duties that would follow marriage. It was time, she wrote, for Laura to acquaint herself with "the *minutia* of housekeeping."[26]

Although their preparations for Laura's debut caused the Wirts to reorient her education, Laura's response to circumstances following her coming out forced the Wirts to reconsider their approach to female education more seriously. Following her formal debut during the capital city's winter "season" of 1820–1821, Laura complained bitterly of the "disagreeable occupations" of housekeeping and "the empty frivolities of the Beau Mode." At the end of her first season, she looked forward to spending the summer with a good supply of books "that I might have some chance of improvement." Laura had little direction in her attempts to continue her studies, however. During the long period between the end of schooling and marriage, William occasionally suggested that his intellectually inclined daughter undertake some new study, but he provided no guidance; meanwhile, Elizabeth and William both subjected their daughter to a litany of reminders that her future depended on a successful match. "Give my love to dear Laura," William wrote home in late 1823, "and tell her that I recommend to her . . . to display a respectful interest in every one that approaches her." Laura was not easily converted from books to belledom, however. For more than five years, she tried to improve her mind, putting off her suitors and deflecting parental pressure to marry. When her efforts to continue her studies proved fruitless, she fell prey to depression and to a series of vague but troubling health problems that her parents labeled "hysteria." Laura's poor health and erratic behavior as she questioned her future and her parents' prescriptions for a woman's relationship to society caused the Wirts much anxiety until she finally married in 1827 at the relatively late age of twenty-three.[27]

Laura's crisis was decisive in the Wirts' approach to educating their younger daughters. Recognizing that the disjuncture between Laura's advanced education and her closely prescribed future had prompted Laura's unhappiness, Elizabeth and William Wirt reevaluated their approach to female education and attempted to ease their younger daughters more gracefully from girlhood to womanhood. As they did so, they began a serious search for a useful education for southern women, a search that would lead them to redefine southern womanhood as well as to redesign their daughters' curriculum.

The Wirts' reassessment of female education also provoked them to redistribute their responsibilities as parents. Inspired by the post-Revolutionary enthusiasm for female education, Elizabeth and William Wirt initially had cooperated in a design to make their girls, as William expressed it, "classical scholar[s]." When the Wirts reevaluated their child-rearing strategies in the 1820s, however, they also began to shift responsibility for girls' education from William to Elizabeth. William, who reluctantly relinquished his role as family tutor, labored to produce a theory of female learning that justified classical education. Elizabeth, who was responsible for the day-to-day supervision of the Wirts' daughters, followed her brother-in-law's advice and assumed the task of training the girls in domestic matters. During the 1820s, the Wirt daughters were caught between the seemingly incompatible directives of their mother and father. As the decade drew to a close, however, the Wirts' shifting strategies of female education hastened the process by which William, preoccupied with work and politics, reduced his direct involvement in child rearing. Left on her own to shepherd their daughters from girlhood to womanhood, Elizabeth Wirt made it her mission to give the Wirts' "grown girls" a suitably feminine education. Ultimately, the route she chose, which curbed the intense learning that her husband continued to defend, enabled the Wirts' daughters to find new outlets for their talents and ambitions in organized female benevolence and in lifelong self-improvement in the company of other women.

William had designed the plan to make Laura a "classical scholar," but Elizabeth took a more active role in the Wirts' search for a suitable education for their other daughters. Following Laura's difficult adolescence, Elizabeth resolved to train the Wirts' five younger daughters differently. Her brother-in-law's comments on the inadvisability of emphasizing intellectual culture over household management may not have been the only criticism of Elizabeth's child-rearing methods. Margaret Smith, an educated woman who was a pillar of Washington society and a popular domestic author, worried that "Mrs. W.'s artificial and refined system of education" made her daughters "fragile," "hot-house plants, that will never bear an exposure to the cold and rude air of common life."[28] By the mid-1820s Elizabeth was inclined to agree with her critics both that the responsibility for raising daughters was hers and that a daughter's education should emphasize preparation for the "common life" of southern women: courtship, marriage, and domestic responsibilities.

Elizabeth's concern and responsibility for preparing her daughters for their seemingly predetermined futures as wives and mothers was shared by other women in antebellum America. Like Williana Lacy in Steven M. Stowe's study of a North Carolina planter family, Elizabeth Wirt, more than her husband, believed that it was necessary to prepare young women for the specific tasks they would confront in their lives, rather than to bombard them with empty exhortations to fulfill their places in society, as some scholars have contended was common among the South's elite.[29] Elizabeth emphasized practical training in housewifery. Laura's difficulties, Elizabeth averred, could be traced to her lack of involvement in housekeeping. Laura found Washington "dull," noted Elizabeth, but it was "not dull for *me*—for my active & incessant avocations fill up my time completely."[30] Elizabeth's acerbic tone indicates that, like Margaret's mother, she may have been inspired to redirect the girls' education in part because she was unable to participate fully in the education of her clever oldest daughter.[31] Beginning in the 1820s she began to insist that the Wirts prepare their daughters for the "incessant avocations" that would fall to them as grown women. Eager to direct her maturing daughters toward domestic pursuits, Elizabeth provided them with a practicum in housewifery. During the summer of 1823, while Elizabeth and William traveled, they wrote letters home directing Liz to supervise the slaves at work in the garden and the house. The following year, Liz assured her grandmother that her experience had made her an accomplished director of household matters. "You had a specimen . . . of my *good management* when you were here," she noted, "and as 'practise makes perfect' I assure you that I am now at all points *une femme de charge*." Elizabeth also expected her daughters to perform basic household tasks themselves. "This is [Liz's] week for housekeeping," she noted in May 1824. "She made on yesterday a most famous *poundcake* . . . to day [brought] forth a *boiled custard*, of superlative quality. . . ." Later that year, Liz informed her father that all the girls had been initiated into a new regime. "We have quite a sewing club this morning," she reported, "every . . . woman and child from Alpha to Omega is plying her needle most assiduously."[32]

William, whose faith in the value of female education remained strong, hoped for more success in combining intellectual and social achievements with the Wirts' younger daughters. His letters took on a contradictory quality as he encouraged Liz and Catharine to work to their full capacities, yet continually reminded them of the need to harmonize high academic standards and feminine "graces." "Quiet and unpretending simplicity of disposition and manners" were essential to the "secret of female power and witchcraft," he began one of his lengthy letters to Liz. Echoing his letter to Laura at the conclusion of her schooling, he warned: "a rattling and voluble tongue, with rattling and volatile spirits, and noisy grace and brilli[ance, dem]anding admiration and exacting homage as their right, may strike and gain eclat and even admiration & external hommage, but they will never win hearts." Modesty, however, did not mean that Liz, then fifteen years old, should shrink from rigorous standards of learning. "Cultivate solid judgment, solid graces, solid kindness and goodness," William urged, "and leave light, frothy, brilliant affectations and pretensions to others—at the same time, *cultivate the solid graces and valuable accomplishments—this is your father's advice*." William's messages to Catharine were similarly mixed. In early 1824 William urged his thirteen-year-old daughter to "application intense, persevering and indefatigable," couching his argument in terms of her eventual debut. "I must strongly inculcate upon you the necessity of making a good use of your time," he began his lecture. "You will soon be a woman and be expected to enter society with a mind highly cultivated and stored with knowledge."[33]

As Liz and Catharine neared the end of their home schooling and prepared to leave for a final stint at a female academy, William struggled to find a rationale for rigorous female education and a suitably feminine goal for intellectual development. William viewed education as a necessary and valuable stage of personal development. Recommending to the girls "close and unwearied assiduity," he argued that self-improvement was its own reward. "Indolence will spoil all—mind, heart, . . . and habits," he warned. "You will be discontented with yourself. . . ." However, "progress in knowledge," William asserted, would prove a source of happiness. "The consciousness that you are making solid and useful acquisitions will animate you," he predicted.[34] Education and character-building, to William's mind, often went together. He urged both girls to improve mind and morals, frequently advising them to take advantage of their school years to build strength of character. Liz should "play the busy bee," he reminded her in 1824, "not the lazy drone."[35]

Although William emphasized that the girls should pursue knowledge for its own sake, he evidently agreed with his wife that, for women, education should be more clearly related to future responsibilities. For William, as for Elizabeth, one acceptable goal of education was preparation for marriage. "Are you practising the graces?" he asked Liz in 1822. "I have set my heart on your making a figure in society which I know you can do if you please. . . . it is early in life to write to you on this subject," he admitted to his thirteen-year-old daughter, "and much too early for you even to dream of the conquests of a *belle*—but not too early for you to begin to form your character to loveliness and enchantment, as they operate on all ages and sexes. . . ."[36] Christie Anne Farnham's recent study of southern women's academies suggests that, properly managed, higher education could be an asset in the marriage market. Parents could send their daughters to female academies without contradicting their purpose of finding good matches for them because a classical, liberal arts education could be perceived as the final polish necessary to gentility. William understood the advantages of education as an indication of elite standing. "I shall have no fortune to give you," he reminded Catharine in 1824, "and your only attractions [will] be those which you will possess in your own person. A good disposition, good [man]ners, an improved mind, an affectionate heart, and good habits of industry [will m]ake you a fortune in yourself."[37] By suggesting that a proper education could give the girls both an asset on the marriage market and valuable knowledge, William hoped to reconcile his enthusiasm for learning with his wife's emphasis on utility. Shortly before Liz's debut, William stepped up the pace of his letters. "The great purpose of education at your time of life is to store the mind with useful knowledge—with *solid, useful, practical* knowledge," he reminded Liz in 1825.[38]

For Liz and Catharine, the Wirts' former enthusiasm for academic achievement was combined with their new concern for the girls' futures. Schooling would henceforth mean not simply intellectual development but also preparation for life. Although Elizabeth and William Wirt directed their daughters toward different pursuits in the early 1820s, both parents emphasized the utility of learning. Like their former neighbors, discussed in Jan Lewis's study of Jeffersonian Virginia, the Wirts were in search of a practical education for their children. Solid, useful, and practical were all words that the Wirts used to remind their daughters that the lessons they learned as girls would serve them well as women. William urged the girls to "cultivate solid judgment, solid graces, solid kindness and goodness," while Elizabeth taught them to cook, sew, and supervise the family's slaves. The purpose of the education that both parents proposed for Liz and Catharine was now clearly related to their futures after the end of schooling. While Laura appears to have been unprepared for the end of her schooling, with no sense of purpose or direction other than cultivating her mind and pleasing her beloved father, Liz and Catharine learned that each of them would "soon be a woman and be expected to enter society with a mind highly cultivated and stored with knowledge"—and with basic housekeeping skills.[39]

Liz and Catharine, like Laura, attended a female academy for the final months of their schooling. In his search for a suitable school for Liz and Catharine, William Wirt revealed his growing concern with providing the girls all that the liberal arts tradition had to offer, while also preparing them for their eventual debut into society. Like the planter parents in Steven Stowe's study of female academies in the Old South, William viewed the academy as an indispensible step from girlhood to womanhood. In late 1823 William asked a friend to discuss "the comparative merits . . . of the Female academies in Balto." He was "anxious," he explained, to send the girls "to a good institution, by way of *finale* to [their] education, if one can be found." A "good institution" was not only a place for the Wirt daughters to receive their final polish but also a place to cap the girls' regime of home study and local schools with a rigorous education. William intended that the full range of subjects—including chemistry, botany, and natural philosophy or physics—would be a part of the curriculum. In the female academy, William hoped to reconcile higher learning with feminine accomplishments.[40]

Elmwood, the school where Liz and Catharine enrolled in late 1824, seemed ideal for William's purposes. The school, located near Fredericksburg, Virginia, was run by Episcopalians, Mr. and Mrs. Garnett and two of their daughters. "The family," reported Liz, "are quiet, unpretending, gentle & ladylike. Their minds are highly cultivated and polished. They are very good and kind and benevolent—there is no hollow and ostentatious display. . . . The school has been conducted with . . . order & methed." The Garnetts offered a full curriculum. "I have undertaken French, Philosophy, Geography (the use of the Globes), Grammar, Dictionary, Musick, Rhetorick & writing," reported Liz. In addition, the Garnetts offered history, Latin, Italian, English, geography, chemistry, astronomy, and drawing.[41]

Anya Jabour

In curriculum, the Garnetts' school offered much the same courses—and even used many of the same textbooks—as male colleges, with the addition of fine arts courses. The curriculum anticipated that of later southern women's colleges described in Christie Anne Farnham's study of higher education for women in the Old South. William urged the girls to take advantage of all the courses offered at Elmwood. "There is nothing to be done without labor," he reminded Liz. "The best schools afford only the facilities for instruction; it rests with the scholar to make the most of these advantages." William wrote frequent and lengthy letters to both girls, urging them to write home "at least once a week if it be only to cultivate and improve your epistolary style" and to write summaries of works as "a *trial* of your *reasoning powers*."[42]

While Elmwood's curriculum acquainted the girls with the classics that had been so essential to Laura's training, time not spent in class was tailored more specifically for women. Domesticity, piety, and charity were all combined in Saturday activities, which prepared the students for a lifetime of service not only to their husbands but also to society at large. "On Saturday we were incorporated as members of the Liberian Society," Liz informed her mother, "whose object is the transportation of emancipated slaves to their newly founded colony. We will make very slow, snail-like progress as all our profits are derived solely from the *works of our hands*. The girls are most of them employed for 2 hours on Saturday in making pincushions, bags and divers other works of ingenuity. . . ."[43]

Liz and Catharine's induction into the Liberian Society was an entree into the world of female reform more commonly associated with the North. Liz's description of the school days suggests that the Garnetts incorporated other reforms in women's education into their school as well. "The school hours are from 9 to 3," explained Liz; the girls dressed and read the Bible before the start of classes and devoted the after-school hours to "musick & exercise." Mrs. Garnett recommended "violent and bracing exercise" for the young women in her charge. "The girls established *Olympic games*," wrote Liz, "and I am so distinguished for my Antelope fleetness. . . . But there is no *horseplay* or tomboy-romping in *our plays*," she assured her mother. "I take care never to forget that I am a lady. . . ."[44]

Liz and Catharine's school went far beyond most female seminaries. Elmwood was run along the principles that would become the basis of college education for southern women in the 1850s and 1860s: academic achievement in both the classics and the fine arts, ladylike deportment, moral fortitude, and public service. In all respects the Garnetts' school sought to prepare its students for a woman's world of home, church, and society, in which hardy exercise, assiduous study, and political opinions were not only acceptable but welcome as long as they were couched in terms of feminine propriety and female duty.

At the Garnetts' school, Liz and Catharine gained a sense of mission and a justification for their ambitions, while never forgetting that they were ladies. But their stay was brief; less than two months after their arrival, Catharine's poor health prompted the Wirts to withdraw both girls from the school.[45]

Following their return home from Elmwood, Liz and Catharine were again subjected to a bewildering set of contradictory demands by both parents. Despite his growing concern for the girls' future, William at first continued to support their studies. In 1825 sixteen-year-old Liz dubbed herself a "Tyro in Botany." Stumping her teachers with her questions, she ransacked her mother's garden for samples and, with the aid of a book, spent her days "reading & anatomising every unfortunate flower which chanced to be within the reach of my rapacious fingers. I think I have a good disposition for such research," she told her father, "and when I surmount the formidable orders & classes hope to make *beaucoup de progres*." William supported Liz's fervor for learning, suggesting that she take lessons from a (male) professor at the Baptist college to supplement her education at the local female school she was attending. The following year, while she visited her relatives in Richmond during the summer of 1826, Liz conceived a plan with her cousin, Catharine Gamble, "to study in uninterrupted peace" for the rest of the summer. "We want you to chalk out a course of history for us," she informed her father, urging him to reply immediately. "Do not forget that we await the word of command from you to begin our march of science," she prompted.[46] Both Liz and Catharine wrote to William to request his opinion of their ambitious plans for the fall of 1826, including chemistry. William responded with a ringing endorsement of a liberal education for women. "I am well pleased that your [*sic*] going to study chemistry," he replied. Although women had been poorly represented in the sciences, William saw no reason that his daughters should not surpass them. Like other advocates of female education in antebellum America, he saw no contradiction in extolling women's intellectual equality while denying them social equality. "I think it is high time for you all to assert your equal rights in this regard," he declared, "and I have not the slightest objection to my daughters being among the foremost in the race[.]"[47]

While William guided his daughters' curriculum, Elizabeth shepherded them through the preparatory stages of their debut by accompanying the two girls to Richmond during the summer of 1826. The trip was an extended exercise in the art of socializing; "Any letter I get seems to tell of parties they have been at or are going to," remarked William. After Elizabeth returned home, leaving the girls in the care of their grandmother, Liz wrote letters home that were designed to please both her parents. She emphasized that religious devotions, care for her clothing, and sewing shared time with French and Plutarch. In addition, she kept up her socializing. "I had a charming ride on horseback the other evening with Adeline Marx & Frederic—Anna Brown John Broken-bury and Catharine," she noted. "Frederic rode by my side all the way. He is the mirror of gallantry, & knightly attention."[48]

Despite their mother's plans for their preparation for marriage, the girls hoped to continue their educations with their father's support. Following their return to Washington in the fall of 1826, Liz and Catharine laid plans to attend a course of lectures on chemistry as well as to study history, arithmetic, moral philosophy (physics), logic, grammar, geography, and music. Liz, who was seventeen and anticipating her debut in the winter of 1826–1827, planned to finish her formal education that fall but hoped to continue her studies on a part-time basis thereafter. "I shall labour unweariedly to my last moment and to the very day of my entrance into the beau-monde," she vowed. "Nor do I then intend to throw my books in the fire nor ever again turn the key in the library door tho' I know I must then relinquish them in a measure for fashionable visitting '*and all the et ceteras of modern life*' as mama says." Catharine, at fifteen, anticipated sufficient time to embark on new subjects. She wrote to her father to ask his permission to learn Italian as well as French, and his response was encouraging: "I mentioned to your dearest mother that I had no objection to your learning Italian," he wrote. "I am very willing to take advantage of a stray inclination of this sort in my children. . . ."[49]

Elizabeth, who had borne the brunt of Laura's erratic behavior at the conclusion of her studies, had other ideas, however. "I have just glanced over Catharine's letter," she wrote William, "and find that *Italian* is still the theme.— I for my part, think one foreign language enough," she reproved. "The time passed in acquiring *many* languages," opined Elizabeth, "would be much better employed, in gaining more solid information, or in more useful employment." The Wirts had erred in their education of Laura, Elizabeth implied, and they ought to learn from experience that their girls should be prepared for courtship and marriage. "We are not fitting our girls to be useful members of society," worried Elizabeth, "to be happy themselves, or make other [*sic*] so—Because, we are devoting them—exclusively to their Books—to the exclusion of every other pursuit or duty. . . . [D]oes our own experience prove the policy of making the devoting to study, the main object of a woman's care?" queried Elizabeth. "I think not." Already, Elizabeth feared, it was too late to fit their second eldest for her intended future as a wife. "Elizabeth is busy with the Boys below, teaching them to make pens—& reading to them the fool of Quality—She is a good sister—And a good daughter—But, I have my fears that, she will never *like* anything but her books[.] I have allowed her to the *First of January* to be devoted to them, after which, I must try if she can do any thing else."[50]

To Elizabeth, it seemed that the Wirts had not thus far been successful in avoiding the apparent mistakes they had made with their first daughter.

Although Liz's and Catharine's academic training had been tempered with charity work and some domestic experience, William had continued to make "Books" the central focus of the girls' education. Despite Liz's keen awareness that she had a deadline for the completion of her studies (an awareness that Laura seems to have lacked), she displayed no eagerness to prepare for life after school, devoting all her free time to reading, writing, and tutoring her younger siblings. Like academy-educated women both North and South, the Wirt girls seemed content to continue as "grown girls," suspended between girlhood and womanhood. "I am in no hurry" to marry, Liz confided to her father in 1828, "nor can I bear the idea of, even at a remote period ceasing to be the *spoilt child* that I have always been. My eyes are filled with tears now. I shall always be a baby!"[51] Elizabeth, however, like Margarett Fuller and Williana Lacy, was anxious to see her daughters cross the threshold from girlhood to womanhood. It was imperative, she wrote, that Liz and Catharine should learn to be, not "a good sister" or "a good daughter" but a good candidate for marriage. In her letter to William, Elizabeth shared the blame for the Wirts' apparent errors but made it clear that she planned to mend her ways and hinted that he would do well to follow suit.[52]

William did little to counter his wife's growing influence over their daughters' education in the late 1820s. Throughout the Wirts' years in Washington, he spent most of his time in his study or in court. William's far-flung practice, common among southern lawyers, necessitated frequent travel; during 1825 he spent only two months in Washington. During his absences, William rarely found time to respond to his daughters' letters. "I owe Lizzy and Catharine a letter," he commented in 1827, "but they must trust me yet a little longer—My cases will detain me I fear much longer than I anticipated[.]"[53] William's letter marked a shift in the girls' schooling as their father withdrew from active supervision of their studies to devote himself to his career.

William's lack of interest in his daughters' preparation for marriage also contributed to his retreat from parenthood. While supervising the girls at the Virginia Spring during the summer of 1826, William found that it took constant effort to prevent them from crossing the invisible but all-important boundaries on young ladies' behavior that were stringently enforced in the Old South. "They are very glad to get clear of my supervision in all their rides that they may ride as fast as they please," he commented, "and in all their walks, that they may climb and crawl into all possible dangers—and in all their dances that they may not fall under the criticism of my eye. . . . I have not had to scold them much," he summed up, "that is—not a great deal—that is—not continually. . . ." The tasks of chaperoning young ladies were very different from those of supervising girls' education, William discovered to his chagrin, and he did not welcome the change. By the end of the summer, William was eager to relinquish his parenting role. "If you were with me," he wrote to Elizabeth, "you wd. take all this off my hands. . . . without you," determined William, "I cannot get along with girls—and this is the last time that I will attempt it[.]" Preparation for Liz's debut left William similarly bewildered: "I am entirely out of my element in all this matter." He despaired of the difficulty of outfitting a daughter for the winter season. "I am always afraid of doing wrong," he excused himself to his wife, "and you must equip her according to your own taste."[54]

After their debuts in the late 1820s, the older Wirt girls were drawn further into their mother's orbit. By the spring of 1828 both Liz and Catharine had, as their father expressed it, "swains, who . . . are very much in earnest." It was up to Elizabeth to supervise this "critical and most interesting Epoche, for our dear children." William's difficulties with supervising the girls in their courtships had lasting effects. "I confess that after the contempt with which Elizabeth treated my admonition to her in Baltimore, I have no great opinion of the virtue of my lectures," he wrote to his wife. "The time has been when she attached some consequence to my advice," he sighed, "but unfortunately for her as well as me, but more unfortunately for herself, it seems to have passed away. . . . It grieves me to say this and still more to know it to be true," William concluded sadly. A disagreement with Elizabeth over the proper pace of Catharine's courtship further dissuaded William from attempts to intervene in the girls' marriage prospects. "[Y]ou can instruct them better in this subject than I can," he wrote, relinquishing the duty to Elizabeth.[55]

Liz and Catharine, like Laura, responded with melancholy and poor health to the end of their schooling and to their father's swift withdrawal. Elizabeth and William described Liz variously as "dispeptic," "morbidly sensitive," and "nervous." Catharine also exhibited symptoms of poor health, including "an affection of the *muscular system*" and "a *chronic catarrh*."[56] Both girls also delayed marriage; Catharine became engaged in 1828 but later broke off the engagement, and Liz refused the man her mother favored. Elizabeth continued to correspond with the suitor, and Liz wrote to her father to plead for understanding. "I believe that mama wishes me to love him," she wrote plaintively, "but she thinks too highly of him." Liz despaired of ever finding a mate she could love and respect. Like her older sister, she idolized her father. "I feel that whatever be my fate I shall never love any body as I do you my beloved father. I can't help crying. Good bye," she closed her heartbroken letter. "Love me as you have always done & I shall be happy." Preoccupied with legal business, William did not offer reassurances in response to his daughter's plea for her father's love. In matters pertaining to courtship, he indicated, the Wirt girls should look to their mother, not their father. "Confide freely in your dear Mother," he advised. "Her opinions are infinitely better than mine, and she will advise you tenderly as well as wisely."[57]

The education of the Wirt girls in the late 1820s and early 1830s reflected the Wirts' growing conviction that Elizabeth's plan for girls' education was "infinitely better" than her husband's preference for classical learning. The adolescent crises of the Wirts' three eldest daughters had confirmed Elizabeth's suspicion that it was not advisable to make intellectual development "the main object of a woman's care." At the same time that Elizabeth resolved to train her daughters in more "useful employments," such as housewifery, she also recognized that the Wirts' bright, talented daughters would never be satisfied with her prescriptions that they find fulfillment exclusively at home. After the family's move to Baltimore in 1829, Elizabeth began to participate in organized female benevolence and to introduce her daughters—from Liz down to Agnes, the youngest Wirt daughter—to Baltimore's female world of sociability, social reform, and self-improvement. By replacing schooling with social commitments, Elizabeth Wirt pioneered a different kind of education for women that was, in its own way, as revolutionary as her husband's plans for Laura's classical education.[58]

The Wirt girls' uncertain health bolstered Elizabeth's intention to take over their education. They had many physical ailments, ranging from nagging colds and headaches to bouts of scarlet fever and malaria, and during the 1820s and 1830s all six of them frequently traveled to the seashore and to the restorative springs for their health. Reinforcing the Wirts' concern, sixteen-year-old Agnes died in late 1830 of what doctors diagnosed as dysentery. The Wirt girls' fragile health may have convinced their parents that rigorous education would make them, as Mrs. Smith charged, "hot-house flowers" who could not bear the demands of marriage and motherhood. Physicians in the antebellum era issued warnings about the delicacy of adolescent females, presaging the Victorian fear that educating teenage women would draw vital energy away from their reproductive organs to their minds and would cause permanent physical and mental illnesses. Certainly the adolescent crises of their three oldest daughters could have caused the Wirts to worry that excessive intellectual development might not only endanger their daughters' futures as wives and mothers but also their mental stability. Agnes's premature death may have served as a warning that even the girls' lives were at stake. Letters that Elizabeth wrote in the late 1820s indicate that she was convinced that a mother was the only proper caretaker for girls. "[W]ho could supply the vigilant care of a mother?" she demanded in one letter to her own mother. "I say that no one could. . . ."[59]

Elizabeth was referring specifically to the "vigilant care" of nursing Catharine through a prolonged illness, but her comments indicated a fundamental shift in the Wirts' approach to educating their daughters. Although Elizabeth experimented with day schools for the Wirts' three youngest daughters, she always returned them to home instruction and maternal supervision. In 1824 and 1825 "the girls"—twins Ellen and Rosa, born in 1812, and the youngest daughter Agnes, born in 1814, sporadically attended with "the Boys"—William Cabell (b. 1815), Dabney Carr (b. 1817), and Henry (b. 1818)—a local school run by Mr. Plumley. Although the boys attended the school regularly for two years, the girls' education was frequently interrupted. The Wirts learned to their dismay that Plumley used corporal discipline in the classroom. "He must be a coarse, rude, blackguard," wrote William, declaring that "he is not fit to have the charge of gentlemen's children." Elizabeth withdrew the girls from Plumley's school, planning to teach Ellen, Rosa, and Agnes at home. The boys continued to attend. Elizabeth's decision may have indicated a greater concern for her daughters' education, perhaps motivated by a belief that girls—but not boys—needed the gentler tuition of a mother. The girls were briefly reenrolled at Plumley's in early 1825 (as Elizabeth "can find no better School for them") but were again withdrawn. They next studied with a Mr. Bonfils but were withdrawn in 1827. The girls' schoolmaster had "excessively shocked" his class—and Elizabeth Wirt—by making references to *the corruption of virgin innocence* in dictation. "He so often says such improper things," exclaimed Elizabeth, "that I do not think him a proper teacher for girls of any delicacy or refinement." Elizabeth kept the girls home from school, and when her letter to Bonfils reproving him for "his improper vulgarity" did not elicit an acceptable response, she withdrew them entirely.[60]

Home instruction proved to be a dramatic change for the youngest Wirt girls. During the girls' time at Mr. Bonfils's school, William praised them for their awards and encouraged them to make the most of their opportunities. His pleasure in the girls' academic prizes indicated that he did not share the growing concern in antebellum America about the propriety of encouraging ambition and competitiveness among female students. "Thank my dear Rosa for her letter," William wrote to Agnes in 1826, "and tell her that I enjoy her school honors quite as much as she does. . . . Tell her to be industrious and press on in the race of education, and she will be an ornament and an honor to her family." Rosa's example was to be imitated by the others, William indicated. "You have capacity enough to acquire any accomplishment you please," he encouraged Agnes, "but none of them will come of their own accord—they all require to be wooed and courted assiduously." Recognizing their father's interest in their schoolwork, the girls kept him informed of all their academic triumphs.[61]

The girls' intellectual development stalled after their mother withdrew them from school. Their father's letters came infrequently, while their mother exerted constant pressure on them to substitute preparation for marriage for the pursuit of academic honors. The girls' letters to their father indicated that they missed intellectual stimulation. When William appended a list of history questions for them in a letter to Elizabeth in 1828, the girls were "delighted," reported Ellen. "I know they will be beneficial to us & teach us to study," she wrote, "& I hope you will continue to question us provided it does not interfere with your business[.]" William's "business" did prevent him from writing often with the encouragement that the girls found so "beneficial," however. "I go now for money," he wrote in 1828. "In trying to accomplish this, I have so little time or strength to spare, that I am anxious to make every blow tell[.]"[62]

Left in charge of the girls' daily lessons, Elizabeth de-emphasized studiousness in favor of practical training in housewifery.[63] She made one more attempt to continue the girls' classical education in late 1828, allowing the younger girls to study Latin informally with the Wirts' friend Mr. Chase. Mr. Chase's visits were intended to replicate their father's instruction of the older girls, but Elizabeth soon concluded that Chase's lessons were no substitute for William's. Chase's style was too harsh, she complained, and he did not soften his criticisms with praise. "[H]e . . . is in fact a *hard task Master*," she concluded, "and not the gentle and encouraging friend, that they had a right to expect—and that they have been accustomed to in their Father."[64]

Elizabeth's experiment with Mr. Chase exhausted her interest in continuing the younger girls' education. Lessons in fashionable accomplishments soon replaced tutorials in Latin. "My Girls all, have commenced Dancing & French," Elizabeth informed her mother in late 1828, "with a young Lady lately come to the place, with a high reputation. She attends them 4 times a week at home. . . ." Elizabeth's pleasure in the girls' new lessons indicated her eagerness to prepare the girls for the marriage market. As Dan Kilbride has suggested in his study of French finishing schools in Philadelphia, which were popular with well-to-do southerners, the ability to speak and read French was an indicator of elite status and could help the girls marry well. Furthermore, the new lessons, to Elizabeth's relief, offered an excuse to end the girls' instruction in advanced subjects. "I was very glad of an opportunity to break off from the Latin with Mr C[hase]," Elizabeth admitted to Laura, "and the Girls undertaking to learn french & dancing with a Miss Sutherland, was a good reason to give, as it took up so much of their time, as even to put a stop to their English lessons."[65]

Elizabeth initially began her campaign to curtail the girls' academic preparation because she, more than her husband, saw that higher education for women was more likely to lead to frustration than to a rewarding career. While northern women of Elizabeth's generation, like Margarett Fuller, also expressed reservations about their husbands' enthusiasm for educating their daughters, Elizabeth's concerns were especially appropriate for the South. In the Northeast, at least some schools, such as Mary Lyons's Mount Holyoke, emphasized education as a preparation for teaching, and at least some students seemed to view education as part of a life plan that included a prolonged period as self-supporting women.[66] In the South fewer options existed for young, single women. Indeed, the Wirts' most significant contact with unmarried women was with their hired housekeepers and seamstresses—a subordinate role that Elizabeth and William certainly did not envision for their own daughters.[67] Initially, then, Elizabeth demonstrated an interest in curtailing female education, rather than searching for broader horizons for the Wirts' educated daughters. However, once Elizabeth gained control of the girls, she began to experiment with ways to redesign, rather than retrench, female education.

In the late 1820s Elizabeth's search for a suitable education for the Wirts' three youngest girls reflected the lessons she had learned from their older sisters' dramatic adolescent crises. The younger girls' schedule was also affected by the continuing presence of their older, and still unmarried, sisters at home. (Liz did not marry until late 1831, and Catharine delayed marriage until 1842.) During the late 1820s, Liz, like Laura, began to experience debilitating depression. As they had with Laura, the Wirts recommended that Liz undertake some engaging activity to give her life direction during the hiatus between the end of her formal education and engagement and marriage. "Inaction," worried William, would "relax your whole system, and enervate your intellect." William recommended "constant, regular, persevering exercise" as an antidote to ennui and asked Elizabeth to make her care of Liz's health "*a sacred and indispensible duty.*" Elizabeth found another cure for her daughter's low spirits by introducing her to a woman's world of sociability, social reform, and self-improvement.[68]

In 1827 Elizabeth reported with satisfaction that "our dear Elizabeth is much improved." Riding horseback, taking baths, and keeping warm, she noted, had improved Liz's health. Perhaps more important was Elizabeth's scheme of "making her unbosom herself to me continually, & trying to reason away her perverted & beclouded views of things, & of herself. . . ." Perhaps through these conversations, Elizabeth became convinced that her earlier prescriptions—learning the "minutia" of domesticity—were insufficient. She began to experiment with new ways to occupy her daughter. "Besides the rides on horseback," she continued, "I have taken Elizabeth out every day in the carriage . . . and filled up the time until four O'clock in visiting & shopping—and in the evening have kept her in company, either at home or abroad—after the reading was over, in which they have been engaged—They have gone this even[in]g to read at Mrs Elzeys with her nieces."[69]

In the late 1820s Elizabeth introduced the Wirt daughters to a social realm inhabited by other women. Following their departure from school, the girls filled their letters with news of their female friends and neighbors, rather than their fellow scholars and schoolmasters. "I have been out *visittin* all day long," announced Catharine in January 1828.[70] Socializing was not simply a sideline to the girls' debut. "Visittin" introduced the girls to a female world of domesticity, piety, reform, and self-improvement. In this world of southern women, as in the "female world of love and ritual" that Carroll Smith-Rosenberg found among northeastern women in the nineteenth century, "men made but a shadowy appearance." In the Wirt girls' letters, men appeared as ministers and escorts, but women occupied center stage. A typical account was contained in a letter that Catharine wrote in late 1827. "We spent last evening at Mrs. Elzey's very pleasantly," Catharine remarked of the Wirts' friend and neighbor. "We went over very early in the evening to read a book which we are all anxious to finish this week and after reading several chapters we concluded the evening with conversation and tea. . . . *We all* went to a prayer meeting held by Mr. Johns at Mr. Hewitt's last Wednesday evening—Mrs. Wade went in the carriage with us—and her sister & Mr. King accompanied those of us who walked—."[71] The girls' letters revealed the existence of a close-knit group of younger and older women who came together to chat, read, and attend religious services. In 1828 Elizabeth escorted Catharine and her cousin, Emma Cabell, who was on an extended visit to the Wirts, "to the Unitarian Church Calling to take up Mrs. French, who is making an effort to get up an oratoria."[72] The oratorio took place the following month, and "Catharine performed to admiration" on the harp.[73]

The women's world inhabited by the Wirt daughters and their neighbors was designed to prepare young women to take up their future duties as wives and mothers. The neighbor women, particularly Mrs. Elzey, assisted Elizabeth in initiating the girls into their new routines at home. During a trip that William and Elizabeth made to the springs in the summer of 1831, the girls' close ties with the neighborhood matrons became apparent. "You ought to see what nice managers Lizzy & Mrs. Elzey are—and how well they *talk* about economy," Rosa reported.[74] In her mother's absence, Liz took over the household, paying bills, sorting papers, arranging closets, and sending forgotten supplies to her parents. Liz wrote with pride to her mother: "We are going on famously. Mrs. Elzey pronounces me to be an excellent *Major Domo* in the absence of the heads of the family."[75] As William concluded at the end of the summer, "Mrs Elzey had staid with the girls to matronize them, and they all got through the summer very well. . . ."[76]

As Elizabeth and her neighbors worked to "matronize" the girls, they also redefined what it meant to be a southern woman. Elizabeth Fox-Genovese has suggested that southern women, as girls' guides from childhood to adulthood, socialized younger women by acting as examples of their class, with gender-specific roles to play as wives, mothers, and mistresses of households. Mothers were central to this process. "Slaveholding daughters," she asserts, "grew up in their mothers' shadows and under their tutelage. They learned the fundamentals of adult responsibilities from their mothers. . . ." Elizabeth Wirt and her female kin and neighbors, like other well-to-do women in the Old South, had primary responsibility for socializing young women into their roles as adult women. In the late 1820s and early 1830s as Elizabeth undertook, with vigor and decisiveness, to socialize her daughters, she also determined to broaden her definition of a southern woman's role. While obviously concerned with preparing her "grown girls" for marriage and housework, Elizabeth decided to give them a social, as well as a domestic, education. As she withdrew the girls from school, Elizabeth introduced them to a new sort of education—pious benevolence and quiet study with the support of other women.[77]

As the century progressed, more and more ministers and their predominantly female constituents became convinced that women, whose duties as economic producers were reduced, should undertake the sacred duty of religious guidance. The growing popularity of so-called domestic piety and what Ann Douglas has dubbed the "feminization" of religion encouraged Elizabeth to demand greater recognition of her role as moral instructress and William to accept her suggestions.[78] Elizabeth concluded that her duties included preparing her children for early conversion, a form of maternal influence that drew special attention in antebellum America. "I wish them all to prepare, without delay, to make a public confession of their faith & dependence upon the Savior, in obedience to his command," she wrote in 1827. Elizabeth enclosed a copy of an article from a religious publication for her husband's perusal; apparently the work addressed the advantages of early religious instruction. Such tracts entrusted women in antebellum America with cultivating children's consciences, preparing their souls for salvation through a gradual process of religious instruction and teaching by example. William approved of his wife's activities, but his reply made it clear that he saw no role for himself in the plan. "I have not time to pursue this subject," he explained. "You view it rightly—and consider me as consenting to all you propose."[79]

Elizabeth made religious instruction central to the younger children's training. She took the children to several churches presided over by different ministers, expressing to William her pleasure that the children, like herself, were more pleased by Episcopal services than by their own Presbyterian ones (following William's death in 1834, Elizabeth became an Episcopalian). Elizabeth herself was the children's principal religious guide, however. Criticizing one minister as "a *pompous formalist*," Elizabeth noted, "I have the vanity to think, that I would make a better instructor of youth myself—in practical religion, and in the duties that infirm, weak, human nature is equal to."[80]

Although all the children attended religious services and gathered around for religious readings, Elizabeth's new role as the "instructor of youth" in "practical religion" had special significance for the Wirts' daughters. Piety was particularly important for girls in antebellum America. Religious conversion was a rite of passage that often coincided with puberty and was attended with great parental concern. For many southern parents, a religious experience was the desired culmination of a girl's schooling. Because piety was central to antebellum ideals of womanhood, the conversion experience gave young women an appropriately feminine way to explore their individuality. Religious conviction also gave women a source of common identity and provided them with the opportunity to engage in charitable work in the community. While Catherine Clinton and Jean Friedman have suggested that for plantation women, religious belief often involved intense self-scrutiny and encouraged submission to male church and community leaders, women in southern cities frequently made piety the basis for female organizations and charitable benevolence. Suzanne Lebsock's study of Petersburg, Virginia, and Barbara L. Bellows's investigation of Charleston, South Carolina, suggest two different routes that southern women took to benevolent work, both as the primary instigators of charitable organizations and as men's followers and allies. Shortly before their departure from Mr. Bonfils's school, Elizabeth encouraged the girls to join the Dorcas society, a group that made clothing for the poor. Such church-related charitable organizations drew on women's talents within the home—in this case, sewing— to serve the wider community. Although, initially, work for the Dorcas society was a sideline to the girls' schooling—Elizabeth mentioned "there being no school this week" when the girls joined—it soon replaced school entirely.[81]

The Wirt daughters' participation in organized benevolence modified the intense academic program that had been favored by educators in the early republic, but it also provided an outlet for their talents and ambitions in those areas of public life that fell within women's domain as moralists. Like women in Petersburg and Charleston, the Wirt daughters had access to a number of female organizations. In the economically uncertain environment of antebellum Baltimore, charitable organizations, nearly all of them church-based, flourished. Elizabeth frequently escorted the girls to charity events, such as a Catholic "Fair" to benefit an "orphan-school."[82] She especially approved of the Dorcas society, which, like the Liberian Society that Liz and Catharine had joined at the Garnetts' school, used domestic skills in the service of society beyond the home. "Your sisters have become active members of the aforesaid society," she informed Laura, "& pass their evenings in working for them which I very much approve of, as it gives them a greater stimulus to industrious habits—and improves them rapidly, in the use of the needle."[83]

Religious charity provided the girls with a new awareness of their duties to others. In the 1830s the girls began catechizing the Wirts' house slaves, holding family prayers and hymns in which the servants were included, and teaching the children to read. As Ellen explained, "how much happier do *we* feel, in the consciousness of discharging our duty aright. . . ."[84]

The Wirt daughters soon began to practice charity in a broader sense. Like the well-to-do wives and daughters in Bellows's study of Charleston, they donated money to poor relief. In 1831 Catharine noted with satisfaction that a local lawyer had made "a munificent donation . . . to the suffering poor" of Baltimore.[85] The Wirt daughters, with their mother's full support, soon joined the effort to ameliorate the condition of "the suffering poor," and, following the example of the charitable lawyer, Liz reported that the family had donated five dollars "for the Poor of the 11th Ward."[86] Like the women in Lebsock's study of Petersburg, Elizabeth and her daughters paid special attention to the unfortunate of their own sex. When "a poor but honest woman" appealed to Elizabeth for charity, Catharine devoted an entire page in a letter to an account of the woman's sad plight, her gratitude for the Wirts' castoff clothing, and her "Christian spirit" of resignation. "[M]y heart ascended in gratitude to God that we were permitted to be the instruments of assisting one of his children in her poverty."[87]

By the 1830s the Wirts were involved with the temperance movement. Temperance in the antebellum South was a male-led effort, but wealthy women like Elizabeth Wirt often gave financial support. Furthermore, like the women in Carroll Smith-Rosenberg's study of New York's social purity movement, some southern women, through social reform, developed a critical perspective on their society, particularly its men. At a party that the Wirts gave in Baltimore in 1830, Elizabeth declared herself "completely disgusted" with several of the male guests. Although the Wirts had planned to serve only lemonade, wine, and water, "the gentlemen called for *brandy & whisky* & wd not rest satisfied till they had completely drained the bottles *five* or *six* times," according to Ellen's description of the evening. Several became "so much *intoxicated*," she wrote, outraged, "that they staggered about the rooms, & were at last compelled to leave the house, for fear of disgracing themselves." Furious, Elizabeth wrote in a postscript to Ellen's letter: "If I were equal to it, I would put a piece in the papers recommending to the ladies to lend their aid to the efforts of the *Temperate society* in every possible way." Baltimore girls, Elizabeth complained further, "all dress in the extreme of the fashion & talk of nothing else"; her daughters, she resolved, would henceforth withdraw from the social season and devote themselves to the improvement of "the present society" of the town.[88]

Conversing and crusading in the company of other women, the Wirt girls also crafted a new mode of learning in a female community. In Baltimore, Elizabeth arranged private lessons in singing and the harp for the youngest three girls, noting that they "h[ave] had no Masters of any sort since they hav[e been] in Baltimore—but they have been doing very [well] at home."[89] William, by the 1830s thoroughly disillusioned with female education, was no longer the family tutor. When Catharine wrote to her father to ask him for help in writing poetry, William recanted from his former encouraging stance. "It will not hurt your fortune my dear to be no poet," he consoled her. "[Y]ou will be just as sweet and beloved a daughter, sister, friend and wife (if you ever should be one) without the poetic talent as with it—to be perfectly frank I had rather you should be without it—for I suspect that female poets are very poor domestic characters." Claiming to be "really too busy" to help his daughter "polish" her writing, William counseled her to turn her ambitions elsewhere. "Be sensible and graceful and winning in the *prose* of domestic life, and you will be the poet's theme—however un-poetic yourself," he advised. "Shew me in a fine girl the qualities too of the good housewife, and that is my *beau ideal* of female excellence—more especially if religion crown the composition."[90] In a joint letter to Laura, Catharine, and Liz in 1829, William even more strongly repudiated female learning. "The *ostentatious* display of intellect in a young lady is revolting," he pronounced.[91]

Unlike their oldest sister, Laura, whose studies had stagnated following William's withdrawal, the younger girls found a way to continue their education informally through group study. Though a network of older women helped initiate the girls into charity and reform, a group of "grown girls," beginning with the Wirt sisters, formed the study group. Piety helped pave the Wirt girls' way to self-improvement. "I sent the girls last evening to visit the Tayloes," Elizabeth informed William in late 1827. "This even[in]g Henrietta Wilson is with them, & they have been reading a portion of Beckersteth together, as they have agreed to do, every even[in]g, instead of their Philosophy, for the rest of the week—I thought it right that they should do so—and I hope you will think it right also[.]" Elizabeth may have considered the substitution of biblical studies for philosophy to be salutary; in any case, the girls did not abandon a classical liberal arts curriculum. In April, Rosa informed her father that "We rose at 6 this morning . . . and then read our Chemistry,—which we like exceedingly. We intend beginning a little chatechism [*sic*] of Botany tomorrow also,—which I expect we shall *like exceedingly too*."[92]

The antebellum introduction of the lyceum system, with lectures on a variety of subjects either open to the general public or tailored specifically for women, allowed northern and southern urban women to hope for intellectual stimulation throughout their lives.[93] Many of the lecture topics were religious. While the Wirt sons attended to their Latin lessons, Elizabeth noted in early 1828, "The girls are . . . attending their bible class, or lecture upon the Jewish antiquities."[94] After they became accustomed to attending public lectures, the girls used them to continue their education on a variety of subjects. Although they were preparing for their "*debut* in company" in 1830, Ellen and Rosa went with their older sisters to an introductory lecture in Chemistry at the Medical Hall.[95]

In 1831 Catharine Wirt wrote a letter to her father that succinctly summed up the girls' new routine of continued study, domestic work, and religious contemplation in the company of other women. "We are all going on very quietly," she reported. "We pass our days in sewing, reading & conversing—with a little exercise. . . . I have been reading aloud to [Miss Susan, the Wirts' hired housekeeper] & the girls today (whilst they sewed) an article in the 'Christian Examiner' lent to dear mother by our neighbour Mrs. Sumners. . . ."[96]

The Wirts' family correspondence declined in frequency and detail following William's death in 1834, and the efficacy of the girls' education in terms of preparing them for life after marriage is difficult to evaluate. All of them did eventually marry. Laura, after a stormy adolescence, finally married her most persistent suitor, Thomas Randall, in 1827.[97] Despite her earlier reluctance to commit herself to marriage, Liz married Navy Lieutenant Louis Malesherbes Goldsborough in 1831. Catharine, who delayed marriage to care for her mother after William's death, married Alexander Randall, Thomas Randall's brother, in 1842.[98] The younger girls apparently were spared the wrenching transition to adult responsibilities that their older sisters experienced. Rosa married in 1832, several months before her twentieth birthday, and Ellen married in 1837, after moving to Florida with her mother to help manage the properties William bequeathed to his widow.[99]

Although the Wirts' success in preparing their daughters for marriage is difficult to measure, their experience nevertheless casts light on the debate over female education and women's role in society in a critical era. The experience of this southern family suggests that, like their northern neighbors, southerners in antebellum America devoted significant attention to the content and the purpose of female education. Like the better-known pioneers of female education in the North—such as Emma Willard and Catharine Beecher—the Wirts sought an education that would fit women for their futures. These southern parents, unlike northern educational reformers of the antebellum era, did not envision their daughters as teachers. However, they did begin to experiment with another role for their "grown girls, highly cultivated"—as members of a female community devoted to social and personal improvement.[100]

During the first three decades of the nineteenth century, Elizabeth and William Wirt and others like them developed a template for later institutions of higher education for women in the Old South. Curbing their daughters' academic development in order to attend to the social positions of the young women, the Wirts redefined their daughters' pursuits to include church-based reform and self-development in the company of other women. By the 1840s and 1850s, female seminaries and colleges thickly sprinkled the southern landscape. Southern women's institutions of higher learning in the later antebellum era reinstated a formal curriculum in the classics, to which the Wirts had exposed all of their daughters for varying (and decreasing) lengths of time. In addition, southern women's academies and colleges offered their female students an "informal curriculum" in domesticity, piety, and charity—lessons that they learned in the company of other women.[101] In these schools, a new generation of southern women, following in the footsteps of the Wirts' "grown girls," experienced a particularly feminine form of education that "cultivated" them to be good neighbors, benevolent churchwomen, and industrious seekers of mental and spiritual enlightenment.

Notes

1. William H. Cabell to Elizabeth Wirt, June 28, 1824, William Wirt Papers (Ms. # 1011, Manuscripts Division, Maryland Historical Society Library, Baltimore) (hereinafter cited as MHS), microfilm at Rice University, reel 6. (Hereinafter, citations to microfilm reel numbers in this collection relate to the holdings of Rice University.)

2. On education and republican motherhood, see Linda K. Kerber, *Women of the Republic: Intellect and Ideology in Revolutionary America* (Chapel Hill, 1980), Chap. 7; and Mary Beth Norton, *Liberty's Daughters: The Revolutionary Experience of American Women, 1750–1800* (Boston and Toronto, 1980), Chap. 9.

3. Catherine Clinton, *The Plantation Mistress: Woman's World in the Old South* (New York, 1982), Chap. 7.

4. Anne Firor Scott, "Education of Women: The Ambiguous Reform," in Scott, *Making the Invisible Woman Visible* (Urbana and Chicago, 1984), 298–312. See also Susan Phinney Conrad, *Perish the Thought: Intellectual Women in Romantic America, 1830–1860* (New York, 1976), Chap. 1.

5. Nancy F. Cott, *The Bonds of Womanhood: "Woman's Sphere" in New England, 1780–1835* (New Haven and London, 1977), especially Chap. 3; Clinton, *Plantation Mistress*, 136–37; Florence Pearl Davis, "The Education of Southern Girls from the Middle of the Eighteenth Century to the Close of the Antebellum Period" (Ph.D. dissertation, University of Chicago, 1951); Christie Farnham Pope, "Preparation for Pedestals: North Carolina Antebellum Female Seminaries" (Ph.D. dissertation, University of Chicago, 1977); Jane Turner Censer, *North Carolina Planters and their Children, 1800–1860* (Baton Rouge and London, 1984), Chap. 3; and Daniel Blake Smith, *Inside the Great House: Planter Family Life in Eighteenth-Century Chesapeake Society* (Ithaca and London, 1980), Chap. 3. Elizabeth Fox-Genovese, *Within the Plantation Household: Black and White Women of the Old South* (Chapel Hill and London, 1988), 46–47, 110–13, and 256–59.

6. Most studies of southern women's education focus on the later antebellum period. See Christie Anne Farnham, *The Education of the Southern Belle: Higher Education and Student Socialization in the Antebellum South* (New York, 1994); Daniel Kilbride, "Philadelphia and the Southern Elite: Class, Kinship, and Culture in Antebellum America" (Ph.D. dissertation, University of Florida, 1997), Chap. 5; Steven M. Stowe, "Growing Up Female in the Planter Class," *Helicon Nine*, XVII/XVIII (1987), 194–205; and Stowe, "The Not-So-Cloistered Academy: Elite Women's Education and Family Feeling in the Old South," in Walter J. Fraser Jr., R. Frank Saunders Jr., and Jon L. Wakelyn, eds., *The*

Web of Southern Social Relations: Women, Family, and Education (Athens, Ga., 1985), 90–106 (see pp. 92 and 104n6 for discussion of "Southron" education).

7. For background on the Wirts, see especially John B. Boles, *A Guide to the Microfilm Edition of the William Wirt Papers* (Baltimore, 1971); Joseph Charles Burke, "William Wirt: Attorney General and Constitutional Lawyer" (Ph.D. dissertation, Indiana University, 1965); John P. Kennedy, *Memoirs of the Life of William Wirt, Attorney-General of the United States* (2 vols., 1849; revd. ed., Philadelphia, 1850); Joseph C. Robert, "William Wirt, Virginian," *Virginia Magazine of History and Biography*, LXXXI (October 1972), 387–441; and Sarah P. Stetson, "Mrs. Wirt and the Language of the Flowers," ibid., LVII (October 1949), 376–89.

8. George Wythe Munford, *The Two Parsons* (Richmond, 1884), 265–75; Virginius Dabney, *Richmond: The Story of a City* (rev. ed., Charlottesville, 1990), 77–78; and Stetson, "Mrs. Wirt and the Language of the Flowers."

9. "On the Condition of Women" is printed in [William Wirt et al.], *The Rainbow: First Series* (Richmond, 1804), 10–15. The rough draft is included in miscellaneous papers in Wirt Papers, MHS, reel 24. In *The Old Bachelor* (3d ed.; Baltimore, [1818]), William responded to "letters" he wrote under fictional names. For quotations, see [Wirt], *Old Bachelor*, 70–71, 98. On women's republican responsibilities, see Jan Lewis, "The Republican Wife: Virtue and Seduction in the Early Republic," *William and Mary Quarterly*, 3d ser., XLIV (October 1987), 689–721; and Rosemarie Zagarri, "Morals, Manners, and the Republican Mother," *American Quarterly*, XLIV (June 1992), 192–215.

10. William Wirt to Dabney Carr, December 21, 1809, Wirt Papers, MHS, reel 1.

11. See William Wirt to Elizabeth Wirt, September 22, 1809, reel 1; and William Wirt to Laura Wirt, July 14, 1810, reel 2, Wirt Papers, MHS. On southern fathers and family, see Censer, *North Carolina Planters*, 39; Sally G. McMillen, *Motherhood in the Old South: Pregnancy, Childbirth, and Infant Rearing* (Baton Rouge and London, 1990), 161–63; McMillen, "Antebellum Southern Fathers and the Health Care of Children," *Journal of Southern History*, LX (August 1994), 513–32; and Smith, *Inside the Great House*, 53. On men's important role as their daughters' educators, see Fox-Genovese, *Within the Plantation Household*, 111. As Clinton explains, mothers were generally ill-equipped to teach advanced subjects and were forced to rely on male tutors. See *Plantation Mistress*, 126–27. On northern fathers' interest in their daughters' education, see Conrad, *Perish the Thought*, 12, 51–54, 187, 191, and 238; and Barbara Welter, "Coming of Age in America: The American Girl in the Nineteenth Century," in *Dimity Convictions: The American Woman in the Nineteenth Century* (Athens, Ohio, 1976), 6.

12. William Wirt to Elizabeth Wirt, September 22, 1809, reel 1, and on Laura's teaching supplies, see William Wirt to Elizabeth Wirt, July 22, 1810, reel 2, Wirt Papers, MHS. On the Fuller and Alcott households, see Charles Capper, *Margaret: An American Romantic Life. Vol. I: The Private Years* (New York and Oxford, 1992), Chaps. 1–2; and Charles Strickland, "A Transcendentalist Father: The Child-Rearing Practices of Bronson Alcott," *Perspectives in American History*, III (1969), 3–73, especially pp. 35, 38, and 47–48.

13. For quotation, see William Wirt to Laura Wirt, July 14, 1810, Wirt Papers, MHS, reel 2. On Laura's teachers and schools, see, for example, Elizabeth Wirt to William Wirt, October 30, 1811; Leroy Anderson to William Wirt, February 7, April 7, 8, 13, May 1, 1813; Laura Wirt to William Wirt, January 16, 1815; William Wirt to M. W. Hancock, July 28, 1815 (all on reel 2); Elizabeth Wirt to William Wirt, January 4, 1816; John H. Rice

to William Wirt, November 8, 1816; and Elizabeth Wirt to William Wirt, November 5, 1817 (all on reel 3), all in Wirt Papers, MHS.

14. For quotations, see William Wirt to Elizabeth Wirt, September 9, 1810 (first quotation), reel 1, and September 11, 1809 (second quotation), reel 2, Wirt Papers, MHS. On justifications for women's education, see Clinton, *Plantation Mistress*, 124–38; Kerber, *Women of the Republic*, Chap. 7; Lewis, "Republican Wife"; Norton, *Liberty's Daughters*, Chap. 9; and Zagarri, "Morals, Manners, and the Republican Mother."

15. See, for example, Elizabeth Wirt to William Wirt, September 22, 26, 1809 (reel 1); July 18, 1810; September 2, 1811; July 11, September 12, 1813 (reel 2), Wirt Papers, MHS. On Abigail Alcott, see Strickland, "Transcendentalist Father," 7–8. Alcott later began to subtly undermine, although not to overtly criticize, her husband's child-rearing strategies.

16. William Wirt to M. W. Hancock, July 28, 1815 (quotations) and three enclosed "System of Study" schedules, Wirt Papers, MHS, reel 2. For information on Jefferson and his daughters, I am indebted to Ron Hatzenbuehler for sharing with me his paper "Hearts Over Head: Thomas Jefferson, His Daughters, and Maria Cosway," delivered at the conference of the Society for Historians of the Early American Republic, held in Chapel Hill, North Carolina, July 23, 1993 (copy in my possession).

17. William Wirt to Robert Wirt, August 20, 1812 (first quotation); Laura Wirt to William Wirt, September 7, 1814 (second quotation), both on reel 2; November 24, 1817 (third quotation), Wirt Papers, MHS, reel 3.

18. See, for example, Elizabeth Wirt to William Wirt, July 11, 1813 (reel 2); September 22, 23, 1818 (reel 3), Wirt Papers, MS.

19. See William Wirt to Laura Wirt, November 26, 1817, Wirt Papers, MHS, reel 3; William Wirt to Peachey Gilmer, September 5, 1818 (quotations), in William Wirt Papers (Manuscript Division, Library of Congress, Washington) (hereinafter LC), reel 1. See also Censer, *North Carolina Planters*, 44.

20. On the female academy, see William Wirt to Laura Wirt, November 26, 1817, Wirt Papers, MHS, reel 3. On Laura's departure from the seminary, see William Wirt to Peachey Gilmer, September 5, 1818, Wirt Papers, LC, reel 1. On Laura's scarlet fever, see, for example, Elizabeth Wirt to William Wirt, April 14, 15, 16, 1819, Wirt Papers, MHS, reel 3. On her stint in Virginia, see William Wirt to Elizabeth Wirt, ca. April/May 1819, Wirt Papers, MHS, reel 3 (quotation); Laura Wirt Randall Papers (Typescript, Virginia Historical Society, Richmond) (hereinafter cited as VHS), preface. Louisa was the daughter of William H. Cabell and his first wife, Elizabeth Cabell. Following Elizabeth Cabell's death, William Cabell married Elizabeth Gamble Wirt's sister, Agnes Sarah Bell, known as Nancy. On "aunt adoption," see Clinton, *Plantation Mistress*, 51. For William's "neglect," see Laura Wirt to Elizabeth Wirt, June 7, 1820, Wirt Papers, MHS, reel 4. On Laura's domestic training, see, for example, Laura Wirt to Catharine Gamble, May 24, 1818, Wirt Papers, MHS, reel 3; Laura Wirt to Elizabeth G. Wirt, January 20, 1825, Wirt Papers, LC, reel 1.

21. See especially Anne Scott MacLeod, "American Girlhood in the Nineteenth Century: Caddie Woodlawn's Sisters," in MacLeod, *American Childhood: Essays on Children's Literature of the Nineteenth and Twentieth Centuries* (Athens, Ga., and London, 1994), 3–29.

22. Laura Wirt to William Wirt, November 27, 1817 (first and second quotations); William Wirt to Elizabeth Wirt, November 22, 1817 (third and fourth quotations); Elizabeth Wirt to William Wirt, November 18, 19, 1817, all in Wirt Papers, MHS, reel 3. On maternal supervision, see especially Fox-Genovese, *Within the Plantation Household*, 111–13. For comparisons to the family of Margarett, see Capper, *Margaret*, Chaps. 2–3.

23. On the Fuller family, see Capper, *Margaret*, Chaps. 2–3; for a contrasting study, see Sharon O'Brien, "Tomboyism and Adolescent Conflict: Three Nineteenth-Century Case Studies," in Mary Kelley, ed., *Woman's Being, Woman's Place: Female Identity and Vocation in American History* (Boston, 1979), 351–72.

24. Fox-Genovese, *Within the Plantation Household*, 113.

25. Elizabeth Wirt to William Wirt, September 22, 23, 1818, Wirt Papers, MHS, reel 3. For quotations, see William Wirt to Laura Wirt, December n.d., 1818 (reel 3), and May 23, 1820 (reel 4), Wirt Papers, MHS. See also Conrad, *Perish the Thought*, Chap. 1.

26. Elizabeth Wirt to Laura Witt, May 10, 1820 (first and second quotation), reel 3; May 26, 1820 (third quotation), reel 4, Wirt Papers, MHS.

27. For quotations, see Laura Wirt to Louisa Cabell, May 3, 1819, Randall Papers, VHS; Laura Wirt to Robert Wirt, January 20, February 25, 1823; and William Wirt to Elizabeth Wirt, December 14, 1823, Wirt Papers, MHS, reel 5. For Laura's debut, see Robert Wirt to Elizabeth Wirt, February 26, 1821, Wirt Papers, MHS, reel 4; for Laura's self-directed studies, see, for example, Laura Wirt to Louisa Cabell Carrington, June 23, 1820, and February 8, 1821, Randall Papers, VHS; for William's recommendations that Laura undertake a new subject, see William Wirt to Laura Wirt, December 22, 1824, Wirt Papers, MHS, reel 6; for Laura's illness, see, for example, William Wirt to Robert Wirt, December 15, 1824, Wirt Papers, MHS, reel 6. On young women and marriage, see Lee Virginia Chambers-Schiller, *Liberty, a Better Husband: Single Women in America: The Generations of 1780–1840* (New Haven and London, 1984). On hysteria, see Carroll Smith-Rosenberg, "The Hysterical Woman: Sex Roles and Role Conflict in Nineteenth-Century America," in *Disorderly Conduct: Visions of Gender in Victorian America* (New York, 1985), 197–216.

28. Gaillard Hunt, ed., *The First Forty Years of Washington Society, Portrayed by the Family Letters of Mrs. Samuel Harrison Smith* (Margaret Bayard) (New York, 1906), 318.

29. On Lacy, see Stowe, "Growing Up Female," 198–200. On parents' exhortations and contradictory advice to their daughters, see, for example, Clinton, *Plantation Mistress*, 19.

30. Elizabeth Wirt to William Wirt, November 22, 1824, Wirt Papers, MHS, reel 6.

31. Capper, *Margaret*, Chaps. 1–2.

32. Elizabeth Wirt, postscripts to William Wirt to Elizabeth G. Wirt, August 26, 28, 1823, and Elizabeth G. Wirt to Catharine Grattan Gamble, August 31, 1824 (first quotation), all in Wirt Papers, LC, reel 1; Elizabeth Wirt to William Wirt, May 13, 1824 (second quotation), reel 5, and Elizabeth G. Wirt, postscript to Catharine G. Wirt to William Wirt, November 9, 1824 (third quotation), reel 6, both in Wirt Papers, MHS.

33. William Wirt to Elizabeth G. Wirt, August 4, 1822; William Wirt to Catharine Wirt, February 24, 1824, Wirt Papers, LC, reel 1.

34. William Wirt to [Catharine] Wirt, February 24, 1824, ibid.

35. William Wirt to Elizabeth G. Wirt, November 1, 1824, ibid.

36. William Wirt to Elizabeth G. Wirt, July 17, 1822, ibid.

37. William Wirt to Catharine Wirt, February 24, 1824, ibid. See also Farnham, *Education of the Southern Belle*, esp. the introduction.

38. William Wirt to Elizabeth G. Wirt, January 15, 1825, Wirt Papers, LC, reel 1.

39. William Wirt to Elizabeth G. Wirt, August 4, 1822, and William Wirt to Catharine Wirt, February 24, 1824, Wirt Papers, LC, reel 1. See Jan Lewis, *The Pursuit of Happiness: Family and Values in Jefferson's Virginia* (Cambridge, Eng., and New York, 1983), 152–68.

40. William Wirt to James Meredith, September 26, 1823, Wirt Papers, MHS, reel 5 (misfiled with November 9, 1823, letters in microfilm edition). See also Stowe, "Not-So-Cloistered Academy."

41. Elizabeth G. Wirt to Elizabeth Wirt, November 18, 1824 (quotations); see also Catharine G. Wirt to William Wirt, November 9, 1824; Elizabeth G. Wirt to William Wirt, November 10, 1824; Elizabeth Wirt to William Wirt, November 14, 1824; William Wirt to Elizabeth Wirt, November 26, 1824, all in Wirt Papers, MHS, reel 6.

42. William Wirt to Elizabeth G. Wirt, November 1, December 19–20, 24, 1824, Wirt Papers, LC, reel 1. See also Farnham, *Education of the Southern Belle*, Chap. 3.

43. Elizabeth G. Wirt to Elizabeth Wirt, November 25, 1824, Wirt Papers, MHS, reel 6.

44. Elizabeth G. Wirt to Elizabeth Wirt, November 26, 1824, ibid.

45. Laura Wirt to William Wirt, January 13, 1825, Wirt Papers, MHS, reel 6. On female seminaries in the South, see Pope, "Preparation for Pedestals"; compare to Farnham, *Education of the Southern Belle*, on southern women's colleges. See also Davis, "Education of Southern Girls," Chaps. 5 and 6. On female education in the Northeast, see Cott, *Bonds of Womanhood*, Chap. 3.

46. Elizabeth G. Wirt to William Wirt, May 6, 1825, and William Wirt to Elizabeth G. Wirt, May 3, 8, 1825, all in Wirt Papers, LC, reel 1; Elizabeth G. Wirt to William Wirt, May 27, 1826, Wirt Papers, MHS, reel 8.

47. William Wirt to Catharine Wirt, November 12, 1826, Wirt Papers, MHS, reel 8. See also Elizabeth G. Wirt to William Wirt, October 24, 1826, and Catharine Wirt to William Wirt, November 13, 1826, both in Wirt Papers, MHS, reel 8. See also Conrad, *Perish the Thought*, 34.

48. William Wirt to Elizabeth Wirt, May 21, 1826, and Elizabeth G. Wirt to William Wirt, June 1, 1826, Wirt Papers, MHS, reel 8.

49. Elizabeth G. Wirt to William Wirt, November 14, 1826, Catharine Wirt to William Wirt, November 13, 23, 1826, and William Wirt to Catharine Wirt, November 18, 1826, all in Wirt Papers, MHS, reel 8.

50. Elizabeth Wirt to William Wirt, November 21, 1826, ibid.

51. Elizabeth G. Wirt to William Wirt, May 4, 1828, Wirt Papers, MHS, reel 10. "Growing Up Female," 203; and "Not-So-Cloistered Academy," 94. In the North, young women often experienced a similar "marriage trauma." See Cott, *Bonds of Womanhood*, 80–83.

52. For comparisons to Margarett and Williana Lacy, see Capper, *Margaret*, Chap. 3; and Stowe, "Growing Up Female," 198–200. Fuller wrote to her husband: "I am so well convinced that we have *erred* in our system of educating S[arah] M[argaret] that I intend with your excellent advice [to] reform our method as much as possible." See Capper, *Margaret*, 72–73.

53. William Wirt to Elizabeth Wirt, April 15, 1827, Wirt Papers, MHS, reel 9. See also Maxwell Bloomfield, *American Lawyers in a Changing Society, 1776–1876* (Cambridge, Mass., 1976).

54. William Wirt to Elizabeth Wirt, September 3, August 31, December 12, 19, 1826, Wirt Papers, MHS, reel 8. On rules in southern courtships, see Clinton, *Plantation Mistress*, 59–65; and Steven M. Stowe, *Intimacy and Power in the Old South: Ritual in the Lives of the Planters* (Baltimore and London, 1987), Chap. 2.

55. For quotations, see William Wirt to Laura Wirt Randall, May 2, 1828 (first quotation); Elizabeth Wirt to William Wirt, May 15, 1828 (second quotation); William Wirt to Elizabeth Wirt, April 27 (continued on April 28) (third quotation), May 11, 1828 (fourth

quotation), all in Wirt Papers, MHS, reel 10. See also Elizabeth Wirt to William Wirt, May 6, 15, 26, 1828, reel 10; and June n.d., 2, 29, 1828, reel 11, Wirt Papers, MHS.

56. Elizabeth Wirt to William Wirt, January 2 (first quotation), 4, 1828, reel 10; July 8, 1828 (fourth quotation), reel 11; William Wirt to Elizabeth Wirt, March 30, 1828 (second and third quotations), reel 10; August 10, 1828 (fifth quotation), reel 11, all in Wirt Papers, MHS.

57. For quotations, see Elizabeth G. Wirt to William Wirt, January 2, 1829 (misfiled in 1828), reel 10; and William Wirt to Elizabeth G. Wirt, January 3, 1829, Wirt Papers, MHS, reel 12. On Catharine's engagement, see Elizabeth Wirt to William Wirt, May 6, 15, 26, 1828 (reel 10); June n.d., 2, 29, 1828 (reel 11), Wirt Papers, MHS.

58. Elizabeth Wirt to William Wirt, November 21, 1826, Wirt Papers, MHS, reel 8.

59. For quotation, see Elizabeth Wirt to Catharine Gamble, October 18, 1828, Wirt Papers, MHS, reel 11. For the Wirts' poor health and travels, see, for example, Elizabeth Wirt to Catharine Gamble, April 28, May 2, June 26, July 6, 1830; Rosa Wirt to Laura Wirt Randall, May 27, 1830; Catharine G. Wirt to Catharine Gamble, July 17, September 3, 1830 (all on reel 13); William Wirt to Elizabeth Wirt, July 29, 31, August 18, 24, 1826 (all on reel 8); August 10, 18, 19, 20, 1828; July 22, 26, 29, August 1, 11, 15, 16, 18, 19, 20, 21, 22, 1830 (all on reel 11), all in Wirt Papers, MHS. On Agnes's death, see Elizabeth Wirt Baker, "A Sketch of William Wirt," February 22, 1899, Wirt Family Papers (Southern Historical Collection, Chapel Hill, North Carolina) (hereinafter cited as SHC). On sociobiological theories on women's mental and sexual development, see Carroll Smith-Rosenberg, "Puberty to Menopause: The Cycle of Femininity in Nineteenth-Century America," in *Disorderly Conduct*, 182–96, especially 183–88. See also Barbara Ehrenreich and Deirdre English, *For Her Own Good: 150 Years of the Experts Advice to Women* (Garden City, N.Y., 1978), 120–21 and 125–31; and Joseph F. Kett, *Rites of Passage: Adolescence in America, 1790 to the Present* (New York, 1977), 134 and 140–42. Southerners shared these fears. According to Christie Farnham Pope, southern parents saw their daughters' puberty as "a threat to female virtue." See "Preparation for Pedestals," 214.

60. William Wirt to Elizabeth Wirt, September 6, October 30, 1824 (on Mr. Plumley's use of corporal discipline); Laura Wirt to William Wirt, January 7, 1825 (first two quoted phrases and reenrollment of Wirt girls), all on reel 6; and Elizabeth Wirt to William Wirt, October 24, November 7 (Mr. Bonfils's use of improper language), 8 (on her letter to Bonfils), and 15, 1827 (all on reel 9), Wirt Papers, MHS.

61. William Wirt to Agnes Wirt, May 23, 1826, and Rosa Wirt to William Wirt, [May 1826], both in Wirt Papers, MHS, reel 8. See also Nancy Green, "Female Education and School Competition: 1820–1850," in Kelley, ed., *Woman's Being, Woman's Place*, 127–41.

62. Ellen Wirt to William Wirt, May 8, 1828, and William Wirt to Thomas Randall, February 1, 1828, both in Wirt Papers, MHS, reel 10.

63. Laura Wirt to William Wirt, January 7, 1825, Wirt Papers, MHS, reel 6.

64. Elizabeth Wirt to William Wirt, September 22, 1828, Wirt Papers, MHS, reel 11.

65. Elizabeth Wirt to Catharine Gamble, October 18, 1828, and Elizabeth Wirt to Laura Wirt Randall, November 1, 1828, Wirt Papers, MHS, reel 11. On French and French finishing schools in Philadelphia, see Kilbride, "Philadelphia and the Southern Elite," Chap. 5.

66. On Margarett, see Capper, *Margaret*, Chaps. 1–3. On Mount Holyoke, see David F. Allmendinger Jr., "Mount Holyoke Students Encounter the Need for Life Planning, 1837–1850," *History of Education Quarterly*, XIX (Spring 1979), 27–46; and Kathryn

Kish Sklar, "The Founding of Mount Holyoke College," in Sklar and Thomas Dublin, eds., *Women and Power in American History: A Reader.* Vol. I: *To 1880* (Englewood Cliffs, N.J., 1991), 199–215.

67. See, for example, William Wirt to Elizabeth Wirt, June 12, 1827, Wirt Papers, MHS, reel 9.

68. William Wirt to Elizabeth G. Wirt, May 15, 1827; William Wirt to Elizabeth Wirt, October 6, 1827, ibid.

69. Elizabeth Wirt to William Wirt, October 18, 1827, ibid.

70. Catharine G. Wirt to William Wirt, January 7, 1828, Wirt Papers, MHS, reel 10.

71. Carroll Smith-Rosenberg, "The Female World of Love and Ritual: Relations between Women in Nineteenth-Century America," in *Disorderly Conduct: Visions of Gender in Victorian America* (New York and Oxford, 1985), 53–76 (quotations on p. 53); Catharine G. Wirt postscript dated October 19, 1827, to Elizabeth Wirt to Laura Wirt Randall, October 15, 1827, Wirt Papers, MHS, reel 9. On female friendship in the South, which often revolved around a central core of kin, see Melinda S. Buza, "Pledges of Our Love: Friendship, Love, and Marriage among the Virginia Gentry, 1800–1825," in Edward L. Ayers and John C. Willis, eds., *The Edge of the South: Life in Nineteenth-Century Virginia* (Charlottesville and London, 1991), 9–20 and 28–29; Joan E. Cashin, "The Structure of Antebellum Planter Families: The Ties That Bound Us Was Strong," *Journal of Southern History*, LVI (February 1990), 55–70, especially pp. 64–65; Cashin, "Decidedly Opposed to the Union: Women's Culture, Marriage, and Politics in Antebellum South Carolina," *Georgia Historical Quarterly*, LXXVIII (Winter 1994), 735–59; and Steven M. Stowe, "The *Thing*, Not Its Vision: A Woman's Courtship and Her Sphere in the Southern Planter Class," *Feminist Studies*, IX (Spring 1983), 113–30.

72. Elizabeth Wirt to Laura Wirt Randall, April 19, 1828, Wirt Papers, MHS, reel 10.

73. Rosa Wirt to William Wirt, May 5, 1828, ibid.

74. Rosa Wirt to Elizabeth and William Wirt, July 21, 1831, Wirt Papers, MHS, reel 14.

75. Elizabeth G. Wirt to Elizabeth Wirt, July 25, 1831, ibid.

76. William Wirt to Thomas Randall, September 15, 1831, ibid.

77. Fox-Genovese, *Within the Plantation Household*, 113.

78. Ann Douglas, *The Feminization of American Culture* (New York, 1977), especially Chaps. 2 and 3. On women and religion, see also Cott, *Bonds of Womanhood*, Chap. 4; and Ryan, *Cradle of the Middle Class*, Chap. 2; also on domestic religion, see Colleen Mc-Dannell, *The Christian Home in Victorian America, 1840–1900* (Bloomington, 1986); and A. Gregory Schneider, *The Way of the Cross Leads Home: The Domestication of American Methodism* (Bloomington and Indianapolis, 1993).

79. Elizabeth Wirt to William Wirt, October 14 (first quotation), 15, 1827; William Wirt to Elizabeth Wirt, October 17, 1827 (second quotation), Wirt Papers, MHS, reel 9. On maternal influence and conversion, see Anne Boylan, "Sunday Schools and Changing Evangelical Views of Children in the 1820s," *Church History*, XLVTII (September 1979), 320–33; Bunkle, "Sentimental Womanhood and Domestic Education"; and Anne Scott MacLeod, "Child and Conscience," in MacLeod, *American Childhood*, 99–113.

80. Elizabeth Wirt to William Wirt, October 18, 20 (quotations), Wirt papers, MHS, reel 9.

81. Elizabeth Wirt to William Wirt, October 24, 1827 (quotations), reel 9; see also Ellen Wirt to Catharine Gamble, January 3, 1828; Elizabeth Wirt to William Wirt, January 5, 1828; Rosa Wirt to William Wirt, May 5, 9, 1828; William Wirt to Elizabeth Wirt, May 7, 1828; Elizabeth G. Wirt to William Wirt, May 8, 1828, all on reel 10, Wirt Papers,

MHS. On female adolescence and conversion, see Kett, *Rites of Passage*, 75–79; and Pope, "Preparation for Pedestals," 230–35; for female religiosity, see Clinton, *Plantation Mistress*, 95–96, 161–63; and Jean E. Friedman, *The Enclosed Garden: Women and Community in the Evangelical South, 1830–1900* (Chapel Hill and London, 1985); and on women's organizations, see Suzanne Lebsock, *The Free Women of Petersburg: Status and Culture in a Southern Town, 1784–1860* (New York and London, 1984), Chap. 7; and Barbara L. Bellows, *Benevolence among Slaveholders: Assisting the Poor in Charleston, 1670–1860* (Baton Rouge and London, 1993), 40–50, 115.

82. Elizabeth Wirt to William Wirt, October 24, 1827, reel 9; Elizabeth Wirt to Laura Wirt Randall, April 19, 1828 (quoted phrases); see also Ellen Wirt to Catharine Gamble, January 3, 1828; Elizabeth Wirt to William Wirt, January 5, 1828; Rosa Wirt to William Wirt, May 5, 9, 1828; William Wirt to Elizabeth Wirt, May 7, 1828; Elizabeth G. Wirt to William Wirt, May 8, 1828, all on reel 10, Wirt Papers, MHS. On female benevolence in Petersburg and Charleston, see Lebsock, *Free Women of Petersburg*, Chap. 7; and Bellows, *Benevolence among Slaveholders*, 40–50. On such organizations in Baltimore, see Gary Larson Browne, *Baltimore in the Nation, 1789–1861* (Chapel Hill, 1980), 102, 193–95.

83. Elizabeth Wirt to Laura Wirt Randall, October 4, 1827, Wirt Papers, MHS, reel 9.

84. For quotation, see Ellen Wirt to William Wirt, January 9, 1831, Wirt Papers, MHS, reel 13. See also Rosa Wirt to William Wirt, January 4, 12, 1831; Elizabeth G. Wirt to William Witt, January 7, 10, 1831; Catharine G. Wirt to William Wirt, February 6, 13, 1831, all in Wirt Papers, MHS, reel 13.

85. Catharine G. Wirt to William Wirt, January 16, 1831, Wirt Papers, MHS, reel 14. See also Bellows, *Benevolence among Slaveholders*, 43–44.

86. Elizabeth G. Wirt to William Wirt, January 19, 1831, Wirt Papers, MHS, reel 14.

87. Catharine G. Wirt to William Wirt, January 25, 1831, ibid. See also Lebsock, *Free Women of Petersburg*, Chap. 7. Contrast Lebsock's study with Bellows, *Benevolence among Slaveholders*, 44–45, who contends that women in Charleston did not have a gender-distinctive agenda.

88. Ellen Wirt to William Wirt, January 21, 1830, with postscript by Elizabeth Wirt, Wirt Papers, MHS, reel 12. See also Bellows, *Benevolence among Slaveholders*, 115; and Smith-Rosenberg, "Beauty, the Beast, and the Militant Woman: A Case Study in Sex Roles and Social Stress in Jacksonian America," in *Disorderly Conduct*, 109–28.

89. Elizabeth Wirt to Catharine Gamble, April 28, 1830, Wirt Papers, MHS, reel 13.

90. William Wirt to Catharine G. Wilt, December 4, 1828, Wirt Papers, MHS, reel 11.

91. William Wirt to Laura, Catharine, and Elizabeth G. Wirt, May 23, 1829, Wirt Papers, MHS, reel 12.

92. Elizabeth Wirt to William Wirt, October 16, 1827, reel 9; and Rosa Wirt to William Wirt, April 28, 1828, reel 10, both in Wirt Papers, MHS. The reference here is probably to Edward Bickersteth (1786–1850), the author of *A Scripture Help: Designed to Assist in Reading the Bible Profitably* (Boston, 1817).

93. See, for example, Capper, *Margaret*, Chap. 4.

94. Elizabeth Wirt to William Wirt, January 5, 1828, Wirt Papers, MHS, reel 10.

95. Rosa Wirt to Catharine Gamble, October 30, 1830, Wirt Papers, MHS, reel 13.

96. Catharine G. Wirt to William Wirt, February 10, 1831, Wirt Papers, MHS, reel 13.

97. See, for example, Laura Wirt to Catharine Wirt, August 22–24, 1826, Wirt Papers, MHS, reel 8. The wedding took place August 21, 1827. See Catherine Wirt to Emma Cabell, September 8, 1827, Carrington Family Papers, VHS; Robert Gamble to James

Breckinridge, August 16, 1827, Breckinridge Family Papers, VHS; and F. Edward Wright [comp.], *Marriage Licenses of Washington, D.C., 1811–1830* (Silver Spring, Md., 1988).

98. See Catharine W. Randall to Elizabeth W. Goldsborough, August 25, 1842, Wirt Family Papers, SHC; and Rosa Wirt to Elizabeth Wirt, November 3, 1831, Catharine G. Wirt to Elizabeth Wirt [?], November 4, 1831, and Ellen Wirt to Catharine Gamble, November 5, 1831, all in Wirt Papers, MHS, reel 14.

99. On Rosa's engagement and wedding, see William Wirt to Thomas Randall, May 31, 1832, and Catharine G. Wirt to Laura Wirt Randall [?], July 5, 1832, Wirt Papers, MHS, reel 15. On Ellen's marriage, see Jerrell H. Shofner, *History of Jefferson County* (Tallahassee, 1976), 31, 40, 128, 135; see also Catharine Wirt to Dabney C. Wirt, January 12, June 8, 29, 1839, Wirt Family Papers, SHC.

100. On Willard, see Anne Firor Scott, "The Ever-Widening Circle: The Diffusion of Feminist Values from the Troy Female Seminary, 1822–72," in Scott, *Making the Invisible Woman Visible*, 64–88; on Beecher, see Kathryn Kish Sklar, *Catharine Beecher: A Study in American Domesticity* (New Haven and London, 1973) especially Chap. 12. Lebsock, *Free Women of Petersburg*, 205–7, notes that educated women were in the forefront of the Virginia towns' charitable and reform organizations.

101. On the "informal curriculum," see especially Farnham, *Education of the Southern Belle*, Chap. 5. On the proliferation of female schools in the early antebellum, see Trey Berry, "A History of Women's Higher Education in Mississippi, 1819–1882," *Journal of Mississippi History*, LIII (November 1991), 303–19; and Sheldon Hanft, "Mordecais Female Academy," *American Jewish History*, LXXIX (Autumn 1989), 72–93.

CHAPTER 3

"Oh I Love Mother, I Love Her Power"

Shaker Spirit Possession and the Performance of Desire

Susan McCully

Ecstatic religious trance and spirit possession occur across a broad cultural and socioeconomic range, from Pentecostal possession by the Holy Ghost to Ethiopian zar possession cults. Interestingly, this phenomenon is most frequently experienced by young women in their early teens. Folklorists such as Felicitas Goodman postulate that this generational and gendered proclivity for trance reception is a response to the powerlessness of girls within their communities.[1] As such, spirit possession allows young women to claim a degree of cultural power through the performance of a spiritual manifestation. Although I want to make it clear that I am not questioning the very real physical (and perhaps metaphysical) effects of the trance state during religious ecstasy, I argue that the trance state is a consciously induced performance[2] and the enactment of spiritual power.

A fascinating example of mass possession led by young women occurred in the Shaker communities across the United States in the 1830s and '40s. I contend that these female Shaker spiritualists used mass possession manifestations to gain power within Shaker society. My focus here is to chart and historicize the rapid repression within the paternalistic sect of the sexualized, somewhat homoerotic, performances by the girls, the most disenfranchised of an already marginalized and sexually deviant society.

Critical to my understanding of the Shaker performances as an access to power is the use of feminist historiography. By using a feminist revisionist approach, I read documentation of the possession as well as the Shaker communities' reaction to these events. Through these readings, I will attempt to illustrate that the rapid repression and containment of these trances points to them as performative moments during which the girls enacted spiritual power to access a culturally unacceptable amount of social power.

By using Foucaultian theory to interpret the meanings and subtexts of several songs and rituals that were created while the girls were in trance, I argue further that the performances were highly sexualized and latently homosexual. This rereading of Shaker history illuminates both the radical transgressiveness of these performances and the paternalistic need for the swift repression of their expression. Critical to this interpretation is my reading of spirit possession as a performative moment rather than an externally induced "supernatural" occurrence. Irrelevant to my discussion are any issues of the subjects' psychological intent, the origin of the phenomenon or the authenticity of the experience.

The Shakers were, and still are, a group of Pentecostal Quakers, originally given the moniker "Shaking Quakers," but known among themselves as "The Society of True Believers in Christ's Second Appearing." From their origin in the 1770s, the basic tenets of Shakerism have put the sect's members in conflict with the larger social order both where they began in England, and in their adopted home, the United States. These tenets include: the belief in Christ's second appearance in female form in the person of Mother Ann Lee, founder of the Shaker movement in the United States; the "equality" of the sexes[3]; mandatory celibacy and the strict separation of the sexes within the community in order to avoid the temptations of sexuality; the belief that carnality is the root of all evil; and communal living with the sharing of both labor and profit.

In his authoritative collection of Shaker hymns and rituals, ethnomusicologist Daniel Patterson breaks the formative years of Shaker history into several periods; an early American period during Mother Ann's life from 1774 to 1784; a middle period from Lee's death until the revival period beginning in 1837; the period of spiritual manifestations by the girls from 1837 until approximately 1850; and a later period until the decline of the Shaker population following the Civil War.[4] I will follow this breakdown because he charts clear distinctions in the rituals before, during, and after the period of mass possession led by the young Shaker women.

From the time of Mother Ann and following her death, the pre-revival worship services were open to the public and were similar in style to contemporary Pentecostal services.[5] The formal structure of these early worship services were centered around memorized dances and songs that were created by Mother Ann and the other elders of the sects. As Patterson documents, the songs were original, but they were drawn from traditional Protestant hymnal themes. "Heavenly Feast in Zion," "Ezekial's Vision," and "We Bless Our Lord and Savior" are typical titles from the period. The structured dances that these songs accompanied were "line dances," "circular dances," and "square dances" that were borrowed primarily from the members' English and Scottish folk traditions.

A print from the late 1700s, which is now widely reproduced in literature about the Shakers, depicts a line dance from this period. The picture shows a folk dance composed primarily of Shaker dancers who are tightly regimented into six straight lines; three lines are made up of only women and three are of only men. On the left side of the room as it is represented, the three female columns march, each in step with the next, toward the center of the room. On the right hand, the three columns of men march in symmetrical unity toward the women of the opposing side. Order and synchroneity dominate the representation. The style of the dance appears to be highly presentational as it is shown in the print. It is as if the church service is also a performance for the non-Shaker visitor in the corner of the lithograph. The female guest who, in contrast to the Shakers is elegantly dressed, watches on as the succinctly unified line dancers walk in formation. The image is reminiscent of a spectator watching a marching band or a dowdy and subdued version of the Radio City Rockettes' Holiday Extravaganza. Clearly represented in the lithograph is both the high degree of structure in the pre-revival services and the fact that the worship was open to the public spectatorship. The picture also suggests that the non-Shaker guests were viewing a kind of theatricalized public performance.

Although the picture does show an outsider apparently enjoying the spectacle of a Shaker service, not all contemporaries approved of this form of Christian worship. Whether because of their radical social tenets or because the services were simply deemed inappropriate by conservative Christian colonists, numerous attacks were launched against the sect. In a tract entitled *The Rise and Progress of the Serpent from the Garden of Eden to the Present Day with a Disclosure of Shakerism Exhibiting a General View of Their Real Character and Conduct from the First Appearance of Ann Lee*, Mary Marshall Dyer documents her disapproval of this type of service. She made the following observation of her 1822 visit to a pre-revival Shaker service: "Their family and church service is to sing songs of their own composition (no form or appearance of prayer) in adoration of Mother Ann Lee, in the most merry tunes, such as 'Yankee

Doodle' and 'Over the River to Charley' with the most ridiculous gestures and motion and dance and their appearance is so farcical, that it is difficult for the spectator to tell whether they are in church or a theatre!"[6]

Marshall's words are actually some of the most civil of the charges leveled against the Shakers during their early period. From the 1770s through to the beginning of the mass spirit possessions in 1837 hundreds of tracts were published claiming that the Shakers were practicing witchcraft and that their services involved drunken revels and sexually deviant public displays. From the beginning of their history, the cultural anxiety surrounding Mother Ann's public performances enticed the non-Shakers to start "smear campaigns" against their "deviant" behavior, and yet none of these charges led the Shaker leaders to close their services to the public.

Despite many scandalous public documents designed to vilify the Shakers and their leaders during the formative years, the Shaker service remained open to the public. Marshall published an extensive collection of court documents and affidavits given between 1781 and 1826 by those who had grievances against the Shakers. In these documents, Mother Ann was frequently characterized as a sexual deviant or some sort of highly sexualized dominatrix. Former Shaker Asa Pattee's sworn testimony of 1818 says:

> I have seen Mother . . . come into a room where many are gathered for a meeting and were, by her own orders, stripped naked. I have seen her slap the men, rub her hands on all parts of their bodies. All the time she was humming and making an enchanted noise . . . Once in a meeting in Petersham, Mass., the Mother came in, leading with her a naked man, whom she committed to another (man) . . . (who) whirled him around, threw him on the floor, hauled him by the hair of the head, calling out, "you bestial devil!" . . . after other indecent conduct, Mother told the women to dog him off, who clapped their hands, and cried out, "Stu-boy! stu-boy!" The man crawled off as best he could.[7]

Despite such charges, the Shakers kept their services open and the worship continued in its highly structured song and dance format. During the period of mass possession known by the Shakers as "Mother Ann's work" and the "Era of Manifestions," that would change.

In August of 1837, nearly fifty years after Ann Lee's death, a group of young women from ten to fourteen years of age began exhibiting strange behavior at the Watervliet, New York, settlement. The accounts of the behavior are typical of trance possession enactments. Rapid spinning, speaking in tongues, mortification, and convulsive movements are among the phenomena attributed to the girls. These behaviors seemed to have been contagious in the settlement; slowly, more girls (and a few young boys) were affected. In November 1837,

Ann Mariah Goff, a woman of fourteen who had been experiencing trance possession, began receiving visions from Mother Ann. She claimed to see Mother as "a spirit dressed in white, [who] kissed all the sisters, labored with them . . . and sang songs of mourning for sinners."[8] Eventually, other girls began receiving Mother as well. At first, these visions were considered to be divinely inspired, but once the girls began experiencing visions during the worship, the visions became disruptive. A lithograph showing a worship service during the "Era of Manifestation" shows a very different atmosphere and focus than the earlier description.

In a lithograph from the 1840s entitled "Whirling Girls," a young girl lies on the floor in the center of the picture. Flanking her in a semicircular arch are other Shakers who appear to be performing a "circular dance," but the dance seems to be interrupted by the girl on the floor. Like the earlier lithograph, the sexes are separated into left and right sides. While some of the women (and a few of the men) have their backs turned to the girl and continue the dance, others are distracted and out of step with the rest. Their focus is shifted to the subject who is writhing on the floor. This picture suggests that the possessed subjects became the focus of the service through their possession manifestations. It also suggests that the structure of the service itself was threatened by these performances. Whereas the earlier representation of the "line dance" typified order and symmetry, the overwhelming imagery in "Whirling Girls" represents chaos. A palpable tension between those who are struggling to continue the dance and those enthralled by this performance of possession can be felt.

By the winter of 1837, visions and the messages interpreted from them became increasingly severe. In the beginning, the messages from Mother Ann's spirit were benign and loving, but over time her warnings (as performed by the girls) grew strident. Both during the actual manifestations and afterward when the girls would relay the visions, they claimed that Mother had returned in spirit to demand the end of all carnality and lust. In trance, the girls would dictate the creation of new dances and songs. As the obsession with carnality grew, the new dances became ritualized enactments of sexual self-denial and the purgation of lustful feelings. The songs created by the girls to accompany the rites—replacing the earlier traditional-style songs—were new anthems professing Mother's power and love. Songs like "Oh Mother, How Blessed Thou Art," and "Oh I Love Mother, I Love her Power" became the standard hymns during this period.

The entranced visionists claimed that Mother's love was the only force powerful enough to rid the Shakers of their worldly and fleshy temptations. In response to these visions, Shaker communities created humility rites to enact Mother's divine cleansing powers and to rid one another of lust. With men and women completely separated, the rites involved the sponging, rubbing, and shaking of one another. During the "cleansing rite," each member of the community was scrubbed.

> The rite consisted of placing "two large white tubs," one for the sisters, on either side of the fountain. In the ensuing pantomime dippers and baskets of sponges were placed near the tubs; these were filled from the fountain and when all were ready for bathing, the sisters and brethren on separate sides of the enclosure went through the motions of scrubbing each other clean.[9]

One of the songs created for the rite included the words: "Come to the fountain and strip off your garment that's old. O what an ocean of pure love I'll strip off my garment that's old. I'll wash and be clean pure and holy. Then Mother will love me she'll own me and bless me."[10]

The performance of this "love" was considered not only permissible, but advisable. Mother Ann, it was thought, counseled them to vent evil yearnings through ecstatic pleasures.

Edward Deming Andrews, one of the first scholars of Shaker ritual, sees cleansing rite as a "curious mortification or humility rite," but I read it quite differently. Because the ritual focuses on the separation of the sexes while the participants obsess about the purgation of their sexuality, this cleansing rite becomes an exotic representation of sexual repression through homoerotic ecstatic pleasure.

In *The History of Sexuality Volume 1*, Michael Foucault says that when sex is deployed in ways such as the Shaker "scrubbing"—the ritualized performance of the repression of sexuality—sex becomes discursive:

> The "putting into discourse of sex," far from undergoing a process of restriction, on the contrary has been subjected to a mechanism of increasing incitement; that the techniques of power exercised over sex have not obeyed a process of rigorous selection, but rather one of dissemination and implementation of polymorphous sexualities.[11]

By reading the cleansing rite through Foucault's "repressive hypothesis" of sexuality, it is clear that this performance of repression thinly disguises the simultaneous performance of polymorphic desire.

Perhaps the most blatantly homoerotic ritual practice that came out of the period of manifestation is a ritual that took place after the humility rites in the service. Once the carnality had been scrubbed out of each individual, they enacted what Andrews refers to as a "promiscuous dance." The separation of the sexes was still strictly upheld that the women and men, in segregated groups, mingled among themselves and "circulated mother's love." A brief essay written by an outsider who observed a Shaker service in 1787 says that the "blowing of mother's love into each other, by breathing in their face,[12] was typical of early services, so I cannot say that the circulation of mother's love was unique to this period. Nonetheless, a wood engraving from the revival period entitled "The Religious Dance" depicts an eroticized representation of this type of ritual. The focus of the image revolves around two Shaker women. One woman faces front, while the other stands at her side as they brush lips. At either side of these figures are women standing in pairs. On one side, the two are women lightly embracing; on the other side, the two are pressing cheeks. While the "kiss" is not represented as a "sexual kiss," I find that an undeniably erotic tone pervades this depiction. This picture is one of the only Shaker representations I have found that has elements typical of 19th century Romanticism. The figures are rendered in a night scene, with the female Shakers bathed in soft light. The result is that the entire image suggests an inherent sensuality. While the eroticism between the women may be seen as stylized convention, it is at least worth noting that this is the event this artist found conducive to a sensualized Roman depiction.

While I am not suggesting that either the trance possessions or the subsequent rituals were representations of homosexuality or homosexual practice, I do believe they were the performance of polymorphic desire. I also believe that this emphasis on the repression of sexuality caused the then newly formed Shaker's Central Ministry to focus on the possibility of polymorphic practices that might not otherwise have been noticed or considered. In *Divine Book of Holy and Eternal Wisdom*, first published in 1845, the Shaker elders admonished all to "Cease to mingle in fleshy defilements with the beasts of the fields, or with your domestic animals. Cease to gratify your carnal desires with your own sex, man with man and woman with woman; neither become defilers of your own bodies, working self-pollution in ways which are unseemly, and against the laws of nature."[13]

During the period of manifestation, the central ministry began to codify rules for all areas of living, not just sexual expression. I do not want to make a direct correlation between the performance of sexual expression and the tightening of restrictions on social behavior. If for no other reason, this causal link would make little sense because the practices that I am suggesting are much more subtle than the charges leveled against Mother Ann during her lifetime. I definitely do see the codification of social rules as a direct result of the girls claiming a culturally "inappropriate" amount of social power through the performance of spirit possession. Clearly these manifestations began to threaten the stability of the Central Ministry's power, because they took immediate action to control the meanings of the manifestations.

As I have charted earlier, the Shakers were much maligned from without by the antebellum American society. As such, the community at Watervliet initially supported the girls, endorsing the possession to justify their own spiritual and political goals. As news of the manifestations in New York spread to the other eighteen Shaker villages throughout the eastern United States, the elders claimed these girls as true visionaries. In their spiritual performances, the leaders found divine validation for their community, but as early as 1837, evidence of the elder's need to control the meanings of the performances appears. Drawing from the Central Ministry Journal 1830–1839, Stephen J. Stein outlines Elder Rufius Bishop's mandate for the "growing public spectacle":

> He judged that these evidences of the condescending goodness of God were intended to strengthen faith in the work of God and to highlight the state of rewards and punishments beyond the grave. He warned the instruments [the girls] against letting their senses rise or taking the honor of those gifts to themselves and he urged that they keep to their elders and to the living body or they would suffer great loss. The central ministry's position was clear; the gifts were of God, but they must be used to support union and order within the society.[14]

By the time of the manifestations, the Shakers maintained more than eighteen communities throughout the eastern United States. An increasingly greater number of youths, particularly girls, were affected as word of the manifestations in Watervliet spread to the other communities. Within a year most of the closely linked northeastern Shaker communities and a few of the midwestern ones as well were beginning to experience similar and sometimes bizarre and frightening physical occurrences.[15] Eventually the girls claimed to be possessed by such women as Mary Magdalene, Pocahantas, Queen Isabella, and Queen Elizabeth. Although the girls were also possessed by George Washington, Christopher Columbus, and even an entire "tribe of Indians," I think it is important to note that these were young women performing extremely powerful historical figures and that many of these figures were female.

These performances of insubordinate power disrupted and fundamentally altered both the sect's governance and the structure of their worship service. The threat of female power overturning the hierarchical structures from within the organization achieved what no external attack on the Shakers could do. By order of the Central Ministry, all Shaker rituals were closed to the public in 1845. Stein, Andrews, and other traditional Shaker scholars read these manifestations as absurd and silly. As a result, they relate the closing of the services to the ministry's desire to hide the "ridiculousness" of the performances. I would argue that the Central Ministry was not concerned with "appearing silly to the outside world"; charges more scandalous than "silliness" had been leveled against them for years. The elders were not concerned with controlling the interpretations that outsiders made of the performances, but rather they needed to control the power the girls were gaining by becoming the focus of attention for both other Shakers and the outside world.

In order to reclaim both spiritual and cultural power, the elders were forced to contain the manifestations. The first strategy employed by the elders was to close the services in order to limit the girls' access to public attention. The second strategy was to claim that only the elders were in a high enough spiritual position to understand the meanings of the possessions. By 1845 the Central Ministry declared the possessions authentic yet unintelligible because they were being transmitted through "unlearned instruments." Eldress Paulina Bates chided them as those "who pretend to be sanctified ministers of the gospel"[16] before they were prepared through confession, obedience, and submission to order. Eventually the spiritualists were required to "confess" their visions to the elders so that they could test for the validity of the communication. According to Foucault, containment through confession is an attempt "to transform your desire, your every desire into discourse."[17] Yet, as Foucault argues, making sex discursive represses physical expression, but desire is never fully containable. Likewise the Central Ministry's attempt to control the possessions by making them discursive and interpreting their meanings did ultimately repress the physical manifestations of possession. By 1847, Shakers were rid of many of the most disruptive members because all of the most severely affected mediums, particularly the young girls, left the society.[18] Yet I argue that their desire for both erotic possession and social power left lasting effects on the structure of the Shaker worship services.

During the early period, Shaker services were open to the public. While charismatic behavior was exhibited during these services, it was performed by the elders who led the services. Ritualized worship services from the early period included structured folk dances and traditional-style hymns. The manifestations and the resultant rituals broke the order of the service. The trance possession performances often disrupted the services; the hymns turned into praises of Mother Ann; and the rites created were raucous representations of sexual repression. Spirit possession phenomena had all but ended in the Shaker communities by 1850, and the services returned to ordered, highly codified private proceedings that continued to be closed to the public.

The elders' ability to reinscribe their power is reflected in the subdued song and dance styles performed during services following the revival. Standardized presentational movements performed to music replaced the rites and dances. Photographs from the early twentieth century show Shaker sisters enacting stilted, standardized gestures that were "acted out" in unison while singing.[19] During the late Shaker periods, rather than "blowing Mother's love," "cheek to cheek" was enacted by standing at arm's length across from a same sex partner. The "giver of the love" would first cross her arms in an "x" over her chest, then bring the arms down and out toward the partner with the giver's palms up. The partner then "receives the love" by repeating the motions in reverse. During the revival, the Shaker's body was scrubbed, shaken, thrown, and rubbed against another to rid the subject of evil, yearning lust. Following this period, a Shaker woman would stand in a pugilistic pose and give her fists several brisk forward pulses to enact the "fighting off" of carnality.

The changes in the ritual reflect the patriarchal attempt to contain both the expression of a female power structure and the expression of sexuality. By charting the material changes in Shaker services from the time of Mother Ann to the decline of the Shaker's spiritual enterprise, a correlation between the repression of sexuality and the repression of the cultural power employed by the women through the performance of spirit possession begins to emerge. From the beginnings of Shaker history the obsessive repression of sexual practice made their ritualized sexual expression discursive in a Foucaultian sense. Also, by embracing Mother Ann as a messianic figure, they allowed a potential female-based power structure to brew under the surface of their patriarchally controlled sect. During the revival the conflation of sexuality and a female-based spiritual power erupted through the performance of religious ecstasy. The effect was the rapid repression of this expression. But the access to power available in the performative moment of spirit possession is the performance of Foucaultian desire, and so was beyond containment by the Shaker leadership. In the ten-year revival period, the elder's containment strategies progressed from an initial appropriation of the manifestations to the ultimate radical stricture of the ritual structures. Yet the power available to the girls in the very moment of performance lingered. Moments of desire possession, both spiritual and erotic, defy regulation.

Notes

1. Felicitas D. Goodman, *How About Demons?: Possession and Exorcism in the Modern World* (Bloomington: Indiana University Press, 1988).
2. I want to stress that my understanding of "consciously induced" implies that the subject of the spirit possession is the causal agent of the trance. In other words, I consider spirit possession an altered state of consciousness that is brought forth both mentally and physically by the subject.
3. Feminist scholar Marjorie Procter-Smith has written extensively about feminism and Shaker religious practice. She accurately points out that even though there appears to be the potential for woman-centered or at least non-phallocratic religion in the Shakers, the governance of both church and community remained hierarchical and male-controlled. This was especially true during the revival period. In *Women in Shaker*

Community and Worship: A Feminist Analysis of the Uses of Religious Symbolism (Lewiston, N.Y.: Edwin Mellen Press, 1985), Proctor-Smith says that by the 1830s any remnant of female leadership had given way to "an ordered community structure, the newly organized Shaker communities were called 'Families,' and were as tightly ordered as a military regiment" (42).

4. Daniel W. Patterson, *The Shaker Spiritual* (Princeton, N.J.: Princeton University Press, 1979).

5. I use the term Pentecostal mostly as a descriptor for a charismatic, emotionally charged spiritual worship that is, in fact, highly codified and framed by a minister and structured song and dance. I want to make it clear that I am not conflating Shakerism with Charles Fox Pakhams's Pentecostal movement that began during this same period and in the same approximate geographical area as Shakerism. For an excellent feminist account of Pentecostalism in the 1980s, see Elaine Lawless's *God's Peculiar People* (Lexington: University Press of Kentucky, 2005). Her focus on Pentecostal women and their social empowerment accessed through charismatic performance resonates nicely with my reading of Shaker women.

6. Mary Marshall Dyer, *The Rise and Progress of the Serpent in the Garden of Eden to the Present with a Disclosure of Shakerism Exhibiting a General View of Their Real Character and Condition from the First Appearance of Ann Lee* (Concord, N.H.: printed for the author, 1847), 279.

7. Mary Marshall, *A Portraiture of Shakerism Exhibiting a General View of Their Character and Conduct from the First Appearance of Ann Lee Down to the Present Time* (Micro-published in *History of Women* [New Haven, Conn.: Research Publications, Inc., 1975]), 28.

8. Stephen J. Stein, *The Shaker Experience in America: A History of the United Society of Believers* (New Haven: Yale University Press, 1992), 158.

9. Edward Deming Andrews, *The Gift to Be Simple: Songs, Dances and Rituals of the American Shakers* (New York: Dover Publications, Inc., 1940), 7.

10. Andrews, 78.

11. Michel Foucault, *The History of Sexuality Volume 1: An Introduction*, trans. Robert Hurley (New York: Vintage Books, 1990), 12.

12. Stein, 37.

13. Louis J. Kern, *An Ordered Love: Sex Roles and Sexuality in Victorian Utopias—The Shakers, Mormons and the Oneida Community* (Chapel Hill: The University of North Carolina Press, 1981), 89.

14. Quoted in Stein, 169.

15. Ibid., 69.

16. Ibid., 196.

17. Foucault, 51.

18. Lawrence Foster, *Religion and Sexuality: Three American Communal Experiments of the Nineteenth Century* (New York: Oxford University Press, 1981), 50.

19. These photographs suggest that the gestures are similar to the "motions" that go along with contemporary children's songs (like "The Inky Dinky Spider").

CHAPTER 4

Women on the Town

Sexual Exchange and Prostitution

Christine Stansell

As urban reformers and writers told it, no tale of working-class life was more chilling in its revelations of vice than the prostitute's. From the 1830s on, prostitutes flitted wraithlike across the pages of urban social commentary, a class of women rendered human only by the occasional penitent in their ranks. Prostitutes had long been familiar to New Yorkers, but between 1830 and 1860 women "on the town" became the subject of a sustained social commentary. By the 1850s, urban prostitution was troubling enough to lead city fathers to lend the services of their police force in aiding William Sanger in conducting a massive investigation. Dr. Sanger's report, the compendious *History of Prostitution*, represents the coming of age of prostitution as a social "problem" in America, and its integration into the new discourse of secular urban reform.

The very fact that reformers in the 1850s were thinking about prostitution had to do with tensions over gender relations and female sexuality. To them, prostitution was simply a verifiable empirical reality synonymous with the degradation of morals and public health. But between the lines of their

considerations ran another discussion, barely delineated, about the dangerous impulses of girls and young women. In New York culture, the image of
the Bowery Gal was one side of the coin of youthful pleasures; that of the
hardened girl on the streets was the other. The alarm over prostitution was
one response to the growing social and sexual distance that working-class
women—especially working-class daughters—were traveling from patriarchal
regulation.

The problem of prostitution as reformers defined it had no necessary relation to the experience of the women involved. For laboring women, prostitution was a particular kind of choice presented by the severities of daily life. It
was both an economic and a social option, a means of self support and a way
to bargain with men in a situation where a living wage was hard to come by,
and holding one's own in heterosexual relations was difficult. The reasons girls
and women went into prostitution, the uses they made of it, and the relation it
bore to the rest of their lives varied greatly. The reformers' image of prostitution
as an irreversible descent into degradation obfuscated more of this complex
reality than it revealed.[1]

The Problem

In 1818, when the city watch published its latest statistics on crime, the
authorities took a complacent view of prostitution. Although the numbers of
known prostitutes and bawdy houses in the city had doubled in a dozen years,
they reported, the women and their patrons had never been more quiet and
law-abiding.[2] In subsequent years, an offensive against urban vice put an end
to such laissez-faire attitudes. After 1831, when the evangelical women of New
York's Magdalene Society first took up the battle to banish prostitution from
the city, denunciations of what was purported to be an urgent problem became
common currency among moral reformers and public authorities. "We have
satisfactorily ascertained the fact that the numbers of females in this city, who
abandon themselves to prostitution is not less than TEN THOUSAND!!!!!"
announced John McDowall, agent for the Magdalene Society, in its first annual report in 1832. McDowall's figure was up by more than eight times from
the 1818 estimate, a supposed increase that should give us pause.[3] Whatever
number reformers picked, however, they used it to stress the reason for alarm.
The National Trades' Union in the 1830s, the Ladies' Industrial Association in
1845, and reformers Matthew Carey and later Horace Greeley all promoted a
similar view that prostitution was making heavy incursions into the female
poor.[4] By 1855, public concern was sufficiently strong to move the aldermen
to commission William Sanger to conduct a statistical investigation in New

York of the kind Parent-Duchâtelet had published for Paris in 1836. Sanger's researches confirmed to him and to his public (as such researches often do) that the city was indeed prey to an "enormous vice." It was, he gravely concluded, "a fact beyond question that this vice is attaining a position and extent in this community which cannot be viewed without alarm."[5]

Was, indeed, prostitution on the rise, expanding along with the manufacturing system, as many people believed? Given the fragmentary statistics, it is hard now to answer conclusively, but the reformers' and officials' estimates tend (contrary to their own conclusions) to disprove the argument. In fact, prostitution seems only to have increased along with the population, at the rate one would expect in a city that multiplied in size more than six times between 1820 and 1860. There was certainly an increase in the absolute number of prostitutes. Police Chief Matsell estimated there were 5,000 women on the town in 1856, as compared to the watch's 1,200 in 1818.[6] But these figures, tenuous as they are, actually indicate a slight *decrease* in the numbers of prostitutes proportional to the urban population. On the level of numbers alone, then, it seems there were more prostitutes simply because there were more people.

Of course, this does not mean there were no problems. The increase in absolute numbers had important effects. Commitments of women to prison for vagrancy, the statutory offense under which prostitution fell, more than doubled between 1850 and 1860; imprisonments for keeping disorderly houses, often the rubric under which houses of prostitution fell, multiplied by more than five times between 1849 and 1860.[7] These statistics cannot tell us how many women were convicted for prostitution, since the police could arrest women in the streets simply because they were homeless. But since the majority of female arrests were of girls and young women ten to thirty years old, the age bracket into which the majority of the women Sanger interviewed fell,[8] it seems likely that prostitution played some role in the increase in vagrancy arrests from 3,500 in 1850 to nearly 6,500 in 1860. In itself, this spectacular rise must have convinced New Yorkers they were living

Table 4.1.

Year	Number of Men	Number of Women	Total	Percentage of Women
1850	1,148	2,204	3,552	62
1851	1,305	2,225	3,530	63
1852	1,797	3,396	5,193	65
1853	2,417	3,824	6,241	61
1855	1,656	3,598	5,254	68
1860	1,816	4,736	6,552	72

Source: Commissioners of the Almshouse. *Annual Reports.* There are no complete figures for 1849, 1854, 1856–59.

amidst an epidemic of female vice, insofar as they closely associated female homelessness and poverty with depravity.

The urgency of the discussion, however, was also a response to the changing character of the trade. What disturbed observers was not just the number of women who bargained with men for sex, but the identity of those women. For if the numbers of known professional prostitutes were not growing disproportionally, those of casual prostitutes—girls or women who turned to prostitution temporarily or episodically to supplement other kinds of livelihoods—probably were. Moreover, the entire context of the transaction was changing, as prostitution moved out of the bawdy houses of the poor into cosmopolitan public spaces like Broadway. "It no longer confines itself to secrecy and darkness," lamented Sanger, "but boldly strikes through our most thronged and elegant thoroughfares."[9]

Prostitution was becoming urbane. The trade was quite public in the business district as well as in poor neighborhoods, a noticeable feature of the ordinary city landscape. Since prostitution was not a statutory offense, there was no legal pressure to conceal it. By 1857, William Sanger could catalog a wide range of establishments catering to prostitution. "Parlor houses," clustered near the elegant hotels on Broadway, were the most respectable, frequented by gentlemen; the second-class brothels served clerks and "the higher class of mechanics."[10] In some theaters, prostitutes solicited and consorted with patrons in the notorious third tier, reserved for their use, although the high-toned Park Theater had closed its third tier in 1842, and Sanger noted that other theaters patronized by the genteel were following suit. Except for the parlor and bawdy houses, however, the trade was informal rather than organized; that is, a woman could easily ply it on her own outside a brothel. Prostitution was still a street trade of independent workers; pimps were a phenomenon of the early twentieth century, a consequence of the onset of serious police harassment.[11] The places where "street-walkers" resorted served other erotic functions as well. Houses of assignation, where much casual prostitution took place, were private establishments where a couple could rent rooms by the hour; illicit lovers used them for trysting places. There was a hierarchy of houses of assignation: the respectable brownstones off Broadway, where ladies carried on affairs during the hours of the afternoon promenade; the shabby-genteel houses, where shopgirls, milliners, and domestic servants went with gentlemen "sweethearts" with whom their work brought them in contact; and the cheap houses where working-class couples and prostitutes resorted and where fast young men set up their working-class mistresses to live. Around the waterfront were the lowest class of establishments, basement dramshops with rooms in the back frequented by sailors, immigrants, and poor transients, and better-kept dancing houses with adjoining rooms for girls and their clients.[12]

In the same working-class neighborhoods, prostitution also went on in the tenements themselves. In the district near City Hall, where there was a lively interest in commercial sex from the many men of all classes doing business there, an investigating commission found that "it is a well-known fact that in many of the tenant-houses of this district such persons [prostitutes] occupy suites of apartments interspersed with those of the respectable laboring classes, and frequently difficult to be distinguished from them." In the lowest neighborhoods, near-destitute residents sometimes rented out corners of their rooms to prostitutes.[13]

There were specialized services as well. In the 1840s, a nascent commercial sex trade began to offer variegated sexual experiences beyond the prostitute's bed, mostly to gentlemen. The sex trade was centered in the area between City Hall Park, the commercial heart of the city, and the Five Points. There, crime and amusement rubbed elbows, laboring people mixed with gentlemen and the quick scam flourished. Visitors and men about town could, within an easy walk from most places of business, gain entrance to dance halls featuring naked performers, brothels with child prostitutes, eating places decorated with pornographic paintings, pornographic book shops, and "model artist" shows, where naked women arranged themselves in edifying tableaux from literature and art (Susannah and the Elders, for example)—as well as a variety of facilities for having sex. The network of sexual experiences for sale was certainly troubling evidence of the centrality of sex to metropolitan life; indeed, its presence in the most cosmopolitan areas of the city was one indication of just how closely a particular kind of sex (bourgeois men with working-class women) was linked to an evolving mode of sophisticated urbanity.[14]

In a city so concerned with defining both women's proper place and the place of the working class, the alarm over prostitution stemmed in part from general hostilities to the milieu of laboring women from which prostitutes came. "Prostitution" evolved in the nineteenth century as a particular construction, the grouping of a range of sexual experiences, which in actual life might be quite disparate. The discourse about prostitution was embedded in genteel preoccupations; while working-class people had their own concerns about prostitution, they remained marginal to the developing public discussion. Bourgeois men and women, who understood female sexuality within the terms of the cult of true womanhood, tended to see any woman who was sexually active outside of marriage as a prostitute. While their judgments were not inherently class bound ("true" women who strayed were equally liable to condemnation), they obviously weighed more heavily on poor women, who did not adhere to standards of premarital (or sometimes even extramarital) chastity. Although working-class men and women could judge and condemn with the same severity as reformers, they did so by the standards of a sexual morality with more fluid definitions of licit and illicit, good and bad, respectability and transgression.

Going to Ruin

For laboring people as well as bourgeois moralists, prostitution was closely linked to "ruin," a state of affairs to be avoided at all costs. But while bourgeois men and women viewed ruin as the consequence of prostitution, working-class people reversed the terms. It was ruin, occasioned by a familial or economic calamity (for women the two were synonymous), that precipitated the "fall" into prostitution. The disasters that afflicted women's lives—male desertion, widowhood, single motherhood—propelled adult women into prostitution as a comparatively easy way to earn a living. The prospect of prostitution was, like the possibility of these other misfortunes, a part of everyday life: a contingency remote to the blessed, the strong, and the fortunate, right around the corner for the weak and the unlucky. Prostitution was neither a tragic fate, as moralists viewed it (and continue to view it), nor an act of defiance, but a way of getting by, of making the best of bad luck.

Prostitution was indeed, as reformers liked to point out, tied to the female labor market. Women on their own earned such low wages that in order to survive; they often supplemented waged employment with casual prostitution. There is a good deal of information on this practice in the 1850s because William Sanger asked about it. "A large number of females," he observed, "earn so small wages that a temporary cessation of their business, or being a short time out of a situation, is sufficient to reduce them to absolute distress."[15] A quarter of Sanger's subjects, about 500 of the 2,000 women interviewed, had worked in manufacturing employment, mostly in the needle trades. More than a quarter again had earned wages of a dollar or less a week; more than half earned less than three dollars. Some 300 were still working at a trade; 325 had only left their work within the six months previous.[16]

From this information, we can infer something about the earning patterns of young women on their own. Their wages alone could not have financed nights on the Bowery. Casual prostitution, exchanging sexual favors with male escorts for money or food and drink (what a later generation called "treating"[17]), may have been one way young women on the town got by. The stories Sanger collected from his errant subjects, however, also chronicled the grimmer side of female employment, when there was no money to buy food, let alone theater tickets. "M. M., a widow with one child, earned $1.50 a week as a tailoress." "E. H. earned from two to three dollars a week as tailoress, but had been out of employment for some time." "M. F., a shirt-maker, earned one dollar a week."

"S. F., a widow with three children, could earn two dollars weekly at cap-making, but could not obtain steady employment even at those prices."[18]

Many of the women with whom Sanger and his police interviewers talked had turned to prostitution as the closest employment at hand after suddenly losing male support. Many had been left alone in the city by husbands or family: 471—almost one-fourth—were married women who had become single and self-supporting through circumstances beyond their control. Eight percent had been deserted by their husbands; fifteen percent were widowed. Fifty-seven percent had lost their fathers before they reached the age of twenty.[19] In themselves, such statistics tell us nothing about the role that destitution played in prostitution. Taken together, however, they do reveal the forces that made prostitution a reasonable choice in a society in which economic support from a man was a prerequisite for any kind of decent life. "No work, no money, and no home," was the succinct description one woman gave of her circumstances. The stark facts that others recited illuminate some of the urgent situations that pushed women out onto the streets. "My husband deserted me and four children. I had no means to live." "My husband eloped with another woman. I support the child." "I came to this city, from Illinois, with my husband. When we got here he deserted me. I have two children dependent on me."[20] These were the painful female actualities from which popular culture would fashion its own morality tales of sexual victimization and depravity.

Sanger veered away from the blanket moral condemnations of early reform literature toward the more dispassionate and environmentalist perspective of early British and French social science. While moral categories entered into his analysis, he preferred to focus on exterior forces and social solutions rather than on the spiritual transformation of the working class that the evangelicals sought.[21] Women were victims of poverty, the wage system, orphanage, abandonment, and seduction. For Sanger, even their "passion" became a kind of environmental factor, divested of moral choice and existing apart from their conscious agency.

Yet ultimately Sanger's survey yields a very different picture than his own preferred one of the victim of circumstance, the distressed needlewoman, and the deserted wife at starvation's door. His exhaustive queries revealed a great deal about the roots of prostitution in economic desperation, but they also produced compelling evidence about more complex sources. When Sanger asked his subjects their reasons for taking up prostitution, over a quarter—a number almost equal to those who cited "destitution"—gave "inclination" as their answer. "Inclination," whatever its moral connotations, still indicated some element of choice within the context of other alternatives. "C. M.: while virtuous, this girl had visited dancehouses, where she became acquainted with prostitutes, who persuaded her that they led an easy, merry life." "S. C.: this girl's

86   *Christine Stansell*

inclination arose from a love of liquor." "E. C. left her husband, and became a prostitute willingly, in order to obtain intoxicating liquors which had been refused her at home."[22]

The historical issues are complicated. One can imagine a sullen woman trapped in the virtual jail that was the Blackwell's Island venereal disease hospital, flinging cynical answers—"drink," "amusement"—to the good doctor's questions as those most likely to shock him or to appeal to the preconceptions she sensed in him. But although this may have been true in some encounters, the dynamic between the doctor and his subject is an unlikely explanation of why so many women rejected a paradigm of victimization (which, if anything, Sanger himself promoted) for answers that stressed their own agency in entering prostitution. Altogether, 918 of the subjects implied motives other than hardship. Sanger classified their responses as: "too idle to work," "persuaded by prostitutes," "an easy life," "drink, and the desire to drink," "ill-treatment of parents, relatives or husbands."[23] Whatever the ways in which the women constructed their stories in consort with Sanger, there seems to have been some common self-understanding, widely enough shared to seem independent of the doctor, that one might choose prostitution within the context of other alternatives.

Of course we cannot separate such answers from the economic difficulties laboring women faced. But structural factors alone cannot clarify why some women took up prostitution and others in similar straits did not. Nor can they illuminate the histories of women who entered prostitution from comparatively secure economic positions. Almost half of Sanger's subjects, for instance, were domestic servants; servants were long notorious (at least since 1820) for turning to prostitution not because they were desperate for work but because they longed for a change.[24] And although the poorest New Yorkers, new immigrants, were well-represented in the 1855 sample—35 percent of Sanger's subjects were Irish, 12 percent German—there were also significant numbers of the native-born: 38 percent, or 762 of the total. Daughters of skilled workers were also present to a surprising extent—30 percent—surprising, since one would suspect their family's prosperity would protect them.[25] True, divisions between immigrant and native-born, skilled and unskilled in themselves mean little. Plenty of native-born laboring people found themselves in distressed circumstances by 1855, and the economic distinction between skilled and unskilled broke down in many trades. The point is more general, however. It is possible to see from Sanger's statistics that while a substantial proportion of prostitutes came from the ranks of unskilled immigrants, as one might expect, a large number did not. Even more significantly, a sizable group of women (73) had fathers in the elite artisanal trades—ship carpentry, butchering, silversmithing—and a scattering (49) claimed to be daughters of professional men—physicians, lawyers and clergymen. Still others came from small property-owning families in the city and country, the daughters of shopkeepers, millers, and blacksmiths.

Sanger threw up his hands over an array of data that defied his preconceptions. "The numerous and varied occupations of the fathers of those women who answered the question renders any classification of them almost impossible."[26] But the range of family circumstances is confounding only if one assumes that indigence was the major cause of prostitution. In fact, a variety of factors led women into the trade. The daughter of a prosperous ship carpenter could end up on the streets because she was orphaned and left to support herself; she could also use prostitution as a way to escape a harsh father's rule. A country girl, abandoned by a suitor, might go on the town because she knew no other way to earn her bread, or because she was determined to stay in the city rather than return to the farm. A married woman might even hazard the prospects of a hand-to-mouth independence, supported in part by prostitution, rather than submit to a drunken and abusive spouse.

Prostitution as an economic choice dictated by extreme need cannot be understood apart from women's problems in supporting themselves and their consequent forced dependency on men. Prostitution as a social choice, an "inclination," cannot be separated from the entire fabric of that dependency. Sexual mores must have varied among Catholics and Protestants, immigrants and native-born, country and city folk (the evidence is silent on this point). Whatever the differences, however, by the 1850s urban culture exposed all working-class women to modes of sexual exchange which, in certain situations, easily merged with casual prostitution. Sexual favors (and, for wives, domestic services) were the coin with which women, insofar as they could, converted that dependency into a reciprocal relation. Sexual bartering, explicit and implicit, was a common element in relations with men from the time a girl became sexually active. Girls and women traded their sexual favors for food, lodgings, and drink. This is not to say that all sexual relations with men were coterminous with prostitution; there were boundaries. Working-class women seem to have known when their daughters and peers threatened to slip over the line into "ruin." Mothers, we shall see, sensed when their girls were approaching "trouble," and "whore" was an insult that women flung about in neighborhood quarrels.

But while middle-class people clearly demarcated opposing erotic spheres of darkness and light, working-class people made more accommodating distinctions. Some women who had "gone to ruin" could find a way back before they became too old to marry. Of all that went on the town, one out of five sooner or later left prostitution, reported the Almshouse commissioners. "They find some way of earning an honest livelihood."[27] The parents of Sarah Courtney, an Irish serving girl, sent her to the House of Refuge in 1827 for having "yielded her virtue for gain"; six years later, the warden noted, Sarah had married a respectable workingman. Sarah Freeman, detained a year earlier, had taken up prostitution after the man who kept her died; she was contrite when she entered, the superintendent noted, and some years later he appended the information that she had married respectably.[28] One wonders about these women. Were there difficulties with their husbands? Was there atonement, and what was its price? What was the nature of repentance? The answers remain veiled. Perhaps for the minority of working-class Protestant churchgoers, the boundaries between licit and illicit sex were more rigid, the road back to propriety a difficult one. Christian observance, however, did not necessarily entail strict condemnations of female transgression. It is likely, for example, that free blacks, a highly devout community, held to the permissive views of premarital female sexuality that characterized Afro-American culture throughout the nineteenth century. And even Irish Catholics, whom one would guess to be subject to strict interdictions from the church, seem generally to have been immune to the conception of irredeemable female transgression (perhaps because the American church had not yet embarked on the surveillance of sexual mores for which it later became so well known). In general, laboring people seem to have made their judgments of female vice and virtue in the context of particular situations rather than by applying absolute moral standards.

For working-class women, the pressures of daily life took the form both of need and desire: the need for subsistence, the desire for change. Either could be urgent enough to push a girl or woman into that shady zone not too many steps removed from the daily routines in which she was raised. The resemblance of prostitution to other ways of dealing with men suggests why, for many poor women, selling themselves was not a radical departure into alien territory.

Girls

It was in large part the involvement of young girls in prostitution—or more important, the relationship to the family that juvenile prostitution signified—that brought prostitution to public attention in the 1850s.

Indeed, the discourse of prostitution expressed and deflected popular anxieties about what happened when daughters ventured out on the town. Adolescents and young women found casual prostitution inviting as metropolitan life made it an increasingly viable choice for working girls. Casual prostitution bordered on working-class youth culture; both provided some tenuous autonomy from family life. Of course, there were other reasons for widespread public concern about this kind of youthful sex. Prostitution was inseparable from venereal disease, economic distress, unwanted pregnancy, the sexual degradation of women, and class exploitation. The public discourse about prostitution, however, also addressed deeper changes in gender relations within the working class.

Prostitution was by no means a happy choice, but it did have advantages that could override those of other, more respectable employments. The advantages were in part monetary, since prostitution paid quite well. The gains could amount to a week or even a month's earnings for a learner, a servant, or a street seller; for girls helping their mothers keep house or working in some kind of semi-indentured learning arrangement, money from men might be the only available source of cash. As a thirteen-year-old in the 1830s tartly answered the moralizing warden of the House of Refuge when he insisted on the point, she would, indeed, sell herself for a shilling if she could get no more, and she would prefer to do so (or "play the Strumpet," as he interpolated) to her usual work, scrubbing up in public houses in exchange for food for her family.[29] Earnings could be far more substantial than this culprit's shilling. In 1825, for example, fifteen-year-old Jane Groesbeck, who also ended up in the House, earned a glorious five dollars (a poor girl's fortune) when she went to the races and met Mr. G., a merchant storekeeper, who hired Jane and her girlfriend to spend the night with him. Ten years later, Mary Jane Box made between twenty shillings and three dollars every time she slept with a man at a bawdy house; the serving girl Harriet Newbury, a country girl from Pennsylvania, came into a windfall of luck in 1828 when a navy captain gave her ten dollars each time they had intercourse.[30] These were gentlemen's prices. Prostitution with workingmen yielded smaller gains, "trifling things"—a few shillings, a meal or admission to the theater. But even to sell oneself for a shilling was to earn in an hour what a seamstress earned in a day in the 1830s.

The lively trade in juvenile prostitution is one of the most striking—and least explored—features of the Victorian sexual landscape. Who were the men who created the demand for young girls' sexual services? It is easy to assume they were bourgeois gentlemen. Certainly gentlemen had money for such pleasures, and Victorian men could use sex with prostitutes to satisfy longings they could not express to their supposedly asexual wives. What we know most about in this regard, the illicit sexuality of the British late Victorians, tends to bear out the assumption that pedophilia was a gentleman's vice that grew out of the bourgeois eroticization of working-class life and depended upon the availability of poor girls for purchase. Dickens's deliciously vulnerable Little Nell was an early, less self-conscious representation of an erotic interest that Lewis Carroll—to take a well-known example—pursued in private photographic sessions with naked little working-class girls, and that fueled a London trade in child prostitutes that became by 1885 a national scandal.[31]

Christine Stansell

Contrary to this parable of bourgeois (male) depredation, however, the erotic sensibilities of workingmen were also involved. Juvenile prostitution stemmed not just from class encounters but from the everyday relations of men and girls in working-class neighborhoods. Rape trials, one source of information about illicit sexuality, show that sex with girl children was woven into the fabric of life in the tenements and the streets: out-of-the ordinary, but not extraordinary.[32] Child molestation figured significantly among reported rapes between 1820 and 1860.[33] Poor girls learned early about their vulnerability to sexual harm from grown men, but they also learned some ways to turn men's interest to their own purposes. Casual prostitution was one.

The men who made sexual advances to girls were not interlopers lurking at the edges of ordinary life, but those familiar from daily routines: lodgers, grocers (who encountered girls when they came into their stores on errands), and occasionally fathers. Sometimes the objects of their attentions could be very young. For the men, taboos against sexual involvement with children seem to have been weak; in court, they often alluded to their actions as a legitimate and benign, if slightly illicit, kind of play. A soldier, for example, charged with the rape of a five-year-old in 1842, claimed that he had only done what others had. "It is true I lay the child in the Bunk as I often have done before as well as other men in the same company. I did not commit any violence upon the child."[34] This man and others accused seem to have respected a prohibition against "violence," or actual intercourse, while they saw fondling, masturbation, and exhibitionism as permissible play. "He then pulled my clothes up," seven-year-old Rosanna Reardon testified of her assailant in 1854, "and carried me behind the counter . . . he unbuttoned his pantaloons and asked if I wanted to see his pistol." "I did not intend to hurt the girl," a grocery clerk protested of his four-year-old victim. He had only taken her on his lap and petted her. "I will never do it again and had no wish to hurt her."[35] Episodes like these did not necessarily involve severe coercion; rather, child molestation often involved child's play. "He danced me about," remembered Rosanna Reardon. Michael O'Connor, another girl's assailant, claimed he had merely come visiting on a summer's night—as he said, "took off my hat coat and shoes and went to the front door and sat down with the others"—when two girls out on an errand "commenced fooling around" in the doorway "about which would go upstairs first." He gave one a push and told her to go upstairs and the other to stay. Soon thereafter the mother of the remaining child charged downstairs "and accused me of having put my hands under her Daughter's clothes."[36] Whatever really happened, the mother thought there were grounds for suspicion when a grown man took to tumbling about with two girls. Roughhousing, teasing, fondling, and horseplay were the same tokens of affection that men gave to children in the normal course of things. Similarly, the favors men offered in exchange for sexual compliance—pennies and candy—were what they dispensed in daily life to garner children's affection. Men's erotic attention to girls, then, was not a discrete and pathological phenomenon but a practice that existed on the fringes of "normal" male sexuality.

Child molestation could blur into juvenile prostitution. The pennies a man offered to a girl to keep quiet about his furtive fumblings were not dissimilar to the prostitute's price. Adult prostitutes were also highly visible throughout the city, and their presence taught girls something about sexual exchange. A baker's daughter in 1830 learned about the pleasures of the bawdy houses in carrying sewing back and forth between her mother and the prostitutes who employed her to do their seamstressing.[37] John McDowall was shocked in 1831 to see little girls in poor wards playing unconcernedly in the streets around the doors of dramshops that served prostitutes; two decades later, Charles Loring Brace observed packs of girls on Corlears Hook hanging about the dance saloons prostitutes frequented and running errands for the inhabitants and their customers.[38] For the great majority of girls, however, it was not the example of adult prostitutes that led them into "ruin" but the immediate incentive of contact with interested men. Laboring girls ran across male invitations in the course of their daily rounds—street selling, scavenging, running errands for mothers or mistresses, in walking home from work, in their workplaces and neighborhoods, and on the sophisticated reaches of Broadway. Opportunities proliferated as New York's expanding industry and commerce provided a range of customers extending well beyond the traditional clientele of wealthy rakes and sailors. Country storekeepers in town on business, gentlemen travelers, lonely clerks, and workingmen were among those who propositioned girls on the street.

Men made the offers, but girls also sought them out. "Walking out" in groups, hanging about corners, flirting with passersby, and generally being "impudent & saucy to men" (as parents committing a girl to the House of Refuge described it) could lead to prostitution.[39] The vigilant John McDowall at watch on fashionable Broadway observed "females of thirteen and fourteen walking the streets without a protector, until some pretended gentleman gives them a nod, and takes their arm, and escorts them to houses of assignation."[40] Catharine Wood, fifteen years old in 1834, was a girl with two trades, stocking making and book folding, and thus more advantaged than an ordinary servant or slop worker. Still, when a girlfriend took her out walking on the Bowery, she could not resist the prospects of nearby Five Points, and began to take men to houses of assignation there. Sarah White, a fur worker in 1840 and likewise from respectably employed working folk, took to walking out at night with her workmates from the shop and soon left her parents to go "on the town."[41]

Christine Stansell

Girls actively sought out other girls, tempting friends and acquaintances with the comparative luxuries of a life spent "walking out" to places like the Bowery Theater, where Sarah White's brother found her, stressing such pleasures to the still-virtuous as, in the words of one reprobate "how much better clothes she could wear who worked none."[42] By the 1850s, respectable New Yorkers were appalled at the eroticization of public space girls like these had brought about. "No one can walk the length of Broadway without meeting some hideous troop of ragged girls," an outraged George Templeton Strong reported.[43]

As witnesses to men's sexual initiatives to adult women, and occasionally objects themselves of those advances, girls must have learned early about the power—and danger—of male desire. As they grew up, however, they could also learn to protect themselves; even more, to bargain for themselves. Girls saw older women trade sex for male support, lodgings, drink, and dress; these lessons in exchange educated them about sexual bargaining. As a result, adolescents could sometimes engage in it with considerable entrepreneurial aplomb. The testimonies of a gang of girls committed to the House of Refuge in 1825 for prostitution and pickpocketing give some insight into the mentality and mechanics of sexual bargaining on the street in the early part of the century. Eleven to fifteen years old, the girls had all worked off and on in service but at the time of their apprehension were living at home. They went out during the days street-scavenging for their mothers and eventually went for higher stakes, first by prostituting themselves with strangers on the streets, next by visiting a bawdy house behind the Park Theater "where they used to accommodate the men, for from two to twelve shillings." The series of episodes that finally landed them in the House of Refuge began one day when, along with a neighbor boy, they fell into company with a country merchant on Broadway. They took him to a half-finished building near City Hall, where two of the girls went down to the basement with him. While he was having intercourse with one, the other picked his pocket. Their next client was an old man they also met on Broadway. The transaction with him took place right on the street, in a dark spot under the wall of St. Paul's churchyard. While one "was feeling of him," another took his money. Finally apprehended at the theater, where they were spending their spoils, the girls were taken to the House where most of them remained intractably unrepentant: one, put in solitary confinement to soften her heart, "singing, Hollowing, and pounding," pretending to be beaten by the discomfited warden and screaming "Murder."[44]

City life allowed such girls to find a wide range of customers and to travel far enough to thwart their mothers' vigilance. Early experiences with men, which girls may have shared round with their peers, perhaps bequeathed a bit of knowledge and shrewdness; perhaps the streets taught them how to turn sexual vulnerability to their own uses. To be sure, there were no reliable means of artificial contraception; only later, with the vulcanization of rubber, did condoms become part of the prostitute's equipment. Any sexually active girl would have risked an illegitimate pregnancy, attended by moral and financial burdens that could bring her to the edge of "ruin." Nonetheless, there were ways to practice birth control. Most likely, a girl engaging in sexual barter stopped short of sexual intercourse, allowing the man instead to ejaculate between her legs, the client's customary privilege in the nineteenth century. Recipes for abortifacients and suppositories probably circulated among young women. If other measures failed, abortions, provided by midwives and "irregular" physicians (as those outside the medical establishment were called), were widely available in American cities. Indeed, ferreting out abortions—both medically induced and self-induced—was a major task of the city coroner. In 1849, the chief official of public health in the city reported that stillbirths were increasing at an alarming rate, and he concluded darkly that the role of "crime and recklessness"—that is, abortion—in this phenomenon "dare not be expressed."[45]

To us now, and to commentators then, selling one's body for a shilling might seem an act imbued with hopelessness and pathos. Such an understanding, however, neglects the fact that this was a society in which many men still saw coerced sex as their prerogative. In this context, the prostitute's price was not a surrender to male sexual exploitation but a way of turning a unilateral relationship into a reciprocal one. If this education in self-reliance was grim, the lessons in the consequences of heterosexual dependency were often no less so.

On the Town

Prostitution offered more than money to girls. Its liaisons were one important way they could escape from or evade their families. For young girls, the milieu of casual prostitution, of walking out, could provide a halfway station to the urban youth culture to which they aspired. For older girls, casual prostitution could finance the fancy clothes and high times that were the entrée to that culture. For all ages, support from lovers and clients could be critical in structuring a life apart from the family.

Prostitution and casual sex provided the resources for girls to live on their own in boardinghouses or houses of assignation—a privilege that most workingwomen would not win until after the First World War.[46] Before factory work began to offer a more respectable alternative, sex was one of the only ways to finance such an arrangement. The working-class room of one's own offered a girl escape from a father's drunken abuse or a mother's nagging, the privilege of seeing "as much company as she wished," and the ability to keep her earnings for herself.[47] Sanger touched on this aspect when he identified "ill treatment" in the family as one of the primary reasons girls went into prostitution. The testimony he collected bears witness to the relationship between youthful prostitution and the relations of the household: "My parents wanted me to marry an old man, and I refused. I had a very unhappy home afterward." "My step-mother ill-used me." "My mother ill-treated me." "My father accused me of being a prostitute when I was innocent. He would give me no clothes to wear." "I had no work, and went home. My father was a drunkard, and ill-treated me and the rest of the family."[48] Sexuality offered a way out. For this reason, while petty theft was the leading cause of boys' commitments to the House of Refuge, the great majority of girls were there for some sexually related offense. Bridget Kelly was the daughter of a dock laborer who drank and beat his children, making her (in the experience of the House of Refuge warden) "an easy prey for Care less persons who persuaded her from home." A washerwoman's daughter made the acquaintance of a young man in 1845 on the Bowery and began meeting him regularly without her mother's knowledge, sometimes at a house of assignation. Her mother found out and put a stop to the courtship, afterward upbraiding the girl so relentlessly that she finally ran away to live in the house of assignation where she had already lost her virtue; from there it was only a short step to incarceration. A foundry worker brought his daughter to the House in 1850 because, he claimed, she had gone to live in a bad house; the girl said she had left because her parents beat her.[49]

The inducement was freedom from domestic and wage labor. From the parents' point of view, running about the streets went hand in hand with laziness and idleness at home and abnegating one's obligations to earn one's keep. Elizabeth Byrne, her father claimed in 1827, thought he "should support her like a Lady"; he sent her to the House of Refuge to save her from ruin. Other families took the same step. Mary Ann Lyons, a "hard" girl given to singing vulgar songs, had been living with her mother for several months in 1830 "doing little or nothing." "Her brother undertook to punish her for not bringing chips [scavenged wood] to help her Mother in Washing Clothes." Amelia Goldsmith, daughter of a cartman, expected more help from her family "than she ought and because she did not get it, she left her trade" in 1840 for an all-female lodging house.[50]

For many young girls the most immediate restraint on sexual activity was not the fear of pregnancy but rather family supervision. A girl's ability to engage quietly in casual prostitution or sexual bartering depended largely on whether she used streetwalking openly to defy her obligations to her family. She might earn a little money now and then from casual liaisons; as long as she hid the luxuries she gained thereby and continued to earn her keep at home, she might evade suspicion. But part of the allure of prostitution was precisely the chance it offered to break free of work and authority. The "ruin" working people feared for their girls was not sexual activity alone, but sex coupled with irresponsibility; the defiance of the claims of the family went hand in hand with working-class conceptions of immorality. Parents became alarmed and angered, for example, when their girls moved about from one servant's position to another without consulting them. They saw such independent ways as a prelude to trouble. Sometimes the girl had changed to a place in a "bad house," a dance hall or house of assignation where the temptation to dabble in prostitution would have been nearly irresistible. Sometimes, however, the girl provoked her parents' wrath simply by shifting from one place to another. Mary Galloway, for instance, fifteen in 1838 and a shoemaker's daughter, had been enamored of walking the streets since she was thirteen. She left house to go into service "thinking that then she would have a better opportunity to walk out evenings," but this led her continually to change places in search of a situation where she would have more time to herself, and she changed so often that her mother finally thought it best to send her for "correction" to the House of Refuge, where incarceration and the strictest of daily routines would presumably set her straight.[51]

Fancy dress also played into prostitution. As in the cases of domestic servants and factory girls, fancy dress signified a rejection of proper feminine behavior and duties. For the girls who donned fine clothes, dress was an emblem of an estimable erotic maturity, a way to carry about the full identity of the adult, and a sign of admission into heterosexual courting. Virtuous girls, who gave over their wages to their families, had no money to spare for such frivolities; from a responsible perspective, fancy dress was a token of selfish gratification at the expense of family needs. The longtime warden of the House of Refuge, who had seen plenty of girls come and go, declared in the 1830s that "the love of dress was the most efficient cause of degradation and misery of the young females of the city."[52] Sarah Dally is a case in point. Her involvement in prostitution stemmed from a set of circumstances in which fine clothes, freedom from work, and resentment of her mother were all combined. In 1829 she was the fifteen-year-old daughter of poor but respectable Irish people. In one of her places at service she befriended another serving girl who was in the habit of staying privately with gentlemen. In walking out with her friend "in pursuit of beaux," Sarah met a Lawyer Blunt and stayed with him several times. In return, Mr. Blunt liberally set her up with ladies' clothes: a silk coat and dresses, a chemise and lace handkerchief, a gilt buckle (all which she put on to go out walking with him), and a nightgown and nightcap for their private meetings. Sarah successfully concealed the new clothes from her family, but her mother's watchfulness began to chafe. When she complained, her friend convinced her to accompany her to Philadelphia, where Sarah would be free to go out fully on the town. To pay for the trip, the pair tried to rob a house, failed, and ended up in jail. The journey back to virtue, however, was far more possible than it would have been for a girl from polite society who had similarly chosen "ruin." Eight years later, Sarah was reported to be respectably married and doing well. She had presumably renounced the delights of ladies' clothes.[53]

Country girls from New England and upstate New York were also open to the inducements of prostitution in the city. Refugees from the monotony and discipline of rural life, they were drawn by the initial excitement of the life, its sociability and novel comforts. Rachel Near, for instance, came from Poughkeepsie to New York in 1835 to learn the trade of tailoressing from her sister. About three months after she arrived she ran into another Poughkeepsie girl on the street whom a man was supporting in a house of assignation. "She persuaded her to go into her House, which was neatly furnished by her ill gotten gain, and asked her to come and live with her, and persuaded her until she consented to do so." There Rachel met a Dr. Johnson, visiting the city from Albany, who supported her in style for six weeks, and she supplemented her earnings from him with visits to a bawdy house "where she used to get from 5 to 7 $ pr night, some weeks she used to make 40 & 45$." Rachel's kin found her and sent her back home, but the next summer she ran away from Pough-keepsie and "fully turned out again." Fifteen-year-old Susannah Bulson also followed a well-trodden path. She was an Albany girl who had been "seduced" by a young cabinetmaker. For a few weeks after they began their liaison in 1835, he supported her in a room across the river in Troy, but she did not want to disgrace her family by her presence, so the two left for New York, where he took a room for them in a boardinghouse. A number of the other boarders were single women who came and went as they pleased, and after seeing this kind of life, Susannah "felt she should prefer this kind of pleasure" to living with her young man and left for a house where she set up on her own. Several months later, the man who would have played the part of heartless seducer in a melodramatic rendition of their story was still trying to persuade Susannah to come back to him."[54]

Rural courtships often played a part in urban prostitution. Some young women had sex with their suitors, were "kept" by them and eventually married: they make no appearance in the historical record. For others, the adventure ended badly; unlike Susannah Bulson, they were the ones left behind, not the ones who did the leaving. It was from such experiences that nineteenth-century popular culture would eventually create the seduced and abandoned tale. A virtuous country girl succumbs to her lover's advances; he persuades her, against her better judgment, to follow him to the big city. Once there he cruelly deserts her, leaving her penniless, alone, shamed before her family and the world. William Sanger gave an early version of this plot in his interpretation of the category "seduced and abandoned" that 258 of his subjects had cited as the reason for their fall. "Unprincipled men, ready to take advantage of women's trustful nature, abound, and they pursue their diabolical course unmolested," Sanger explained. The woman, "naturally unsuspicious herself . . . cannot believe that the being whom she has almost deified can be aught but good, and noble, and trustworthy."[55] Women's generous and undiscriminating nature made them an easy mark.

In truth, it was a bad bargaining position, not a too-compliant nature, that made women a mark for "unprincipled men." Courtship was a gamble; elopement, the possibility of rape, and male mobility made it all the more treacherous. Country girls were especially vulnerable to the process whereby desertion led to prostitution. Sanger found that 440 of his subjects were farmers' daughters.[56] Left alone in the city, often without friends to help them, country girls sometimes had no choice but to turn to the streets for their bread. The sanctions of rural communities gave some protection to young women, but once they isolated themselves from neighbors, family, and other women, they could find themselves caught in an escalating series of circumstances in which intercourse, voluntary or involuntary, led to prostitution.

Once again, however, we should avoid interpreting prostitution as a desperate measure. It could also be an act of shrewdness, prompted by a woman's comprehension of the power relations in which she found herself. Once a farm girl perceived the possibilities the city held out, to sell her favors for money was a logical countermove in a sexual system in which men might take what they could get—sometimes through rape—and turn their backs on the consequences. To exact a price from a man, hard cash, must have held some appeal to a woman whose last lover had just skipped off scot-free.

But it would also be wrong to cast prostitution as a deliberate bid for control; mostly, farm girls—like their urban peers—just wanted to live on their own. Once abandoned by a suitor, a young woman could easily want to stay away from the family she had deserted or defied. Cornelia Avery ran away from home in Connecticut in 1827 with a stagecoach driver her father had forbidden her to marry; when the man deserted her, she took up prostitution instead of going back. And what else could Marian Hubbard do, tired of the farm, and taken in by a scoundrel? Marian's second cousin Joe Farryall from New York, visiting his kin in Vermont in 1835, convinced her to return with him to the city. Although she knew nothing of his character, he persuaded her—or so she later recounted—that she worked too hard, and that he would make a lady of her if she came to New York. Halfway there she slept with him, only to find on arriving that he was the keeper of a brothel inhabited by a dozen other country girls he had lured there under similar pretenses. When the warden of the House of Refuge, where Marian ended up, inquired about Farryall, the watchmen told him that the man made three or four such recruiting trips to the countryside each year. [57]

The money and perquisites from casual prostitution opened up a world beyond the pinched life of the tenements, the metropolitan milieu of fashion and comfort. Every day girls viewed this world from the streets, as if in the audience of a theater: the elaborate bonnets in shop windows, the silk dresses in the Broadway promenade, the rich food behind the windows of glittering eating places. Bonnets, fancy aprons, silk handkerchiefs, pastries were poor girls' treasures, coveted emblems of felicity and style. There were serious drawbacks to prostitution: venereal disease, physical abuse, the pain of early intercourse, and the ever-present prospect of pregnancy. While the road back to respectable marriage was not irrevocably closed, it must have been rocky, the reproaches and contempt of kin and neighbors a burden to bear. Still, casual prostitution offered many their best chance for some kind of autonomy—even for that most rare acquisition for a poor girl, a room of her own.

In this context, the imagery of unregeneracy served to interpret a particular kind of adolescent female rebellion. The debauched juvenile would become central to the bourgeois construction of a pathological "tenement class." "Hideous and ragged" girls and young women moved attention away from other villains—capitalist exploitation, deceiving seducers, deserting husbands, the ordinary and sometimes cruel nature of erotic experience between the sexes—to the supposedly pitiable nature of working-class childhood and the supposedly disintegrating moral standards of working-class families.

The urgency that discussions of prostitution took on in the 1850s indicates just how disturbing youthful female independence could be in a society structured culturally on women's dependence on the household. In the public spaces of New York, as well as in domestic service and on the Bowery, the evidence of girls' circumvention of family discipline was deeply troubling, especially (but not exclusively) to people who saw the family as woman's *only* proper place and asexuality as a cardinal tenet of femininity. The stress on the female reprobate's active pursuit of her appetites was the reformers' rendition of an obvious fact of youthful prostitution: It was not solely the resort of hopelessness and misery.

Antebellum Victorian culture generated two opposing images of the prostitute. One was the preyed-upon innocent, driven by starvation's threat or by a seducer's treachery to take to the streets. Women reformers—especially the ladies of the Female Moral Reform Society—played an important role in popularizing this construction. The prostitute-as-innocent was a sister to the familiar figure of the downtrodden sewing woman and similarly allowed genteel women to stretch their sexual sympathies across class lines. The other image was the hard, vice-ridden jade, who sold her body to satisfy a base appetite for sex or, more likely (such was the difficulty of imagining that women could have active sexual desires), for liquor. This creature was almost wholly beyond redemption, certainly forever cast out from the bonds of womanhood. The prostitute-as-reprobate depended upon older conceptions of the vicious poor, but the figure also assimilated moral "viciousness" into the new environmentalist thought promoted by the secular reformers of the 1840s and 1850s.

In the 1850s it was the "abandoned" female, not the betrayed innocent, who captured public attention. Her popularity reflects the generally hardening tone social commentators were taking toward the poor, as an emerging "scientific" comprehension of urban problems gripped their imagination. The ascendancy of the abandoned woman may also signify a weakening of women's influence in urban reform movements. Women had drawn their reforming energies from evangelicalism. As reformers moved away from a religious to a secular orientation, women's evangelical language of the heart and their empathy with the "fallen" of their sex may have seemed less than relevant to the new breed of scientific philanthropists concerned with environmental solutions to problems of public health and disorder.

We are still too much influenced by the Victorians' view of prostitution as utter degradation to accept easily any interpretation that stresses the opportunities commercial sex provided to women rather than the victimization it entailed. Caution is certainly justified. Prostitution was a relationship that grew directly from the double standard and men's subordination of women. It carried legal, physical, and moral hazards for women but involved few, if any, consequences for men. Whatever its pleasures, they were momentary; its rewards were fleeting and its troubles were grave. But then, the same could be said of other aspects of laboring women's relations with men. Prostitution was one of a number of choices fraught with hardship and moral ambiguity.

Charles Loring Brace, who labored to redeem girls from New York's streets, spoke to the heart of the issue. By the time he began his mission in 1853, poor girls knew enough about the politics of interpretation to invoke the sentimentalist imagery of prostitution in their own defense when dealing with reformers and police. "They usually relate, and perhaps even imagine, that they have been seduced from the paths of virtue suddenly and by the wiles of some heartless seducer. Often they describe themselves as belonging to some virtuous, respectable, and even wealthy family." "Their real history," scoffed the streetwise Brace, "is much more commonplace and matter-of-fact. They have been poor women's daughters, and did not want to work as their mothers did."[58] In the 1850s, the opportunities for girls to repudiate their mothers' lot in this way were greater than ever.

Notes

1. Two recent works, Judith R. Walkowitz, *Prostitution and Victorian Society: Women, Class, and the State* (Cambridge: Cambridge U. Press, 1980), and Ruth Rosen, *The Lost Sisterhood in America, 1900–1918* (Baltimore, Md.: Johns Hopkins U. Press, 1982), set the historical discussion of prostitution on a new footing.

2. *Columbian* (New York), December 30, 1818. Larry Howard Whiteaker also notes the general tolerance for prostitution in the eighteenth and early nineteenth centuries. Larry Howard Whiteaker, *Moral Reform and Prostitution in New York City, 1830–1860* (Ph.D., Princeton University, 1977), 21–26.

3. J. R. McDowall, *Magdalen Facts* (New York: J. McDowall, 1832), 69. A grand jury investigation of the extent of the problem in 1831 found only 1,388 prostitutes in a ward-by-ward survey. *Working Man's Advocate*, August 20, 1831.

4. National Trades' Union "Report . . . on Female Labor," in John R. Commons et al., *A Documentary History of American Industrial Society* (Cleveland: A. H. Clark, 1910–11), 6:217, 282: *Working Man's Advocate*, March 8, 1845; Mathew Carey, "Essays on the Public Charities of Philadelphia," *Miscellaneous Essays* (Philadelphia: Carey and Hart, 1830), 154, 161; *Daily Tribune*, June 8, 1853. In the comments of the *Working Man's Advocate* on prostitution and on the Magdalen Society, one can see the similarities of the evangelical analysis to that of supporters of labor. Ibid., September 11, 1830, July 30, 1831.

5. William W. Sanger, *The History of Prostitution: Its Extent, Causes, and Effects Throughout the World* (New York: American Medical Press, 1895), 29. Public interest in New York was also prompted by concerns about syphilis. See the comments in the reports from the Penitentiary Hospital contained in Commissioners of the Almshouse, *Annual Reports* (1849–60).

6. Matsell's letter is reprinted in Sanger, *History of Prostitution*, 576.

7. Commitments of disorderly housekeepers to the First District Prison rose from 17 in 1849 to 90 in 1860. Commissioners of the Almshouse, *Annual Reports*. The magnitude of vagrancy commitments in the 1850s is especially striking compared to the figure of 3,173 commitments for the entire *decade* 1820–30 that a grand jury gave for commitments exclusive of assault and battery (which mostly comprised drunkenness and vagrancy). Report quoted in *Working Man's Advocate*, August 20, 1831.

   Commitments to the city prisons for vagrancy rose from 3,552 in 1850 to 6,552 in 1860. Commitments of females aged ten to thirty years old comprised between 49 and 65 percent of the total female commitments in those years in the 1850s when age breakdowns are available (for the First District Prison, the largest in the city).

8. Eighty-eight percent of Sanger's interviewees were fifteen to thirty years old. *History of Prostitution*, 452. These women were around marrying age, and there was a demographic undercurrent to their situations; the disproportional sex ratio in New York lessened their chances of marrying.

9. Sanger, *History of Prostitution*, 29.

10. Ibid., 549–59.

11. Rosen, *The Lost Sisterhood*, 32–33.

12. Sanger, *History of Prostitution*, 559–73.

13. Citizens' Association, *Report of the Council of Hygiene and Public Health* (New York: D. Appleton and Co., 1865), 26. For descriptions of a similar variety of establishments in London, see Dr. Fernando Henriques, *Modern Sexuality* (London: MacGibbon and

Kee, 1968); Kellow Chesney, *The Victorian Underworld* (London: Maurice Temple Smith, 1970), 307–365.

14. The beginnings of the sex trade were already evident in the 1830s, when John McDowall sought to expose the traffic in pornography in the city. Whiteaker, "Moral Reform and the Prostitute," 182. George Foster provides a tour of commercial sex establishments in *New York by Gas-Light and Other Urban Sketches* (New York: 1850). See also Michael Batterberry and Ariane Batterberry, *On the Town in New York, From 1776 to the Present* (New York: Scribner, 1973), 102, 104 for some of the "lowest" of the city's night spots. Indictments for various kinds of "indecent exhibitions" can be found in Court of General Sessions (hereafter cited CGS), *People v. Brennan* and *People v. Fowler et al.*, March 22, 1848; *People v. Hamilton et al.*, March 24, 1848 and for obscene reading matter and prints, *People v. Ryan*, September 28, 1842, *People v. Shaw*, July 1844, *People v. Carns*, June 21, 1844, *People v. Miller et al.*, October 16, 1835.

15. Sanger, *History of Prostitution*, 492. Sanger estimated that the Panic of 1857 had sent 500–1,000 new prostitutes out on the streets. Ibid., 34.

16. Ibid., 524, 528, 529; see also 532.

17. Peiss, "'Charity Girls' and City Pleasures: Historical Notes on Working-Class Sexuality" in Ann Snitow, Christine Stansell, and Sharon Thompson, eds., *Powers of Desire: The Politics of Sexuality* (New York: Monthly Review Press, 1983), 74–87.

18. Sanger, *History of Prostitution*, 491.

19. Ibid., 473, 475, 539.

20. Ibid., 506–508.

21. The European writers are analyzed in Walkowitz, *Prostitution in Victorian Society*, 36–47.

22. Sanger, *History of Prostitution*, 488–89.

23. Ibid., 488.

24. Ibid., 524; see also McDowall, *Magdalen Facts*, 53.

25. The Irish were overrepresented in Sanger's sample (28 percent of the total population was Irish in 1855); the Germans (16 percent of the population) were underrepresented. Ibid., 460, 536.

26. Ibid.

27. Commissioners of the Almshouse, *Annual Report* (1849), 160–61.

28. House of Refuge Case Histories (hereafter cited HRCH), cases # 232 (1827), # 191 (1826).

29. Quoted in Robert S. Pickett, *House of Refuge: Origins of Juvenile Reform in New York State, 1815–57* (Syracuse: Syracuse U. Press, 1969), 3.

30. HRCH, cases # 60 (1825), # 1559 (1835), # 538 (1828). My interpretations of children's lives in this chapter and elsewhere are based on my reading of 455 girls' cases from the House of Refuge—all girls committed each year at five-year intervals 1825–60—and assorted other cases of both boys and girls, totaling about 700 cases.

31. On the Victorian gentleman's erotic fascination with working-class life, see Davidoff, "Class and Gender in Victorian England." The pedophilic propensities of late Victorian men are described in Eric Trudgill, *Madonnas and Magdalens: The Origins and Development of Victorian Sexual Attitudes* (New York: Holmes and Meier, 1976), 90–100, and Ronald Pearsall, *The Worm in the Bud: The World of Victorian Sexuality* (London: Weidenfeld and Nicolson, 1969), 350–63. Many of Carroll's photographs are in Graham Ovenden and Robert Melville, eds., *Victorian Children* (New York: St. Martin's Press, 1972).

32. Obviously there are problems with using rape records as evidence of sexual expectations and practices; the investigation of a crime is necessarily limited in what it can tell us about legitimated forms of sexuality. Court cases themselves, as I have noted before, present many problems in the authenticity of evidence, which was, after all, constructed to persuade a judge and/or jury. Nonetheless, much can be learned. The descriptions of rape, however distorted in the courtroom setting, reveal something of where people, especially women, drew the line between licit and illicit sex. And conflicting evidence in the trials themselves can also be a source of historical understanding, illuminating the different ways in which the (female) victims and the (male) perpetrators perceived and experienced certain sexual acts.

33. In a random sample of 101 rape cases between 1820 and 1860 tried before the Court of General Sessions, 26 involved complainants who were under 16 years of age. Of these, 19 were under 12 years old (the youngest was 4), 5 under 16, and 2 of age unknown.

34. CGS, *People v. Hynes*, February 17, 1842.

35. *People v. Foyce*, May 11, 1854, *People v. Plonsha*, June 14, 1848.

36. *People v. O'Connor*, August 10, 1849.

37. HRCH, case # 712 (1830).

38. McDowall, *Magdalen Facts*, 53; Charles Loring Brace, *The Dangerous Classes of New York, and Twenty Years' Work among Them* (New York: Wynkoop and Hallenbeck, 1872), p. 135.

39. HRCH, case # 61 (1825).

40. McDowall, *Magdalen Facts*, 53.

41. HRCH, case # 1421 (1834), # 2480 (1840).

42. Ibid., case # 209 (1826).

43. George Templeton Strong, *The Diary of George Templeton Strong* (New York: MacMillan, 1952), 2:57 (July 7, 1851); see also Robinson, *Hot Corn: Life Scenes in New York* (New York: DeWitt and Davenport, 1854),267.

44. Society for the Reformation of Juvenile Delinquents in the City of New York, *Examination of Subjects Who Are in the House of Refuge* (Albany, N.Y., 1825); HRCH, case # 5 (1825).

45. Records of the County Coroner, passim; New York City Inspector, *Annual Report* (1849); Gordon, *Woman's Body, Woman's Right: A Social History of Birth Control in America* (New York: Grossman, 1976), 26–71.

46. Ibid., pp. 203–204.

47. HRCH, case # 2513 (1840).

48. Sanger, *History of Prostitution*, 488, 500, 502.

49. HRCH, cases # 2487 (1840), # 3628 (1845), # 4882 (1850).

50. HRCH, cases # 326 (1827), # 737 (1830), # 2555 (1840).

51. Ibid., case # 2442 (1838).

52. Quoted in Catherine Maria Sedgwick, *The Poor Rich Man and the Rich Poor Man* (New York: Harper and Brothers, 1842), 168.

53. HRCH, case # 576 (1829).

54. Ibid., cases # 1613 (1835), # 1585 (1835).

55. Sanger, *History of Prostitution*, 494, 496, 536; an early example of the seduced-and-abandoned tale is in Samuel Iraenaeus Prime, *Life in New York* (New York: Robert Carter, 1847), 15–30.

56. Ibid., p. 536.

57. HRCH, cases # 261 (1827), # 1548 (1835).

58. Brace, *Dangerous Classes*, 118.

When I saw the lonely figure of my mother vanish
in the distance, a sense of regret settled heavily
upon me. I felt suddenly weak, as if I might fall
limp to the ground. I was in the hands of strangers
whom my mother did not fully trust. I no longer
felt free to be myself, or to voice my own feelings.
The tears trickled down my cheeks, and I buried
my face in the folds of my blanket. Now the first
step, parting me from my mother, was taken, and
all my belated tears availed nothing.

—*Zitkala-Sa*

CHAPTER 5

"If We Get the Girls, We Get the Race"

Missionary Education of Native American Girls

Carol Devens

Mission school education, with its wrenching separation from family, had a profound impact on Native American girls and on their female kin. Zitkala-Sa's description of her departure for boarding school in 1884 characterized the experience of thousands of young girls in the nineteenth century.[1] Most left no written record of their years in school; Zitkala-Sa (Gertrude Bonnin), a Dakota (Sioux) writer and activist on Native American issues, was unusual in that respect. She recorded both her own memories of her school years and her mother's reaction to the Western education of her daughter.

Zitkala-Sa's mother, heartbroken by the child's departure, was convinced that someone had "filled [her daughter's] ears with the white man's lies" to persuade her to leave for school. What else would induce an eight-year-old to quit her mother for the company of strangers? "Stay with me, my little one!" she futilely implored the child, overwhelmed by anxiety about her safety among white people.[2] The woman's fears were not unfounded. Her child's well-being at school was by no means assured, as an examination of the experiences of Ojibwa and Dakota girls suggests.[3] A girl's exposure to Anglo-American religious, economic, and gender values often had a permanent effect on her, whether or not she accepted them. Moreover, the time in school deprived her of the continuing tutelage of her mother and other female relatives— instruction that was the key to assuming her place as a woman within her own cultural tradition.

The history of mission schools is a troubling one in which stories of benevolent, self-sacrificing missionaries contend with accounts of relentlessly rigid discipline, ethnocentrism, and desperately unhappy children.[4] Native Americans received their introduction to Anglo-American education at the hands of British missionaries in 1617, following King James's advocacy of schooling Indians to promote "civilization" and Christianity. Dartmouth College soon was established to teach young Indian men, and both Harvard College and William and Mary College incorporated the education of native youth into their missions. The Church of England's Society for the Propagation of the Gospel in Foreign Parts also regularly instructed Indians until the American Revolution. Following independence, a host of missionary societies were organized with the stated intent of evangelizing native peoples, among them the American Society for Propagating the Gospel among the Indians and Others in North America (1787) and the New York Missionary Society (1796).[5]

The founding of the interdenominational American Board of Commissioners of Foreign Missions (ABCFM) in 1810 ushered in a new era of missionary endeavor. The combined influences of the religious revival known as the Second Great Awakening and heightened nationalism following the War of 1812 added a further goal to the missionary effort: rescuing Indians from destruction by the inexorable march of Anglo-American progress. Numerous denominational organizations were formed, such as the Missionary Society of the American Methodist Episcopal Church in 1820 and the Presbyterian Board of Foreign Missions (BFM) in 1837.[6]

Nineteenth-century missionaries and their sponsors firmly believed in the linear progression of history and in their own elevated place on the ladder of civilization. They clearly understood their charge to be the transformation of native peoples into Christian citizens. Admittedly, it was a monumental undertaking. "We cannot be too grateful that God did not make us heathens," observed Sherman Hall, of ABCFM's La Pointe mission in Wisconsin, in 1833. "It is an aweful calamity to be born in the midst of heathen darkness."[7] Heathenism seemed a surmountable obstacle, however, if children could be brought into the fold at a tender age and raised as Christians. As one missionary put it: "This can only be effectually accomplished by taking them away from the demoralizing & enervating atmosphere of camp life & Res[ervation] surroundings & Concomitants."[8] Although bringing adults to knowledge of gospel truths was important, it was "the rising generation" who provided hope for the salvation of the native population.

Schooling became the primary means of enticing young Native Americans to reject tradition and seek conversion. To missionaries, the abandonment of native ways for Western ones was a creative rather than destructive process that made new Christian citizens out of savages. School, missionaries hoped, was a way to change Indians from "others" into dusky versions of themselves. Rayna Green, a Native American scholar, has offered this observation of a photograph of pupils at the Hampton Institute, a nineteenth-century boarding school in Virginia for African American and Native American pupils: "School put them into drawing classes, where young Indian ladies in long dresses made charcoal portraits of a boy dressed in his Plains warrior best. These Victorian Indians look toward the camera from painting class, their eyes turned away from their buckskinned model."[9]

Missionaries worked diligently to gather girls and boys of all ages into day and boarding schools near villages and reservations, as well as at distant Indian schools such as the Hampton Institute or the Carlisle School in Pennsylvania (founded in 1879 to prove to the public that Native Americans were educable). Because missionary teachers could not forcibly round up and remove Native American children to schools as their government counterparts often did, it was a real challenge to enroll them. Zitkala-Sa was lured to the Quakers' Indiana Manual Labor Institute in Wabash by tales of lush, rich land bursting with sweet fruits for the child's taking.[10] Charles Hall, a minister at the ABCFM's Fort Berthold mission in North Dakota (which served mostly Mandan, Hidatsa, and Arikara rather than Dakota) in the late nineteenth and early twentieth centuries, reported that "getting the children to go to school was as delicate and cautious work as catching trout. To send a child to school meant, to the Indian, the giving up of all his distinctive tribal life, his ancestral customs, his religious beliefs, and sinking himself into the vast unknown, the way of the white man."[11] After several years, Hall developed a recruitment strategy that he later explained in a section of his memoirs entitled "Capturing Children":

> How to reach the children was a problem. They were told by shrewd parents that owls and bears and white men would harm them, so naturally they ran and hid when we approached. . . . White Shield, the old Ree [Arikara] chief, said in regard to our problem, "If you feed the children, they will come to school like flies to syrup." His advice was taken, and a Friday dinner, in the manner of the white man, was provided. This was as attractive as ice cream and lollipops. The school became a popular institution, especially on Friday.[12]

Other missionaries reported similar uses of food and other enticements, such as singing, to get the children into the classroom.[13]

Initially, mission schools concentrated on teaching boys and men, with little emphasis on female schooling. By midcentury, however, they had shifted their approach in response to the growing belief among Americans that women, as mothers, must be educated in order to raise virtuous male citizens.[14] According to Isaac Baird, who served at the Presbyterian BFM Odanah mission in Wisconsin, "The girls will need the training more than the boys & they will wield a greater influence in the future. If we get the girls, we get the race."[15] ABCFM's Santee Normal Training School in Nebraska, founded in 1870, exemplified this position in its annual bulletin, which stated that the school's purpose was the "raising up [of] preachers, teachers, interpreters, business men, and model mothers for the Dakota Nation."[16]

Once the commitment to female education had been made, however, missionaries faced low enrollments and high dropout rates. Presbyterian and ABCFM missions to the Ojibwa and Dakota suffered a shortage of schoolgirls and, moreover, were dissatisfied with the performance of the female pupils they did have. William Boutwell, ABCFM missionary at Leech Lake, Minnesota, reported in the 1830s that girls avoided him and refused to come to school; he was uncertain whether fear or shame motivated their response.[17] At the Presbyterian BFM mission in Omena, Michigan, Peter Dougherty thought he could not go wrong with his female school; he had provided women teachers to instruct girls in domesticity and Christianity as well as some academic subjects. When the school opened in 1848, it had a fine enrollment of twenty-two, but this quickly dwindled, and by 1850 Dougherty was forced to close the school. The boys' school, however, flourished as fathers sent their sons to acquire reading and ciphering skills that allowed them to deal with Anglo-Americans on their own terms.[18] The manual labor boarding school Dougherty opened in 1853 had similar problems, attracting only five girls out of twenty-seven students. The Presbyterians were even more discouraged by the situation at Middle Village, a satellite mission of Omena, where women refused to send any children to school. Their action led to the school's closing in 1858, despite the village men's petition to the BFM to keep it open.[19]

At Sisseton agency in the Dakota Territory, the local U.S. Indian agent, J.G. Hamilton, was shocked by how tenaciously Dakota women clung to their old ways. He urged the Women's Board of Missions (affiliated with the ABCFM) to send a lady to teach the native women. "I was struck, upon my arrival here some two months ago," he wrote to the Women's Board in 1875, "with the vast difference in the general appearance of the men & women. Contrary to the usual rule, the men of this tribe have made far greater progress & have yielded more readily to civilizing forces than the women have."[20] He hoped that female teachers might be able to reach them. His comment suggests that, like the Ojibwa, Dakota women sought to keep distance between themselves and whites and were reluctant to adapt to Anglo-American customs or values. Susan Webb, a missionary teacher at Santee, reported that "the older women could not read and the younger women would not."[21] The female aversion to interaction included an unwillingness to have their daughters involved in mission schooling. When Captain Richard H. Pratt, founder of the Carlisle School, visited Fort Berthold in 1878 to recruit Dakota children for the Hampton Institute, he had a difficult time securing students, especially girls. "The people feared to give up their girls," Charles Hall explained, "not trusting the white people."[22]

One teacher contemplating the enrollment problem suggested that the Ojibwa, at least, saw no point in educating girls. Revealing his poor understanding of Ojibwa gender roles and cultural values, he explained that women were destined for a life of servitude. A more likely explanation, however, came from a perceptive missionary who suggested that close ties between mothers and daughters were to blame—that women who maintained a traditional way of life were loath to relinquish control of their daughters' upbringing. It was with tremendous reluctance, for example, that Zitkala-Sa's mother allowed her to go to school. She eventually consented only after concluding that Western education would provide her daughter greater protection against the growing number of Anglo-Americans settling on Dakota lands than traditional training could.[23]

Much like their Ojibwa counterparts, those Dakota girls who did enroll seldom seemed to conform to the missionaries' expectations. Susan Webb commented that her female students always seemed the opposite of what she hoped they would be. She saw her work with them as a lesson in the depths of the human condition: "I think as I work for these girls I am learning the weakness and depravity of our own human natures."[24]

Despite women's traditionalism and their suspicion of missionaries, many girls did end up attending school for at least short periods of time.[25] Once there, they immediately began the physical transformation that missionaries hoped would be a catalyst for their intellectual and spiritual metamorphosis into Christian citizens. A young girl, whether faced with the total immersion of boarding school or the less comprehensive (but nonetheless thorough) indoctrination attempted by day schools, was presented with an alien world view, behavior code, and language to which she was quickly expected to adhere. It was a confusing and frightening whirlwind of strangers, journeys, haircuts, and loneliness. Zitkala-Sa again provides a window on the experience of starting school: "My long travel and the bewildering sights had exhausted me. I fell asleep, heaving deep, tired sobs. My tears were left to dry themselves in streaks, because neither my aunt nor my mother was near to wipe them away."[26] She recalled how humiliating the mandatory haircuts were for

Native American children. "Our mothers had taught us that only unskilled warriors who were captured had their hair shingled by the enemy. Among our people, short hair was worn by mourners, and shingled hair by cowards!" She had to be dragged out from under a bed before she submitted to having her long braids snipped off. Charles Hall remembered the children's horror of losing their long hair at his school, and the Indian agent, J. C. McGillycuddy, reported that when new Lakota students at Pine Ridge reservation caught a glimpse of teachers giving haircuts, they feared that he intended to disgrace them, and all fled in alarm.[27]

The school world was tough and confusing. Mission schools' programs for girls were intended to indoctrinate them with the ideals of Christian womanhood—piety, domesticity, submissiveness, and purity. By the missionaries' Victorian standards, Native American women were careless, dirty, and unfamiliar with the concept of hard work. Indian girls, they complained, were woefully unfamiliar with the lore, paraphernalia, and routines of female domesticity.[28] Schools therefore trained girls in sewing, knitting, cooking, and other domestic skills and tasks, as well as in academic subjects, such as history, natural sciences, arithmetic, and spelling.[29] The content of the curriculum bore no relationship to the intellectual, social, or philosophical constructs in which the girls had been raised. Indeed, the schools' underlying principle was that Anglo-American history, morality, and health were inherently superior to and should replace those of their students' cultures.

This perspective was reinforced by typical textbooks, such as Webb's *Readers*, Webster's *Spelling Book*, Greenleaf's *Intellectual Arithmetic*, and Colbun's *Mental Arithmetic*, used by Ojibwa children in the 1860s at ABCFM's Odanah Manual Labor Boarding School.[30] These books unabashedly proclaimed the Anglo-American vision of progress and morality subscribed to by the missionaries.

Even texts written specifically for Native American pupils (ABCFM teachers usually taught in their students' language) tended to be literal translations of standard classroom lessons that teachers applied to their pupils with little or no regard for context or appropriateness. The sailboats depicted in Stephen Riggs's *Model First Reader* (1873), for example, were a world away from the experiences of the Dakota children learning to read out of this book at the Santee Normal Training School.[31]

The curriculum often placed an even heavier emphasis on vocational instruction for girls than for boys. The thirty-six girls at the Shawnee Quaker School, for example, in 1827 alone produced 400 pieces of student clothing, 50 sets of sheets and towels, and 80 pairs of socks. They also spun and wove 100 pounds of wool and 40 yards of rag carpet, churned 800 pounds of butter, made 600 pounds of cheese, 2–1/2 barrels of soap, and 100 pounds of candles. In addition, they did daily housekeeping, laundry, cooking, and cleaning. The girls worked in groups, rotating jobs every two weeks in order to learn all aspects of housekeeping.[32] Martha Riggs Morris at ABCFM's Sisseton (Dakota) mission, explained the rationale for this approach, which still held sway in 1881: "The book learning is after all not so important for them, at least after they have learned to read and write fairly well. But to take care of themselves—to learn to keep body and mind pure and clean, to learn to keep house comfortably, these are most important—for the advancement of the people."[33]

Ideally, the missions' female teachers were to be role models for appropriate gender activities, values, and work, showing Native American girls through daily example both the techniques of household economy and a womanly demeanor. In reality, however, the teachers were overworked and often ill. Furthermore, rigid schedules and overcrowding often made the situation impersonal and miserable. At the Wesleyan Methodist Missionary Society's Aldersville School in Ontario, Canada, a report of the girls' schedule in 1841 indicated their rigorous life. The children (mostly Ojibwa) arose at 4:30 A.M. in summer, a lazy 5 A.M. in winter. Between rising and 9 A.M., the girls did the milking, prepared the school breakfast, attended prayers and a lecture, made cheese, and did housework. They then spent six hours in the classroom, with a break for lunch, followed by needlework, supper, evening milking, prayers at 8 P.M. and bed at 8:30.[34]

Throughout the 1880s, Martha Riggs Morris complained that her twenty-eight Dakota students were crowded into two tiny buildings measuring 10 × 24 feet and 17 × 24 feet. At the Santee Normal Training School, the Bird's Nest, a boarding home for small girls, was more spacious, having two kitchens, a dining room, teachers' sitting room and bedrooms, sick bay, laundry room, and three dormitories for the girls. Still, both teachers and students felt cramped and hurried.[35] Zitkala-Sa's account of the Wabash school once again personalizes the depressing impact of frantic school regimes on pupils and teachers alike:

> A loud-clamoring bell awakened us at half-past six in the cold winter mornings . . . There were too many drowsy children and too numerous orders for the day to waste a moment in any apology to nature for giving her children such a shock in the early morning. . . . A paleface woman, with a yellow-covered roll book open on her arm and a gnawed pencil in her hand, appeared at the door. Her small, tired face was coldly lighted with a pair of large gray eyes. She stood still in a halo of authority. . . . It was next to impossible to leave the iron routine after the civilizing machine had once begun its day's buzzing.[36]

Susan Webb's comments about her pupils indicate that the schooling process alienated and confused the girls. "When I look about me," Webb wrote in 1881, "and see how helpless and indifferent apparently are the young women I long to help arouse them to a sense that there is something for them to be doing. I cannot endure the thought that our girls will leave us to settle down with no weight of responsibility."[37] Zitkala-Sa's experience confirmed this: "The melancholy of those black days has left so long a shadow that it darkens the path of years that have since gone by. These sad memories rise above those of smoothly grinding school days."[38]

Stories of her grandmother's experiences in a turn-of-the-century mission school prompted Mary Crow Dog (Lakota Sioux) to write: "It is almost impossible to explain to a sympathetic white person what a typical old Indian boarding school was like; how it affected the Indian child suddenly dumped into it like a small creature from another world, helpless, defenseless, bewildered, trying desperately and instinctively to survive at all."[39] Some young girls at the school killed themselves or attempted suicide to escape an unhappy situation beyond their control.

The demoralizing effect of school programs was often rivaled by their futility. Most of the domestic instruction that girls received was virtually useless when their schooling ended and they returned to the village or reservation. Only if a family had made the transition from tipi or lodge to frame house, as Zitkala-Sa's had, were the girl's Western housekeeping skills applicable— unless she worked as a domestic servant for local Anglo-Americans or at the mission itself. Native American girls' servitude filled a perceived need for trained household help; girls at the government's Phoenix Indian School were pressured to become servants, and this may have been the case at mission schools as well.[40]

The conditions that children reported enduring in school led many Native American parents to become firmly entrenched in their opposition to Anglo-American education. Other factors influenced them as well. The loss of the children to school was, in a way, like death in the family and community. "Since you have been here with your writing . . . the place has become full of ghosts," one person told Charles Hall. In fact, schooling often did end in death, as Hall observed, especially for children at boarding schools, where infectious diseases took a high toll.[41]

The schools' threat to family well-being was heightened for mothers and grandmothers. A girl's participation in mission school undermined the women's ability to oversee her upbringing and to assure that she would take her place as a woman within the tribal tradition. "The grandmothers and many of the parents," reported Eda Ward, a teacher at Fort Berthold, "wish their children to be wholly Indian."[42] Female kin were responsible for instructing the child in both the practical and ritual activities that would shape her life as an adult within the community. Schooling removed a girl from the warmth of her kin's care, left her with no one to teach, comfort, or guide her as they would at home. Zitkala-Sa's mother had warned her departing child that "you will cry for me, but they will not even soothe you."[43]

Overworked, ill, and ethnocentric teachers were no substitute for the female network on which a girl's emotional, spiritual, and intellectual development depended. Although many missionary teachers were well intentioned and some really enjoyed their small charges, all were put off by the unfamiliar habits and values of the girls, and by the physical setting of their new environment. After nine years with the Ojibwa around the La Pointe mission, the ABCFM missionary Sherman Hall told his brother that "it is difficult to reach their hearts, or even their understandings with the truth. They seem almost as stupid as blocks. Yet they are far enough from being destitute of natural endowment. Most of them have superior minds by nature; but they are minds in ruins."[44] Hall lasted a long time in the missionary field and was seemingly better able to adjust to his surroundings than many of his peers, yet he described his pupils as "ragged, dirty, lousy and disgusting little objects trying to learn to read their own language."[45] His attitude was more positive than that of one of his coworkers, however, who complained bitterly about "the effects of crowding from 40 to 70 dirty vicious Indian children" into a small schoolhouse.[46]

Not all teachers were so intolerant; most of the women at ABCFM's Dakota missions, for example, expressed real fondness for their students and jobs.[47] However, their commitment to "civilizing" their pupils precluded any real understanding of or concession to those pupils' culture or values. Most tried to treat their charges as they would Anglo-American youngsters.[48] By regarding their students simply as children rather than as Indian children, teachers essentially denied their very identities. This lack of cultural awareness or empathy contributed to the gulf between student and teacher and to the children's unhappiness and disorientation. Even well-intentioned but uninformed jollity could be a source of alienation and confusion for the newly (dis)located girl. Zitkala-Sa vividly remembered an incident at the Quaker school that to the staff must surely have seemed an inappropriate response to an innocuous action. On the night she arrived, "a rosy-cheeked paleface woman caught me in her arms. I was both frightened and insulted by such trifling. I stared into her eyes, wishing her to let me stand on my own feet, but she jumped me up and down with increasing enthusiasm. My mother had never made a plaything of her wee daughter. Remembering this I began to cry aloud."[49] Indeed, Native American parents treated their children with respect and reserve. In general, mothers were satisfied to scold a young offender or to threaten that an animal might kidnap her. The rare physical punishment was a light switching with a twig on the hands or knees, and only serious problems warranted it. Mission teachers, however, often were quite free with corporal punishment. Because such punishment was an accepted, even required, part of their own culture, beatings and other methods were frequently used. At ABCFM's Fond-du-Lac mission in Minnesota, Edmund Ely, a contemporary of Sherman Hall, moved Ojibwa parents and children to outrage when he pulled children's hair to discipline them.[50] Both the rough play that Zitkala-Sa was subjected to and the strict discipline and corporal punishment that were standard fare in most schools went against Native American child-rearing methods, frightening and humiliating students.

The difference in educational methods between Anglo-American and Native American cultures exacerbated the disorienting impact of the mission schools on girls. Native peoples did not confine either schooling or pupils to classrooms. Children roamed freely, exploring and learning individually and in groups. "I was a wild little girl of seven," Zitkala-Sa recalled. "Loosely clad in a slip of brown buckskin, and light-footed with a pair of soft moccasins on my feet, I was as free as the wind that blew my hair, and no less spirited than a bounding deer. These were my mother's pride,—my wild freedom and overflowing spirits. She taught me no fear save that of intruding myself upon others."[51]

A girl's education took place constantly, through listening to and working with elders or in games with peers. Dakota girls engaged in "small play"—impersonating their mothers, and mimicking marital and domestic roles, conversations, and manners. Little girls worked companionably alongside their mothers, cooking, cleaning, and imitating them in beadwork and preparing medicinal plants. Zitkala-Sa's mother attracted her daughter's interest in beadwork by having her assist in designing and working on her own new moccasins. The woman's guidance made the child feel responsible and secure in her skill: "she treated me as a dignified little individual."[52]

Grandmothers also played a critical role in educating girls, enticing them with stories and reminiscences that illustrated tradition and history, drawing them toward an understanding of tribal philosophy and values. In *Waterlily*, Ella Deloria, a Dakota ethnologist, described a girl's relationship with her grandmother. The older woman's role was to make "well-behaved women" of her young charges. She tutored them in how to move, how to interact with elders, where to sit in the tipi. Only with constant and relentless reminding could she be sure that the girls had absorbed the lessons vital to their success in life. Moreover, the grandmother frequently talked with the girls about the children's early years in the camp, furthering their sense of belonging and place.[53] In the evenings, mothers often sent daughters—proudly bearing presents of tobacco or a favorite food—to invite grandmothers to instruct the girls in the myths and lessons that established their own place within the group and their people's place in the world.[54]

Women also guided their daughters and granddaughters through the ritual activities preparing them for womanhood. For example, Ojibwa girls of four or five undertook their first vision quests, heading into the forests with their little laces blackened, hoping to establish a relationship with supernaturals. Over the next few years the length of the quests gradually increased; eventually a girl might spend four or more days fasting, sleeping, and dreaming for power. She was ritually greeted and feasted by her mother or a female relative upon her return home, and all listened attentively as she reported on her guardian spirit dreams.[55]

Mothers and grandmothers also presided over a girl's first menstruation. The Ojibwa built a special small wigwam near the main lodge, to isolate the adolescent's newly expanded spiritual powers from men's hunting powers and infants' weak natures. During these days of seclusion and fasting for dreams, the mother instructed the girl in the responsibilities of adult women and oversaw her beadwork and sewing. When a daughter's first menstrual period had ended, her female kin feasted her upon her return to the household and entry into womanhood. Thereafter, she was chaperoned by a grandmother or aunt until marriage.[56] Dakota girls similarly retired to a new tipi set up beyond the circle of the camp, and female relatives cared for them and instructed them in the duties of a wife and mother. When seclusion had ended, the Buffalo Ceremony took place, and female relatives set up a ceremonial tipi. A medicine man then called upon the spirit of the buffalo to infuse the girl with womanly virtue, and he informed the community that her childhood had ended. The mother now attempted to protect her daughter, insisting that she wear a rawhide chastity belt, and her grandmother took it upon herself to constantly accompany the girl.[57]

Clearly, it was difficult if not impossible for a girl at day or boarding school to engage in vision fasts or menstrual seclusion, both for practical reasons of time and distance from women relatives and because of the missionaries' opposition to such practices.[58] Girls who went to school were inevitably less immersed in their cultures and frequently felt less obligated or able to maintain traditional ways. Otter, daughter of Hidatsa shaman Poor Wolf, was only seven years old in 1881 when Charles Hall sent her to the Santee boarding school, 300 miles from her home near Fort Berthold. When she and her sister returned home, their father felt compelled to move because his daughters no longer fit into the old village life. Moreover, Otter, "having found the Christ-road, told her father how to become a 'child of God'" and convinced him to abandon his lifelong beliefs.[59] Similarly, Zitkala-Sa related that after three years at the mission school she felt that she had no place in the world, that she was caught in between two cultures. Four uncomfortable years as a misfit among her people prompted her to return to school and go on to college—without her mother's approval.[60]

Mission education clearly threatened and sometimes eliminated Native American women's ability to supervise their daughters. Its goal was to alienate girls from the cultural values and practices of their mothers and turn them instead to Christianity and the Anglo-American work ethic and material culture. Although missionaries were not overwhelmingly successful in achieving their goal of shaping a new generation of assimilated citizens, their programs did have a long-term and often devastating impact both on girls and on the daughter-mother-grandmother relationship. For Zitkala-Sa, it was a bitter experience. "Like a slender tree," she remembered, "I had been uprooted from my mother, nature, and God."[61]

Notes

1. Zitkala-Sa (Gertrude Bonnin), *American Indian Stories* (Washington, D.C.: Hayworth Publishing, 1921; rpt. Glorieta, N.M.: The Rio Grande Press, 1976), pp. 44–45.
2. Ibid., pp. 40–41.
3. The Ojibwa (also known as Chippewa) are Algonquian-speaking peoples in the western Great Lakes region, southern Ontario, and Manitoba. See Frances Densmore, *Chippewa Customs*, Smithsonian Institution Bureau of American Ethnology Bulletin 86 (Washington, D.C.: Government Printing Office, 1929); A. Irving Hallowell, *Culture and Experience* (Philadelphia: University of Pennsylvania Press, 1955); Harold Hickerson, "The Chippewa of the Upper Great Lakes: A Study in Sociopolitical Change," in Eleanor Burke Leacock and Nancy Oestreich Lurie, eds., *North American Indians in Historical Perspective* (New York: Random House, 1971), pp. 169–99. Roy W. Meyer, *History of the Santee Sioux: United States Indian Policy on Trial* (Lincoln: University of Nebraska Press, 1967); Marla N. Powers, *Oglala Women: Myth, Ritual, and Reality* (Chicago: University of Chicago Press, 1986).
4. Robert F. Berkhofer, Jr., *Salvation and the Savage: An Analysis of Protestant Missions and American Indian Response, 1787–1862*, 2d ed. (New York: Atheneum, 1976); Henry Warner Bowden, *American Indians and Christian Missions: Studies in Conflict* (Chicago: University of Chicago Press, 1981); Mary Lou Hullgren and Paulette Fairbanks Molin, *To Lead and to Serve: American Indian Education at Hampton Institute, 1878–1923* (Virginia Beach: Virginia Foundation for the Humanities and Public Policy, 1989); Elizabeth Muir, "The Bark School House: Methodist Episcopal Missionary Women in Upper Canada, 1827–1833," in John S. Moir and C. T. McIntire, eds., *Canadian Protestant and Catholic Missions, 1820s-1960s: Historical Essays in Honor of John Webster Grant* (New York: Peter Lang, 1988), pp. 23–74; Francis Paul Prucha, *The Churches and the Indian Schools, 1888–1912* (Lincoln: University of Nebraska Press, 1979); Robert A. Trennert, Jr., *The Phoenix Indian School: Forced Assimilation in Arizona, 1891–1935* (Norman: University of Oklahoma Press, 1988). See also James Axtell, *The School upon a Hill: Education and Society in Colonial New England* (New Haven: Yale University Press, 1974).

   For contemporary studies, see Estelle Fuchs and Robert J. Havighurst, *To Live on This Earth: American Indian Education* (Garden City, N.Y.: Doubleday, 1972); Margaret Connell Szasz, *Education and the American Indian: The Road to Self-Determination since 1928*, 2d ed. (Albuquerque: University of New Mexico Press, 1977).

Several Native American women have written about their school experiences. In addition to Zitkala-Sa, see Mary Crow Dog and Richard Erdoes, *Lakota Woman* (New York: Grove Weidenfeld, 1990); Polingaysi Qoyawayma (Elizabeth Q. White), *No Turning Back: A Hopi Indian Woman's Struggle to Live in Two Worlds* (Albuquerque: University of New Mexico Press, 1964). Maria Campbell, *Halfbreed* (Lincoln: University of Nebraska Press, 1973), relates her school experiences as a métis woman in Canada.

On Native American girls and school, see Robert A. Trennert, "Educating Indian Girls at Nonreservation Boarding Schools, 1878–1920," in Ellen Carol DuBois and Vicki L. Ruiz, eds., *Unequal Sisters: A Multicultural Reader in U.S. Women's History* (New York: Routledge, 1990), pp. 224–37; Ruey-Lin Lin, "A Profile of Reservation Indian High School Girls," *Journal of American Indian Education* 26 (1987): 18–28; Beatrice Medicine, "The Interaction of Culture and Sex Roles in the Schools," in Shirley M. Hufstedler et al., eds., *Conference on the Educational and Occupational Needs of American Indian Women* (1976) (Washington, D.C.: National Institute of Education, 1980), pp. 141–58; Agnes F. Williams, "Transition from the Reservation to an Urban Setting and the Changing Roles of American Indian Women," in Hufstedler et al., eds., *Conference on the Educational and Occupational Needs of American Indian Women*, pp. 251–84.

5. Fuchs and Havighurst, *To Live on This Earth*, pp. 2–3; Charles L. Chancy, *The Birth of Missions in America* (South Pasadena, Calif.: William Carey Library, 1976), pp. 70–71; Ernest Hawkins, *Historical Notices of the Missions of the Church of England in the North American Colonies, Previous to the Independence of the United States: Chiefly from the M.S. Documents of the Society for the Propagation of the Gospel in Foreign Parts* (London: B. Stowes, 1845), p. 342. On French missionary education, see James Axtell, *The Invasion Within: The Contest of Cultures in Colonial North America* (New York: Oxford University Press, 1985): Cornelius J. Jaenen, *Friend and Foe: Aspects of French-AmerIndian Cultural Contact in the Sixteenth and Seventeenth Centuries* (New York: Columbia University Press, 1976); and J. H. Kennedy, *Jesuit and Savage in New France* (New Haven: Yale University Press, 1950). On Spanish efforts to educate Indians in California, see Sherburne F. Cook, *The Conflict between the California Indians and White Civilization, Ibero-Americana* 21–24 (1943).

6. Berkhofer, *Salvation and the Savage*, pp. 2–3, 12–13; Wade Crawford Barclay, *History of Methodist Missions, Part One: Early American Methodism, 1769–1844* (New York: Board of Missions and Church Extension of the Methodist Church, 1949–50), p. 164; Timothy L. Smith, *Revivalism and Social Reform: American Protestantism on the Eve of the Civil War* (Baltimore: Johns Hopkins University Press, 1980), pp. 58–62. For a detailed examination of the ABCFM, see William R. Hutchison, *Errand to the World: American Protestant Thought and Foreign Missions* (Chicago: University of Chicago Press, 1987).

7. Sherman Hall to Lydia Hall, 15 June 1833, Sherman Hall Papers, Minnesota Historical Society (hereafter cited as SH), St. Paul.

8. John C. Lowrie, 2 March 1877, *American Indian Correspondence: The Presbyterian Historical Society Collection of Missionaries' Letters, 1833–1893* (Westport, Conn.: Greenwood Press, 1979), C:31O (hereafter cited as AIC).

9. Rayna Green, "'Kill the Indian and save the Man': Indian Education in the United States," introduction to Hultgren and Molin, *To Lead and to Serve*, p. 9.

10. Szasz, *Education and the American Indian*, pp. 9–10; Zitkala-Sa, *American Indian Stories*, pp. 39–40; Trennert, *The Phoenix Indian School*, pp. 113–14.

11. Charles Hall, "The Story of Fort Berthold," Papers of the American Board of Commissioners for Foreign Missions: Missions to the North American Indians, Houghton Library, Harvard University, Cambridge, Mass., 26: 6.48–49 (hereafter cited as ABC).

12. Ibid., pp. 17–18.

13. See, for example, Carol Devens, *Countering Colonization: Native American Women and Great Lakes Missions, 1630–1900* (Berkeley: University of California Press, 1992), chap. 5.

14. On nineteenth-century views of women and education, see Polly Weltz Kaufman, *Women Teachers on the Frontier* (New Haven: Yale University Press, 1984); *Mary Beth Norton, Liberty's Daughters: The Revolutionary Experience of American Women, 1750–1800* (Boston: Little, Brown, 1980); Mary Ryan, *Cradle of the Middle Class: The Family in Oneida County, New York, 1790–1865* (Cambridge: Cambridge University Press, 1981); Barbara Leslie Epstein, *The Politics of Domesticity: Women, Evangelism, and Temperance in Nineteenth-Century America* (Middletown, Conn.: Wesleyan University Press, 1981). On Native American women and missionaries, see Kendall Blanchard, "Changing Sex Roles and Protestantism among the Navajo Women in Ramah," *Journal for the Scientific Study of Religion* 14 (1975): 43–50; Devens, *Countering Colonization*; Lillian A. Ackerman, "The Effect of Missionary Ideals on Family Structure and Women's Roles in Plateau Indian Culture," *Idaho Yesterdays* 31 (1987): 64–73; Karen Anderson, "Commodity Exchange and Subordination: Montagnais-Nasakapi and Huron Women, 1600–1650," *Signs: Journal of Women in Culture and Society* II (1985): 49–62; Mary C. Wright, "Economic Development and Native American Women in the Early Nineteenth Century," *American Quarterly* 33 (1981): 525–36.

15. Isaac Baird to John C. Lowrie, 14 July 1883, AIC, G:I:III.

16. *Woonspe Wankantu* (Santee, Nebr.: Santee Normal Training School, 1879), ABC, 18.3.7. v.5, 85.

17. William Thurston Boutwell, "Diary Kept by the Reverend William Thurston Boutwell, Missionary to the Ojibwa Indians, 1832–1837," entry for 11 November 1833, William T. Boutwell Papers, Minnesota Historical Society, St. Paul.

18. Peter Dougherty to Mr. McKean, 25 September 1850, AIC, 7:1:13.

19. Peter Dougherty to Walter Lowrie, 25 December 1848, AIC, 7:3:167; 1 May 1849, AIC, 7:3:166; 4 September 1850, AIC, 7:1:7; 26 September 1853, AIC, 7:1:91; 16 January 1854, AIC, 7:1:108. Dougherty to P. Babcock, superintendent of Indian affairs, Grand Traverse, 14 October 1850, AIC, 7:1:8; J. G. Turner to Walter Lowrie, 5 January 1858, AIC, 7:2:47. For further explanation of these incidents, see Devens, *Countering Colonization*, chap. 5.

20. J. G. Hamilton, U.S. Indian agent, to Mrs. E. W. Blalchford, secretary of Women's Board, Chicago, 7 July 1875, ABC, 183.3.7, v.5, 170.

21. Susan Webb to J. O. Means, 8 February 1881, ABC,18.3.7, v.4, 274.

22. Hall, "Ford Berthold," p. 46.

23. Isaac Baird to J. C. Lowrie, 30 December 1876, AIC, C:287; Baird to D. C. Mahan, U.S. Indian agent, 30 March 1878, AIC, E:1:3; Zitkala-Sa, *American Indian Stories* (n. 1 above), pp. 42–43. Also see Devens, *Countering Colonization*, chaps. 3,5.

24. Susan Webb to J. O. Means, 18 March 1881, ABC, 18.3.7, v. 7, 276.

25. The reasons for their enrollment are not often clear. Many appear, like Zitkala-Sa, to have been enticed by the material goods promised them. Polingaysi, a Hopi, recalled that she was fascinated by the cotton dresses and food that the children received at school. See Qoyawayma, *No Turning Back* (n. 4 above), p. 23.

26. Zitkala-Sa, *American Indian Stories* (n. 1 above), p. 51.

27. Ibid., p. 54; Hall, "Fort Berthold," p. 49; J. C. McGillycuddy, *McGillycuddy, Agent* (Stanford: Stanford University Press, 1941), pp. 205–206, quoted in Medicine, "Culture and Sex Roles" (n. 4 above), pp. 149–50.

28. Leonard Wheeler to David Greene, 23 January 1843, ABC, 18.3.7., v. 2, 219. See Berkhofer, *Salvation and the Savage* (n. 4 above); and Michael Coleman, *Presbyterian Missionary Attitudes toward American Indians, 1837–1893* (Jackson: University Press of Mississippi, 1985), for thorough explications of the workings of a mission classroom. Barbara Welter, "The Cult of True Womanhood, 1820–1860," *American Quarterly* 18 (1966): 151–74.

29. Fuchs and Havighurst, *To Live on This Earth* (n. 4 above), p. 19, observe that current pedagogy and curriculum in most schools for Native American children still are intended to alienate them from their own cultures.

30. Leonard Wheeler, First Report of Manual Labor Boarding School, 11 January 1869, ABC (n. 11 above), 18.4.1, v. 2, 14.

31. R. David Edmunds, "National Expansion from the Indian Perspective," in Frederick E. Hoxie, ed., *Indians in American History* (Arlington Heights, Ill.: Harlan Davidson), pp. 159–77.

32. Berkhofer, *Salvation and the Savage* (n. 4 above), p, 39.

33. Martha Riggs Morris to J. O. Means, 6 May 1881, ABC (n. 11 above), 18.3.7, v.6, 165.

34. John Sunday to Robert Alder, 7 April 1841, Wesleyan Methodist Missionary Society Archives, London–North American correspondence, microfiche. United Methodist Archives and History Center, Madison, N.J., Box 102,1841/42, 12C.

35. Martha Riggs Morris to J. O. Means, 6 May 1881, ABC (n. 11 above), 18.3.7, v. 6, 165; Alfred L. Riggs to John O. Means, Report of Santee Agency Station for the Year ending March 31, 1882, ABC, 18.3.7, v. 5, 64; M. A. Shepard to J. O. Means, 17 June 1881, ABC, 18.3.7, v. 7, 241.

36. Zitkala-Sa, *American Indian Stories* (n. 1 above), pp. 65–66. This pattern continued in government boarding schools well into the twentieth century. At the Rice Boarding School in Arizona in the 1910s, children were up at 5 A.M., spent half the day in school and half working, and made their own clothing and shoes. They did this on a diet of bread, coffee, and potatoes, which cost the school nine cents per day per child. (The minimum standard expenditure for healthy growth in those years was set by the government at thirty-five cents per day per child.) See Szasz, *Education and the American Indian* (n. 4 above), p. 19.

37. Susan Webb to J. O. Means, 8 February 1881, ABC (n. 11 above), 18.3.7, v. 7, 274.

38. Zitkala-Sa, *American Indian Stories* (n. 1 above), p. 67.

39. Crow Dog and Erdoes, *Lakota Woman* (n. 4 above), p. 28.

40. Berkhofer, *Salvation and the Savage* (n. 4 above), pp. 17–42; Leonard Wheeler to Selah B. Treat, 21 July 1857, ABC (n. 30 above), 18.4.1, v. 1, 265. See Hall to Laura Hall, 4 February 1835, SH (n. 7 above); Trennert, *The Phoenix Indian School* (n. 4 above), p. 137.

41. Hall, "Fort Berthold" (n. 11 above), pp. 41, 49; Szasz, *Education and the American Indian* (n. 4 above); Trennert, *The Phoenix Indian School* (n. 4 above); Berkhofer, *Salvation and the Savage* (n. 4 above); and Zitkala-Sa, *American Indian Stories* (n.1 above), all address the issue of children's deaths at school.

42. Eda Ward to J. O. Means, 13 March 1881, ABC (n. 11 above), 18.3.7, v. 7, 27.

43. Zitkala-Sa, *American Indian Stories* (n. 1 above), pp. 40–41.

44. Sherman Hall to Aaron Hall, 2 February 1842, SH (n. 7 above).

45. Sherman Hall to Laura Hall, 4 February 1835, SH (n. 7 above).

46. A. P. Truesdell, quoted in S. G. Clark to S. L. Pumroy, 11 May 1858, ABC (n. 11 above), 18.4. I, v. 2, 19.

47. Adele Curtis (Sisseton) reported, "I enjoy my work very *much indeed.*" Susan Webb (Santee) claimed that her years at the mission were the happiest of her life, as did Martha Paddock (Santee). Adele M. Curtis to Selah B. Treat, 9 December 1875, ABC (n. 11 above), 18.3.7, v. 6, 29; Susan Webb to J. O. Means, 8 February 1881, ABC, 18.3.7, v. 7, 274; Martha M. Paddock to J. O. Means, 20 June 1881, ABC, 18,3,7, v. 6, 187.

48. Fuchs and Havighurst, *To Live on This Earth*, p. 199; Williams, "Changing Roles of American Indian Women," p. 262.

49. Zitkala-Sa, *American Indian Stories* (n. 1 above), p. 50.

50. Sister M. Inez Hilger, *Chippewa Child Life and Its Cultural Background*, Smithsonian Institution, Bureau of American Ethnology Bulletin 146 (Washington, D.C.: Smithsonian Institution, 1951), pp. 58–59; Laurence French, *Psychocultural Change and the American Indian: An Ethnohistorical Analysis* (New York: Garland, 1987), p. 107; Edmund F. Ely, Writing, 1 January 1835, Ely Family Papers, Minnesota Historical Society, St. Paul. For a discussion of Anglo-American child-rearing practices, see Philip Greven, *The Protestant Temperament: Patterns of Child Rearing, Religious Experience, and the Self in Early America* (New York: Meridian, 1977), pp. 87–99.

51. Zitkala-Sa, *American Indian Stories* (n. 1 above), p. 8.

52. Ibid., pp. 20, 21; French, *Psychocultural Change*, pp. 107–108; Medicine, "Culture and Sex Roles" (n. 4 above), p. 146; Powers, *Oglala* Women (n. 3 above), p. 58.

53. Ella Caria Deloria, *Waterlily* (Lincoln: University of Nebraska Press, 1988), pp. 52–53, 70. The book, based on twenty years of scholarly field work about her people, was written in the form of a novel, with the goal of making it more accessible to a general readership.

54. Hilger, *Chippewa Child Life*, pp. 153–62; Ruth Landes, *Ojibwa Woman* (New York: Columbia University Press, 1938), p. 11; Williams, "Transition from the Reservation" (n. 4 above), p. 254; Medicine, "The Interaction of Culture and Sex Roles" (n. 4 above), p. 146; Zitkala-Sa, *American Indian Stories* (n. 1 above), pp. 13–15.

55. Hilger, *Chippewa Child Life*, pp. 39–50. Mountain Wolf Woman, *Mountain Wolf Woman, Sister of Crashing Thunder: The Autobiography of a Winnebago Indian*, ed. Nancy Oestreich Lurie (Ann Arbor: University of Michigan Press, 1961), pp. 21–22.

56. Hilger, *Chippewa Childlife*, pp. 50–55.

57. Powers, *Oglala Women* (n. 3 above), pp. 66–70.

58. Medicine, "Culture and Sex Roles" (n. 4 above), p. 153, has pointed out that the matter of learning appropriate gender roles of a child's particular tribe continues to be a problem in contemporary boarding schools.

59. Hall, "Fort Berthold" (n. 11 above), pp. 32, 98, 117 (quote).

60. Zirkala-Sa, *American Indian Stories* (n. 1 above), pp. 69–75; (Qoyawayma, *No Turning Back* [no. 4 above], p. 76). A study of Navajo women who had accepted Christianity found that they tended to view themselves as outside traditional structures and did not feel obliged to maintain older social patterns, such as matrilocal residence: Blanchard, "Changing Sex Roles" (n. 14 above), p. 48.

61. Zitkala-Sa, *American Indian Stories* (n. 1 above), p. 97.

CHAPTER 6

"Rosebloom and Pure White,"
Or So It Seemed

Mary Niall Mitchell

We have a picture of Rosa Downs, though we do not know what she thought about having it made. In a photograph taken in a studio in New York in 1864, she appears to have been a little girl born into the Victorian middle class, like the unnamed child who sat for a photographer in Philadelphia the same year. Both girls' portraits were rendered in vignette, a style popular at the time in which only the head of the sitter was visible, surrounded by soft white space—a style that made young children look very much like angels.[1] But the similarity between these young girls ended at appearances. Their faces had been photographed for very different reasons. Their prospects, too, would never be the same. And those viewers who, at first glance, took Rosa for a white child would have seen her otherwise once they read the words that were beneath her portrait: "Rosa [her name in lovely script], A Slave Girl from New Orleans."

Rosina (known as Rosa) Downs, age "not quite seven," was one of five children and three adults freed at the city of New Orleans by Union Major General N. P. Banks in 1863. Colonel George Hanks, serving on a commission appointed by Banks that was responsible for the education and labor of freedpeople, took this group of eight emancipated slaves north that year with the help of representatives from the American Missionary Association and the National Freedman's Relief Association.[2] Their tour involved both public appearances and visits to photographers' studios to sit for portraits, which were in turn sold to raise money to fund newly established schools for freedpeople in Louisiana.[3] A photographic portrait of the entire group from Louisiana was made into an engraving and printed on a full page of *Harper's Weekly* in 1864 with an accompanying letter to the editor from one of the missionary sponsors, appearing under the provocative headline, "White and Colored Slaves." Nearly all of the individual and small group portraits made, however, featured the children—Isaac, Augusta, Rosa, Charles, and Rebecca. Of these portraits, most included only the whitest-looking children: Rosa, Rebecca, and Charles.[4]

The decision to display white-looking children was due, in part, to the earlier success of a girl child named Fanny Lawrence (to whom we shall return) who had been "redeemed" in Virginia.[5] As Fanny had done, Rosa, Rebecca, and Charles captivated white northern audiences. In an account of the group's appearance in New York, these children were singled out: "three of the children," said the *Evening Post*, "were perfectly white, and had brown hair."[6] Isaac and Augusta, both darker-skinned than the others, along with the clearly black adults, were mostly absent from the photographs. When the sponsors opted to take the children on to Philadelphia for more appearances and sittings in photography studios, Isaac and Augusta were left behind.[7]

The whitest-looking girls, however, seem to have received the most attention. There are more surviving *cartes de visite* of them in archives than of the others, suggesting that perhaps more people bought pictures of them. And unlike photographs of Charles, the white-looking boy, representations of Rosa and Rebecca seemed especially tailored to pique viewers' interest. In *Harper's Weekly*, Rosina Downs was described as "a fair child with blonde complexion and silky hair." Her rather mature-sounding name was shortened to "Rosa" for the photographic portraits, presumably to emphasize her innocence and youth. Rebecca Huger, age eleven, was a little older, and photographers often dressed and posed her to seem more a young lady than a child. Of Rebecca, the missionary wrote to *Harper's*: "to all appearance, she is perfectly white. Her complexion, hair, and features show not the slightest trace of negro blood."[8] These white-looking girls, in sweet, innocent form, troubled notions of racial difference and fostered an unease laced with fascination among white northern viewers. Indeed, what made Rosa and Rebecca so beguiling for nineteenth-century audiences was that these lovely white girls were not "white."

The photographic portraits of Rosa, Rebecca, and Fanny Lawrence were spectacles with multiple meanings, inviting a combination of sympathy, speculation, voyeurism, and moral outrage.[9] Because the girls looked white, their images appealed to Victorian sentiments about white rather than black or "colored" girlhood; indeed, while they pressed for the abolition that would free white-skinned children like Rosa, they left the black child and her plight in the shadows. Furthermore, the pictures played upon fears that white people could become enslaved in the South, should slavery continue to spread, fears that had become more prominent as the sectional debate deepened. They also raised for consideration the interracial sex that had produced seemingly white nonwhite progeny, and they fanned northern fascination with light-skinned "fancy girls" sold as slaves in the New Orleans market. Indeed, in the invitation to scrutiny and in their sale price, these photographs mirrored the activities of the slave market itself. Further still—no doubt, unintentionally—they raised anxieties about emancipation and what place there would be in American society for freedpeople who perhaps looked white but who were not considered to be white.

These tangled interpretations are most readily explained, perhaps, with a portrait of Isaac (the darkest-skinned child in the group) shown arm-in-arm with Rosa. Both of the children were dressed fancily, with Isaac in a suit and starched collar and Rosa wearing a flowered hat and tailored cloak over a dress with full petticoats. From first glance, the contrast in skin color between the two is striking (what Roland Barthes might have called the photograph's "punctuation"), and this was, no doubt, the point.[10] Isaac's dark skin served to accentuate Rosa's paleness. Next to her black-skinned companion, she appeared unmistakably "white." But placing Isaac and Rosa together had the opposite effect as well. It assured viewers that their own eyes deceived them, that Rosa could not have been "white" since a white girl never would have appeared in public on the arm of a black boy.[11] For playing upon uncertainty, Rosa's image was the perfect metaphor, one that signified blackness and whiteness, racial mixture and racial purity, sexual innocence and sexual promise, and slavery and freedom.[12] In the ambiguous, vulnerable body of a white-looking "slave" girl, white northern audiences saw the precarious future of their divided nation—a nation many of them still considered (despite increasing doubts) to be a "white" one.[13]

If the portraits of Rosa and the others presented a nation's uncertain future, however, they also illustrate the nature of its past. Rosa's image, so full of meaning, makes manifest the inextricable histories of black children and white children in the nineteenth century. Both in image and in reality, these two groups were bound together by what one historian has termed the "relational nature of difference"—that is, white children lived as they did because black children lived as they did, and both white and black childhoods were shaped (and still are) by race.[14] In the nineteenth century, images of black and white childhood were mutually defining and mutually reinforcing; representations of the two, like the real lives of children themselves, were forged together out of prejudice and privilege. Although historians have paid childhood little heed in their discussions of race, adult ideas about race and racism have often been reproduced and put into practice through the lives of children.[15] To study the history of white children and black children in isolation, then, is to see only part of the story. As these pictures so cleverly remind us, we cannot look at one group of children, black or white, without seeing the other.

———

To fully understand the appeal of these portraits and the particular ways in which audiences might have read them, we must look in several directions: to Civil War stories of "white slaves," to popular representations of white and black children in the nineteenth century and those of girls in particular, to antislavery ideas and white audiences' fantasies about light-skinned slave women, to the significance of the new "truth-telling" medium of photography, and into the labyrinth of race that both guided and confused white northern sympathies. Although it is difficult to know who saw these images or purchased them, their production at a time when white working-class people were openly opposing the Civil War—most notably during the New York Draft Riots of 1863—suggests that they were aimed at a broad northern audience rather than just limited to middle-class viewers.[16] Indeed, the girls' portraits seem to have been, in part, an effort to circumvent issues of class by pressing the argument that southern slavery threatened the freedoms and privileges of all white people.[17]

By the 1850s and 1860s, white slaves had become some of the peculiar institution's most "vile" specters, and accounts of white people enslaved in the South proliferated in newspapers and antislavery journals in the northern states. These reports sprang from fears that if slavery went unchecked—if the southern slave power had its way—it would soon deny the liberties of non-slaveholding white people.[18] In one such story, a correspondent from the New York *Tribune* reported in 1863 that a white woman, "through whose veins courses the Anglo-Saxon blood, and who has no negro taint about her," had been sold into slavery near Beaufort, South Carolina, apparently by her own husband, with whom she had had a dispute. "The selling of wives is not uncommon in South Carolina," the writer explained, "especially when their health is broken down and they are unable to do hard work." Mrs. Cribb, the woman in question, even produced a bill of sale for herself for the (suspiciously meager) sum of five dollars.[19]

Another story reported by the *Tribune* involved the son of a white woman. The woman, the paper explained, had been the product of a planter's daughter's "seduction" out of wedlock by a white man and was given to a slave woman to raise. The child grew up to be a planter's mistress, and the children she then had by him were treated as his slaves. One of them, a son by the name of Charles Grayson, was sold away from her, but not before the truth about his parentage was revealed to him by his mother. According to the *Tribune*, Grayson had "straight, light hair, fair, blue eyes, a sandy beard, and evidently is a white man, with no drop of black blood in his veins." Perhaps even more frightening to readers was the writer's description of Grayson's demeanor: "He is totally ignorant. He scarcely knows what freedom is," the writer remarked. Although "a negro slave has a subdued, and yet, at times a gay air, Charles Grayson is continually abject and gloomy." Grayson managed to escape into Union lines in 1862 where he was aided by members of the 3rd Michigan Cavalry.[20] A story like Grayson's proved quite useful to the Union military and to abolitionists. Given the increasing unpopularity of the Civil War in the North, abolitionists and Union officials hoped to divert northern eyes from the largely black slave population for whom the war was, arguably, fought. Instead of black freedom, these stories implied, it was the white man's freedom that needed to be defended against the inevitable encroachments of southern slavery.

Tales of "white slaves" had more dramatic appeal, however, when they concerned beautiful white girls, for whom not only freedom but virtue was at stake. The *National Antislavery Standard*, for instance, ran a two-part story, around the time the correspondences from the *Tribune* appeared in 1863, entitled "Sold at Savannah." The apparently fictional story featured an Irish girl named Ellen Neale who, while in the South, had lost all of her kin to cholera.[21] Although taken in by kindly Quakers, Ellen soon was seized as a fugitive slave under orders from the "yellow-eyed" Elder Mathewson who had been propositioning Ellen without success for several months. Ellen's face, the narrator explained, was "more than pretty, for it was downright beautiful, with its rosebloom and pure white and the dark, lustrous eyes and well-shaped mouth." Ellen eventually found herself on the auction block, subjected to the scrutiny of the "chivalry" (white male spectators who attended her sale). "They did not come to buy," the narrator observed, "but for the most part to look on, scrutinize, and exercise their critical powers." The auctioneer informed his audience, "high bids are expected, for it isn't every day such angeliferous loveliness comes to the hammer." He proclaimed her "a very white mulatto, ... but I have never heard a fair skin objected to in a slave. A housekeeper, gentlemen, governess, *or* companion." Ellen was rescued at the last moment when her Quaker friends brought forward proof of her British citizenship, but her story was a harrowing one meant to show white readers how little distance remained between a white woman's purity and the abominations of slavery.[22]

Accounts of *white-looking* people who had been born into slavery—that is, those who had "African" blood yet appeared to be "perfectly" white—were effective in ways both similar to and different from stories of white people enslaved. William H. DeCamp, for instance, working among black regiments in Tennessee, wrote home to the *Grand Rapids Eagle* that he had discovered a number of soldiers in the "negro enlistment" who appeared to be white men: "When one sees standing before him a man of mature years, who possesses not the slightest trace of negro blood in a single feature or complexion, and hair straighter than you can generally find in the pure Anglo-Saxon race and he tells you that his father is Col. Higgins, now of the rebel army, [then the] ruling passion in the South" became quite clear. Encountering white-looking former slaves seemed to further convince DeCamp of the righteousness of his duty: "I never was an Abolitionist," he wrote, "but I am not in favor of white slaves in a white country, and that where we call our nation a white one."[23]

In one sense, then, DeCamp viewed the soldier as a white man, and his outrage stemmed from the thought of white men enslaved. By the same token, audiences were horrified to imagine white-looking children like Rosa as the chattel of southern slaveholders. Yet because of their African ancestry, the furor that white-looking enslaved people inspired was more complex than reactions to accounts of "Anglo-Saxon" people "accidentally" enslaved. Both the soldiers DeCamp encountered and the "white slaves" brought north by abolitionists did more than demonstrate white people's vulnerability to enslavement. Such white-looking people were the embodiment of racial transgression, living proof of the "ruling passion of the South." Historian Martha Hodes (writing about sexual relations between white women and black men in the nineteenth-century South) observes that "it was the problem of the child that brought the illicit liaison into the public realm beyond the confines of gossip and scandal. . . ." Although relations between white male slaveholders and their black female slaves were not illicit in the antebellum South, the "mulatto" children resulting from those encounters were nonetheless public manifestations of the relations between master and slave. One need only recall southern diarist Mary Chestnut's famous quip: "every lady tells you who is the father of all the mulatto children in everybody's household, but those in her own she seems to think drop from the clouds, or pretends so to think."[24] But very light-skinned slaves were, for whites, the most problematic group since they were capable of claiming to be white even though they were of "mixed" race. Photographic images of white-looking slaves, in particular—through which viewers could see for themselves—simultaneously fascinated and tormented viewers because of both the subjects' "invisible" ancestry and the sexual history that produced them.[25]

For white northern viewers, the act of reading the images of Rosa, Rebecca, and Fanny was further complicated by the girls' status as children. White childhood was increasingly sentimentalized in the nineteenth century as middle-class children became separated from both the world of adults and the world of work. Instead of contributing to the family income, they became "priceless" members of the middle-class family: innocent, unproductive, and primarily the focus of nurture and attention.[26] Images of white childhood, in turn, idealized in fiction, advertisements, and illustrations, highlighted the supposed "innocence" and "vulnerability" of white children. These sentiments were reflected, as well, in family portraiture of the middle and late nineteenth century. The soft vignettes in which both Rosa and Rebecca appeared and the image of Fanny perched on a chair, holding a bouquet of flowers, were the sorts of children's pictures that would have been familiar to most Northerners.[27] By 1860, the widespread production of cartes de visite made portraits affordable to middle-class people, and pictures of one's children—surrounded by all the trappings of middle-class domesticity—were an increasingly common sight in the homes of many Americans.[28] Using the genre of the child's portrait, then, the producers of these images of white-looking girls sent a pointedly political message. With each child framed in the vignettes and parlor scenes associated with white northern middle-class girlhood, these images of "slave girls" brought antislavery into the homes, perhaps even the family photograph albums, of many white Northerners.[29]

The language and ideals of middle-class domesticity had often been employed by abolitionists to condemn southern slavery. The domestic disorder slavery produced—slave-owning fathers who sold their own children, slave women forever subject to the sexual desires of their owners, and slave families torn apart by the market in human beings—made enslavement terrifying, both for slaves themselves and in the eyes of northern abolitionists. Both former slaves and white abolitionists highlighted stories of outraged motherhood and torn families in order to bring enslaved people into the realm of Victorian sentiment.[30] And yet the supposed distance (both geographical and racial) that separated Northerners from southern slavery's evils must have shrunk considerably at the sight of little Rosa.[31] Although white abolitionist writers often fantasized about their own enslavement as well as the enslavement of their children as a means of sympathizing and empathizing with slaves, Rosa's photograph introduced something quite new.[32] Fixing visions of seemingly white slave children through photography was for northern viewers a step away from fantasy, closer to "truth," and ultimately more frightening. The effect of these photographs—both despite and because of their Victorian veneer— was that they asked white northern viewers to look upon the enslavement of their own children.

Pure sentimentality is perhaps not the only light in which these images can be understood, however. The reform literature of the nineteenth century, for instance, introduced another facet of the white child. In the idealized American home of nineteenth-century reform literature and child-rearing manuals, love and affection replaced punishment as the proper means of disciplining children.[33] Yet domestic order achieved through affection rather than harsh reprimand involved a reciprocal role on the part of the child. Children, and girl children in particular, appeared often in temperance literature "not only as objects of discipline but also . . . as its agents."[34] In narratives verging on the incestuous, for instance, drunken fathers found salvation in the tender embraces of their young daughters. (He swore never to drink again; she showered him with forgiving kisses.) The purity, innocence, and vulnerability of young children made them powerful disciplinary agents of reform, able to subdue their fathers despite and because of the child's inherently weak position. Likewise, in the images of Rosa and Rebecca, notions about white little girls as pure and precious things may have been employed to redeem those viewers who had yet to rally around the antislavery cause and encourage them to act on the girls' behalf.

The meanings that audiences would have invested in photographs of white-looking slave girls, however, were founded also on nineteenth-century ideas about racial difference. Images of innocent white children in the nineteenth century, whether sentimental or moralistic, developed largely in relation to their imagined opposite.[35] Popular images of black children in the nineteenth century often rendered them not as virtuous ideals of feminine beauty but rather as tricksters of untamed and immoral stripe. Harriet Beecher Stowe's characters Little Eva and Topsy were the most well-known symbols of young, white, feminine purity juxtaposed with young, unschooled black devilishness. In one scene in *Uncle Tom's Cabin*, Stowe explicitly compared her two characters to one another:

> Eva stood looking at Topsy, . . . the two children, representatives of the two extremes of society. The fair, high-bred child, with her golden head, her deep eyes, her spiritual, noble brow, and prince-like movements; and her black, keen, subtle, cringing, yet acute neighbor. They stood as the representatives of their races. The Saxon, born of ages of cultivation, command, education, physical and moral eminence; the Afric, born of ages of oppression, submission, ignorance, toil, and vice![36]

The two little "representatives of their races" in Stowe's narrative existed in contrast with one another, like good and evil. Through the details of their features and their behavior—Eva's "prince-like movements" and Topsy as her "black, keen, subtle, cringing" counterpart—the author aimed to reveal the true nature of the difference between them. Stowe even explained that Eva was fond of Topsy and her antics "as a dove is sometimes charmed by a glittering serpent."[37]

The invidious distinctions that Stowe drew between Eva and Topsy were drawn in real life as well. In the letters of northern missionaries, black children were described with far less affection than white ones. Strangely, such prejudices become clearer when the "white" child in question looked white, but was not. For example, a northern missionary woman in New Orleans during the war was shocked to learn that an orphaned child named Clara Wilbur was the property of a man who lived on the Red River. "Oh! The thought that that child had been a slave!" she wrote. "It was almost naked, but its little rosy cheeks and dimpled chin, all told too plainly that Saxon blood was in those veins."[38] Of a freedchild named Bess, on the other hand, a missionary teacher wrote: "She is very black, and in outward appearance stupid and unprepossessing," even though the woman admitted that Bess was one of her best students.[39]

Even when black children were depicted as good but unfortunate (rather than "devilish" or "stupid"), the tragic stories of their lives still served to shore up an idealized white childhood. This opposing, mutually defining relationship between white childhood and black childhood comes across most directly in antislavery appeals to white children. The "Children's Department" of the *American Missionary*, for instance, was particularly keen to link the lives of its young white readers and black children; yet inevitably white childhood's preciousness and separation from the evils of the world was affirmed through the telling of these stories, while slave children's lives remained wretched and forlorn. "Don't you pity the poor slave children?" read one column. "Will you do all you can, as you grow up, to put away slavery from the land? O, be thankful that you are not slaves." The writer then asked each young reader to say aloud, thankfully:

> I was not born a little slave,
> To labor in the sun.
> And wish I was but in my grave,
> And all my labor done.
> My God, I thank Thee, who hast planned
> A better lot for me;
> And placed me in this favored land
> Where I may hear of Thee.
> Placed me in the *free* States!
> O, how thankful I am and how kind I shall be to
> all who are not so well off as me.[40]

Even while persuading white children to identify with the plight of their black counterparts—thus disciplining the conscience of the white child by pointing to the misfortunes of the slave child—antislavery writers continued to draw lines of difference between the two groups. In a column from the *American Missionary*, the writer explained to his young readers that enslaved children lived a life of sadness and fear of being torn from their parents, and that though they (as white children) might empathize with the black child, they would never be subject to the ravages of the slave trade. "We should remember that parents and children are separated every day by the cruelties of slavery, never more to meet on earth. And such separations are just as wicked and cruel as it would be for the same men to come and separate *you* and *your parents*, and sell you into all the horrors of bondage!"[41] The sentiment aroused by sympathy for the black child's plight not only privileged white childhood but also placed the white child readers in a position of power by asking them to "remember" enslaved children in their prayers.[42] White children also read of "a poor little heathen girl" in Africa whose father sold his own children. "Dear children," the magazine asked, "are you not thankful that you have Christian parents, who love you, and teach you what is right and good. . . . Will you not then remember the poor little heathen children who have not the priceless blessings you enjoy?"[43]

In the most familiar of all antislavery narratives, *Uncle Tom's Cabin*, Harriet Beecher Stowe seemed to bestow happy, intact families and sugared sentiment upon only the white and light-skinned children in the story. Little Eva, of course was the precious child of loving parents. Harry—"a small quadroon boy . . . beautiful and engaging" with "glossy curls about his round, dimpled face"—avoids being sold from his mother, Eliza, and when she bravely runs away with him, Harry is later reunited with his father, too, and grows up in freedom.[44] Uncle Tom's children, however, lose their father to slave traders early in the story. And the infamous Topsy was altogether parentless. After Miss Ophelia (a northern white woman with abolitionist sympathies living in the home of her slaveholding brother) was given charge of Topsy, she asked the child where her mother was. Topsy explained that she had never had one. "Never was born," she said. "Never had father nor mother, nor nothin', I was raised by a speculator, with lots of others. Old Aunt Sue used to take car on us."[45] Through such renderings of black slave children, the white (and near-white) child was re-created again and again as precious, protected, and fortunate, while the black child remained woeful and alone.

In fact, much of the horror and sympathy elicited from *Harper's Weekly* readers concerning the three "white" slave children was gleaned from their status as members of families. Rebecca "was a slave in her father's house, the special attendant of a girl little older than herself." Her mother and grandmother (to whom the writer had spoken) "live in New Orleans, where they support themselves comfortably by their own labor." Rosina had a father "in the rebel army" while her mother, "a bright mulatto, lives in New Orleans in a poor hut and has hard work to support her family." And of Charles readers learned: "three out of five boys in any school in New York are darker than he. Yet this white boy has been twice sold as a slave. First by his father and 'owner,' Alexander

Wethers, of Lewis County, Virginia, to a slavetrader named Harrison, who sold [him and his mother] to Mr. Thornhill of New Orleans."[46] By providing detailed information about these three children and their origin, the writer was intent to prove that these "white" children had indeed been enslaved, should anyone in the North doubt the veracity of their former status or their nonwhiteness.[47] Still, readers learned almost nothing of Augusta and Isaac or how they lived and with whom. Of Augusta (the lighter-skinned of the two) the reader learned that she was nine years old and that her "almost white" mother still had two children in bondage. Isaac's parents were never mentioned. He was "a black boy of eight years; but none the less intelligent than his whiter companions," and had made admirable progress in school. Despite praise of Isaac's schoolwork, the personal histories the others received—histories that were denied Isaac and Augusta—served to distance black children and their childhoods from the conscience and sympathies of white northern audiences.

By the eve of the Civil War, abolitionists recognized the potential of white-looking slave children for stirring up antislavery sentiment. They could evoke the precious sentiments that surrounded white children (rather than the indifference and scorn black ones received), yet they were real (not fictional) children who had been born into the clutches of slavery. In 1860, in an event that foreshadowed Fanny Lawrence's presentation to his congregation a few years later, the Reverend Henry Ward Beecher brought before his church a girl (still enslaved and apparently not quite as white-skinned as Rosa, Rebecca, and Fanny) who had been separated from her mother and was living with her grandmother, a freedwoman. The slave traders who owned the child had agreed to let her stay with her grandmother, but when offered enough money from an interested buyer, they decided to sell her. According to a report in the "Children's Corner" of the *American Missionary*, the girl had tried to hide but the slave traders "burst in the door and dragged her away." ("How would you feel, children, if the slave traders should come and tear you away from your home and friends?" the writer asked. "And why should they do so to this little girl any more than to you?") As Beecher recounted the girl's story to the congregation, the girl stood quietly beside him, a representative of the kind of innocent, near-white girlhood toward which his audience already felt such tender sentiment and sympathy:

> She was very pretty, of a light complexion, with brown, wavy hair. There was in her face an expression of innocence and gentleness, and a look of sadness too. As she stood there, in her brown frock and little red sack, and Mr. Beecher with his arm thrown protectingly around her, it made a pretty tableau. Tears came into the people's eyes as they gazed at this child, and thought of the

thousands of little slave girls in our land, held in a cruel and hopeless bondage. While we looked at her, we seemed to see them all.[48]

Beecher's intent was for the audience to see the "little slave girl" as a child very like their own children, and he drew pointed parallels between the enslaved girl and the children of his parishioners. "Mothers," said Beecher, "how would you feel if your little daughters were to be sold away from you? I know you will not let this child go back to slavery." With the presentation of the light-skinned "little slave girl," then, the black slave child was replaced in the minds of sympathetic white Northerners with visions of their own (white) children enslaved. The collection plates were passed around Plymouth Church for the "little slave girl" until enough money had been raised to buy her from the slave traders. When Beecher at last exclaimed, "*the child is free!*" the audience "clapped their hands for joy."[49]

The photographs of Rebecca, Rosa, and Fanny, then, were more than a visual trick, a *trompe l'oeil* meant to play on the emotions of white viewers. Lines of sympathy had already been drawn in the antislavery rhetoric of the day, lines that held the white child in a cherished and protected light and the black child in a tearful, motherless place. Empathy for white-looking slave children, rather than dissolving racial differences, only reaffirmed the viewers' sense of themselves as privileged and white.[50] And although it was the image of a raggedy, motherless, Topsy-like black child that viewers might have expected to see above the words "slave girl," it was the "innocent," "pure," and "well-loved" white child Rosa who appeared, a child who needed the protection of the northern white public.

Rosa's image, however, combined the unprotected child with the figure of the white female slave, inspiring the fears white audiences associated with both. Nineteenth-century viewers, North and South, were quite familiar with the figure of the white female slave in the form of American sculptor Hiriam Powers's *The Greek Slave* (1844), a work that attracted crowds of museum goers and spawned reams of commentary in the American press. Though Powers did not set out to make an abolitionist symbol, one historian has argued that the sculptor borrowed the image of the naked female in chains from American antislavery emblems.[51] Yet public reception of the sculpture—which toured in the 1840s and 1850s from the Northeast to as far south as New Orleans—suggests that audiences read Powers's slave (meant to represent a Greek woman enslaved by Turks) as an emblem of ideal feminine purity, submissiveness, and Christian faith. Among abolitionists, feminists, even anti-abolitionists, however, the sculpture became a point of reference to the enslavement of African Americans in the South and to the enchained status of all women in American society. Indeed, many antislavery feminists were outraged by the depiction of the "ideal" woman as submissive and resigned to her terrible fate.[52]

Although less popular than Powers's sculpture, Erastus Dow Palmer's *The White Captive* (1859) also made the marble body of a white woman enslaved a point of public reflection. Palmer, also American, was responding to the popularity of Powers's earlier work but brought his sculpture closer to his audience by providing an American setting for his female figure. Instead of a Greek woman, Palmer sculpted a young white woman (indeed, almost girllike in expression if not form) captured by Indians. Palmer himself described her as "the young daughter of a pioneer," suggesting that she was not yet mature and was still living with her parents when captured. As historian Joy Kasson has pointed out, the parallels between *The Greek Slave* and *The White Captive* were deliberate and striking. The figures were similarly posed, each one bound by the hands to a post and gazing resignedly over her shoulder. They were victims in desperate need of saving, but beyond reach. Yet they also seemed, by their very powerlessness, to have a hold over the viewer. As an article in *Harper's Weekly* observed of *The White Captive*, "No: it is not she, it is we who are captive."[53]

What makes these sculptures useful for interpreting the photographs at hand is not simply that they share with the girls' images the theme of the white (or white-looking) female enslaved. Rather, they are most instructive for what they prepared audiences to do. Nineteenth-century audiences, with clues from their creators, read in these marble sculptures a narrative about the impending violation of the white woman enslaved. Given the information that *The Greek Slave* was a young, white, Christian woman in a Turkish slave mart, stripped of her clothing and all her possessions but for her cross, viewers imagined for themselves the fate that awaited her at the hands of lecherous men.[54] Similarly, the white girl captured by "savage" Indians and tied tightly to a stake would soon lose her girlish innocence in the wilderness, where no white man could save her. Nineteenth-century writers mused in just this way about these sculptures, embellishing the stories with their own commentary about their posture and expressions betraying "the sudden thought of coming trial."[55]

Although the material clues given in the photographs of Rosa, Rebecca, and Fanny were quite different from those belonging to *The Greek Slave* and *The White Captive*, the invitation for a narrative of lust was common to both. If the sculpted women were poised at the threshold of a horrifying scene, the white-looking slave girls stood on the slim ground of girlhood—their young age, their skin, and the knowledge that they had been enslaved combined to suggest a harrowing future. Also, by their perceived powerlessness, both the sculptures and the white-looking girls seemed to hold viewers in sway. Yet, although audiences had no control over the fate of *The Greek Slave* or *The White Captive*, abolitionists made the point that for other little slave girls in the

South, it was not too late. Where the sculptures could only inspire agony, the images, as propaganda, could inspire action. The endangered virtue of white and white-looking little girls, in turn, made appeals for their protection all the more urgent and made the thought of *not* helping them a scandalous one.

Within the context of white, middle-class Victorian culture, white little girls (perhaps even more so than white women) embodied the "Victorian ideal" of femininity—childlike, dependent, and sexually pure. Yet they nevertheless exuded (in the eyes of mostly male artists and photographers) a budding sexuality. Scholars have noted the irony implicit in nineteenth-century notions of white girls' sexual innocence and untouchability. White girls' association with innocence and purity gave their images the allure of the forbidden, thus making them all the more enticing and seemingly sexually vulnerable.[56] The eroticism inherent in pictures of "innocent" white girls—pure yet alluring— seems to have contributed to the appeal of white girlhood as the subject of paintings and mass-reproduced prints that sold by the thousands in the mid– and late nineteenth century.[57] Renderings of little white girls such as John Everett Millais's mass-reproduced *Cherry Ripe* (1879) captured at once little girls' innocence, their sexual allure, and their popular appeal.[58] This theme is especially clear in Seymour Smith Guy's *Making a Train* (1867) in which the young girl slips her dress from her shoulders, baring her just-developing breasts, in order to make the train of a grown woman's gown. Lewis Carroll's pictures of young Alice Liddell also play on the idea of the "incipient woman" within the child. In his photograph of *Alice Liddell as "The Beggar Maid"* (c. 1859) for instance, Carroll cleverly made the suggestion of the fallen woman using the bared limbs and shabby dress of an unfallen upper-class child.[59]

The idea of the woman within the child, however, was even more easily projected onto the bodies of white-looking slave girls from the South, since their sexuality, or at the very least their anticipated fertility, would have been part of their purchase price. Allusion to the sexuality of Rosa, Rebecca, and Fanny did not require pointed visual or verbal clues like those attached to Guy's *Making a Train*. Because they looked white but had been slaves and because they were female, their portraits no doubt summoned the familiar figure of the "tragic mulatta," a woman noted for her beauty, her near-whiteness, and her unspeakable violation by the white men of the South. From the mid–nineteenth century, in fact, abolitionist propaganda and rhetoric reflected an increasing preoccupation among middle-class white Northerners with sexuality, and the unrestrained sexuality of southern slaveholders in particular.[60] Fictional portrayals of mulatta slaves became a familiar trope of nineteenth-century sentimental fiction, their popularity stemming from the notion that white, often female, readers would more readily identify with the plight of white-looking women.[61]

Whereas white Northerners might have imagined the mournful life of a light-skinned woman from lines of fiction or the accounts of former slaves, it was the *imperiled future* of a white-looking girl that presented itself in the bodies of Rosa, Rebecca, and Fanny. This becomes especially clear in the well-documented story of Fanny Lawrence. Although we have very little record of the appearances made by the children from Louisiana, we do have accounts of Fanny's presentation and baptism in Brooklyn, New York, before the Reverend Henry Ward Beecher's Plymouth Church in 1863. Every account of Fanny's appearance reads much like the following, penned in the dramatic tones of sentimental fiction:

> When the audience supposed that the ceremony was ended, Mr. Beecher carried up into the pulpit a little girl about five years of age, of sweet face, large eyes, light hair, and fair as a lily. Pausing a moment to conquer his emotion, he sent a shiver of horror through the congregation by saying "This child was born a slave, and is just redeemed from slavery!" It is impossible to describe the effect of this announcement. The fact seemed so incredible and so atrocious that at first, the spectators held their breath in their amazement, and were then melted to tears.[62]

Beecher then addressed his audience, explaining that the child, baptized Fanny Virginia Casseopia Lawrence, had been discovered "sore and tattered and unclean" by a nurse tending Union soldiers in Fairfax, Virginia, who adopted Fanny as her own. "Look upon this child," said Beecher, "tell me if you ever saw a fairer, sweeter face?" Beecher then made explicit the fate that awaited little girls like Fanny. "This is a sample of the slavery which clutches for itself everything fair and attractive," he explained. "The loveliness of this face, the beauty of this figure, would only make her so much more valuable for lust."[63] Like "Ellen," who had been saved from yellow-eyed Elder Matthewson, Fanny was presented as a white-looking female rescued from the grips of a lecherous slaveholder. Beecher's rhetoric (as it had with the otherwise anonymous "little slave girl" before her) also placed Fanny alongside the children of his own congregation, bemoaning slavery's trespasses not upon black children but on "fair and attractive" white ones. While their children were sheltered from the ravages of slavery, he intoned, Fanny (until "redeemed") had been left exposed.

Ironically, we cannot even be certain that Fanny was *not* a free white child. In the autobiography of Catherine Lawrence, Fanny's benefactor, the author consistently evaded the question of whether the child had, in fact, ever been enslaved or whether both of her parents may have been white.[64] Fanny's ambiguous past, however, makes it all the more clear that Beecher, and perhaps Lawrence herself, saw a profit in the presentation of a white-looking slave girl no matter what her true status. As long as children who looked so white were enslaved, he could argue, no white child was safe. "While your children are brought up to fear and serve the Lord," Beecher declared, "this little one, just as beautiful, would be made, through slavery, a child of damnation."[65] The lines of sentimentality and sexuality crossed at the point of sympathy, thereby deepening the audience's response to each girl's possibly tragic end and spurring them to act in order to preserve her from it.[66] Winning the war, in turn, was the only way to protect the virtue of white-looking little girls like Fanny: "let your soul burn with fiery indignation against the horrible system which turns into chattels such fair children of God! May God strike for our armies and the right that this accursed thing may be utterly destroyed!"[67] Instead of a battle for black freedom, the war to end slavery, in Beecher's words, became a means to preserve the freedom and purity of the white race, both things that slavery seemed to threaten. The future of the Union—embodied in a young unspoiled "white" girl rather than a black one—was at stake.

It is chilling to consider, however, how closely Beecher's description of Fanny follows that of an auctioneer in a slave market.[68] As with the antislavery story about Ellen, "Sold in Savannah" (recall the auctioneer's words: "it isn't every day such angeliferous loveliness comes to the hammer"), Beecher made his appeal by pointing to Fanny's "fair, sweet face," and thus to the price she could have commanded. White northern viewers, in turn, valued each girl's presentation for much the same qualities that would have brought her owner a considerable sum in the slave market: her gender and the whiteness of her skin.[69] The kind of looking encouraged by the public presentation of Fanny and the others, in turn, was unmistakably akin to the very acts of "reading" bodies that occurred in the slave market. Like white-looking girls and women on the auction block, Fanny, Rosa, and Rebecca were subject to scrutiny by northern audiences and viewers. With the help of the Union army and well-meaning missionaries, the girls once again had a price attached to them—with the words "slave girl" used as a point of sale—although this time it was only their image to be bought and not their bodies. If their resemblance to white girls made them more valuable in the market, in Beecher's view, it also made them even more worthy of rescue than a child who did not look white.

The photographic medium used for the presentation of white-looking slave girls had its own particular effects and their black and white images reached a far broader audience than did the children themselves. Though the sponsors of these photographs (abolitionists and the Union Army) hoped to spark Northerners' outrage towards the institution of slavery, the effect these images had on their audiences may have been far more complicated. The power of photographs, as far as Victorian Americans were concerned, lay in their ability to "speak" truths otherwise inaudible. Every photographic image was a testimonial with the capacity to turn "the narrative status of its subject from fiction to fact."[70] Before the invention and spread of photography, the most compelling evidence of the cruelties of slavery was to be found in eyewitness accounts of slavery's atrocities, both written and oral—accounts that carried even more weight when delivered to audiences aloud, by former slaves.[71] Yet there was a vast difference between *reading* about slavery and *seeing* its effects for oneself. The surgeon who examined a fugitive slave named Gordon—the subject of the widely reproduced photograph "Scourged Back"—observed that "few sensation writers ever depicted worse punishments than this man must have received."[72] Indeed, a photograph allowed northern viewers to see Gordon's mutilated body for themselves, witnessing "firsthand" the evil effects of slavery. Images like the "Scourged Back" testified to slavery's atrocities in a way that written ex-slave narratives could not, since the cruel effects of slavery had been inscribed on the ex-slave's person *by the slaveholder himself*, rather than onto a page by a former slave. On seeing the "Scourged Back" in 1863, an editor at the New York *Independent* remarked that the photograph "tells the story in a way that even Mrs. Stowe cannot approach, because it tells the story to the eye."[73]

The "reality" introduced by the photograph, in turn, opened up new avenues of sympathy and, further still, of imagined pain and suffering. The sight of Gordon's back, covered in hundreds of thickened scars, forced viewers not only to see the effects of slavery but to imagine the scene of the slave's punishment, the very laying on the lash. Indeed, the image even placed them in the position—behind Gordon's back—of the punisher. Photographs of these white-looking slave girls, no less than the picture of Gordon, exposed the evils of southern slavery. Yet the fantasy they inspired was a quite different one. In the images of Rosa, Rebecca, and Fanny, the slaveholder's violence was read by viewers on the unmarked surfaces of their light-skinned bodies rather than, as with Gordon, stated in firm welts on the skin. The girls' portraits invited viewers—particularly male viewers—to imagine them as the light-skinned "fancy girls" for sale in the New Orleans slave market, young women highly valued for their service as concubines to the wealthy white men of New Orleans.

These photographs presented a female body that existed for the viewer somewhere between the real and the imagined, and in this respect were much like pornographic photography of the nineteenth century. With the invention of photography, pornographers let the direct gazes of *real* women return the stares of the male spectator rather than those of fictionalized or painted figures. Like pornographic photographs, images of white-looking slave girls did not replace fantasies of beautiful mulatto and octoroon women enslaved and violated but rather further encouraged them.[74] Seeing the portrait of Rebecca kneeling in prayer, a white northern audience could have read in her white skin a history of "miscegenation," generations of it, resulting from the sexual

Mary Niall Mitchell

interaction of white masters with their female slaves.[75] And Rebecca's girlish form, as with Fanny's, raised the possibility of future violations (whereas the image of a woman might have represented virtue already lost) and further invited the exercise of viewers' imaginations as they looked at her photograph.

If viewers read a sexual future in the photographs of these girls, however, they were also doing their utmost to read their race. We can imagine that viewers studied the portraits carefully, searching each photograph for the curve of the nose or the shape of the head that might indicate the child's African ancestry. Nineteenth-century scholars and scientists valued the "mute testimony" that photography provided as a means to scrutinize human subjects for physical signs of intelligence, potential for criminality, or evidence of a deranged mind.[76] A physician writing in 1859 insisted that one could uncover the physical and psychological essences of a person with photography because only in photographs could one rely on the "silent but telling language of nature."[77] The medium of photography also developed in tandem with theories concerning the separate origins of the races and the biology of racial difference proffered by the "American School" of anthropology (Louis Agassiz and Samuel Morton the most prominent among them) in the 1850s and 1860s.[78] With the popularity of the easily reproducible *carte de visite*, photographic images had just begun to provide a new way of gathering anthropological knowledge—a new way of presenting and seeing race—using the body as evidence.[79] Louis Agassiz himself had several daguerreotype portraits of slaves taken in South Carolina in 1850, presumably to provide visual "proof" of the written observations he made during his visit concerning the purported differences in limb size and muscle structure between African-born slaves and whites.[80] As a means of discovering an underlying "truth" not directly visible to the eye, in turn, photography in the nineteenth century enhanced the act of looking itself.[81]

The desire to see certain people's "true" racial identity surfaces throughout Northerners' accounts of their visits to the South during the Civil War. What confounded them was that one could not always observe traces of "African blood" in a person. A Boston "traveler" who visited a New Orleans jail reported that among those people of color imprisoned for not having a pass were "several women that in New York or Boston would pass for white women, without the slightest difficulty or suspicion" and a young girl "with a beautiful face . . . whose complexion was that of a pretty Boston brunette."[82] And a correspondent for the *New York Times* encountered a "colored soldier" in the Louisiana Native Guards whom he took for a white man, only to be corrected by the commanding officer. "And do you really think him white?" the colonel asked. "Well you may, Sir: but that man is a 'negro'—one who carries the so-called curse of African blood in his veins." And yet the writer concluded after studying the "fine-looking young man, not unlike General McClellan in mould of features," that he "would have defied the most consummate expert in Niggerology, by the aid of the most powerful microscope, to discover the one drop of African blood in the man's veins."[83]

Similarly, the ways in which the children from Louisiana were described, photographed, and publicly presented as freed slaves suggests that although audiences were scandalized by the children's whiteness, they may also have been troubled by the inability to see their blackness. If the end of slavery is what the children's sponsors sought, their careful presentations of white-looking slave girls also must have had an unintended effect—that is, they hinted at the dangers of emancipation. Though slavery was inscribed in the lives and on the skins of the adults in the group—Wilson Chinn had the initials of his former master branded on his forehead, Mary Johnson bore on her left arm "scars of three cuts given her by her mistress with a rawhide" and on her back "scars of more than fifty cuts given her by her master," and Robert Whitehead's history was marked by the dollar amounts at which he had been bought and sold—the unscarred, racially ambiguous bodies of the children made it clear that the old ways of "reading" slavery and race were insufficient.[84] Images such as these, in fact, may have further endorsed the determination of a person's blackness through blood and descent, since they rendered physical manifestations of race unreliable.[85] If the words "slave child" beneath the girls' portraits kept them from walking out into the world as white, how else would one be able to discern nonwhiteness when slavery no longer held such people in check?

Further still, what would this state of affairs mean for those who considered themselves white? If even photographs could not detect "African" blood, then was the race of every white person soon to be in question? Consider the story that accompanied the picture of "white and colored slaves" in *Harper's Weekly*. With indignation, the writer recounted the ejection of the three whitest-looking children, Rebecca, Charles, and Rosa, from the St. Lawrence Hotel in Philadelphia while on tour there. The hotel's proprietor insisted that since the children had been slaves they "must therefore be colored persons" and that he kept a hotel for "white people."[86] Beneath a photographic portrait of the three children taken in Philadelphia after the incident, this story served as part of the caption: "These children were turned out of the St. Lawrence Hotel, Chestnut St, Philadelphia, on account of Color." The story was a critique of northern white supremacy and prejudice against "colored" people, but for viewers already unsettled by the appearances of the children, it also must have confirmed their fears. If white-looking children could be denied entrance to a public establishment on the suspicion that they had been ("colored") slaves, then any white person's race might be open to question.

It was to counter such fears, perhaps, that the children's sponsors staged a few photographs that were far less subtle than the vignette portraits of Rosa and Rebecca, and which made explicit the threat slavery (and not emancipation) posed to the liberties of white people. In one, Rebecca is by herself, seated and gazing up at the American flag. The caption beneath her reads: "Oh! How I Love the Old Flag," representing the Union as a refuge for white-looking children from the evils of slavery. Another portrait shows the three children, Rosa, Charles, and Rebecca, each wrapped in their own flag, with the words "Our Protection" printed beneath them. One interpretation might be that these patriotic photographs critiqued the system of slavery, which denied white-looking children the protections enjoyed by free white children and threatened the safety of any who looked like them. But another reading of these images finds a young, white face on emancipation—rather than a young black one—and suggests that the postbellum United States, despite its millions of black inhabitants, would remain a white nation.[87]

If appeals for slavery's demise took the form of white-looking slave girls, the work of northern "civilization" in the South after emancipation was embodied in a black child. The photographic portrait of a woman named Harriet Murray with two of her students, Elsie and Puss, taken in South Carolina in 1866, would have been a familiar sort of picture to northern readers and reformers after the war. In the photograph, Murray, a white woman, occupies the role of the civilizer as she directs the attention of the two girls to the book in her lap. (As one writer has observed, Murray's arm around the smallest child, Elsie, "compels her attention as much as it embraces."[88]) Instead of the sentimental poses and velvet-trimmed frocks in which Rosa, Rebecca, and Fanny had appeared, Elsie and Puss stand plainly before the viewer in boots without laces and hand-me-down dresses. Further still, the "setting" given to them was not a Victorian parlor but a cultivated field.

The disparities between Rosa's portrait and the photograph of Elsie and Puss reflect both the passage of time—from the height of the Civil War to the years immediately following—and the importance of children, black and white, to the sectional politics of the nineteenth century. Onto the bodies of white-looking slave girls, abolitionists and generals had hoped that white Northerners could project their hatred and fear of slavery, even their fascination with it. After emancipation, however, missionaries sought to quiet anxieties about the responses of millions of black freedpeople to freedom (that they would migrate to the North, kill their former masters, or refuse to work, letting cotton and sugarcane rot in the fields[89]) with images of black freedgirls in a rural landscape under the civilizing influence of a white female teacher.

Although the picture of a white-looking slave child may have fueled northern indignation toward the South during the war, Rosa's image would not have been a welcome one once slavery (and the caption "slave child") no longer kept her from "passing" as the "white" child she appeared to be. Rather, what most white Northerners wanted to imagine about the South after emancipation was just what they saw in the picture of Elsie and Puss with their teacher: dutiful black children (so "black" that they could not pass for "white") ready to receive the order and discipline of a victorious northern white "civilization."

The photograph was staged, of course: the white woman in broad skirts with her young black charges, the painted backdrop, the open book. Yet like the images of Rosa and Rebecca, this propaganda photograph placed ideas about black and white childhood at the political center of emancipation. If Rosa and Rebecca seemed to represent the endangered future of both the white race and the Union itself, then Elsie and Puss embodied the future of freedpeople under the careful guidance of white northern "civilization." Just as Rosa (a white-looking girl) made white children seem more vulnerable than a white-skinned boy might have, Elsie and Puss (black girls) may have represented freedpeople as more gentle and compliant than would their male counterparts. As little girls, they could be posed more closely to their white female guardian, thereby appearing to be tightly under her influence. (Though there were pictures of freed boys in the series that included Elsie and Puss's portrait, they never appeared in close contact with their teachers. They either stood stock-still behind her or were in group photographs unaccompanied by an adult.[90])

Yet by underscoring the freed girls' need for "civilization" (the white woman pointing toward the book), rather than their innocence or vulnerability (Rosa's doleful, pleading gaze), the creators of this image devised a distance between the white child and the black child, an imaginary space at once racial and geographical—orchestrating what was, in fact, an inversion of Rosa's image. In the eyes of northern viewers, children like Elsie and Puss once "civilized" would dutifully cook and clean in the rural, plantation setting into which they had been born and in which they appeared beside their teacher. Unlike Rosa's photograph, this image was not staged to bring the enslaved into the parlors of the white northern middle class, except perhaps as maids.[91] Such an image assured viewers of the existence of a stable supply of industrious black workers in the South, labor that would continue to support the nation's economy and undergird the privileged, labor-free existence of middle-class white children. The portrait of Harriet Murray, Elsie, and Puss, then, was an image to counter the fright that Rosa had inspired: a sign that the Union had been preserved, that black freedchildren were under the civilizing influence of white northern women, and that white children were protected at last from the "vile" enslavement that had threatened them.

Mary Niall Mitchell

Notes

The author would like to thank the following people for reading drafts of this article or otherwise lending support for its completion: Connie Atkinson, Kathleen Barry, Adrienne Berney, Lisa Brock, Erin Clune, Ada Ferrer, Martha Hodes, Walter Johnson. Robin D.G. Kelley, Ellen Noonan, Lucy Maddox, Meg Mitchell, Evelyn and Walter Mitchell, Jr., Margaret and William Mitchell, Jon Pult, Kate Sampsell, Julius Scott, participants at the Berkshire Conference on the History of Women and Gender, the History Department of the University of New Orleans, and anonymous reviewers for this journal. Any errors are my own. Much of the research and writing of this article was completed with the support of a Harry Frank Guggenheim Foundation Dissertation Fellowship. Thanks, as well, to Kathleen Collins for her work on the photographic history of many of the images used here; to John Magill at the Historic New Orleans Collection; and to archivists from all of the repositories cited here for their assistance with reproductions and permissions for publication of images from their holdings.

1. Robert Taft, *Photography and the American Scene* (1938; New York: Dover Publications, 1964), ch. 8. For a technical index of *cartes de visite* and their uses, see William C. Darrah, *Cartes de Visite in Nineteenth-Century Photography* (Gettysburg, Penn: William C. Darrah, 1981).

2. General Order No. 64, Headquarters, Dept of the Gulf, New Orleans, Aug. 29, 1863. *War of the Rebellion: Official Records of the Union and Confederate Armies*. Series I, vol. 26, p. 704; Kathleen Collins, "Portraits of Slave Children," *History of Photography* 9 (July–Sept. 1985): 187–88.

3. Banks appointed a Board of Education in March of 1864 to direct the establishment of freedpeople's schools. But by then at least seven black schools already had been established and fourteen hundred students enrolled in what was, arguably, the first major effort at public education for freed people in the South. See Donald R. Devore and Joseph Logsdon, *Crescent City Schools: Public Education in New Orleans 1841–1991* (Lafayette: Center for Louisiana Studies, 1991), 57.

4. Collins, "Portraits of Slave Children," 187–210; and *Harper's Weekly*, Jan. 30, 1864, p. 69 and 71.

5. Ibid., 203.

6. Quoted in the *National Antislavery Standard*, Dec. 5, 1863.

7. Collins, "Portraits of Slave Children," 189.

8. *Harper's Weekly*, Jan. 30, 1864, p. 71; curator Adrienne Berney at the Louisiana State Museum has traced Rebecca to a group of slaves belonging to an inhabitant of the (now) historic Pontalba buildings in New Orleans's French Quarter. In 1860, she appears in the census rolls as the seven-year-old "mulatto" slave of John M. Huger. Huger also owned her mother and her grandmother.

9. In images, according to W. J. T. Mitchell, "what expression amounts to is the artful planting of certain clues in a picture that allow us to form an act of ventriloquism, an act which endows the picture with eloquence, and particularly with a nonvisual and verbal eloquence." W. J. T. Mitchell, *Iconology: Image, Text, Ideology* (Chicago: Univ. of Chicago Press, 1986), 41. See also Allan Sekula, "On the Invention of Photographic Meaning," in Victor Burgin, ed., *Thinking Photography* (London: MacMillan Education Press, 1982).

10. Roland Barthes, *Camera Lucida: Reflections on Photography*, trans. Richard Howard (New York: Hill and Wang, 1981), 26.

11. Thanks to Martha Hodes for this point.

12. The figure of the child often becomes a metaphor for adult desires and political aims. See Carolyn Steedman, *Past Tenses: Essays on Writing, Autobiography, and History* (London: Rivers Oram Press, 1992), 194. Steedman makes a theoretical distinction between this figure and children as a group: "'the child' is an historical construct," the product of adult imagination and projection, whereas "children" are individuals experiencing childhood. For further explorations of this idea see Carolyn Kay Steedman, *Landscape for a Good Woman: A Story of Two Lives* (New Brunswick, N.J.: Rutgers Univ. Press, 1986); and Carolyn Steedman, *Strange Dislocations: Childhood and the Idea of Human Interiority 1780–1930* (Cambridge: Harvard Univ. Press, 1995).

13. The notion of the United States as a "white nation" was not new. Historian Joanne Pope Melish has noted that in the eighteenth century, many residents of the New England states imagined that gradual emancipation in the North would somehow "restore" the region's homogeneity, that "a free New England would be a white New England." Joanne Pope Melish, *Disowning Slavery: Gradual Emancipation and "Race" in New England, 1780–1860* (Ithaca, N.Y.: Cornell Univ. Press, 1998), 164. On race and emancipation, see Saidiya V. Hartman, *Scenes of Subjection: Terror, Slavery, and Self-Making in Nineteenth-Century America* (New York: Oxford Univ. Press, 1997), 117–18.

Visual images (as well as print media like newspapers, maps, and census rolls) are a vital part of the production of a nation, both as an idea—an "imagined community"—and a political entity. Benedict Anderson, *Imagined Communities: Reflections on the Origin and Spread of Nationalism* (New York: Verso, 1983), passim; on visual images, race, and nationhood, see Shawn Michelle Smith, "Photographing the 'American Negro': Nation, Race, and Photography at the Paris Exposition of 1900," in Lisa Bloom, ed., *With Other Eyes: Looking at Race and Gender in Visual Culture* (Minneapolis: Univ. of Minnesota Press, 1999).

14. Elsa Barkley Brown makes this point about the "relational nature of difference" in the lives of black women and white women. See Barkley Brown, "Polyrhythms and Improvisation: Lessons for Women's History," *History Workshop* 31 (Spring 1991): 86, 88.

15. Thomas Holt poses the question of how race and racism are "reproduced" in "Marking: Race, Race-Making, and the Writing of History," *American Historical Review* 100 (Feb. 1995): 1–20.

16. Iver Bernstein, *The New York City Draft Riots: Their Significance for American Society and Politics in the Age of the Civil War* (New York: Oxford Univ. Press, 1990). Most abolitionists came from the middle class, although there were substantial numbers of "skilled" workers and artisans and a very small percentage of "unskilled" workers involved in the movement as well. See Paul Goodman, *Of One Blood: Abolitionism and the Origins of Racial Equality* (Berkeley: Univ. of California Press, 1998), ch. 11, esp. 145–47; Edward Magdol, *The Antislavery Rank and File: A Social Profile of the Abolitionist Constituency* (Westport, Conn.: Greenwood Press, 1986), ch. 6.

17. The "displacement" of class issues with the language of race and gender was characteristic of antebellum sentimental fiction. See Amy Schrager Lang, "Class and the Strategies of Sympathy," in Shirley Samuels, ed., *The Culture of Sentiment: Race, Gender, and Sentimentality in Nineteenth-Century America* (New York: Oxford Univ. Press, 1992). Ex-slave and abolitionist Frederick Douglass believed that the defeat of slavery could

come only with the support of the working class. "It is not to the rich that we are to look," he said in 1852, "but to the poor, to the hardhanded working men of the country; these are to come to the rescue of the slave." Quoted in Herbert Aptheker, *Abolitionism: A Revolutionary Movement* (Boston: Twayne Publishers, 1989), 36.

18. Carol Wilson and Calvin D. Wilson, "White Slavery: An American Paradox," *Slavery and Abolition* 19 (Apr. 1998): 1–23. I have chosen to use the term "white slaves" instead of "white slavery" in the interest of clarity and historical accuracy. Most accounts I have seen pertaining to the subject at hand discuss "white slaves" rather than "white slavery." The latter term also has a trickier history. White northern workers and labor advocates used "white slavery" (as well as "wage slavery") in the 1830s and 1840s as a critique of the labor system. As historian David Roediger has noted, "white slavery" was a complicated term that seemed to identify white workers with slaves (problematic since many laborers did not favor any association with black Americans), while it also suggested that the enslavement of whites was more objectionable than that of blacks. By the 1850s, labor advocates dropped the term in favor of "free labor." See David E. Roediger, *The Wages of Whiteness: Race and the Making of the American Working Class* (New York: Verso, 1991), ch. 4. "White slavery" was also a term associated with female prostitution but did not come into common usage until Progressive-era anti-prostitution campaigns in the early twentieth century, a time when "formal" networks of prostitution had become regional and even international in scope. In the mid–nineteenth century, however, prostitution was referred to simply as a "social evil." See Barbara Meil Hobson, *Uneasy Virtue: The Politics of Prostitution and the American Reform Tradition* (New York: Basic Books, 1987), 141–45; and Margit Stange, *Personal Property: Wives, White Slaves, and the Market in Women* (Baltimore: The Johns Hopkins University Press, 1998).

19. "A White Woman Sold into Slavery," correspondence of the *Tribune*, repr. in *The National Anti-Slavery Standard*, Jan. 3, 1863.

20. "A White Slave," correspondence of the *Tribune*, repr. in *The National Anti-Slavery Standard*, Apr. 4, 1863.

21. Another fictional account of white slavery was William Wells Brown's *Clotel; or The President's Daughter* (1853). See Joanne Pope Melish's discussion of *Clotel* in Melish, *Disowning Slavery*, 272–77.

22. "Sold at Savannah, in Two Chapters," repr. from *Chamber's Journal* in the *National Anti-Slavery Standard*, Sept. 12 and 19, 1863.

23. "The White Slaves of the South," correspondence of *The Grand Rapids Eagle*, repr. in *The National Anti-Slavery Standard*, Sept. 5, 1863. Another story involved a white soldier in the 78th Ohio, who had been sold into slavery "out of some charitable institute [in Kentucky] to which he had been committed as a vagrant." "Peculiarities of the Peculiar Institution," correspondence of the Cincinnati *Commercial* repr. in *The National Anti-Slavery Standard*, Apr. 11, 1863.

24. Martha Hodes, *White Women, Black Men: Illicit Sex in the 19th-Century South* (New Haven: Yale Univ. Press, 1997), 48. *Mary Chestnut's Civil War*, ed., C. Vann Woodward (New Haven: Yale Univ. Press, 1981), 29.

25. The life of Alexina Morrison illustrates well the furor that racially ambiguous people could create in the antebellum South. See Walter Johnson, "The Slave Trader, the White Slave, and the Politics of Racial Determination in the 1850s," *The Journal of American History* 87 (June 2000): 13–38.

26. Viviana A. Zelizer, *Pricing the Priceless Child: The Changing Social Value of Children* (Princeton, N.J.: Princeton Univ. Press, 1985).

27. Leslie Williams, "The Look of Little Girls: John Everett Millais and the Victorian Art Market," and Carol Mavor, "Dream Rushes: Lewis Carroll's Photographs of the Little Girl," both in Claudia Nelson and Lynne Vallone, eds., *The Girl's Own: Cultural Histories of the Anglo-American Girl, 1830–1915* (Athens: Univ. of Georgia Press, 1994); Anne Higonnet, *Pictures of Innocence: The History and Crisis of Ideal Childhood* (New York: Thames and Hudson, 1998), ch. 3; Karin Calvert, *Children in the House: The Material Culture of Early Childhood, 1600–1900* (Boston: Northeastern Univ. Press, 1992).

28. Taft, *Photography and the American Scene*, 140. Heinz K. Henisch and Bridget A. Henisch, *The Photographic Experience 1839–1914: Images and Attitudes* (University Park: Pennsylvania State Univ. Press, 1994), ch. 2. Nell Irvin Painter has noted the importance of dress and "props" in *cartes de visite* portraits "self-fashioned" by antislavery activist and former slave Sojourner Truth. Truth used knitting yarn, reading glasses, and books to convey motherliness and wisdom. Nell Irvin Painter, *Sojourner Truth: A Life, A Symbol* (New York: W.W. Norton and Co., 1996), 196.

29. Sojourner Truth was also one of the first antislavery activists to employ the camera's potential for representation (through portraiture) and the *carte de visite* as a means of fund-raising. See Painter, "Representing Truth: Sojourner Truth's Knowing and Becoming Known," *The Journal of American History* 81 (Sept. 1994): 461–92; and Painter, *Sojourner Truth*, ch. 20. Fund-raising through the sale of photographs became especially popular during the Civil War. Kathleen Collins, "Photographic Fundraising: Civil War Philanthropy," *History of Photography* 11 (July–Sept. 1987): 173–87; and Collins, "Living Skeletons: *Cartes de visite* Propaganda in the American Civil War," *History of Photography* 12 (Apr.–June 1988): 103–20. On the invention of the photograph album to display *cartes de visite* see Taft, *Photography and the American Scene*, 140 and ch. 8.

30. Gillian Brown, "Getting in the Kitchen with Dinah: Domestic Politics in *Uncle Tom's Cabin*," *American Quarterly* 36 (Fall 1984): 505; Harriet A. Jacobs, *Incidents in the Life of a Slave Girl, Written by Herself*, ed., L. Maria Child (Boston, 1861), repr. and reedited by Jean Fagan Yellin (Cambridge: Harvard Univ. Press, 1987). What made Jacobs's narrative so effective was her description of the household in the slaveholding South as "the ground of the institution's most terrifying intimacies." See Hortense J. Spillers, "Changing the Letter: the Yokes, the Jokes of Discourse or, Mrs. Stowe, Mr. Reed," in Deborah E. McDowell and Arnold Rampersad, eds., *Slavery and the Literary Imagination* (Baltimore: The Johns Hopkins Univ. Press, 1987), 28. See also Philip Fisher, *Hard Facts: Setting and Form in the American Novel* (New York: Oxford Univ. Press, 1987), ch. 2.

31. Laura Wexler, "Seeing Sentiment: Photography, Race, and the Innocent Eye," in Marianne Hirsch, ed., *The Familial Gaze* (Hanover, N.H.: Univ. Press of New England, 1999), 256. On the "geographical distance" (more felt than real) between the North and South in this period, see Ronald G. Walters, *The Antislavery Appeal: American Abolitionism after 1830* (Baltimore: The Johns Hopkins Univ. Press, 1976), 59.

32. Elizabeth B. Clark, "Sacred Rights of the Weak: Pain and Sympathy in Antebellum America." *Journal of American History* 82 (Sept. 1995), 476. Similar expressions of empathy arose in the writings of antislavery feminists, who paralleled their plight as women with that of the enslaved population of the South. See Jean Fagan Yellin, *Women & Sisters: The Antislavery Feminists in American Culture* (New Haven: Yale Univ. Press, 1989), 50; and "Introduction: Familial Looking," in Hirsch, ed., *The Familial Gaze*.

33. Bernard Wishy, *The Child and the Republic* (Philadelphia: Univ. of Pennsylvania Press, 1968); Mary Ryan, *Cradle of the Middle Class: The Family in Oneida County, New*

York, 1790–1865 (Cambridge: Harvard Univ. Press, 1981); Mary Ryan, *The Empire of the Mother: American Writing about Domesticity 1830–1860* (New York: Institute for Research in History and the Haworth Press, 1982); Richard Broadhead, "Sparing the Rod: Discipline and Fiction in Antebellum America," *Representations* 21 (Winter 1988): 67–96.

34. Karen Sánchez-Eppler, "Temperance in the Bed of a Child: Incest and Social Order in Nineteenth-Century America," *American Quarterly* 47 (Mar. 1995): 4. The figure of the "daughter-as-redeemer" displayed both moral purity and strength of character. See Deborah Gorham, *The Victorian Girl and the Feminine Ideal* (Bloomington: Indiana Univ. Press, 1983), 42.

35. Although her concern is not race, Deborah Gorham notes that the image of the good girl in Victorian culture was often contrasted with her opposite. Gorham, *The Victorian Girl*, 49.

36. Harriet Beecher Stowe, *Uncle Tom's Cabin or, Life among the Lowly* (1852; New York: Harper and Row, 1965), 247. See also "The Meaning of Little Eva," the introduction to Ann Douglas, *The Feminization of American Culture* (New York: Alfred A. Knopf, 1977).

37. Stowe, *Uncle Tom's Cabin*, 249.

38. *Freedmen's Journal*, quoted in the *American Missionary*, Nov. 1864, p. 276.

39. *American Missionary*, June 1865, p. 126.

40. *American Missionary*, Mar. 1859, p. 68.

41. *American Missionary*, Oct. 1860, p. 234.

42. Hartman, *Scenes of Subjection*, p. 5.

43. *American Missionary*, Mar. 1859, p. 67.

44. Stowe, *Uncle Tom's Cabin*, 43, 496.

45. Stowe, *Uncle Tom's Cabin*, 242.

46. "White and Colored Slaves," *Harper's Weekly*, Jan. 30, 1864, p. 71.

47. Ex-slave narrators throughout the nineteenth century had to concern themselves with the authentication of their narratives. This involved using specific names and places in their accounts and providing a written introduction by a white sponsor in order to prove their autobiographies were true and not simply the creation of abolitionists. William L. Andrews, *To Tell a Free Story: The First Century of Afro-American Autobiography, 1760–1865* (Urbana: Univ. of Illinois Press, 1986), 26. See also Charles T. Davis and Henry Louis Gates, Jr., *The Slave's Narrative* (New York: Oxford Univ. Press, 1985); John Sekora, "Black Message/White Envelope: Genre, Authenticity, and Authority in the Antebellum Slave Narrative," *Callaloo* 32 (Summer 1987): 482–515; Marion Wilson Starling, *The Slave Narrative: Its Place in American History*, 2nd ed. (Washington, D.C.: Howard Univ. Press, 1988), ch. 4.

48. *American Missionary*, Mar. 1860, p. 68–69.

49. *American Missionary*, Mar. 1860, p. 69.

50. Hartman, *Scenes of Subjection*, esp. 19–21. On the imaginings of abolitionists, see Clark, "Sacred Rights of the Weak," 479.

51. Jean Fagan Yellin, *Women & Sisters: The Antislavery Feminists in American Culture* (New Haven: Yale Univ. Press, 1989), 100.

52. Joy S. Kasson, *Marble Queens and Captives: Women in Nineteenth-Century American Sculpture* (New Haven: Yale Univ. Press, 1990), ch. 3; Yellin, *Women & Sisters*, ch. 5.

53. Kasson, *Marble Queens and Captives*, 75, 82. The quote from *Harper's Weekly* is also from ibid., 82.

54. Ibid., 55.

55. The quotes from Palmer and a nineteenth-century viewer (responding to *The White Captive*) are taken from ibid., 75–76.

56. Sánchez-Eppler, "Temperance in the Bed of a Child," 15. James Kincaid, *Child Loving: The Erotic Child and Victorian Culture* (New York: Routledge, 1992), 13; Higonnet, *Pictures of Innocence*, 36–39, 122–32. These views of girl children as sexually alluring dispute Deborah Gorham's idea that little girls somehow resolved the "tensions inherent in the Victorian view of female sexuality" and that idealized womanhood (in which women were seen as "pure" or "innocent") could "more appropriately be applied to daughters than to wives." I think there is truth in both interpretations of white little girls in the nineteenth century. Gorham, *The Victorian Girl*, 6–7.

57. Leslie Williams, "The Look of Little Girls: John Everett Millais and the Victorian Art Market," in *The Girls' Own: Cultural Histories of the Anglo-American Girl, 1830–1915* (Athens: Univ. of Georgia Press, 1994), 124.

58. Millais's *Cherry Ripe* sold six hundred thousand copies in England when it was reproduced as a color centerfold in a Christmas annual. Higonnet, *Pictures of Innocence*, 51. See also Pamela Tamarkin Reis and Laurel Bradley, "Victorian Centerfold: Another Look at Millais's *Cherry Ripe*," *Victorian Studies* 35 (Winter 1992): 201–6; Robert M. Polhemus, "John Millais's Children: Faith, Erotics, and *The Woodsman's Daughter*," *Victorian Studies* 7 (Spring 1994): 433–50.

59. Nina Auerbach, *Romantic Imprisonment: Women and Other Glorified Outcasts* (New York: Columbia Univ. Press, 1985), ch. 9. See also David M. Lubin's discussion of Guy and Carroll in Lubin, *Picturing a Nation: Art and Social Change in Nineteenth-Century America* (New Haven: Yale Univ. Press, 1994), ch. 5.

60. Ronald J. Walters, "The Erotic South: Civilization and Sexuality in American Abolitionism," in John R. McKivigan, ed., *History of the American Abolitionist Movement*, vol. I, *Abolitionism and American Reform* (New York: Garland Publishing, 1999).

61. On the literature of the "tragic mulatto," see Jean Fagan Yellin, *Women & Sisters*, 71–76; Karen Sánchez-Eppler, *Touching Liberty: Abolition, Feminism, and the Politics of the Body* (Berkeley: Univ. of California Press, 1993), ch. 1; and Susan Gillman, "The Mulatto, Tragic or Triumphant? The Nineteenth-Century American Race Melodrama," in Samuels, *The Culture of Sentiment*.

62. *American Missionary*, June 1863, p. 131.

63. Ibid., 131.

64. Catherine S. Lawrence, *Autobiography or Sketch of Life and Labors of Miss Catherine S. Lawrence Who in Early Life Distinguished Herself as a Bitter Opponent of Slavery and Intemperance, and Later in Life as a Nurse in the Late War; and for Other Patriotic and Philanthropic Services*, rev. ed. (Albany, N.Y.: James B. Lyon Printer, 1896), 140. Thanks to Mary L. White, a participant at the 1999 Berkshire Conference for the History of Women & Gender, for bringing Lawrence's memoir to my attention.

65. *American Missionary*, June 1863, p. 132.

66. Sentimental fiction was intended to have similar effects on readers. See Samuels, ed., *Culture of Sentiment*; and Fisher, *Hard Facts*, ch. 2.

67. *American Missionary*, June 1863, p. 132.

68. Walter Johnson, *Soul by Soul: Life Inside the Antebellum Slave Market* (Cambridge: Harvard Univ. Press, 2000), passim.

69. Ibid., ch. 5.

70. Jennifer Green-Lewis, *Framing the Victorians: Photography and the Culture of Realism* (Ithaca, N.Y.: Cornell Univ. Press, 1996), 100, 3–4.

71. Clark, "'The Sacred Rights of the Weak,'" 467–68.

72. S. K. Towle, Surgeon, 30th Massachusetts Volunteers, to W. J. Dale, Surgeon-General of the State of Massachusetts, Apr. 16, 1863, cited in Kathleen Collins, "The Scourged Back," *History of Photography* 9 (Jan.–Mar. 1985), 44. Towle's comments were printed on the verso of the *cartes de visite* made of Gordon, printed in Philadelphia. The photographic printers titled the image "Scourged Back."

73. Quoted in the *National Anti-Slavery Standard*, June 20, 1863, beneath the heading: "The 'Peculiar Institution' Illustrated." Like the group portrait of "Emancipated Slaves White and Colored," this photograph was made into an illustration and printed in *Harper's Weekly*, appearing on July 4, 1863. See Kathleen Collins, "The Scourged Back," 43–45.

74. See Abigail Solomon-Godeau, "The Legs of the Countess," *October* 39 (Winter 1996), 98.

75. Sánchez-Eppler, *Touching Liberty*, 18, 23. On Southerners' readings of a "white" woman enslaved, see Johnson, "The Slave Trader, the White Slave, and the Politics of Racial Determination in the 1850s"; and of slaves in the market, see Johnson, *Soul by Soul.*

76. John Tagg, *The Burden of Representation: Essays on Photographies and Histories* (Amherst: Univ. of Massachusetts Press, 1988), 78. The phrase "mute testimony" comes from Allan Sekula. "The Body and the Archive," *October* 39 (Winter 1986), 6. The invention and proliferation of photography in the nineteenth century was part of a developing system of surveillance and subjection of particular groups of society, most especially children, workers, the insane, and criminals. Michel Foucault, *Discipline and Punish: The Birth of the Prison*, trans. Alan Sheridan (New York: Vintage Books, 1977), 170–94.

77. H.W. Diamond, *Lancet*, Jan. 22, 1859, p. 89, quoted in Tagg, *The Burden of Representation*, 79.

78. For a history of the "American School," see William Stanton, *The Leopard's Spots: Scientific Attitudes toward Race in America, 1815–1859* (Chicago: Univ. of Chicago Press, 1960). Agassiz is quoted in Stephen Jay Gould, *The Mismeasure of Man* (1981; New York: W. W. Norton, 1996), 77. See also Gould's analysis of Agassiz, Morton, and their "evidence" in ch. 2.

79. See Brian Street, "British Popular Anthropology: Exhibiting and Photographing the Other," in Elizabeth Edwards, ed., *Anthropology and Photography 1860–1920* (New Haven: Yale Univ. Press, 1992), 130.

80. These images, found in a cabinet in 1976, were never published by Agassiz. See Alan Trachtenberg, *Reading American Photographs: Images as History Matthew Brady to Walker Evans* (New York: Hill and Wang, 1989), 53–56; Painter, *Sojourner Truth*, 196–97.

81. Green-Lewis, Framing the Victorians, 3–4; Jonathan Crary, *Techniques of the Observer: On Vision and Modernity in the Nineteenth Century* (Cambridge, Mass.: MIT Press, 1990), 23–24.

82. *National Anti-Slavery Standard*, Feb. 21, 1863. New Orleans was particularly well-known for its light-skinned slave women and free women of color, glamorized by stories of "quadroon balls" where white men chose mistresses from among fair-skinned young women of color. Monique Guillory, "Some Enchanted Evening on the Auction Block: The Cultural Legacy of the New Orleans Quadroon Balls" (Ph.D. diss., New York Univ., 1999); Caryn Cossé Bell, *Revolution, Romanticism, and the Afro-Creole Protest Tradition in Louisiana, 1718–1868* (Baton Rouge: Louisiana State Univ. Press, 1997), 112–14.

83. Quoted in *Harper's Weekly*, Feb. 28, 1863.

84. *Harper's Weekly*, "White and Colored Slaves," p. 71.

85. Thanks to an anonymous reviewer for this point.

86. *Harper's Weekly*, Jan. 30, 1864, p. 71.

87. On white nationalism and "free soil" ideology in the antebellum and Civil War years, see George M. Frederickson, *The Black Image in the White Mind: The Debate on Afro-American Character and Destiny 1817–1914* (1971; Hanover, N.H.: Wesleyan Univ. Press, 1987), ch. 5. See also Melish, *Disowning Slavery*, ch. 6.

88. Sánchez-Eppler, *Touching Liberty*, 7. One can find similar images of white women and black slaves in antislavery literature. For example, the frontispiece to an almanac printed in London in 1853 in honor of Harriet Beecher Stowe's *Uncle Tom's Cabin* depicts Liberty as a white woman reading from the Bible to a group of black children with chains around their feet, repr. in Clare Midley, *Women against Slavery: The British Campaigns, 1780–1870* (London: Routledge, 1992), 147.

89. The Freedmen's Bureau tried to counter these and other rumors (i.e., that "[the freed-people] are dying off," or "they are killing their children") with published reports from military officials in the field. *Letters from the South, relating to the condition of freedmen, addressed to Major General O.O. Howard, commissioner Bureau R., F., and A.L. by J.W. Alford, gen. sup't education, Bureau R., F., & A.L.* (Washington, D.C.: Howard Univ. Press, 1870), found in the collection of the Library of Congress, "From Slavery to Freedom: The African American Pamphlet Collection, 1824–1909."

90. For a fuller discussion of these photographs, see Mary Niall Mitchell, "Raising Freedom's Child: Race, Nation, and the Lives of Black Children in Nineteenth-Century Louisiana" (Ph.D. diss., New York Univ., 2001), ch. 3.

91. On some missionaries' attempts to fill white Northerners' requests for young black workers after emancipation, see Mitchell, "Raising Freedom's Child," ch. 3.

CHAPTER 7

The Female World of Love and Ritual

Relations Between Women in
Nineteenth-Century America[1]

Carroll Smith-Rosenberg

The female friendship of the nineteenth century, the long-lived, intimate, loving friendship between two women, is an excellent example of the type of historical phenomenon that most historians know something about, few have thought much about, and virtually no one has written about.[2] It is one aspect of the female experience which, consciously or unconsciously, we have chosen to ignore. Yet an abundance of manuscript evidence suggests that eighteenth- and nineteenth-century women routinely formed emotional ties with other women. Such deeply felt same-sex friendships were casually accepted in American society. Indeed, from at least the late eighteenth through the mid–nineteenth century, a female world of varied and yet highly structured relationships appears to have been an essential aspect of American society. These relationships ranged from the supportive love of sisters, through the enthusiasms of adolescent girls, to sensual avowals of love by mature women. It was a world in which men made but a shadowy appearance.[3]

Defining and analyzing same-sex relationships involves the historian in deeply problematical questions of method and interpretation. This is especially true since historians, influenced by Freud's libidinal theory, have discussed these relationships almost exclusively within the context of individual psychosexual development or, to be more explicit, psychopathology.[4] Seeing same-sex relationships in terms of a dichotomy between normal and abnormal, they have sought the origins of such apparent deviance in childhood or adolescent trauma and detected the symptoms of "latent" homosexuality in the lives of both those who later became "overtly" homosexual and those who did not. Yet theories concerning the nature and origins of same-sex relationships are frequently contradictory or based on questionable or arbitrary data. In recent years such hypotheses have been subjected to criticism, both from within and without the psychological professions. Historians who seek to work within a psychological framework, therefore, are faced with two hard questions: Do sound psychodynamic theories concerning the nature and origins of same-sex relationships exist? If so, does the historical datum exist which would permit the use of such dynamic models?

I would like to suggest an alternative approach to female friendships— one that would view them within a cultural and social setting rather than from an exclusively individual psychosexual perspective. Only by thus altering our approach will we be in the position to evaluate the appropriateness of particular dynamic interpretations. Intimate friendships between men and men and women and women existed in a larger world of social relations and social values. To interpret such friendships more fully, one must relate them to the structure of the American family and to the nature of sex-role divisions and of male-female relations, both within the family and in society generally. The female friendship must not be seen in isolation; it must be analyzed as one aspect of women's overall relations with one another. The ties between mothers and daughters, sisters, female cousins, and friends, at all stages of the female life cycle, constitute the most suggestive framework the historian can use to begin an analysis of intimacy and affection between women. Such an analysis would not only emphasize general cultural patterns rather than the internal dynamics of a particular family or childhood; it would shift the focus of the study from a concern with deviance to that of defining configurations of legitimate behavioral norms and options.[5]

This analysis will be based upon the correspondence and diaries of women and men in thirty-five families between the 1760s and the 1880s. These families, though limited in number, represented a broad range of the American middle class, from hard-pressed pioneer families and orphaned girls to daughters of the intellectual and social elite. It includes families from most geographic regions, rural and urban, and a spectrum of Protestant denominations ranging from

Mormon to orthodox Quaker. Although scarcely a comprehensive sample of America's increasingly heterogeneous population, it does, I believe, reflect accurately the literate middle class to which the historian working with letters and diaries is necessarily bound. It has involved an analysis of many thousands of letters written to women friends, kin, husbands, brothers, and children at every period of life from adolescence to old age. Some collections encompass virtually entire life spans; one contains over a hundred thousand letters as well as diaries and account books. It is my contention that an analysis of women's private letters and diaries which were never intended to be published permits the historian to explore a very private world of emotional realities central both to women's lives and to the middle-class family in nineteenth-century America.[6]

The question of female friendships is peculiarly elusive; we know so little, or perhaps have forgotten so much. An intriguing and almost alien form of human relationship, they flourished in a different social structure and amid different sexual norms. Before I attempt to reconstruct the social setting, therefore, it might be best to describe two not atypical friendships. These two friendships, intense, loving, and openly avowed, began during the women's adolescence and, despite subsequent marriages and geographic separation, continued throughout their lives. For nearly half a century these women played a central emotional role in one another's lives, writing time and again of their love and of the pain of separation. Paradoxically to twentieth-century minds, their love appears to have been both sensual and platonic.

Sarah Butler Wistar first met Jeannie Field Musgrove while vacationing with her family at Stockbridge, Massachusetts, in the summer of 1849.[7] Jeannie was then sixteen, Sarah fourteen. During two subsequent years spent together in boarding school, they formed a deep and intimate friendship. Sarah began to keep a bouquet of flowers before Jeannie's portrait and wrote complaining of the intensity and anguish of her affection.[8] Both young women assumed *noms de plume*, Jeannie a female name, Sarah a male one; they would use these secret names into old age.[9] They frequently commented on the nature of their affection: "If the day should come," Sarah wrote Jeannie in the spring of 1861, "when you failed me either through your fault or my own, I would forswear all human friendship, thenceforth." A few months later Jeannie commented: "Gratitude is a word I should never use toward you. It is perhaps a misfortune of such intimacy and love that it makes one regard all kindness as a matter of course, as one has always found it, as natural as the embrace in meeting."[10]

Sarah's marriage altered neither the frequency of their correspondence nor their desire to be together. In 1864, when twenty-nine, married, and a mother, Sarah wrote to Jeannie, "I shall be entirely alone [this coming week]. I can give you no idea how desperately I shall want you. . . ." After one such visit Jeannie, then a spinster in New York, echoed Sarah's longing: "Dear darling

Sarah! How I love you & how happy I have been! You are the joy of my life. . . . I cannot tell you how much happiness you gave me, nor how constantly it is all in my thoughts. . . . My darling how I long for the time when I shall see you. . . ." After another visit Jeannie wrote: "I want you to tell me in your next letter, to assure me, that I am your dearest. . . . I do not doubt you, & I am not jealous but I long to hear you say it once more & it seems already a long time since your voice fell on my ear. So just fill a quarter page with caresses & expressions of endearment. Your silly Angelina." Jeannie ended one letter, "Goodbye my dearest, dearest lover—ever your own Angelina." And another, "I will go to bed. . . . [though] I could write all night—A thousand kisses—I love you with my whole soul—your Angelina."

When Jeannie finally married in 1870, at the age of thirty-seven, Sarah underwent a period of extreme anxiety. Two days before Jeannie's marriage, Sarah, then in London, wrote desperately: "Dearest darling—How incessantly have I thought of you these eight days—all today—the entire uncertainty, the distance, the long silence—are all new features in my separation from you, grievous to be borne. . . . Oh Jeannie. I have thought & thought & yearned over you these two days. Are you married I wonder? My dearest love to you wherever and *who*ever you are."[11] As was true for many other women in this collection of thirty-five families, marriage brought Sarah and Jeannie physical separation; it did not cause emotional distance. Although at first they may have wondered how marriage would affect their relationship, their affection remained unabated throughout their lives, underscored by their loneliness and their desire to be together.[12]

During the same years that Jeannie and Sarah wrote of their love and need for each other, two slightly younger women began a similar odyssey of love, dependence, and—ultimately—physical, though not emotional, separation. Molly and Helena met in 1868, while both attended the Cooper Union Institution of Design for Women in New York City. For several years these young women studied and explored the city together, visited each other's families, and formed part of a social network of other artistic young women. Gradually, over the years, their initial friendship deepened into an intimacy that continued throughout their lives. The tone in the letters Molly wrote to Helena changed over these years from "My dear Helena," and signed "your attached friend," to "My dearest Helena," "My Dearest," "My Beloved," and signed "Thine always" or "thine Molly."[13]

The letters they wrote to each other during these first five years permit us to reconstruct something of their relationship together. As Molly wrote in one early letter:

I have not said to you in so many or so few words that I was happy with you during those few so incredibly short weeks but surely you do not need words to tell you what you must know. Those two or three days so dark without, so bright with firelight and contentment within I shall always remember as proof that, for a time, at least—I fancy for quite a long time—we might be sufficient for each other. We know that we can amuse each other for many idle hours together and now we know that we can also work together. And that means much, don't you think so?

She ended, "I shall return in a few days. Imagine yourself kissed many times by one who loves you so dearly."

The intensity and even physical nature of Molly's love was echoed in many of the letters she wrote during the next few years, as, for instance, in this short thank-you note for a small present:

Imagine yourself kissed a dozen times my darling. Perhaps it is well for you that we are far apart. You might find my thanks so expressed rather overpowering. I have that delightful feeling that it doesn't matter much what I say or how I say it, since we shall meet so soon and forget in that moment that we were ever separated. . . . I shall see you soon and be content.[14]

At the end of the fifth year, however, several crises occurred. The relationship, at least in its intense form, ended, though Molly and Helena continued an intimate and complex relationship for the next half-century. The exact nature of these crises is not completely clear, but it seems to have involved Molly's decision not to live with Helena, as they had originally planned, but to remain at home because of parental insistence. Molly was now in her late twenties. Helena responded with anger and Molly became frantic at the thought that Helena would break off their relationship. Though she wrote distraught letters and made despairing attempts to see Helena, the relationship never regained its former ardor—possibly because Molly had a male suitor.[15] Within six months Helena had decided to marry a man who was, coincidentally, Molly's friend and editor. Two years later Molly herself finally married. The letters toward the end of this period discuss the transition both women made to having male lovers—Molly spending much time reassuring Helena, who seemed depressed about the end of their relationship and her forthcoming marriage.[16]

It is clearly difficult, from a distance of a hundred years and from a post-Freudian cultural perspective, to decipher the complexities of Molly and Helena's relationship. Certainly Molly and Helena were lovers—emotionally if not physically. The emotional intensity and pathos of their love becomes apparent in several letters Molly wrote Helena during their crisis:

I wanted so to put my arms round my girl of all the girls in the world and tell her . . . I love her as wives do love their husbands, as *friends* who have taken each other for life—and believe in her as I believe in my God. . . . If I didn't love you do you suppose I'd care about anything or have ridiculous notions and panics and behave like an old fool who ought to know better. I'm going to hang on to your skirts. . . . You can't get away from [my] love.

Or, as she wrote after Helena's decision to marry: "You know dear Helena, I really was in love with you. It was a passion such as I had never known until I saw you. I don't think it was the noblest way to love you." The theme of intense female love was one Molly again expressed in a letter she wrote to the man Helena was to marry: "Do you know sir, that until you came along I believe that she loved me almost as girls love their lovers. *I know I loved her so*. Don't you wonder that I can stand the sight of you." This was in a letter congratulating them on their forthcoming marriage.[17]

The essential question is not whether these women had genital contact and can therefore be defined as homosexual or heterosexual. The twentieth-century tendency to view human love and sexuality within a dichotomized universe of deviance and normality, genitality and platonic love, is alien to the emotions and attitudes of the nineteenth century and fundamentally distorts the nature of these women's emotional interaction. These letters are significant because they force us to place such female love in a particular historical context. There is every indication that these four women, their husbands and families—all eminently respectable and socially conservative—considered such love both socially acceptable and fully compatible with heterosexual marriage. Emotionally and cognitively, their heterosocial and their homosocial worlds were complementary.

One could argue, on the other hand, that these letters were but an example of the romantic rhetoric with which the nineteenth century surrounded the concept of friendship. Yet they possess an emotional intensity and a sensual and physical explicitness that are difficult to dismiss. Jeannie longed to hold Sarah in her arms; Molly mourned her physical isolation from Helena. Molly's love and devotion to Helena, the emotions that bound Jeannie and Sarah together, while perhaps a phenomenon of nineteenth-century society, were not the less real for their Victorian origins. A survey of the correspondence and diaries of eighteenth- and nineteenth-century women indicates that Molly, Jeannie, and Sarah represented one very real behavioral and emotional option socially available to nineteenth-century women.

This is not to argue that individual needs, personalities, and family dynamics did not have a significant role in determining the nature of particular relationships. But the scholar must ask if it is historically possible and, if possible, important to study the intensely individual aspects of psychosexual dynamics. Is it not the historian's first task to explore the social structure and the worldview that made intense and sometimes sensual female love both a possible and an acceptable emotional option? From such a social perspective a new and quite different series of questions suggests itself. What emotional function did such female love serve? What was its place within the hetero- and homosocial worlds which women jointly inhabited? Did a spectrum of love-object choices exist in the nineteenth century across which some individuals, at least, were capable of moving? Unless we attempt to answer these questions, it will be difficult to understand either nineteenth-century sexuality or the nineteenth-century family.

Several factors in American society between the mid–eighteenth and the mid–nineteenth centuries may well have permitted women to form a variety of close emotional relationships with other women. American society was characterized in large part by rigid gender-role differentiation within the family and within society as a whole, leading to the emotional segregation of women and men. The roles of daughter and mother shaded imperceptibly and ineluctably into each other, while the biological realities of frequent pregnancies, childbirth, nursing, and menopause bound women together in physical and emotional intimacy. It was within just such a social framework, I would argue, that a specifically female world did indeed develop, a world built around a generic and unself-conscious pattern of single-sex or homosocial networks. These supportive networks were institutionalized in social conventions or rituals that accompanied virtually every important event in a woman's life, from birth to death. Such female relationships were frequently supported and paralleled by severe social restrictions on intimacy between young men and women. Within such a world of emotional richness and complexity, devotion to and love of other women became a plausible and socially accepted form of human interaction.

An abundance of printed and manuscript sources exists to support such a hypothesis. Etiquette books, advice books on child-rearing, religious sermons, guides to young men and young women, medical texts, and school curricula all suggest that late-eighteenth- and most nineteenth-century Americans assumed the existence of a world composed of distinctly male and female spheres, spheres determined by the immutable laws of God and nature.[18] The unpublished letters and diaries of Americans during this same period concur, detailing the existence of sexually segregated worlds inhabited by human beings with different values, expectations, and personalities. Contacts between men and women frequently partook of a formality and stiffness quite alien to twentieth-century America, and which today we tend to define as "Victorian." Women, however, did not form an isolated and oppressed subcategory in male society. Their letters and diaries indicate that women's sphere had an essential integrity and dignity that grew out of women's shared experiences and mutual affection and that, despite the profound changes that affected American social structure and institutions between the 1760s and the 1870s, retained a constancy and predictability. The ways in which women thought of and interacted with one another remained unchanged. Continuity, not discontinuity, characterized this female world. Molly Hallock's and Jeannie Field's words, emotions, and experiences have direct parallels in the 1760s and the 1790s.[19] There are indications in contemporary sociological and psychological literature that female closeness and support networks have continued into the twentieth century—not only among ethnic and working-class groups but even among the middle class.[20]

Most eighteenth- and nineteenth-century women lived within a world bounded by home, church, and the institution of visiting—that endless trooping of women to one another's homes for social purposes. It was a world inhabited by children and by other women.[21] Women helped one another with domestic chores and in times of sickness, sorrow, or trouble. Entire days, even weeks, might be spent almost exclusively with other women.[22] Urban and town women could devote virtually every day to visits, teas, or shopping trips with other women. Rural women developed a pattern of more extended visits that lasted weeks and sometimes months, at times even dislodging husbands from their beds and bedrooms so that dear friends might spend every hour of every day together.[23] When husbands traveled, wives routinely moved in with other women, invited women friends to teas and suppers, sat together sharing and comparing the letters they had received from other close women friends. Secrets were exchanged and cherished, and the husband's return at times was viewed with some ambivalence.[24]

Summer vacations were frequently organized to permit old friends to meet at water spas or share a country home. In 1848, for example, a young matron wrote cheerfully to her husband about the delightful time she was having with five close women friends whom she had invited to spend the summer with her; he remained at home alone to face the heat of Philadelphia and a cholera epidemic.[25] Some ninety years earlier, two young Quaker girls commented upon the vacation their aunt had taken alone with another woman; their remarks were openly envious and tell us something of the emotional quality of these friendships: "I hear Aunt is gone with the Friend and wont be back for two weeks, fine times indeed I think the old friends had, taking their pleasure about the country . . . and have the advantage of that fine woman's conversation and instruction, while we poor young girls must spend all spring at home. . . . What a disappointment that we are not together. . . ."[26]

Carroll Smith-Rosenberg

Friends did not form isolated dyads but were normally part of highly integrated networks. Knowing one another, perhaps related to one another, they played a central role in holding communities and kin systems together. Especially when families became geographically mobile, women's long visits to one another and their frequent letters filled with discussions of marriages and births, illnesses and deaths, descriptions of growing children, and reminiscences of times and people past provided an important sense of continuity in a rapidly changing society.[27] Central to this female world was an inner core of kin. The ties between sisters, first cousins, aunts, and nieces provided the underlying structure upon which groups of friends and their network of female relatives clustered. Although most of the women within this sample would appear to be living within isolated nuclear families, the emotional ties between nonresidential kin were deep and binding and provided one of the fundamental existential realities of women's lives.[28] Twenty years after Parke Lewis Butler moved with her husband to Louisiana, she sent her two daughters back to Virginia to attend school, live with their grandmother and aunt, and be integrated back into Virginia society.[29] The constant letters between Maria Inskeep and Fanny Hampton, sisters separated in their early twenties when Maria moved with her husband from New Jersey to Louisiana, held their families together, making it possible for their daughters to feel a part of their cousins' network of friends and interests.[30] The Ripley daughters, growing up in western Massachusetts in the early 1800s, spent months each year with their mother's sister and her family in distant Boston; these female cousins and their network of friends exchanged gossip-filled letters and gradually formed deeply loving and dependent ties.[31]

Women frequently spent their days within the social confines of such extended families. Sisters-in-law visited one another and, in some families, seemed to spend more time with one another than with their husbands. First cousins cared for one another's babies—for weeks or even months in times of sickness or childbirth. Sisters helped one another with housework, shopped and sewed for one another. Geographic separation was borne with difficulty. A sister's absence for even a week or two could cause loneliness and depression and would be bridged by frequent letters. Sibling rivalry was hardly unknown, but with separation or illness the theme of deep affection and dependency reemerged.[32]

Sisterly bonds continued across a lifetime. In her old age, a rural Quaker matron, Martha Jefferis, wrote to her daughter Anne concerning her own half-sister, Phoebe: "In sister Phoebe I have a real friend—she studies my comfort and waits on me like a child. . . . She is exceedingly kind and this to all other homes (set aside yours) I would prefer—it is next to being with a daughter." Phoebe's own letters confirmed Martha's evaluation of her feelings. "Thou knowest my dear sister," Phoebe wrote, "there is no one. . . . that exactly feels [for] thee as I do, for I think without boasting I can truly say that my desire is for thee."[33]

Such women, whether friends or relatives, assumed an emotional centrality in one another's lives. In their diaries and letters they wrote of the joy and contentment they felt in one another's company, their sense of isolation and despair when apart. The regularity of their correspondence underlines the sincerity of such words. Women named their daughters after one another and sought to integrate dear friends into their lives after marriage.[34] As one young bride wrote to an old friend shortly after her marriage, "I want to see you and talk with you and feel that we are united by the same bonds of sympathy and congeniality as ever."[35] After years of friendship, one aging woman wrote of another, "Time cannot destroy the fascination of her manner . . . her voice is music to the ear. . . ."[36] Women made elaborate presents for one another, ranging from the Quakers' frugal pies and breads to painted velvet bags and phantom bouquets.[37] When a friend died, their grief was deeply felt: Martha Jefferis was unable to write to her daughter for three weeks because of the sorrow she felt at the death of a dear friend, and such distress was not unusual. A generation earlier, a young Massachusetts farm woman filled pages of her diary with her grief at the death of her "dearest friend" and transcribed the letters of condolence other women sent her. She marked the anniversary of Rachel's death each year in her diary, contrasting her faithfulness with that of Rachel's husband, who had soon remarried.[38]

These female friendships served a number of emotional functions. Within this secure and empathetic world women could share sorrows, anxieties, and joys, confident that other women had experienced similar emotions. One mid-nineteenth-century rural matron, in a letter to her daughter, discussed this particular aspect of women's friendships: "To have such a friend as thyself to look to and sympathize with her—and enter into all her little needs and in whose bosom she could with freedom pour forth her joys and sorrows—such a friend would very much relieve the tedium of many a wearisome hour. . . ." A generation later Molly more informally underscored the importance of this same function in a letter to Helena: "Suppose I come down . . . [and] spend Sunday with you quietly," she wrote Helena, " . . . that means talking all the time until you are relieved of all your latest troubles, and I of mine. . . ."[39] These were frequently troubles that apparently no man could understand. When Anne Jefferis Sheppard was first married, she and her older sister Edith (who then lived with Anne) wrote in detail to their mother of the severe depression and anxiety they experienced. Moses Sheppard, Anne's husband, added cheerful postscripts to the sisters' letters—which he had clearly not read—remarking on Anne's and Edith's contentment. Theirs was an emotional world to which he had little access.[40]

Carroll Smith-Rosenberg

This was, as well, a female world in which hostility and criticism of other women were discouraged, and thus a milieu in which women could develop a sense of inner security and self-esteem. As one young woman wrote to her mother's long-time friend: "I cannot sufficiently thank you for the kind unvaried affection & indulgence you have ever shown and expressed both by words and actions for me. . . . Happy would it be did all the world view me as you do, through the medium of kindness and forbearance."[41] They valued one another. Women, who had little status or power in the larger world of male concerns, possessed status and power in the lives and worlds of other women.[42]

An intimate mother-daughter relationship lay at the heart of this female world. The diaries and letters of both mothers and daughters attest to their closeness and mutual emotional dependency. Daughters routinely discussed their mothers' health and activities with their own friends, expressed anxiety when their mothers were ill and concern for their cares.[43] Expressions of hostility which we would today consider routine on the part of both mothers and daughters seem to have been uncommon indeed. On the contrary, this sample of families indicates that the normal relationship between mother and daughter was one of sympathy and understanding.[44] Only sickness or great geographic distance was allowed to cause extended separation. When marriage did result in such separation, both viewed the distance between them with distress.[45] Something of this sympathy and love between mothers and daughters is evident in a letter Sarah Alden Ripley, at age sixty-nine, wrote her youngest and recently married daughter: "You do not know how much I miss you, not only when I struggle in and out of my mortal envelop and pump my nightly potation and no longer pour into your sympathizing ear my senile gossip, but all the day I muse away, since the sound of your voice no longer rouses me to sympathy with your joys or sorrows. . . . You cannot know how much I miss your affectionate demonstrations."[46] A dozen aging mothers in this sample of over thirty families echoed her sentiments.

Central to these mother-daughter relations is what might be described as an apprenticeship system. In those families where the daughter followed the mother into a life of traditional domesticity, mothers and other older women had carefully trained daughters in the arts of housewifery and motherhood. Such training undoubtedly occurred throughout a girl's childhood but became more systematized, almost ritualistic, in the years following the end of her formal education and before her marriage. At this time a girl either returned home from boarding school or no longer divided her time between home and school. Rather, she devoted her energies to two tasks: mastering new domestic skills and participating in the visiting and social activities necessary to finding a husband. Under the careful supervision of their mothers and of older female relatives, such late-adolescent girls temporarily took over the household management from their mothers, tended their young nieces and nephews, and helped in childbirth, nursing, and weaning. Such experiences tied the generations together in shared skills and emotional interaction.[47]

Daughters were born into a female world. Their mothers' life expectations and sympathetic network of friends and relations were among the first realities in the life of developing children. As long as the mothers' domestic role remained relatively stable and few viable alternatives competed with it, daughters tended to accept their mothers' world and to turn automatically to other women for support and intimacy. It was within this closed and intimate female world that the young girl grew toward womanhood.

One could speculate at length concerning the absence of that mother-daughter hostility today considered almost inevitable to an adolescent's struggle for autonomy and self-identity. It is possible that taboos against female aggression and hostility were sufficiently strong to repress even that between mothers and their adolescent daughters. Yet these letters seem so alive, and the interest of daughters in their mothers' affairs so vital and genuine, that it is difficult to interpret their closeness exclusively in terms of repression and denial. The functional bonds that held mothers and daughters together in a world that permitted few alternatives to domesticity might well have created a source of mutuality and trust absent in societies where greater options were available for daughters than for mothers. Furthermore, the extended female network—a daughter's close ties with her own older sisters, cousins, and aunts—may well have permitted a diffusion and a relaxation of mother-daughter identification and so have aided a daughter in her struggle for identity and autonomy. None of these explanations are mutually exclusive; all may well have interacted to produce the degree of empathy evident in those letters and diaries.

At some point in adolescence, the young girl began to move outside the matrix of her mother's support group to develop a network of her own. Among the middle class, at least, this transition toward what was at the same time both a limited autonomy and a repetition of her mother's life seemed to have most frequently coincided with a girl's going to school. Indeed, education appears to have played a crucial role in the lives of most of the families in this study. Attending school for a few months, for a year, or longer was common even among daughters of relatively poor families, while middle-class girls routinely spent at least a year in boarding school.[48] These school years ordinarily marked a girl's first separation from home. They served to wean the daughter from her home, to train her in the essential social graces, and, ultimately, to help introduce her into the marriage market. It was not infrequently a trying emotional experience for both mother and daughter.[49]

In this process of leaving one home and adjusting to another, the mother's friends and relatives played a key transitional role. Such older women routinely accepted the role of foster mother; they supervised the young girl's deportment, monitored her health, and introduced her to their own network of female friends and kin.[50] Not infrequently, women who had been friends from their own school years arranged to send their daughters to the same school, so that the girls might form bonds paralleling those their mothers had made. For years Molly and Helena wrote of their daughters' meeting and worried over each other's children. When Molly finally brought her daughter east to school, their first act on reaching New York was to meet Helena and her daughters. Elizabeth Bordley Gibson virtually adopted the daughters of her school chum, Eleanor Custis Lewis. The Lewis daughters soon began to write Elizabeth Gibson letters with the salutation "Dearest Mama." Eleuthera DuPont, attending boarding school in Philadelphia at roughly the same time as the Lewis girls, developed a parallel relationship with her mother's friend, Elizabeth McKie Smith. Eleuthera went to the same school as and became a close friend of the Smith girls, and eventually married their first cousin. During this period she routinely called Mrs. Smith "Mother." Indeed, Eleuthera so internalized the sense of having two mothers that she casually wrote her sisters of her "Mamma's" visits at her "mother's" house—that is, at Mrs. Smith's.[51]

Even more important to this process of maturation than their mother's friends were the female friends young women made at school. Young girls helped one another overcome homesickness and endure the crises of adolescence. They gossiped about beaux, incorporated one another into their own kinship systems, and attended and gave teas and balls together. Older girls in boarding school "adopted" younger ones, who called them "Mother."[52] Dear friends might indeed continue this pattern of adoption and mothering throughout their lives; one woman might routinely assume the nurturing role of pseudo-mother, the other the dependency role of daughter. The pseudo-mother performed for the other woman all the services we normally associate with mothers; she went to absurd lengths to purchase items her "daughter" could have obtained from other sources, gave advice, and functioned as an idealized figure in her "daughter's" imagination. Helena played such a role for Molly, as did Sarah for Jeannie. Elizabeth Bordley Gibson bought almost all Eleanor Parke Custis Lewis's necessities—from shoes and corset covers to bedding and harp strings—and sent them from Philadelphia to Virginia, a procedure that sometimes took months. Eleanor frequently asked Elizabeth to take back her purchases, have them redone, and argue with shopkeepers about prices. These were favors automatically asked and complied with. Anne Jefferis Sheppard made the analogy very explicitly in a letter to her own mother written shortly after Anne's marriage, when she was feeling depressed about their separation: "Mary Paulen is truly kind, almost acts the part of a mother and trys to aid and *comfort me*, and also to *lighten my new cares*."[53]

A comparison of the references to men and women in these young women's letters is striking. Boys were obviously indispensable to the elaborate courtship ritual girls engaged in. In these teen-age letters and diaries, however, boys appear distant and warded off—an effect produced both by the girls' sense of bonding and by a highly developed and deprecatory whimsy. Girls joked among themselves about the conceit, poor looks, or affectations of suitors. Rarely, especially in the eighteenth and early nineteenth centuries, were favorable remarks exchanged. Indeed, although hostility and criticism of other women were so rare as to seem almost tabooed, young women permitted themselves to express a great deal of hostility toward peer-group men.[54] If unacceptable suitors appeared, girls might even band together to harass them. When one such unfortunate came to court Sophie DuPont, she hid in her room, first sending her sister Eleuthera to entertain him and then dispatching a number of urgent notes to her neighboring sister-in-law, cousins, and a visiting friend, who all came to Sophie's support. A wild female romp ensued, ending only when Sophie banged into a door, lacerated her nose, and retired, with her female cohorts, to bed. Her brother and the presumably disconcerted suitor were left alone. These were not the antics of teenagers but of women in their early and midtwenties.[55]

Even if young men were acceptable suitors, girls referred to them formally and obliquely: "The last week I received the unexpected intelligence of the arrival of a friend in Boston," Sarah Ripley wrote in her diary of the young man to whom she had been engaged for years and whom she would shortly marry. Harriet Manigault assiduously kept a lively and gossipy diary during the three years preceding her marriage, yet did not once comment upon her own engagement or, indeed, make any personal references to her fiancé—who was never identified as such but always referred to as Mr. Wilcox.[56] The point is not that these young women were hostile to young men. Far from it: they sought marriage and domesticity. Yet in these letters and diaries men appear as an other or out group, segregated into different schools, supported by their own male network of friends and kin, socialized to different behavior, and coached to a proper formality in courtship behavior. As a consequence, relations between young women and men frequently lacked the spontaneity and emotional intimacy that characterized the young girls' ties to one another.

Indeed, in sharp contrast to their distant relations with boys, young women's relations with one another were close, often frolicsome, and surprisingly long-lasting and devoted. They wrote secret missives to one another, spent long, solitary days with one another, curled up together in bed at night to whisper fantasies and secrets.[57] In 1862 one woman in her early twenties described such a scene to an absent friend:

I have sat up to midnight listening to the confidences of Constance Kinney, whose heart was opened by that most charming of all situations, a seat on a bedside late at night, when all the household are asleep & only oneself & one's confidante survive in wakefulness. So she has told me all her loves and tried to get some confidences in return but being five or six years older than she, I know better. . . . [58]

Elizabeth Bordley and Nelly Parke Custis, teenagers in Philadelphia in the 1790s, routinely secreted themselves until late every night in Nelly's attic, where each wrote a novel about the other.[59] Quite a few young women kept diaries, and it was a sign of special friendship to show their diaries to one another. The emotional quality of such exchanges emerges from the comments of one young girl who grew up along the Ohio frontier:

Sisters CW and RT keep diaries & allow me the inestimable pleasure of reading them and in turn they see mine—but O shame covers my face when I think of it; theirs is so much better than mine, that every time. Then I think well now I *will* burn mine but upon second thought it would deprive me the pleasure of reading theirs, for I esteem it a very great privilege indeed, as well as very improving, as we lay our hearts open to each other, it heightens our love & helps to cherish & keep alive that sweet soothing friendship and endears us to each other by that soft attraction.[60]

Girls routinely slept together, kissed and hugged one another. Indeed, while waltzing with young men scandalized the otherwise flighty and highly fashionable Harriet Manigault, she considered waltzing with other young women not only acceptable but pleasant.[61]

Marriage followed adolescence. With increasing frequency in the nineteenth century, marriage involved a girl's traumatic removal from her mother and her mother's network. It involved, as well, adjustment to a husband, who, because he was male, came to marriage with both a different world view and vastly different experiences. Not surprisingly, marriage was an event surrounded by supportive, almost ritualistic, practices. (Weddings are one of the last female rituals remaining in twentieth-century America.) Young women routinely spent the months preceding their marriage almost exclusively with other women—at neighborhood sewing bees and quilting parties or in a round of visits to geographically distant friends and relatives. Ostensibly they went to receive assistance in the practical preparations for their new homes—sewing and quilting trousseaux and linen—but, of equal importance, they appear to have gained emotional support and reassurance. Sarah Ripley spent over a month with friends and relatives in Boston and Hingham before her wedding;

Parke Custis Lewis exchanged visits with her aunts and first cousins throughout Virginia.[62] Anne Jefferis, who married with some hesitation, spent virtually half a year in endless visiting with cousins, aunts, and friends. Despite their reassurance and support, however, she would not marry Moses Sheppard until her sister Edith and her cousin Rebecca moved into the groom's home, met his friends, and explored his personality.[63] The wedding did not take place until Edith wrote to Anne, "I can say in truth I am entirely willing thou shouldst follow him even away in the Jersey sands believing if thou are not happy in thy future home it will not be any fault on his part. . . ."[64]

Sisters, cousins, and friends frequently accompanied newlyweds on their wedding night and wedding trip, which often involved additional family visiting. Such extensive visits presumably served to wean the daughter from her family of origin. As such they often contained a note of ambivalence. Nelly Custis, for example, reported homesickness and loneliness on her wedding trip. "I left my Beloved and revered Grandmamma with sincere regret," she wrote Elizabeth Bordley. "It was some time before I could feel reconciled to traveling without her." Perhaps they also functioned to reassure the young woman herself, and her friends and kin, that though marriage might alter it would not destroy old bonds of intimacy and familiarity.[65]

Married life too was structured about a host of female rituals. Childbirth, especially the birth of the first child, became virtually a *rite de passage*, with a lengthy seclusion of the woman before and after delivery, severe restrictions on her activities, and finally a dramatic reemergence.[66] This seclusion was supervised by mothers, sisters, and loving friends. Nursing and weaning involved the advice and assistance of female friends and relatives. So did miscarriage.[67] Death, like birth, was structured around elaborate, unisexed rituals. When Nelly Parke Custis Lewis rushed to nurse her daughter who was critically ill while away at school, Nelly received support, not from her husband, who remained on their plantation, but from her old school friend Elizabeth Bordley. Elizabeth aided Nelly in caring for her dying daughter, cared for Nelly's other children, played a major role in making arrangements for the elaborate funeral (which the father did not attend), and frequently visited the girl's grave at the mother's request. For years Elizabeth continued to be the confidante of Nelly's anguished recollections of her lost daughter. These memories, Nelly's letters make clear, were for Elizabeth alone. "Mr. L. knows nothing of this" was a frequent comment.[68] Virtually every collection of letters and diaries in my sample contained evidence of women turning to one another for comfort when facing the frequent and unavoidable deaths of the eighteenth and nineteenth centuries.[69] While mourning for her father's death, Sophie DuPont received eloquent letters and visits of condolence—all from women. No man wrote or visited Sophie to offer sympathy at her father's death.[70] Among rural Pennsylvania Quakers, death and mourning rituals assumed an even more extreme same-sex form, with men or women largely barred from the deathbeds of the other sex. Women relatives and friends slept with the dying woman, nursed her, and prepared her body for burial.[71]

Eighteenth- and nineteenth-century women thus lived in emotional proximity to one another. Friendships and intimacies followed the biological ebb and flow of women's lives. Marriage and pregnancy, childbirth and weaning, sickness and death, involved physical and psychic trauma that comfort and sympathy made easier to bear. Intense bonds of love and intimacy bound together those women who, offering one another aid and sympathy, shared such stressful moments.

These bonds were often physical as well as emotional. An undeniably romantic and even sensual note frequently marked female relationships. This theme, significant throughout the stages of a woman's life, surfaced first during adolescence. As one teenager from a struggling pioneer family in the Ohio Valley wrote in her diary in 1808, "I laid with my dear R[ebecca] and a glorious good talk we had until about 4[A.M.]—O how hard I do *love* her. . . ."[72] Only a few years later, Bostonian Eunice Callender carved her initials and Sarah Ripley's into a favorite tree, along with a pledge of eternal love, and then waited breathlessly for Sarah to discover and respond to her declaration of affection. The response appears to have been affirmative.[73] A half-century later, urbane and sophisticated Katherine Wharton commented upon meeting an old school chum: "She was a great pet of mine at school & I thought as I watched her light figure how often I had held her in my arms—how dear she had once been to me." Katie maintained a long, intimate friendship with another girl. When a young man began to court this friend seriously, Katie commented in her diary that she had never realized "how deeply I loved Eng and how fully." She wrote over and over again in that entry, "Indeed I love her!," and only with great reluctance left the city that summer, since it meant also leaving Eng with Eng's new suitor.[74]

Peggy Emlen, a Quaker adolescent in Philadelphia in the 1760s, expressed similar feelings about her first cousin, Sally Logan. The girls sent love poems to each other (not unlike the ones Elizabeth Bordley wrote to Nelly Custis a generation later); took long, solitary walks together; and even haunted the empty house of the other when one was out of town. Indeed, Sally's absences from Philadelphia caused Peggy acute unhappiness. So strong were Peggy's feelings that her brothers began to tease her about her affection for Sally and threatened to steal Sally's letters, much to both girls' alarm. In one letter that Peggy wrote the absent Sally, she elaborately described the depth and nature of her feelings:

I have not words to express my impatience to see My Dear Cousin, what would I not give just now for an hours sweet conversation with her, it seems as if I had a thousand things to say to thee, yet when I see thee, everything will be forgot thro' joy. . . . I have a very great friendship for several Girls yet it dont give me so much uneasiness at being absent from them as from thee. . . . [Let us] go and spend a day down at our place together and there unmolested enjoy each others company.[75]

Sarah Alden Ripley, a young, highly educated woman, formed a similar intense relationship, in this instance with a woman somewhat older than herself. The immediate bond of friendship rested on their atypically intense scholarly interests, but it soon involved strong emotions, at least on Sarah's part. "Friendship," she wrote Mary Emerson, "is fast twining about her willing captive the silken hands of dependence, a dependence so sweet who would renounce it for the apathy of self-sufficiency?" Subsequent letters became far more emotional, almost conspiratorial. Mary visited Sarah secretly in her room, or the two women crept away from family and friends to meet in a nearby wood. Sarah became jealous of Mary's other young woman friends. Mary's trips away from Boston also thrust Sarah into periods of anguished depression. Interestingly, the letters detailing their love were not destroyed but were preserved and even reprinted in a eulogistic biography of Sarah Alden Ripley.[76]

Tender letters between adolescent women, confessions of loneliness and emotional dependency, were not peculiar to Sarah Alden, Peggy Emlen, or Katie Wharton. They are found throughout the letters of the thirty-five families studied. They have, of course, their parallel today in the musings of many female adolescents. Yet these eighteenth- and nineteenth-century friendships lasted with undiminished, indeed often increased, intensity throughout the women's lives. Sarah Alden Ripley's first child was named after Mary Emerson. Nelly Custis Lewis's love for and dependence on Elizabeth Bordley Gibson only increased after her marriage. Eunice Callender remained enamored of her cousin Sarah Ripley (Stearns) for years and rejected as impossible the suggestion by another woman that their love might someday fade away.[77] Sophie DuPont and her childhood friend Clementina Smith exchanged letters filled with love and dependency for forty years while another dear friend, Mary Black Couper, wrote of dreaming that she, Sophie, and her husband were all united in one marriage. Mary's letters to Sophie are filled with avowals of love and indications of ambivalence toward her own husband. Eliza Schlatter, another of Sophie's intimate friends, wrote to her at a time of crisis: "I wish I could be with you present in the body as well as the mind & heart—I would turn your *good husband out of bed*—and snuggle into you and we would have a long talk like old times in Pine St.—I want to tell you so many things that are not *writable*. . . ."[78]

Such mutual dependency and deep affection are a central existential reality coloring the world of supportive networks and rituals. In the case of Katie, Sophie, or Eunice—as with Molly, Jeannie, and Sarah—their need for closeness and support merged with more intense demands for a love that was at the same time both emotional and sensual. Perhaps the most explicit statement concerning women's lifelong friendships appeared in the letter that abolitionist and reformer Mary Grew wrote at about the same time, referring to her own love for her dear friend and lifelong companion, Margaret Burleigh. Grew wrote, in response to a letter of condolence from another woman on Burleigh's death:

> Your words respecting my beloved friend touch me deeply. Evidently . . . you comprehend and appreciate, as few persons do . . . the nature of the relation which existed, which exists, between her and myself. Her only surviving niece . . . also does. To me it seems to have been a closer union than that of most marriages. We know there have been other such between two men and also between two women. And why should there not be. Love is spiritual, only passion is sexual.[79]

How, then, can we ultimately interpret these long-lived intimate female relationships and integrate them into our understanding of Victorian sexuality? Their ambivalent and romantic rhetoric presents us with an ultimate puzzle: the relationship along the spectrum of human emotions between love, sensuality, and sexuality.

One is tempted, as I have remarked, to compare Molly, Peggy, or Sophie's relationship with the friendships adolescent girls in the twentieth century routinely form—close friendships of great emotional intensity. Helena Deutsch and Clara Thompson have both described these friendships as emotionally necessary to a girl's psychosexual development. But, they warn, such friendships might shade into adolescent and postadolescent homosexuality.[80]

It is possible to speculate that in the twentieth century a number of cultural taboos evolved to cut short the homosocial ties of girlhood and to impel the emerging women of thirteen or fourteen toward heterosexual relationships. In contrast, nineteenth-century American society did not taboo close female relationships but, rather, recognized them as a socially viable form of human contact—and, as such, acceptable throughout a woman's life. Indeed, it was not these homosocial ties that were inhibited but, rather, heterosexual leanings. While closeness, freedom of emotional expression, and uninhibited physical contact characterized women's relationships with one another, the opposite was frequently true of male-female relationships. One could thus argue that within such a world of female support, intimacy, and ritual it was only to be expected that adult women would turn trustingly and lovingly to one another. It was a behavior they had observed and learned since childhood. A different type of emotional landscape existed in the nineteenth century, one in which Molly and Helena's love became a natural development.

Of perhaps equal significance are the implications we can garner from this framework for the understanding of heterosexual marriages in the nineteenth century. If men and women grew up, as they did, in relatively homogeneous and segregated sexual groups, then marriage represented a major problem in adjustment. From this perspective we could interpret much of the emotional stiffness and distance that we associate with Victorian marriage as a structural consequence of contemporary sex-role differentiation and gender-role socialization. With marriage both women and men had to adjust to life with a person who was, in essence, a member of an alien group.

I have thus far substituted a cultural or psychosocial for a psychosexual interpretation of women's emotional bonding. But there are psychosexual implications in this model that I think it only fair to make more explicit. Despite Sigmund Freud's insistence on the bisexuality of us all, or the recent American Psychiatric Association decision on homosexuality, many psychiatrists today tend explicitly or implicitly to view homosexuality as a totally alien or pathological behavior—as totally unlike heterosexuality. I suspect that in essence they may have adopted an explanatory model similar to the one used in discussing schizophrenia. As a psychiatrist can speak of schizophrenia and of a borderline schizophrenic personality as both ultimately and fundamentally different from a normal or a neurotic personality, so they also think of both homosexuality and latent homosexuality as states totally different from heterosexuality. With this rapidly dichotomous model of assumption, "latent homosexuality" becomes the indication of a disease in progress—seeds of a pathology which belie the reality of an individual's heterosexuality.

Yet, at the same time, we are well aware that cultural values can affect choices in the gender of a person's sexual partner. We, for instance, do not necessarily consider homosexual-object choice among men in prison, on shipboard, or in boarding schools a necessary indication of pathology. I would urge that we expand this relativistic model and hypothesize that a number of cultures might well tolerate or even encourage diversity in sexual and nonsexual relations. Based on my research into this nineteenth-century world of female intimacy, I would further suggest that, rather than seeing a gulf between the normal and the abnormal, we view sexual and emotional impulses as part of a continuum or spectrum of affect gradations strongly affected by cultural norms and arrangements, a continuum influenced in part by observed and thus learned behavior. At one end of the continuum lies committed heterosexuality, at the other uncompromising homosexuality; between, a wide latitude of emotions and sexual feelings. Certain cultures and environments permit individuals a great deal of freedom in moving across this spectrum. I would like to suggest that the nineteenth century was such a cultural environment. That is, the supposedly repressive and destructive Victorian sexual ethos may have been more flexible and responsive to the needs of particular individuals than those of the mid–twentieth century.

Notes

1. Research for this chapter was supported in part by a grant from the Grant Foundation, New York, and by a National Institutes of Health trainee grant. I would like to thank several scholars for their assistance and criticism in preparing this chapter: Erving Goffman, Roy Schafer, Charles E. Rosenberg, Cynthia Secor, Anthony Wallace, Judy Breault, who has just completed a biography of an important and introspective nineteenth-century feminist, Emily Howland, served as a research assistant for this chapter, and her knowledge of nineteenth-century family structure and religious history proved invaluable.

2. The most notable exception to this rule is now eleven years old: William R. Taylor and Christopher Lasch, "Two 'Kindred Spirits': Sorority and Family in New England, 1839–1846," *New England Quarterly* 36 (1963); 25–41. Taylor has made a valuable contribution to the history of women and the history of the family with his concept of "sororial" relations. I do not, however, accept the Taylor-Lasch thesis that female friendships developed in the mid–nineteenth century because of geographic mobility and the breakup of the colonial family. I have found these friendships as frequently in the eighteenth century as in the nineteenth, and would hypothesize that the geographic mobility of the mid–nineteenth century eroded them as it did so many other traditional social institutions. Helen Vendler (Review of *Notable American Women, 1607–1950 Notable American*, ed. Edward James and Janet James, *New York Times*, November 5, 1972, sec. 7) points out the significance of these friendships.

3. I do not wish to deny the importance of women's relations with particular men. Obviously, women were close to brothers, husbands, fathers, and sons. However, there is evidence that, despite such closeness, relationships between men and women differed in both emotional texture and frequency from those between women. Women's relations with one another, although they played a central role in the American family and American society, have been so seldom examined either by general social historians or by historians of the family that I wish in this essay simply to examine their nature and analyze their implications for our understanding of social relations and social structure. I have discussed some aspects of male-female relationships in two articles: "Puberty to Menopause: The Cycle of Femininity in Nineteenth-Century America," *Feminist Studies* 1 (1973): 58–72, and, with Charles Rosenberg, "The Female Animal: Medical and Biological Views of Woman and Her Role in 19th-Century America," *Journal of American History* LX (1973): 332–56.

4. See Freud's classic paper on homosexuality, "Three Essays on the Theory of Sexuality," in *The Standard Edition of the Complete Psychological Works of Sigmund Freud*, trans. James Strachey (London: Hogarth Press, 1953), 7:135–72. The essays originally appeared

in 1905. Professor Roy Schafer, Department of Psychiatry, Yale University, has pointed out that Freud's view of sexual behavior was strongly influenced by nineteenth-century evolutionary thought. Within Freud's schema, genital heterosexuality marked the height of human development (Schafer, "Problems in Freud's Psychology of Women," *Journal of the American Psychoanalytic Association* 22 [1974]: 459–85).

5. For a novel and most important exposition of one theory of behavioral norms and options and its application to the study of human sexuality, see Charles Rosenberg, "Sexuality, Class and Role," *American Quarterly* 25(1973): 131–53.

6. See, e.g., the letters of Peggy Emlen to Sally Logan, 1768–72, Wells Morris Collection, box 1, Historical Society of Pennsylvania; the Eleanor Parke Custis Lewis Letters, Historical Society of Pennsylvania, Philadelphia.

7. Sarah Butler Wistar was the daughter of Fanny Kemble and Pierce Butler. In 1859 she married a Philadelphia physician, Owen Wistar. The novelist Owen Wistar was her son. Jeannie Field Musgrove was the half-orphaned daughter of constitutional lawyer and New York Republican politician David Dudley Field. Their correspondence (1855–98) is in the Sarah Butler Wistar Papers. Wistar Family Papers, Historical Society of Pennsylvania.

8. Sarah Butler, Butler Place, S.C., to Jeannie Field, New York, September 14, 1855.

9. See, e.g., Sarah Butler Wistar, Germantown, Pa., to Jeannie Field, New York, September 25, 1862, October 21, 1863; Jeannie Field, New York, to Sarah Butler Wistar, Germantown, July 3, 1861, January 23 and July 12, 1863.

10. Sarah Butler Wistar, Germantown, to Jeannie Field, New York, June 5, 1861; Jeannie Field to Sarah Butler Wistar, November 22, 1861. See also Sarah Butler Wistar, Germantown, to Jeannie Field, New York, February 29, 1864; Jeannie Field to Sarah Butler Wistar, January 4 and June 14, 1863.

11. Sarah Butler Wistar, London, to Jeannie Field Musgrove, New York, June 18. See also August 3, 1870.

12. See, e.g., two of Sarah's letters to Jeannie: December 21, 1873, July 16, 1878.

13. This is the 1868–1920 correspondence between Mary Hallock Foote and Helena DeKay Gilder, a New York friend (the Mary Hallock Foote Papers are in the Manuscript Division, Stanford University). Wallace E. Stegner has written a fictionalized biography of Mary Hallock Foote *(Angle of Repose* [Garden City, N.Y.: Doubleday and Co., 1971]). See, as well, her autobiography: Mary Hallock Foote, *A Victorian Gentlewoman in the Far West: The Reminiscences of Mary Hallock Foote*, ed. Rodman W. Paul (San Marino, Calif.: Huntington Library, 1972). In many ways these letters are typical of those that women wrote to other women. Women frequently began letters to each other with salutations such as "Dearest," "My Most Beloved," "You Darling Girl," and signed them "tenderly" or "to my dear dear sweet friend, good-bye." Without the least self-consciousness, one woman in her frequent letters to a female friend referred to her husband as "my other love." She was by no means unique. See, e.g., Annie to Charlena Van Vleck Anderson, Appleton. Wis., June 10, 1871, Anderson Family Papers, Manuscript Division, Stanford University; Maggie to Emily Howland, Philadelphia, July 12, 1851, Howland Family Papers, Phoebe King Collection, Friends Historical Library, Swarthmore College; Mary Jane Burleigh to Emily Howland, Sherwood, N.Y., March 27, 1872, Howland Family Papers, Sophia Smith Collection, Smith College; Mary Black Couper to Sophia Madeleine DuPont, Wilmington, Del., n.d. [1834] (two letters), Samuel Francis DuPont Papers, Eleutherian Mills Foundation, Wilmington, Del.; Phoebe Middleton, Concordville, Pa., to Martha Jefferis, Chester County, Pa., February 22, 1848; and see in general the

correspondence (1838–49) between Rebecca Biddle of Philadelphia and Martha Jefferis, Chester County, Pa., Jefferis Family Correspondence, Chester County Historical Society, West Chester, Pa.; Phoebe Bradford Diary, June 7 and July 3, 1832, Historical Society of Pennsylvania; Sarah Alden Ripley to Abba Allyn, Boston, n.d. [1818–20], and Sarah Alden Ripley to Sophia Bradford, November 30, 1854, in the Sarah Alden Ripley Correspondence, Schlesinger Library, Radcliffe College; Fanny Canby Ferris to Anne Biddle, Philadelphia, October 11 and November 19, 1811, December 26, 1813, Fanny Canby to Mary Canby, May 27, 1801, Mary R. Garrigues to Mary Canby, five letters, n.d. [1802–8], Anne Biddle to Mary Canby, two letters n.d., May 16, July 13, and November 24, 1806, June 14, 1807, June 5, 1808, Anne Sterling Biddle Family Papers, Friends Historical Society, Swarthmore College; Harriet Manigault Wilcox Diary, August 7, 1814, Historical Society of Pennsylvania. See as well the correspondence between Harriet Manigault Wilcox's mother, Mrs. Gabrielle Manigault, Philadelphia, and Mrs. Henry Middleton, Charleston, S.C., between 1810 and 1830, Cadwalader Collection, J. Francis Fisher Section, Historical Society of Pennsylvania. The basis and nature of such friendships can be seen in the comments of Sarah Alden Ripley to her sister-in-law and long-time friend, Sophia Bradford: "Hearing that you are not well reminds me of what it would be to lose your loving society. We have kept step together through a long piece of road in the weary journey of life. We have loved the same beings and wept together over their graves" (Mrs. O. J. Wistar and Miss Agnes Irwin, eds., *Worthy Women of Our First Century* [Philadelphia: J. B. Lippincott and Co., 1877], p. 195.

14. Mary Hallock [Foote] to Helena, n.d. [1869–70], n.d. [1871–72], folder 1, Mary Hallock Foote Letters, Manuscript Division, Stanford University.

15. Mary Hallock [Foote] to Helena, September 15 and 23, 1873, n.d. [October 1873], [October 12, 1873].

16. Mary Hallock [Foote] to Helena, n.d. (January 1874], n.d. [Spring 1874].

17. Mary Hallock [Foote] to Helena, September 23, 1873; Mary Hallock [Foote] to Richard Gilder, December 13, 1873. Throughout the rest of their lives, Molly's letters are filled with tender and intimate references as when she wrote, twenty years later and from two thousand miles away: "It isn't because you are good that I love you—but for the essence of you which is like perfume" (n.d. [1890s?]).

18. I am in the midst of a larger study of adult gender roles and gender-role socialization in America, 1785–1895. For a discussion of social attitudes toward appropriate male and female roles, see Barbara Welter, "The Cult of True Womanhood: 1800–1860," *American Quarterly* 18 (Summer 1966): 151–74; Ann Firor Scott, *The Southern Lady: From Pedestal to Politics, 1830–1930* (Chicago: University of Chicago Press. 1970), chaps. 1, 2; Smith-Rosenberg and Rosenberg, "The Female Animal."

19. See, e.g., the letters of Peggy Emlen to Sally Logan, 1768–72; the Eleanor Parke Custis Lewis Letters.

20. See especially Elizabeth Botts, *Family and Social Network* (London: Tavistock Publications, 1957); Michael Young and Peter Willmott, *Family and Kinship in East London*, rev. ed. (Baltimore: Penguin Books, 1964).

21. This pattern seemed to cross class barriers. A letter that an Irish domestic wrote in the 1830s contains seventeen separate references to women but only seven to men, most of whom were relatives and two of whom were infant brothers living with her mother and mentioned in relation to her mother (Ann McGrann, Philadelphia, to Sophie M. DuPont, Philadelphia, July 3, 1834, Sophie Madeleine DuPont Letters, Eleutherian Mills Foundation).

22. Harriet Manigault Diary, June 28, 1814, and passim; Jeannie Field, New York, to Sarah Butler Wistar, Germantown, April 19, 1863; Phoebe Bradford Diary, January 30, February 19, March 4, August 11, and October 14, 1832, Historical Society of Pennsylvania; Sophie M. DuPont, Brandywine, to Henry DuPont, Germantown, July 9, 1827, Eleuthenan Mills Foundation.

23. Martha Jefferis to Anne Jefferis Sheppard, July 9, 1843; Anne Jefferis Sheppard to Martha Jefferis, June 28, 1846; Anne Sterling Biddle Papers, passim; Eleanor Parke Custis Lewis, Virginia, to Elizabeth Bordley Gibson, Philadelphia, November 24 and December 4, 1820, November 6, 1821.

24. Phoebe Bradford Diary, January 13. November 16–19, 1832, April 26 and May 7, 1833; Abigail Brackett Lyman to Mrs. Catling, Litchfield, Conn., May 3, 1801, collection in private hands; Martha Jefferis to Anne Jefferis Sheppard, August 28, 1845.

25. Lisa Mitchell Diary, 1860s, passim, Manuscript Division, Tulane University; see also Eleanor Parke Custis Lewis to Elizabeth Bordley [Gibson], February 5, 1822; Jeannie McCall, Cedar Park, to Peter McCall, Philadelphia, June 30, 1849, McCall Section, Cadwalader Collection, Historical Society of Pennsylvania.

26. Peggy Emlen to Sally Logan, May 3, 1769.

27. For prime examples of this type of letter, see Eleanor Parke Custis Lewis to Elizabeth Bordley Gibson, passim; Fanny Canby to Mary Canby, Philadelphia, May 27, 1801; Sophie M. DuPont, Brandywine, to Henry DuPont, Germantown, February 4, 1832.

28. Place of residence is not the only variable significant in characterizing family structure. Strong emotional ties and frequent visiting and correspondence can unite families that do not live under one roof. Demographic studies based on household structure alone fail to reflect such emotional and even economic ties between families.

29. Eleanor Parke Custis Lewis to Elizabeth Bordley Gibson, April 20 and September 25, 1848.

30. Maria Inskeep to Fanny Hampton Correspondence, 1823–60, Inskeep Collection, Tulane University Library.

31. Eunice Callender, Boston, to Sarah Ripley [Stearns], September 24 and October 29, 1803, February 16, 1805, April 29 and October 9, 1806, May 26, 1810.

32. Sophie DuPont filled her letters to her younger brother Henry (with whom she had been assigned to correspond while he was at boarding school) with accounts of family visiting (see, e.g., December 13, 1827, January 10 and March 9, 1828, February 4 and March 10, 1832; also Sophie M. DuPont to Victorine DuPont Bauday, September 26 and December 4, 1827, February 22, 1828; Sophie M. DuPont, Brandywine, to Clementina B. Smith, Philadelphia, January 15, 1830; Eleuthera DuPont, Brandywine, to Victorine DuPont Bauday, Philadelphia, April 17, 1821, October 20, 1826; Evelina DuPont [Biderman] to Victorine DuPont Bauday, October 18, 1816). Other examples, from the Historical Society of Pennsylvania, are Harriet Manigault [Wilcox] Diary. August 17, September 8, October 19 and 22, December 22, 1814; Jane Zook, West Town School, Chester County, Pa., to Mary Zook, November 13, December 7 and 11, 1870, February 26, 1871; Eleanor Parke Custis [Lewis] to Elizabeth Bordley [Gibson], March 30, 1796, February 7 and March 20, 1798; Jeannie McCall to Peter McCall, Philadelphia, November 12. 1847; Mary B. Ashew Diary, July 11, and 13, August 17, summer and October 1858; and, from a private collection, Edith Jefferis to Anne Jefferis Sheppard, November 1841, April 5, 1842; Abigail Brackett Lyman, Northampton, Mass., to Mrs. Catling, Litchfield. Conn., May 13, 1801; Abigail Brackett Lyman, Northampton, to Mary Lord, August 11, 1800. Mary Hallock Foote vacationed with her sister, her sister's children, her aunt, and a female

cousin in the summer of 1874; cousins frequently visited the Hallock farm in Milton, N.Y. In later years Molly and her sister Bessie set up a joint household in Boise, Idaho (Mary Hallock Foote to Helena, July [1874?] and passim). Jeannie Field, after initially disliking her sister-in-law, Laura, became very close to her, calling her "my little sister" and at times spending virtually every day with her. Jeannie Field [Musgrove], New York, to Sarah Butler Wistar, Germantown, March 1, 8, and 15, and May 9, 1863).

33. Martha Jefferis to Anne Jefferis Sheppard, January 12, 1845; Phoebe Middleton to Martha Jefferis, February 22, 1848. A number of other women remained close to sisters and sisters-in-law across a long lifetime (Phoebe Bradford Diary, June 7, 1832, and Sarah Alden Ripley to Sophia Bradford, cited in Wistar and Irwin, *Worthy Women*, p. 195).

34. Rebecca Biddle to Martha Jefferis, 1838–49, passim; Martha Jefferis to Anne Jefferis Sheppard, July 6, 1846; Anne Jefferis Sheppard to Rachel Jefferis, January 16, 1865; Sarah Foulke Farquhar [Emlen] Diary, September 22, 1813, Friends Historical Library, Swarthmore College; Mary Garrigues to Mary Canby [Biddle], 1802–8, passim; Anne Biddle to Mary Canby [Biddle], May 16, July 13, and November 24, 1806, June 14, 1807, June 5, 1808.

35. Sarah Alden Ripley to Abba Allyn, n.d.

36. Phoebe Bradford Diary, July 13, 1832.

37. Mary Hallock [Foote] to Helena DeKay Gilder, December 23 [1868 or 1869]; Phoebe Bradford Diary, December 8, 1832; Martha Jefferis and Anne Jefferis Sheppard letters, passim.

38. Martha Jefferis to Anne Jefferis Sheppard, August 3, 1849; Sarah Ripley [Stearns] Diary, November 12, 1808, January 8, 1811. An interesting note of hostility or rivalry is present in Sarah Ripley's diary entry. Sarah evidently deeply resented the husband's rapid remarriage.

39. Martha Jefferis to Edith Jefferis, March 15, 1841; Mary Hallock Foote to Helena, n.d. [1874–75?]; see also Jeannie Field, New York, to Sarah Butler Wistar, Germantown, May 5, 1863; Emily Howland Diary, December 1879, Howland Family Papers.

40. Anne Jefferis Sheppard to Martha Jefferis, September 29, 1841.

41. Frances Parke Lewis to Elizabeth Bordley Gibson, April 29, 1821.

42. Mary Jane Burleigh, Mount Pleasant, S.C., to Emily Howland, Sherwood, N.Y., March 27, 1872; Emily Howland Diary, September 16, 1879, January 21 and 23, 1880; Mary Black Couper, New Castle, Del., to Sophie M. DuPont, Brandywine, April 7, 1834.

43. Harriet Manigault Diary, August 15, 21, and 23, 1814. Historical Society of Pennsylvania; Polly [Simmons] to Sophie Madeleine DuPont, February 1822; Sophie Madeleine DuPont to Victorine Bauday, December 4, 1827; Sophie Madeleine DuPont to Clementina Beach Smith, July 24, 1828, August 19, 1829; Clementina Beach Smith to Sophie Madeleine DuPont, April 29, 1831; Mary Black Couper to Sophie Madeleine DuPont, December 24, 1828, July 21, 1834. This pattern appears to have crossed class lines. When a former Sunday school student of Sophie DuPont's (and the daughter of a worker in her father's factory) wrote to Sophie, she discussed her mother's health and activities quite naturally (Ann McGrann to Sophie Madeleine DuPont, August 25, 1832; see also Elizabeth Bordley to Martha, n.d. [1797]; Eleanor Parke Custis [Lewis] to Elizabeth Bordley [Gibson], May 13, 1796, July 1, 1798; Peggy Emlen to Sally Logan, January 8, 1786. All but the Emlen/Logan letters are in the Eleanor Parke Custis Lewis Correspondence, Historical Society of Pennsylvania).

44. Mrs. L. L. Dalton, "Autobiography," Circle Valley, Utah, 1876, pp. 21–22, Bancroft Library, University of California, Berkeley; Sarah Foulke Emlen Diary, April 1809; Louisa

G. Van Vleck, Appleton, Wis., to Charlena Van Vleck Anderson, Göttingen, n.d. [1875], Anderson Family Papers; Harriet Manigault Diary, August 16, 1814, July 14, 1815; Sarah Alden Ripley to Sophy Thayer [early 1860s], quoted in Wistar and Irwin, *Worthy Women*, p. 212. The Jefferis family papers are filled with empathetic letters between Martha and her daughters, Anne and Edith. See, e.g., Martha Jefferis to Edith Jefferis, December 26, 1836, March 11, 1837, March 15, 1841; Anne Jefferis Sheppard to Martha Jefferis, March 17, 1841, January 17, 1847; Martha Jefferis to Anne Jefferis Sheppard, April 17, 1848, April 30, 1849. A representative letter is this of March 9, 1837, from Edith to Martha: "My heart can fully respond to the language of my own precious Mother, that absence has not diminished our affection for each other, but has, if possible, strengthened the bonds that have united us together & I have had to remark how we had been permitted to mingle in sweet fellowship and have been strengthened to bear one another's burdens. . . ."

45. Abigail Brackett Lyman, Boston, to Mrs. Abigail Brackett (daughter to mother), n.d. [1797], June 3, 1800; Sarah Alden Ripley wrote weekly to her daughter Sophy Ripley Fisher after the latter's marriage (Sarah Alden Ripley Correspondence, passim); Phoebe Bradford Diary, February 25, 1833, passim. 1832–33; Louisa G. Van Vleck to Charlena Van Vleck Anderson, December 15, 1873, July 4, August 15 and 29, September 19, and November 9, 1875. Eleanor Parke Custis Lewis's long correspondence with Elizabeth Bordley Gibson contains evidence of her anxiety at leaving her foster mother's home at various times during her adolescence and at her marriage, and her own longing for her daughters, both of whom had married and moved to Louisiana (Eleanor Parke Custis [Lewis] to Elizabeth Bordley [Gibson], October 13, 1795, November 4, 1799, passim, 1820s and 1830s). Anne Jefferis Sheppard experienced a great deal of anxiety on moving two days' journey from her mother at the time of her marriage. This loneliness and sense of isolation persisted through her marriage until, finally a widow, she returned to live with her mother (Anne Jefferis Sheppard to Martha Jefferis, April 1841, October 16, 1842, April 2, May 22, and October 12, 1844, September 3, 1845, January 17, 1847, May 16, June 3, and October 31, 1849; Anne Jefferis Sheppard to Susanna Lightfoot, March 23, 1845, and to Joshua Jefferis, May 14, 1854). Daughters evidently frequently slept with their mothers—into adulthood (Harriet Manigault [Wilcox] Diary, February 19, 1815; Eleanor Parke Custis Lewis to Elizabeth Bordley Gibson, October 10, 1832). Daughters also frequently asked mothers to live with them and professed delight when they did so. See, e.g., Sarah Alden Ripley's comments to George Simmons, October 6, 1844, in Wistar and Irwin, *Worthy Women*, p. 185: "It is no longer 'Mother and Charles came out one day and returned the next,' for mother is one of us: she has entered the penetratice [*sic*], been initiated into the mystery of the household gods, . . . Her divertissement is to mend the stockings . . . whiten sheets and napkins, . . . and take a stroll at evening with me to talk of our children, to compare our experiences, what we have learned and what we have suffered, and, last of all, to complete with pears and melons the cheerful circle about the solar lamp. . . ." We did find a few exceptions to this mother-daughter felicity (M. B. Ashew Diary, November 19, 1857, April 10 and May 17, 1858). Sarah Foulke Emlen was at first very hostile to her stepmother (Sarah Foulke Emlen Diary, August 9, 1807), but they later developed a warm, supportive relationship.

46. Sarah Alden Ripley to Sophy Thayer, n.d. [1861].

47. Mary Hallock Foote to Helena [winter 1873] (no. 52); Jossie, Stevens Point, Wis., to Charlena Van Vleck [Anderson], Appleton, Wis., October 24, 1870; Pollie Chandler, Green Bay, Wis., to Charlena Van Vleck [Anderson], Appleton, n.d. [1870]; Eleuthera

DuPont to Sophie DuPont, September 5, 1829; Sophie DuPont to Eleuthera DuPont, December 1827; Sophie DuPont to Victorine Bauday, December 4, 1827; Mary Gilpin to Sophie DuPont, September 26, 1827; Sarah Ripley Stearns Diary, April 2, 1809; Jeannie McCall to Peter McCall, October 27 [late 1840s]. Eleanor Parke Custis Lewis's correspondence with Elizabeth Bordley Gibson describes such an apprenticeship system over two generations—that of her childhood and that of her daughters. Indeed, Eleanor Lewis's own apprenticeship was quite formal. She was deliberately separated from her foster mother so that she could spend a winter of domesticity with her married sisters and her remarried mother. It was clearly felt that her foster mother's (Martha Washington) home at the nation's capital was not an appropriate place to develop domestic talents (October 13, 1795, March 30, May 13, and [summer] 1796, March 18 and April 27, 1797, October 1827).

48. Education was not limited to the daughters of the well-to-do. Sarah Foulke Emlen, the daughter of an Ohio Valley frontier farmer, for instance, attended day school for several years during the early 1800s. Sarah Ripley Stearns, the daughter of a shopkeeper in Greenfield, Massachusetts, attended a boarding school for but three months, yet the experience seemed very important to her. Mrs. S. S. Dalton, a Mormon woman from Utah, attended a series of poor country schools and greatly valued her opportunity, though she also expressed a great deal of guilt for the sacrifices her mother accepted to make her education possible (Sarah Foulke Emlen Journal, Sarah Ripley Stearns Diary, Mrs. S. S. Dalton, "Autobiography").

49. Maria Revere to her mother [Mrs. Paul Revere], June 13, 1801, Paul Revere Papers, Massachusetts Historical Society. In a letter to Elizabeth Bordley Gibson, March 28, 1847, Eleanor Parke Custis Lewis from Virginia discussed the anxiety her daughter felt when her granddaughters left home to go to boarding school. Eleuthera DuPont was very homesick when away at school in Philadelphia in the early 1820s (Eleuthera DuPont, Philadelphia, to Victorine Bauday, Wilmington, Del., April 7, 1821; Eleuthera DuPont to Sophie Madeleine DuPont, Wilmington, Del., February and April 3, 1821).

50. Elizabeth Bordley Gibson, a Philadelphia matron, played such a role for the daughters and nieces of her lifelong friend, Eleanor Parke Custis Lewis, a Virginia planter's wife (Eleanor Parke Custis Lewis to Elizabeth Bordley Gibson, January 29, 1833, March 19, 1826, and passim through the collection). The wife of Thomas Gurney Smith played a similar role for Sophie and Eleuthera DuPont (see, e.g., Eleuthera DuPont to Sophie Madeleine DuPont, May 22, 1825; Rest Cope to Philema P. Swayne [niece], West Town School, Chester County, Pa., April 8, 1829, Friends Historical Library, Swarthmore College). For a view of such a social pattern over three generations, see the letters and diaries of three generations of Manigault women in Philadelphia: Mrs. Gabrielle Manigault, her daughter, Harriet Manigault Wilcox, and granddaughter, Charlotte Wilcox McCall. Unfortunately, the papers of the three women are not in one family collection (Mrs. Henry Middleton, Charleston, S.C., to Mrs. Gabrielle Manigault, n.d. [mid-1800s]; Harriet Manigault Diary, vol. 1; December 1, 1813, June 28, 1814; Charlotte Wilcox McCall Diary, vol. 1, 1842, passim; all in Historical Society of Philadelphia).

51. Frances Parke Lewis, Woodlawn, Va., to Elizabeth Bordley Gibson, Philadelphia, April 11, 1821, Lewis Correspondence; Eleuthera DuPont, Philadelphia, to Victorine DuPont Bauday, Brandywine, December 8, 1821, January 31, 1822; Eleuthera DuPont, Brandywine, to Margaretta Lammont [DuPont], Philadelphia, May 1823.

52. Sarah Ripley Stearns Diary, March 9 and 25, 1810; Peggy Emlen to Sally Logan, March and July 4, 1769; Harriet Manigault [Wilcox] Diary, vol. 1, December 1, 1813, June 28

and September 18, 1814, August 10, 1815; Charlotte Wilcox McCall Diary, 1842, passim; Fanny Canby to Mary Canby, May 27, 1801, March 17, 1804; Deborah Cope, West Town School, to Rest Cope, Philadelphia, July 9, 1828, Chester County Historical Society, West Chester, Pa.; Anne Zook, West Town School, to Mary Zook, Philadelphia, January 30, 1866, Chester County Historical Society, West Chester, Pa,; Mary Gilpin to Sophie Madeleine DuPont, February 25, 1829; Eleanor Parke Custis [Lewis] to Elizabeth Bordley [Gibson], April 27, July 2, and September 8, 1797, June 30, 1799, December 29, 1820; Frances Parke Lewis to Elizabeth Bordley Gibson, December 20, 1820.

53. Anne Jefferis Sheppard to Martha Jefferis, March 17, 1841.

54. Peggy Emlen to Sally Logan, Mount Vernon, Va., March 1769; Eleanor Parke Custis [Lewis] to Elizabeth Bordley [Gibson], Philadelphia, April 27, 1797, June 30, 1799; Jeannie Field, New York, to Sarah Butler Wistar, Germantown, July 3, 1861, January 16, 1863; Harriet Manigault Diary, August 3 and 11–13, 1814; Eunice Callender, Boston, to Sarah Ripley [Stearns], Greenfield, May 4, 1809. I found one exception to this inhibition of female hostility toward other women: the diary of Charlotte Wilcox McCall, Philadelphia (see, e.g., her March 23, 1842, entry).

55. Sophie M. DuPont and Eleuthera DuPont, Brandywine, to Victorine DuPont Bauday, Philadelphia, January 25, 1832.

56. Sarah Ripley [Stearns] Diary and Harriet Manigault Diary, passim.

57. Sophie Madeleine DuPont to Eleuthera DuPont, December 1827; Clementina Beach Smith to Sophie Madeleine DuPont, December 26, 1828; Sarah Foulke Emlen Diary, July 21, 1808, March 30, 1809; Annie Hethroe, Ellington, Wis., to Charlena Van Vleck [Anderson], Appleton, Wis., April 23, 1865; Frances Parke Lewis, Woodlawn, Va., to Elizabeth Bordley [Gibson], Philadelphia, December 20, 1820; Fanny Ferris to Debby Ferris, West Town School, Chester County, Pa., May 29, 1826. An excellent example of the warmth of women's comments about one another and the reserved nature of their references to men is seen in two entries in Sarah Ripley Stearns's diary. On January 8, 1811, she commented about a young woman friend: "The amiable Mrs. White of Princeton . . . one of the loveliest most interesting creatures I ever knew, young fair and blooming . . . beloved by everyone . . . formed to please & to charm . . ." She referred to the man she ultimately married always as "my friend" or "a friend" (February 2 or April 23, 1810.

58. Jeannie Field, New York, to Sarah Butler Wistar, Germantown, April 6, 1862.

59. Elizabeth Bordley Gibson, introductory statement to the Eleanor Parke Custis Lewis Letters [1850s], Historical Society of Pennsylvania.

60. Sarah Foulke [Emlen] Diary, March 30, 1809.

61. Harriet Manigault Diary, May 26, 1815.

62. Sarah Ripley [Stearns] Diary, May 17 and October 2, 1812; Eleanor Parke Custis Lewis to Elizabeth Bordley Gibson, April 23, 1826; see also, Rebecca Ralston, Philadelphia, to Victorine DuPont [Bauday], Brandywine, September 27, 1813.

63. Anne Jefferis to Martha Jefferis, November 22 and 27, 1840, January 13 and March 17, 1841; Edith Jefferis, Greenwich, N.J., to Anne Jefferis, Philadelphia, January 31, February 6 and February 1841.

64. Edith Jefferis to Anne Jefferis, January 31, 1841.

65. Eleanor Parke Custis Lewis to Elizabeth Bordley, November 4, 1799. Eleanor and her daughter Parke experienced similar sorrow and anxiety when Parke married and moved to Cincinnati (Eleanor Parke Custis Lewis to Elizabeth Bordley Gibson, April 23, 1826). Helena DeKay visited Mary Hallock the month before her marriage; Mary Hallock

was an attendant at the wedding; Helena again visited Molly about three weeks after her marriage; and then Molly went with Helena and spent a week with Helena and Richard in their new apartment (Mary Hallock [Foote] to Helena DeKay Gilder [Spring 1874] [no. 61], May 10, 1874 [May 1874], June 14, 1874, [Summer 1874]). See also Anne Biddle, Philadelphia, to Clement Biddle (brother), Wilmington, March 12 and May 27, 1827; Eunice Callender, Boston, to Sarah Ripley [Stearns], Greenfield, Mass., August 3, 1807, January 26, 1808; Victorine DuPont Bauday, Philadelphia, to Evelina DuPont [Biderman], Brandywine, November 25 and 26, December 1, 1813; Peggy Emlen to Sally Logan, n.d. [1769–70?]; Jeannie Field, New York, to Sarah Butler Wistar, Germantown, July 3, 1861.

66. Mary Hallock to Helena DeKay Gilder [1876] (no. 81); n.d. (no. 83), March 3, 1884; Mary B. Ashew Diary, vol. 2, September-January 1860; Louisa Van Vleck to Charlena Van Vleck Anderson, n.d. [1875]; Sophie DuPont to Henry DuPont, July 24, 1827; Benjamin Ferns to William Canby, February 13, 1805; Benjamin Ferris to Mary Canby Biddle December 20, 1825; Anne Jefferis Sheppard to Martha Jefferis, September 15, 1884; Martha Jefferis to Anne Jefferis Sheppard, July 4, 1843, May 5, 1844, May 3, 1847, July 17, 1849; Jeannie McCall to Peter McCall, November 26, 1847., n.d. [late 1840s]. A graphic description of the ritual surrounding a first birth is found in Abigail Lyman's letter to her husband, Erastus Lyman, October 18, 1810.

67. Fanny Ferns to Anne Biddle, November 19, 1811; Eleanor Parke Custis Lewis to Elizabeth Bordley Gibson, November 4, 1799, April 27, 1827; Martha Jefferis to Anne Jefferis Sheppard, January 31, 1843, April 4, 1844; Martha Jefferis to Phoebe Sharpless Middleton, June 4, 1846; Anne Jefferis Sheppard to Martha Jefferis, August 20, 1843, February 12, 1844; Maria Inskeep, New Orleans, to Mrs. Fanny G. Hampton, Bridgeton, N.J., September 22, 1848; Benjamin Ferris to Mary Canby, February 14, 1805; Fanny Ferns to Mary Canby [Biddle], December 2, 1816.

68. Eleanor Parke Custis Lewis to Elizabeth Bordley Gibson, October–November 1820, passim.

69. Emily Howland to Hannah, September 30, 1866; Emily Howland Diary, February 8, 11, and 27, 1880; Phoebe Bradford Diary, April 12 and 13, and August 4, 1833; Eunice Callender, Boston, to Sarah Ripley [Stearns], Greenwich, Mass., September 11, 1802, August 26, 1810; Mrs. H. Middleton, Charleston, to Mrs. Gabrielle Manigault, Philadelphia, n.d. [mid-1800s]; Mrs. H. C. Paul to Mrs. Jeannie McCall, Philadelphia, n.d. [1840s]: Sarah Butler Wistar, Germantown, to Jeannie Field [Musgrove], New York, April 22, 1864; Jeannie Field [Musgrove] to Sarah Butler Wistar, August 25, 1861, July 6, 1862; S. B. Randolph to Elizabeth Bordley [Gibson], n.d. [1790s]. For an example of similar letters between men, see Henry Wright to Peter McCall, December 10, 1852; Charles McCall to Peter McCall, January 4, 1860, March 22, 1864, R. Mercer to Peter McCall, November 29, 1872.

70. Mary Black [Couper] to Sophie Madeline DuPont, February 1827, [November 1, 1834], November 12, 1834, two letters, n.d. [late November 1834]; Eliza Schlatter to Sophie Madeleine DuPont, November 2, 1834.

71. For a few of the references to death rituals in the Jefferis papers, see Martha Jefferis to Anne Jefferis Sheppard, September 28, 1843, August 21 and September 25, 1844, January 11, 1846, summer 1848, passim; Anne Jefferis Sheppard to Martha Jefferis, August 20, 1843; Anne Jefferis Sheppard to Rachel Jefferis, March 17, 1863, February 9, 1868. For other Quaker families, see Rachel Biddle to Anne Biddle, July 23, 1854; Sarah Foulke Farquhar [Emlen] Diary, April 30, 1811, February 14, 1812; Fanny Ferris to Mary Canby,

August 31, 1810. This is not to argue that men and women did not mourn together. Yet in many families women aided and comforted women, and men, men. The same-sex death ritual was one emotional option available to nineteenth-century Americans.

72. Sarah Foulke [Emlen] Diary, December 29, 1808.

73. Eunice Callender, Boston, to Sarah Ripley [Stearns], Greenfield, Mass., May 14, 1803.

74. Katherine Johnstone Brinley [Wharton] Journal, April 26, May 29, and May 30, 1856, Historical Society of Pennsylvania.

75. A series of fourteen letters by Peggy Emlen to Sally Logan (1768–71) has been preserved in the Wells Morris Collection, box 1, Historical Society of Pennsylvania (see especially May 3 and July 4, 1769, January 8, 1768).

76. The Sarah Alden Ripley Collection, the Schlesinger Library, Radcliffe College, contains a number of Sarah Alden Ripley's letters to Mary Emerson. Most of these are undated, but they extend over a number of years and contain letters written both before and after Sarah's marriage. The eulogistic biographical sketch appeared in Wistar and Irwin, *Worthy Women*. It should be noted that Sarah Butler Wistar was one of the editors who sensitively selected Sarah's letters.

77. See Sarah Alden Ripley to Mary Emerson, November 19, 1823. Sarah Alden Ripley routinely, and, one must assume, ritualistically, read Mary Emerson's letters to her infant daughter, Mary. Eleanor Parke Custis Lewis reported doing the same with Elizabeth Bordley Gibson's letters, passim. Eunice Callender Boston, to Sarah Ripley [Stearns], October 19, 1808.

78. Mary Black Couper to Sophie M. DuPont, March 5, 1832. The Clementina Smith Sophie DuPont correspondence of 1,678 letters is in the Sophie DuPont Correspondence. The quotation is from Eliza Schlatter, Mount Holly, N.J., to Sophie DuPont, Brandywine, August 24, 1834. I am indebted to Anthony Wallace for informing me about this collection.

79. Mary Grew, Providence, R.I., to Isabel Howland, Sherwood, N.Y., April 27, 1892, Howland Correspondence, Sophia Smith Collection, Smith College.

80. Helena Deutsch, *Psychology of Women* (New York: Grune and Stratton, 1944), vol. 1, chaps. 1–3; Clara Thompson, *On Women*, ed. Maurice Green (New York: New American Library, 1971).

CHAPTER 8

Psychosomatic Illness in History

The "Green Sickness" among Nineteenth-Century Adolescent Girls

Nancy M. Theriot

In 1975, *Signs: A Journal of Women in Culture and Society* opened its first issue with a now-classic article by Carroll Smith-Rosenberg. In "The Female World of Love and Ritual: Relations between Women in Nineteenth-Century America," Smith-Rosenberg describes an intimate community of mothers, daughters, sisters, and female friends in which women found recognition and support. The core of this female world was the mother/daughter relationship. Smith-Rosenberg argues that mothers and daughters were close friends and confidantes, that daughters learned the skills and arts of domesticity in an informal apprenticeship with their mothers, and that mothers and daughters shared the rituals surrounding sexuality, marriage, and first birth. All of this fostered an easy transition from girlhood to womanhood and an unambivalent mother/daughter tie.[1]

While Smith-Rosenberg has been criticized for painting a rose-colored picture of contentment and solidarity in the female world, her mother/daughter image and her suggestion of smooth adolescent transition have prompted less objection. However, if we consider the changes in middle-class women's lives in the last quarter of the nineteenth century, changes in the material conditions of womanhood and in cultural notions of femininity, it is difficult to imagine that the mother/daughter relationship and the daughter's transition to womanhood were entirely problem free. If some daughters experienced adolescence as difficult, if some daughters experienced ambivalence in their relationships with their mothers, what historical record would there be for this difficulty and ambivalence? How does the historian investigate inter-generational conflict and adolescents' problems with assuming adult roles? Letters between mothers and daughters surely would not indicate much tension or hostility, and, in fact, letters tend to sentimentalize the relationship between the correspondents.[2] It is possible to detect ambivalence in some women's diaries, by reading closely and between the lines, but failure to find ambivalence in diaries does not mean that it was absent. A different kind of evidence is needed to explore possible mother/daughter conflict and uneasy transition from girlhood to womanhood.

One possible source of information about adolescent role conflict in the mid– to late nineteenth century is psychosomatic illness. Many historians have argued convincingly that mental illness and psychosomatic illness can be interpreted functionally; that is, the illness can be viewed as an individual or group response to particular social conditions or cultural values. Carroll Smith-Rosenberg in her study of hysteria, Howard Feinstein in his study of neurasthenia in the James family, and Christopher Lasch in his study of narcissism argue that such illnesses are social phenomena and have wider significance than their individual sufferers.[3] The presence of mental or psychosomatic illness that is induced or aggravated by specific social or cultural conditions suggests that those conditions are also problematic in a less intense way for nonsufferers. Furthermore, the illness itself is merely an extreme response, an overreaction, that the healthy or the sane exhibit in less dramatic ways. In Lasch's words: "[P]athology represents a heightened version of normality."[4]

Viewing psychosomatic illness as social commentary as well as individual malady can provide new information about nineteenth-century adolescence. Although women's letters to their mothers do not indicate hostility or tension and although there is little written evidence of difficult transitions into adulthood, some adolescent girls born in the midcentury period developed a psychosomatic illness known as "chlorosis." Beginning around puberty and ending by age 25, chlorosis was an illness unique to adolescent women. Although the disease was reported as early as the sixteenth century, medical observers agreed that it was an increasingly widespread problem in the mid– to late nineteenth century, some even declaring chlorosis to be of epidemic proportions. By the beginning of the First World War, however, chlorosis had vanished as a commonly diagnosed medical problem.[5] Because it was directly related to adolescence and in fact was "cured" by physical maturity, and because it seemed to flourish in the 1870s and 1880s, chlorosis can provide information about the struggles of adolescent girls in that particular time.

Although chlorosis was named for the greenish color of its victims, medical historians believe this symptom was not actually characteristic. Besides the age and sex of its sufferers and the expectation of recovery, the most outstanding features of the disease were amenorrhoea (the absence of menses), a disturbed mental state, a pronounced disturbance of appetite, loss of weight, and a tendency to relapse in the third or fourth decades of life. Medical historians have puzzled over the nature and cause of chlorosis, but the most common explanation has been that chlorosis was a type of anemia. This explanation does not address the question of the special characteristics of the 1870s and 1880s that might have produced the anemia or made it more noticeable to medical writers. If we add a psychological dimension to the interpretation, a clearer image emerges. I. S. L. Loudon has argued in "Chlorosis, Anemia, and Anorexia Nervosa" that chlorosis was a functional disorder, psychologically rooted, which was closely related to what we today would call anorexia nervosa: willful self-starvation accompanied by a distorted body image.[6] Loudon describes chlorosis in Great Britain and sees it as a manifestation of middle-class concerns over self-control at a time when such control was valued as a sign of middle-class status.

Although I will offer a different interpretation of the meaning of chlorosis, I agree with Loudon that the disease was another name for anorexia. Mid-nineteenth-century medical writers in the United States described chlorosis in terms very similar to twentieth-century descriptions of anorexia. Chlorosis was always associated with "young unmarried women" around the age of fourteen or fifteen sometimes extending from fourteen to twenty.[7] "It never occurs except at or near the age of puberty," one physician noted.[8] Loss of appetite was a characteristic of chlorosis according to nineteenth-century writers. A "capricious appetite," "feeble appetite and digestion," and "eating little" were noted to accompany the disorder.[9] "One of the most frequent causes of the disease . . . is *starvation*, as if the food prepared is at fault," one physician remarked.[10] In addition to appetite loss and age, a second commonly noted symptom of chlorosis was depression and a longing for solitude. Chlorotic girls were said to have "disturbing emotions," to be "low-spirited," and to "weep easily."[11] They also were described as having a "distaste for exertion and society."[12] Prudence Saur, a midcentury physician, described the chlorotic girl: "She is sad, subject to fits of weeping, and prefers to be alone."[13] These three characteristics (puberty-related, appetite disturbance, depression) are also commonly associated with anorexia.

Further indication that chlorosis was what today would be diagnosed as anorexia is the nineteenth-century use of the term "anorexia." Physicians considered anorexia to be a symptom of physiological disorder, not as a disease in an of itself. They used the term "anorexia" to mean "loss of appetite."[14] Many physicians in the mid– to late nineteenth century explained the anorexia of chlorosis as related to the connection between the reproductive system and the digestive system. Some related the symptoms of chlorosis, including anorexia, to low hemoglobin. Even physicians who explained chlorosis as due to cultural or environmental factors, such as overeducation or overwork, believed the symptoms were physiologically induced. In an article entitled "Cases of Neurasthenia or Chlorosis," the physician-authors concluded that their cases were neurasthenia and *not* chlorosis because they displayed only psychological symptoms.[15] Physicians did not see chlorosis as anorexia because they were looking for physical causes for the loss of appetite, refusal of food, and vomiting of food thought to be a symptom of chlorosis. Not until the twentieth century, with the growing influence of Freud and psychoanalysis, did "anorexia nervosa" become a popular diagnostic category and physicians begin to focus on psychological origins. At the same time, chlorosis began to disappear as a disease.[16]

Although most nineteenth-century physicians searched for a physical cause of the symptoms of chlorosis, many recognized the malady as a "nervous disorder" and some even identified malnutrition as the most significant symptom. A French physician quoted in an approving article in an American medical journal noted that "nervous troubles" were "extended," "profound," and "rebellious" in chlorosis.[17] An American physician, William H. Thompson, asserted that chlorosis was caused by a nervous disorder that affected the "nutritive organs." Thompson went on to say that a clear view of "anaemia, chlorosis, hysteria, et cetera" would come only with knowledge of the interrelationship of the "nerves" and the "organs concerned in nutrition."[18] For Dr. Thompson, anorexia and/or the rejection of food (vomiting) was the first manifestation of chlorosis. "The entire alimentary apparatus, from beginning to end, commences to act strangely. First of all, the nervous sensation of hunger disappears, to be replaced perhaps by the most curious and capricious manifestation indicative of perverted nervous transmission. The stomach frequently rejects food, or deals with it most uneasily."[19] James McShane, a Baltimore physician, viewed chlorosis as "essentially a disease of the nervous system." He linked the malady to emotion, disappointment, city life, and a sedentary life, and he described the psychological symptoms as "hysterical."[20] In "Cases of Chlorosis," the physician-author reported two cases of young women who were "afflicted with persistent vomiting" that left them weak and pale.[21] Each of these physicians described symptoms that today would be diagnosed as anorexia.

Nancy M. Theriot

One nineteenth-century physician, Charles E. Simon of Baltimore, came closest to recognizing chlorosis as anorexia. Writing in the *American Journal of the Medical Sciences* of thirty-one cases of chlorosis, Simon reviewed the current theories as to the etiology of the disease and offered his own opinion based on case studies and reading other physicians' case studies. "The writer has been led to the conclusion," he wrote, "that in the great majority of cases chlorosis is essentially a disease of malnutrition, the result very frequently of abnormal feeding in early childhood."[22] He asserted that "every physician probably has seen cases of chlorosis in which body weight was 95 pounds or even less," and he noted that the "capricious appetite" of chlorotic girls is "proverbial." One of his own cases weighed 74 pounds. Simon thought that chlorosis was brought on by emotional or environmental, not physical causes, and he listed early habits of low protein eating, mental strain, sedentary habits, sexual excess (masturbation), worry, and grief as "causes" in his case studies. He also noted the pattern associated with the onset of anorexia by twentieth-century writers: the gradual elimination of various foods from the diet. "This and that article of food is thought to disagree and is abandoned, until finally a condition develops where the patient is practically starving."[23] It shouldn't be surprising that Simon treated chlorosis with a high protein diet (and a pint of dark beer daily).

If chlorosis was an early name for anorexia, what was the meaning of the malady for nineteenth-century girls? One possibility is that the chlorotic girl was simply trying to approximate the maternal generation's ideal of feminine beauty, and, like the modern anorexic, was displaying extreme behavior, which was typical in less dramatic forms of young women in general. In the twentieth century, when most American women are either actively dieting or think they should be, the anorexic takes fashionable thinness to the point of absurdity. In the mid–nineteenth century, when paleness, fainting spells, and general "delicacy" were idealized as romantic and feminine, the chlorotic girl was the romantic heroine *par excellence*. Nineteenth-century writers noted that thinness was part of the ideal of feminine beauty: "invalidism, pallor, small appetite, and a languid mode of speech and manner" were considered fashionable in the midcentury period.[24] A foreign visitor noticed "too much thinness" among American girls.[25] And Jerome Smith, a midcentury physician, wrote: "no calamity is more dreaded than fat in an aspiring young lady." He went on to say that young women's "partial starvation" sometimes "degenerates into an insane determination to be the shadow, rather than the substance, of a live woman,"[26] a very apt comment about the deeper, psychological issues involved in chlorosis/anorexia. A British physician also interpreted the anorexia of chlorosis as prompted by cultural norms: "She thinks of her appearance and tightens her waist. Afraid of getting fat, she stints herself in food, and eats of only dainty things."[27] Like the twentieth-century anorexic, the nineteenth-century chlorotic girl can be interpreted as taking her culture's ideal of feminine beauty to its suicidal limits. Her pathology expressed an exaggerated normality.

While consideration of fashion might have prompted some cases of chlorosis/anorexia, there were deeper issues involved then as now. A 110-pound woman whose normal weight should be 125 could see herself as "fashionably thin"; when her weight drops to 85, different questions must be asked. In the late twentieth century, both clinical psychiatrists and imagistic psychologists have described anorexia as an indication of acute anxiety over the adult feminine role expressed through rejection of the mature female body.[28] Both also view anorexia as a mother/daughter conflict. If applied to chlorosis, this explanation offers several possible meanings of the illness in the 1870s and 1880s adolescent world. When viewed as an earlier name for anorexia, chlorosis can be interpreted at least three ways: as an individual disorder, as a "family system" dysfunction, and as an individual response to social and cultural change. I will argue for the third interpretation because it is the only one that can claim any historical validity. However, I want to respond briefly to the other two interpretations before offering my argument, trusting that the digression will be useful in clarifying my position.

One late-twentieth-century interpretation of anorexia is psychoanalytic. Viewing anorexia in this way, one would argue that it is an individual impulse disorder with pre-oedipal fixations.[29] I find this interpretation of anorexia very problematic since it disregards the specifics of historical time/space in favor of a circular argument that can be proven neither true nor false with empirical evidence. Applying this point of view to a different historical time is even more problematic because we do not have the testimony of chlorotic girls or their parents to analyze for evidence of "impulse disorders." It may or may not be true that some, or even all cases of chlorosis involved "impulse disorder," but we have no way to validate this with historical evidence. Therefore, we say nothing about chlorosis as a nineteenth-century phenomenon when we interpret it psychoanalytically; it is simply not an interpretation that explains anything.

The second possible interpretation, that chlorosis (anorexia) involved a family system dysfunction, is more suggestive. Late-twentieth-century researchers interested in the family dynamics of anorexics have found that sexual abuse is a factor in many anorexics' childhoods.[30] Historians of the nineteenth century have also found that sexual abuse of children was more widespread than we had thought.[31] It is very possible that many cases of chlorosis had sexual abuse as a root cause. However, evidence of sexual abuse of children and evidence that adolescents developed chlorosis does not necessarily mean the two were connected. In order to connect chlorosis with sexual abuse of daughters, we would have to have case studies linking the two. Having no evidence of the

Nancy M. Theriot

link does not mean that the link did not exist, but it does mean that we can say very little about the connection between chlorosis and sexual abuse.

What both of these interpretations have in common is the necessity of detailed case studies in order to make the argument. Unfortunately, cases of chlorosis reported in medical journals contain no information to support (or refute) either a psychoanalytic or a family dysfunction interpretation. The case studies contain enough information about behavior for us to see that chlorotic girls of the nineteenth century and anorexic girls of the twentieth century shared the same symptoms. Just as cases of anorexia can be linked to a variety of causes, including specific family dynamics, there were probably cases of chlorosis brought on by particular family relationships. For the historian, however, chlorosis and anorexia are most interesting because of their concentration in a particular time and in a particular class. The question is not: What one factor causes anorexic behavior (sexual abuse, being the oldest child of an alcoholic parent, etc.)? Regardless of the various situations prompting some girls to develop chlorosis, the question is: Why *these* symptoms at *this* time among *this* social group? Chlorosis and anorexia are historically significant because of the larger social and cultural tensions reflected in chlorotic and anorexic girls.

In the post–Civil War decades when medical men described chlorosis as "epidemic" in the middle class, certain structural characteristics of the middle-class family made anorexic behavior an understandable response to the changing boundaries of female life. As Glenn Davis demonstrated in *Childhood and History in America*, child-rearing patterns both influence and are influenced *by* larger social and cultural developments.[32] Following Davis's lead, I will argue in the remainder of this essay that chlorosis was epidemic in the 1870s and 1880s because it was a product of a particular child-rearing pattern among middle-class mothers and daughters during a time of changing expectations and opportunities for women. Within a particular family structure, chlorosis was an indication of mother/daughter stress and adolescent ambivalence about adulthood at a time when mothers' and daughters' worlds were becoming increasingly different.

Let us turn our attention first to family structure. Throughout the nineteenth century, middle-class women were wives, mothers, and daughters in a nuclear family that was increasingly privatized. As a by-product of the economic and social changes accompanying a rising industrial economy, motherhood became the chief occupation of middle-class women and mothers became the more significant parent for middle-class children. Both clinical observation and social-psychological theory indicate that the child-nurturing context of the privatized nuclear family, in which women provide the primary parenting, produces definite consequences for mothers and daughters.[33] The structure itself leads to an intensely close mother/daughter relationship and overidentification on the part of both mother and daughter. For the girl, gender is personified; the daughter's sense of femininity is fused with her sense of mother-as-female. This structural feature of the middle-class family was accentuated in the nineteenth century by the woman's world Carroll Smith-Rosenberg describes. Not only were daughters raised in constant proximity to their female parent, but they were also part of their mothers' female community from infancy, through girlhood, to womanhood. They were constantly surrounded by live examples of their futures as women.

With the exception of strict behavioralists, there is widespread agreement among all varieties of psychologists that both role modeling in the family and general cultural stimuli are sources of role learning for children and adolescents.[34] Keeping in mind the nineteenth-century middle-class family structure and its particular ramifications for mothers and daughters, what were girls learning about womanhood in the 1870s and 1880s? From their mothers and from the fictional and prescriptive literature written by their mothers' generation, girls received a mixed message about womanhood, a message complicated by changing social conditions.

The mothers, women who were adults by the 1840s, were raised within the cultural expectations of "true womanhood" and "moral motherhood."[35] The conditions of their lives led them to see suffering and submission as essential to womanhood. They described themselves as unhealthy, had numerous female-related illnesses that were not correctable, wanted to control fertility but had only abstinence and frequent abortion as a means of fertility control, and suffered through the first generations of male birth attendants (seen by medical historians as incompetent and dangerous at that time).[36] Because suffering seemed to be "natural" to womanhood, middle-class women writers idealized suffering as a specifically feminine virtue and tied suffering to the necessities of female life. In diaries and letters, in domestic fiction and in prescriptive literature directed to their daughters' generation, middle-class women wrote of self-sacrificial suffering as basic to the feminine role. At the same time, women who described mothering as a health-breaking burden and domesticity as a boring, thankless duty also *advocated* motherhood and self-denying domestic service for their daughters.[37] From their mothers' generation, daughters received the message that womanhood would bring suffering and self-denial and that submission to this fate was both expected and laudable.

By the 1870s and 1880s, however, the necessity of feminine suffering and self-denial was called into question. Adolescents of the mid– to late nineteenth century were the first generation of women to have access to secondary education of a serious nature and university education, both sex-segregated and coeducational. Although female education stressed altruistic service to society, the young woman was encouraged to take active control of her life and prepare herself for a larger-than-domestic world. Furthermore, jobs and professions were available to young middle-class women that were unheard of in their mothers' youth. Women were invited into sales jobs, begrudgingly into medicine and law, and enthusiastically into the new social science fields by the last part of the century.[38] As if to further complicate the young woman's acceptance of her mother's suffering world view, medical advances in anesthesia and aseptic technique rendered childbirth less painful, less dangerous, and less damaging to a woman's body, and birth-related injuries could be surgically repaired. The female body, which to the earlier generation had been a metaphor for the necessity of feminine suffering, was less of a liability to the 1870s and 1880s generation because of scientific management.[39]

The feminine ideology that midcentury mothers passed on to daughters stressed suffering, self-abnegation, and submission as basic to "true womanhood," but the daughters' new experience as women made these "virtues" less relevant. Within the psychosexual structure of same-sex parenting and in a historical situation further encouraging intense mother/daughter identification, struggle between mothers and adolescent daughters would be avoidable only if daughters believed their lives would exactly replicate their mothers' lives. This is precisely what Smith-Rosenberg assumes to have been the case; supposedly, the daughter moved easily, without ambivalence, from girlhood into a womanhood like her mother's, and so mother and daughter felt no conflict and daughter was not concerned about her approaching womanhood.[40] But for daughters born in the midcentury period, this was not the story. The future included different possibilities. The necessity of feminine suffering, the propriety of nondomestic education, the assumption of self-denying motherhood as the natural and exclusive lifework of adult women—these were opened to question by the 1870s.

The growing difference between mothers' and daughters' worlds, within the particular family structure of the nineteenth century, must have led to mother/daughter tension and to adolescent uneasiness over the transition into womanhood in some middle-class families.[41] Anorexic behavior was a manifestation of this tension and uneasiness. Chlorosis can be seen as an exaggerated act of rebellion for the daughter, a temporary refusal to accept the dictates of "true womanhood" by rejecting maturity, resisting other-directedness, and declaring herself different and separate from mother—while at the same time never confronting mother directly, never specifically rejecting mother, and, in fact, imitating mother's own sickliness.

The chlorotic girl's anorexic behavior was rejection of physical maturity, and therefore the adult female role. It was a dramatic acting out of a common adolescent fear carried to its extreme. In the mid–nineteenth century, when adult females continually described their lives in terms of suffering, even the healthy adolescent girl frequently experienced anxiety over her rapidly approaching maturity. Medical and lay observers testified that young women experienced puberty as a time of sickness.[42] Women also described it as a "crisis" and a "supreme emergency."[43] Girls' ignorance as to what was happening to them contributed to this healthy fear of maturity. Women wrote very frequently that mothers did not teach daughters about their bodies. More specifically, writers claimed that daughters were not taught about "the mysterious process of reproduction."[44] One woman wrote of her fear and ignorance on the eve of her midcentury marriage: "The problematic relations of marriage and its mysteries filled me with something akin to terror."[45] Another woman reported that girls commonly started their periods without knowing about menstruation.[46]

Puberty was dramatic not only because of the physical changes involved and because of body ignorance, but more so because the physical changes demanded that a girl think of herself as a woman. As her body began to resemble the mature female form and the onset of menstruation signified her physical readiness for reproduction, the cultural expectations of feminine gender became more acute for the growing girl. Associating puberty with its cultural manifestations, for example hair and dress style, young women often focused rage and disappointment on the symbols of womanhood. One wrote negatively of her dresses being let down and her curls "caught up and fastened with a matronly looking comb."[47] Another described "the traditional weight of an increased length of skirt."[48] Both viewed these womanly demands as a hindrance to activity and a cause of lament. Frances Willard gave a most revealing description of the outward change demanded by culture to signify the girl was now a woman. She wrote in her diary:

> This is my seventeenth birthday, and the date of my martyrdom. Mother insists that at last I *must* have my hair "done up woman fashion." She says she can hardly forgive herself for letting me "run wild" so long. We had a great time over it all, and here I sit . . . My "back hair" is twisted up like a corkscrew; I carry eighteen hair-pins; my head aches, my feet are entangled in the skirt of my new gown. I can never jump over a fence again so long as I live. As for chasing the sheep down in the shady pasture, it's out of the question, and to climb down to my "Eagle's Nest" seat in the big burr oak would ruin this new frock beyond repair. Altogether, I recognize the fact that "my occupation's gone."[49]

The chlorotic girl was an exaggeration of this tension surrounding physical maturity. By reducing her food intake she became physically smaller, caused her menses to cease, and reclaimed maternal solicitude. In effect, she chose childhood over adulthood by refusing to allow her body to take on the characteristic curves and fullness of mature female form. The chlorotic girl expressed in extreme form what her more acquiescent sisters also felt: ambivalence about adult femininity.

This is especially clear when we consider physicians' case studies and the conclusions they drew from their cases. "Abnormal development of the sexual apperatus" and masturbation were cited as causes of chlorosis, indicating that adolescent awakening to sexual urges prompted some girls to stop eating.[50] One physician noted that "the process of sexual development is looked to as the time of most common occurrences of chlorosis."[51] Another noted that chlorosis was one of the most common disorders of women fourteen to twenty-four and concluded: "It is very natural, then, to attribute the disease to the effects of these processes which are going on in the bodies of young girls at the passage of puberty." The physician admitted, however, that no one understood the "physiological connexion" between puberty and chlorosis.[52] Many physicians, based on their experience with the disease, concluded that menstruation must in some sense "cause" chlorosis since physical maturity and chlorosis so often went together.

Physicians' interpretation of chlorosis as brought on by the physical changes associated with puberty should not be taken as necessarily "correct." However, the fact that girls were brought to physicians for chlorotic symptoms around puberty by mothers who saw their daughters as ill is significant. Girls were displaying these symptoms as their bodies were developing into women's bodies. Physicians who connected chlorosis with puberty were simply observing that chlorotic symptoms most often appeared during the transition to physical maturity.

The psychological strains of puberty, specifically the fear of womanhood, was noted by a New York physician, T. Gaillard Thomas. Thomas agreed with his colleagues that chlorosis was brought on by the changes of puberty, but thought that the emotional stress, not the physical stress, was most significant. He claimed that most chlorotic girls were brought to doctors by mothers who were concerned about their daughters' amenorrhea, obstinate constipation (a side effect of anorexia), "or more or less rapid emaciation." Gaillard viewed chlorosis as caused by "some strong mental or emotional disturbance," and noted that "nostalgia" was regarded as "one of its most frequent causes."[53]

Some young women developed chlorosis *after* puberty, but several physician case studies indicate that these women too experienced adult femininity as threatening. Some of the older chlorotic women (between eighteen and thirty) developed chlorosis after being abandoned by lovers. In one case, a young woman developed chlorosis after being sexually aroused to the point of orgasm with her fiancé. Another nineteen-year-old developed chlorosis after the wedding of a friend.[54] Like the younger girls, whose chlorosis was brought on by physical maturation, the older chlorotic young women also demonstrated ambivalence over adult roles.

Besides avoiding physical maturity, the young woman who developed chlorosis could also exert control and exercise self-direction over her life/body without rejecting her mother's world view. According to the maternal message, adult femininity demanded that a woman be passive and receptive. The "true woman" that the young girl was supposed to become was required to wait passively to be chosen in marriage, to endure patiently the physical trials of pregnancy and birth, to go quietly wherever her husband chose to live, to submit lovingly to her husband's wishes. Even in dealing with her own children, the "true woman" was not to be willful; she was to see herself as the transmitter of culture and the guardian of the young, always taking direction from husbands, clergymen, physicians, and counselors. The chlorotic girl, during the time of her illness, symbolically rejected this external control and asserted her will over her body and her environment.[55] She caused her body to diminish or grow according to her desire; she consumed indigestible substances (clay, pebbles, etc.) and elicited concern from her family; she became clinically ill (anemia was a side effect of chlorosis) and required medical attention. Like the twentieth-century anorexic, the chlorotic girl symbolically (and actually) controlled her world by controlling her body—while never directly challenging her mother's world view.

The controlling aspect of chlorosis was clear in many case studies. One writer described the nervous symptoms of chlorosis as "rebellious" and another wrote that chlorosis brought on "hysterical and infantile paralysis."[56] A Baltimore physician presented case studies in 1876 in which chlorosis was said to change the "character." "The individual becomes morose, melancholic, or subject of various *whimsicalities* of disposition."[57] He hinted that such moodiness was manipulative, citing examples of chlorotic girls whose illness was cured by getting their way. A similar conclusion was drawn by a New York City physician whose chlorotic patient was "vomiting every day almost all the solids and fluids which she was prevailed upon to swallow"; the doctor treated her with a placebo and suggested that the girl's behavior was under her control and was manipulative like a hysteric's attack."[58]

The disturbed mental state accompanying chlorosis was described by many physicians as very similar to hysteria, a disease of more mature women that has been interpreted as a temporary release from role performance.[59] Like hysteria, chlorosis gave the young woman the opportunity to reject feminine "other-directedness" by giving her permission to be moody, infantile, and demanding. Instead of following the dictates of a role that sometimes required her to provide care for others (younger siblings), to guard against angry or melancholy emotions, and to minister to the needs and desires of those around

Nancy M. Theriot

her (especially father and brothers), the chlorotic girl was freed by her illness to take, rather than give, and to express negative feelings, rather than hide behind a considerate facade.

Chlorosis put the girl in the center of the family and drew loving concern, patient understanding of moods, and gentle caretaking to her. Especially significant was the fact that the chlorotic girl received increased maternal attention in ways that she had as a very young child: motherly concern over diet and appetite, motherly pampering of fluctuating moods, motherly protection from the demands of household and household members. Regardless of the numerous theories as to what chlorosis actually was, physicians prescribed regimens that demanded increased maternal caretaking. Many recommended complete bed rest with very specific feeding routines. Almost all outpatient chlorotics were treated with some form of iron, administered by the mother. Also, since chlorosis/anorexia always involved constipation, most physicians prescribed some sort of laxative, thus making the girl's mother responsible for keeping track of her daughter's bowel movements in a way reminiscent of infancy. Instead of practicing other directedness as "true womanhood" required, the girl suffering with chlorosis claimed the attention and concern of significant others, especially mother, without eliciting her mother's anger or disapproval.

The deepest mother/daughter questions involved in chlorosis/anorexia cannot be answered positively for the nineteenth-century malady. Although it seems logical to assume that the chlorotic girl was in some sense imitating her mother's "sickliness" or the sickliness the daughter associated with her mother's generation, physicians and therapists who work with twentieth-century anorexics see the mother's symbolic importance differently. For the twentieth-century writers, mother is the symbol of adult femininity that daughter hopes to avoid. Anorexia maintains a distance between mother and daughter by preventing the daughter from becoming her mother, physically.

This interpretation applied to nineteenth-century chlorosis provides a consistent and interesting summation of the mother/daughter dynamic in chlorotic behavior. While avoiding maturity, exerting control, and rejecting other directedness, the chlorotic girl also expressed her difference from mother and her hope for a different future. The maternal body, with its curves, fullness, and fertility, represented the adolescent girl's destiny. In the feminine drama, the young woman was eventually to become her mother. But chlorosis established a physical boundary, albeit temporary, between mother and daughter, and thus hinted at different adult possibilities for the daughter. The chlorotic girl, with her slightly emaciated angularity and childlike, sexless contours, resembled her younger brother more than she did her mother. Perhaps, like him, she could escape the dictates of nature and female body. If her physical form were different enough from her mother's form, perhaps she was not predetermined to repeat her mother's life, but might, instead, have maternal permission for a different future.

Viewed within the context of the adolescent life world of the 1870s and 1880s, chlorosis can be seen as evidence that some daughters feel ambivalent about adult femininity and about their mothers as representatives of womanhood. Daughters at that time grew with a model of womanhood, an inherited feminine script, that was becoming obsolete in the transition to "modern" America. However, the structural and historical conditions defining a "female world of love and ritual" made it difficult for young women to express outright rebellion or to believe fully in a future different from their mothers.' Mother/daughter tension and anxiety over impending womanhood surfaced in psychosomatic symptoms. The nineteenth-century chlorotic girl was the embodiment of this tension and anxiety, but other girls who avoided the extremes of illness indicated similar feelings in their reluctant acceptance of the physical symbols of approaching womanhood, the dress and hairstyle changes which signaled the transition to a social status less free and more demanding. Although chlorosis affected only a small number of middle-class girls, it can be interpreted as an extreme form of a more pervasive, less intense adolescent response to a feminine ideology that was becoming out of touch with the changing material conditions of female life.

Faced with the female adolescent dilemma, the impossibility *and* the necessity of going beyond the maternal vision of womanhood, how did "healthy," "normal" daughters respond? Just as most girls in the late twentieth century do not develop anorexia, most girls in the mid–nineteenth century did not develop chlorosis. Instead, as late-nineteenth-century women, they forged a new feminine synthesis from the contradictions of their mothers' world view and their own experience of a freer, less physically demanding womanhood. Keeping the core of their original sexual script, the daughters retained motherhood as other-directed and as central to a woman's life; however, motherhood came to be a metaphor not for passive suffering and submission, but for active self-directed and altruistic public service. Late-nineteenth-century women transposed "moral motherhood" into "professional motherhood," necessary suffering into chosen altruism, and submission to male authority into devotion to public-spirited female superiority. Like their mothers, most late-nineteenth-century women remained committed to separate spheres and a revised version of "natural" womanhood. They created their own sense of proper femininity *not* by rejecting their inherited sexual script and *not* by accepting it, but by amending it to express their acceptance of a world different from their mothers', while remaining uncritical daughters.[60]

Nancy M. Theriot

Chlorosis marked the beginning of a new mother/daughter tension prompted by the accelerated rate of change in the material conditions defining women's lives. Since girls grow with their mothers' world view into a world unimagined by their mothers, daughters must always adjust their inherited idea of womanhood to fit their new conditions. Because those conditions change more rapidly in a modern, as opposed to traditional society, the modern mother/daughter relationship cannot help but be somewhat problematic for both mothers and daughters. Chlorosis dramatized the mother/daughter ambivalence and the anxiety over mature womanhood which would become more and more characteristic of modern female adolescence.

Notes

1. Carroll Smith-Rosenberg, "The Female World of Love and Ritual: Relations between Women in Nineteenth-Century America," *Signs*, 1(1975), 1–30.
2. Anne Boylan called my attention to this drawback in using letters as sources of information about the relative closeness or tension in relationships.
3. Carroll Smith-Rosenberg, "The Hysterical Woman: Sex Roles and Role Conflict in Nineteenth-Century America," *Social Research*, 39(1972), 562–583; Howard M. Feinstein, "The Use and Abuse of Illness in the James Family Circle," in *Our Selves Our Past*, ed. Robert J. Grugger (Baltimore: The Johns Hopkins University Press, 1981), pp. 228–242; Christopher Lasch, "The Narcissistic Personality in Our Time," in *Our Selves Our Past*, pp. 385–404.
4. Lasch, "The Narcissistic Personality in Our Time," p. 392.
5. I came across references to chlorosis in medical writings and in books dealing with health, such as: Edward H. Dixon, *Woman and Her Diseases* (New York: A. Ranney, 1857); Pye H. Chavasse, *Advice to Mothers on the Management of Their Offspring* (New York: D. Appleton and Co., 1844). William Beach, *An Improved System of Midwifery* (New York: Baker and Scribner, 1850), pp. 179–184 is the most detailed description of the "sickliness" of young women that did not name chlorosis (the writers were not physicians), but the descriptions coincide with the medical symptoms of chlorosis. See Samuel Osgood, *The Hearthstone: Thoughts upon Home-Life in Our Cities* (New York: D. Appleton and Co., 1854), pp. 227–229; William A. Alcott, *The Young Woman's Book of Health* (New York: Auburn, Miller, Orton, and Mulligan, 1855), pp. 30–31, 201; George Sumner Weaver, *Aims and Aids for Girls and Young Women on the Various Duties of Life*; Caroline Louisa Tuthill, *The Young Lady's Home* (Boston: Wm. J. Reynolds and Co., 1847), pp. 74–78; Miss Coxe, *Claims of the Country on American Females* (Columbus: Isaac N. Whiting, 1842), pp. 98–100; Catharine Maria Sedgwick, *Means and Ends, or Self-Training* (Boston: March, Capen, Lyon and Webb, 1840), pp. 34–51; Elizabeth Blackwell, *The Laws of Life, with Special Reference to the Physical Education of Girls* (New York: George P. Putnam, 1852), pp. 138–140; Mary S. Gove, *Lectures to Ladies on Anatomy and Physiology* (Boston: Saxton and Pierce, 1842), p. 227.
6. I. S. L. Loudon, "Chlorosis, Aneamia, and Anorexia Nervosa," *British Medical Journal*, 281(1980), 1669–1975. See also Paul B. Beeson, "Some Diseases That Have Disappeared," *The American Journal of Medicine*, 68(1980), 806–811; K. Figlio, "Chlorosis and Chronic

Disease in Nineteenth Century Britain: The Social Construction of Somatic Illness in a Capitalistic Society," *Social History*, 3(1978), 167–197. Recently chlorosis has attracted the attention of a women's studies scholar, Joan Jacobs Brumberg. In "Chlorotic Girls, 1870–1920: A Historical Perspective on Female Adolescence," *Child Development*, 53(1982), 1468–1477, Brumberg argues that chlorosis allowed daughters to share symptoms with their fashionably sick mothers and that turn-of-the-century changes meant less social approval for "sickliness" in general (thus the decline of chlorosis by World War I). While I am in basic agreement with Brumberg's explanation, I think she does not give sufficient attention to the mother/daughter relationship, and therefore misses the chlorosis/anorexia connection and the deeper psychological significance of chlorosis.

7. Prudence B. Saur, *Maternity: A Book for Every Wife and Mother* (Chicago: L. P. Miller, 1891), p. 37; Eutocia Cook, *Easy Favorable Child Bearing: A Book for All Women* (Chicago: Arcade Publishing Co., 1886, fourth edition), p. 331.

8. George Napheys, *The Physical Life of Woman: Advice to the Maiden, Wife and Mother* (Philadelphia: G. Maclean, 1870), p. 27.

9. Cook, *Easy Favorable Child Bearing*, p. 331; Saur, *Maternity*, p. 43; George Austin, *Perils of American Women; or, A Doctor's Talk with Maiden, Wife, and Mother* (Boston: Lee and Shepard, 1883), p. 189.

10. Napheys, *The Physical Life of Woman*, p. 31.

11. Saur, *Maternity*, p. 43; Napheys, *The Physical Life of Woman*, p. 27; Cook, *Easy Favorable Child Bearing*, p. 331.

12. Napheys, *The Physical Life of Woman*, p. 27.

13. Saur, *Maternity*, p. 44. Other writers described "case studies" of young women with chlorotic symptoms. See: George Taylor (M.D.), *Health for Women* (New York: American Book Exchange, 1879), pp. 290–298; Clarke, *Sex in Education*, pp. 105–106 (Clarke attributed the symptoms to too much "masculine" study); Ada Shepard Badger in *Sex and Education: A Reply to Dr. E.H. Clarke's "Sex in Education,"* ed. Julia Ward Howe (Boston: Roberts Brothers, 1874), p. 83 (Badger attributed the symptoms to the young girl's leaving school). One mid-nineteenth-century woman described her mental state around age 12 when she was diagnosed as having chlorosis: "I became dyspeptic and nervous. I often awoke in the morning bathed in tears; and the most indescribable and horrible sinking of spirits was my portion." She also complained of headache and dizziness. Gove, *Lectures to Ladies*, p. 227, in which the young woman was quoted, attributed the girl's illness to masturbation as did the woman herself.

14. For example, William H. Thompson, "Chlorosis," *The Medical Record*, 1 (1866), 161, wrote of the "first trouble" that brought girls and their mothers to the doctor as "persistent constipation, attended with anorexia."

15. Cherver Bevill and F. R. Fry, "Cases of Neurasthenia or Chlorosis," *St. Louis Courier Medicine*, 17(1887), 229–231.

16. In the first articles on anorexia nervosa, appearing in British medical journals, what is interesting to the authors is that the anorexia does not seem to be brought on by physiological causes but is instead brought on by "nervous" causes; hence the term "anorexia nervosa." See Sir William Gull, "Anorexia Nervosa," *Lancet*, 1(1888), 516–517; and in that same issue, W. S. Playfair, "Notes on the So-Called 'Anorexia Nervosa,'" 817–818. In the twentieth century, medical articles on anorexia nervosa multiply.

17. M. Nonat, "Reflections on Chlorosis, Especially in Children," *Cincinnati Lancet and Observer*, 3(1860), 706–713.

Nancy M. Theriot

18. Thompson, "Chlorosis," p. 161.

19. Ibid., p. 162. Other physicians who saw appetite disturbance as the major characteristic of chlorosis include: J. A. Mayes, "Observations on Chlorosis, with a Case," *Southern Medical and Surgical Journal*, 6(1850), 513–522; Leon L. Solomon, "Chlorosis—Its Etiology, Diagnosis, and Treatment, Based upon Constipation as a Causative Factor in the Production of the Morbid Condition," *The American Therapist*, 6(1897), 101–106. George A. Gibson, "On the Signs of Chlorosis," *Lancet*, 2(1877), 418–420 wrote that "pain in the epigastrium" after eating contributed to the "little appetite and enfeebled digestion" of the chlorotic patient.

20. James F. McShance, "Chlorosis," *Baltimore Physician and Surgeon*, 6(1876), 19.

21. James B. Burnet, "Cases of Chlorosis," *Medical and Surgical Reporter*, 17 (1867), 71. On vomiting and chlorosis, see also William A. Hammond, "On Mental Therapeutics," 38(1878), 383–388.

22. Charles E. Simon, "A Study of 31 Cases on Chlorosis with Special Reference to the Etiology and the Dietetic Treatment of the Disease," *American Journal of the Medical Sciences*, 113(1897), 412.

23. Ibid., p. 417.

24. Helen Ekin Starrett, *Letters to Elder Daughters, Married and Unmarried* (Chicago: A. C. McClury and Co., 1892), p. 132.

25. Marie Therese Blanc, *The Condition of Woman in the United States, A Traveller's Notes*, tr. Abby Landdon Alger (Boston: Roberts Brothers, 1895), p. 26.

26. Jerome Smith, *The Ways of Women in Their Physical, Moral and Intellectual Relation* (New York: Jewett, 1873), p. 115.

27. Sir Andrew Clark, "Anaemia or Chlorosis of Girls, Occurring More Commonly between the Advent of Menstruation and the Consummation of Womanhood," *Lancet*, 2(1887), 1004.

28. The medical (psychiatric and psychological) literature on anorexia is very extensive. For example, see: M. R. Kaufman, M. Heiman, eds., *Evolution of Psychosomatic Concepts: Anorexia Nervosa: A Paradigm* (New York: International Universities Press, 1964); H. Bruch, *Eating Disorders: Obesity, Anorexia Nervosa, and the Person Within* (New York: Basic Books, 1973); Salvador Minuchin, Bernice L. Rosman, and Lester Baker, *Psychosomatic Families: Anorexia Nervosa in Context* (Cambridge: Harvard University Press, 1978); Alan Sugarman, Donald M. Quinlan, and Luanna Devenis, "Ego Boundary Disturbance in Anorexia Nervosa: Preliminary Findings," *Journal of Personality Assessment*, 46(1982), 455–461; Paul E. Garfinkel and David M. Garner, *Anorexia Nervosa: A Multidimensional Perspective* (New York: Bruner/Mazel, 1982); A. H. Crisp, *Anorexia Nervosa: Let Me Be* (London: Academic Press, 1980). For a feminist explanation of anorexia, see Marlene Boskind-Lodahl, "Cinderella's Stepsisters: A Feminist Perspective on Anorexia Nervosa and Bulimia," *Signs*, 2(1976), 342–356. See also Robert Avens, *Imagination is Reality* (Dallas: Spring Publications, 1980); James Hillman, *The Myth of Analysis* (Evanston, Ill.: Northwestern University Press, 1972), especially part 3 "On Psychological Femininity"; Peter L. Berger and Thomas Luckmann, *The Social Construction of Reality: A Treatise in the Sociology of Knowledge* (London: Allen Lane, 1966).

29. This psychoanalytic view of anorexia was suggested in the review of this essay by Casper G. Schmidt, dated 28 September 1987.

30. The possible connection between chlorosis and sexual abuse was suggested by Ardyce Masters as a referee for this essay, citing twentieth-century studies of anorexia that link the behavior with sexual abuse. As I indicated in the text, I believe there could have been

a connection between chlorosis and sexual abuse in some family situations; however, historical evidence does not exist to draw positive conclusions about this point.

31. Masters cited Florence Rush, *The Best Kept Secret: Sexual Abuse of Children* (New York: McGraw-Hill Book Company, 1980) for information about nineteenth-century sexual abuse.

32. Glenn Davis, *Childhood and History in America* (New York: Psychohistory Press, 1976). The assumption that child-rearing patterns influence and are influenced by larger social and cultural change is shared by many historians and psychologists. For example, see Lloyd deMause, ed. *The History of Childhood* (New York: Psychohistory Press, 1974); Erik H. Erikson, *Childhood and Society* (New York: W. W. Norton, 1963); the work of John Demos, Elizabeth Pleck, Nancy Cott, and Charles Rosenberg, just to name a few.

33. Nancy Chodorow, *The Reproduction of Mothering: Psychoanalysis and the Sociology of Gender* (Berkeley: University of California Press, 1978); and David B. Lynn, *Parental and Sex-Role Identification: A Theoretical Formulation* (Berkeley: McCutchen, 1969). For a very clear explanation of object-relations theory as it applies to sex and personality, see Ethel Spector Person, "Sexuality as the Mainstay of Identity: Psychoanalytic Perspectives," in *Women: Sex and Sexuality*, ed. Catharine E. Stimpson and Ethel Spector Person (Chicago: University of Chicago Press, 1980), pp. 36–61; and Jane Flax, "Political Philosophy and the Patriarchal Unconscious: A Psychoanalytic Perspective on Epistemology and Metaphysics," in *Discovering Reality*, ed. Sandra Harding and Merrill B. Hintikka (Boston: D. Reidel Publishing Co., 1983), pp. 245–282.

34. Social psychological theorists who discuss role learning as it applies to gender include the four cited above and also others from social learning theory and symbolic interactionist perspectives such as: Walter Mischel, "A Social-Learning View of Sex Differences in Behavior," in *The Development of Sex Differences*, ed. Eleanor E. Maccoby (Stanford: Stanford University Press, 1966), pp. 56–81; in the same volume, Lawrence Kohlberg, "A Cognitive-Developmental Analysis of Children's Sex-Role Concepts and Attitudes," pp. 82–173; Walter Mischel, "Sex-Typing and Socialization," in *Carmichael's Manual of Child Psychology*, vol. II, ed. Paul H. Mussen (New York: John Wiley and Sons, Inc., 1970), pp. 3–72; Albert Bandura, *Social Learning Theory* (Englewood Cliffs, N.J.: Prentice-Hall, Inc., 1977); Dorothy Z. Ullian, "The Development of Conceptions of Masculinity and Femininity," in *Exploring Sex Differences*, ed. Barbara B. Lloyd and John Archer (London: Academic Press, 1976), pp. 25–48; Regina Yando, Victoria Seitz, Edward Zigler, *Imitation: A Developmental Perspective* (Hillsdale, N.J.: Lawrence Erbaum Associates, Publishers, 1978).

35. Barbara Welter, "The Cult of True Womanhood: 1820–1860," *American Quarterly*, 18(1966), 151–174; Ruth H. Block, "American Feminine Ideals in Transition: The Rise of the Moral Mother, 1785–1815," *Feminist Studies*, 4(1978), 101–125; Mary P. Ryan, *The Empire of the Mother: American Writing about Domesticity, 1830–1860* in the series *Women and History*, Numbers 2/3, ed. Eleanor S. Riemer (The Institute for Research in History and the Haworth Press, 1982).

36. See Richard W. Wertz and Dorothy G. Wertz, *Lying-In: A History of Childbirth in America* (New York: Schocken Books, 1977); Jane B. Donegan, *Women and Men Midwives: Medicine, Morality and Misogyny in Early America* (Westport, Conn.: Greenwood Press, 1978); Richard H. Shryock, *Medicine and Society in America, 1660–1860* (Ithaca: Cornell University Press, 1962); William G. Rothstein, *American Physicians in the Nineteenth Century: From Sects to Science* (Baltimore: The Johns Hopkins University Press, 1972); Paul Starr, *The Social Transformation of American Medicine* (New York: Basic Books, 1982).

37. I have written about the mother/daughter mixed message in more detail in *The Biosocial Construction of Femininity: Mothers and Daughters in Nineteenth-Century America* (Westport, Conn.: Greenwood Press, 1988). On the theme of suffering in women's fiction see Mary Kelley, *Private Woman, Public Stage: Literary Domesticity in Nineteenth-Century America* (New York: Oxford University Press, 1984).

38. About the changing material conditions of women's lives in the post–Civil War period, see Margaret Gibbons Wilson, *The American Woman in Transition: The Urban Influence, 1870–1920* (Westport, Conn.: Greenwood Press, 1979). On changes in women's education, see Susan Ware, *Beyond Suffrage* (Boston: Harvard University Press, 1981), pp. 22–25; Shelia M. Rothman, *Woman's Proper Place: A History of Changing Ideals and Practices, 1870 to the Present* (New York: Basic Books, 1978), pp. 24–40; and Barbara Miller Solomon, *In the Company of Educated Women: A History of Women in Higher Education in America* (New Haven: Yale University Press, 1985). On women's entrance into the professions see Barbara J. Harris, *Beyond Her Sphere: Women and the Professions in American History* (Westport, Conn.: Greenwood Press, 1978).

39. About some of the physical changes in women's lives related to changes in medicine, see Judith Walzer Leavitt, *Brought to Bed: Childbearing in America, 1750–1950* (New York: Oxford University Press, 1986); and Martin S. Pernick, *A Calculus of Suffering: Pain, Professionalization, and Anesthesia in Nineteenth-Century America* (New York: Columbia University Press, 1985).

40. Smith-Rosenberg, "The Female World of Love and Ritual."

41. Erikson, *Childhood and Society*, argues that one "task" of adolescence is to test the parental world view against the experienced *real* world and that sharp discontinuity between the two produces anxiety in the adolescent.

42. Mary Terhune, *Eve's Daughters: or Common Sense for Maid, Wife, and Mother* (New York: J. R. Anderson and H. S. Allen, 1882), p. 85; Jane Croly, *For Better or Worse: For Some Men and All Women* (Boston: Lee and Shepard, 1875), p. 23; Anna Callender Brackett, ed., *The Education of American Girls* (New York: G. P. Putnam and Sons, 1874), p. 124.

43. Terhune, *Eve's Daughters*, p. 97; Frances Willard, *A Great Mother: Sketches of Madam Willard, by Her Daughter* (Chicago: Woman's Temperance Publishing Association, 1894), p. 145.

44. Anna Callender Brackett, *The Education of American Girls* (New York: G. P. Putnam and Sons, 1874), pp. 61–64. Writers who pointed out that mothers did not teach their daughters about their bodies included Croly, *For Better or Worse*, pp. 216–218; Eliza Barton Lyman, *The Coming Woman; The Royal Road to Perfection*, a series of medical lectures, (Lansing, Mich.: W. S. George, 1880), pp. 177, 178; George Fisk Comfort and Anna Manning Comfort, *Women's Education and Women's Health* (Syracuse, N.Y.: T. W. Durston and Co., 1874), p. 60; Catharine Beecher, *Woman's Profession as Mother and Educator, with Views in Opposition to Woman Suffrage* (Philadelphia: George Maclean, 1872); Mary Studley, *What Our Girls Ought to Know* (New York: M. L. Holbrook and Co., 1878), p. 10; Margaret E. Sangster, *Winsome Womanhood: Familiar Talks on Life and Conduct* (New York: F. H. Revell Co., 1900), p. 27.

45. Mary Rossiter, *My Mother's Life, The Evolution of a Recluse* (Chicago: Fleming H. Revell Co., 1900), p. 72.

46. Terhune, *Eve's Daughters*, pp. 79–84. Since this is also true for some twentieth-century American girls, it is probable that it was more common in the nineteenth century when feminine "modesty" was held to be extremely important and when many women were

ignorant of female physiology. It is also probable that many mothers did not have the language with which to describe menstruation (or intercourse) to their daughters, since female medical writers still referred to women's genitals as "the mysterious organs of generation."

47. Martha Jay Coston, *A Single Success, An Autobiography* (Philadelphia: J. B. Lippincott Co., 1886), p. 22.

48. Helen Gilbert Ecob, *The Well-Dressed Woman; A Study in the Practical Application to Dress of the Laws of Health, Art and Morals* (New York: Fowler and Wells, 1892), pp. 29–30.

49. Frances Willard, *How to Win; A Book for Girls* (New York: Funk and Wagnalls, 1888), pp. 16–17.

50. William B. Neftel, "Chlorosis," *Medical Record*, 8(1873), 98–99; Simon, "A Study of 31 Cases of Chlorosis."

51. Frederick P. Henry, "Relations between Chlorosis, Simple Anaemia, and Pernicious Anaemia," *Medical Record*, 36(1889), 353.

52. Willoughby Francis Wade, "Clinical Lecture on the Relation between Menstruation and the Chlorosis of Young Women," *British Medical Journal*, 2(1872), 35.

53. T. Gaillard Thomas, "Clinical Lecture on Chlorosis," *Boston Medical and Surgical Journal*, 103(1880), 389–390.

54. Simon, "A Study of 31 Cases of Chlorosis," p. 418; McShane, "Chlorosis," p. 19; Burnet, "Cases of Chlorosis," p. 71.

55. Control is also a very important aim of the anorexic. See Crisp, *Anorexia Nervosa*, p. 65 and Minuchin, et. al., *Psychosomatic Families*.

56. Nonat, "Reflections on Chlorosis," p. 708; Neftel, "Some Recent Researches in Pathology," p. 98.

57. McShane, "Chlorosis," p. 19, my emphasis.

58. Hammond, "On Mental Therapeutics," 386–388.

59. On hysteria, see Anne Douglas Wood, "'The Fashionable Diseases': Women's Complaints and Their Treatment in Nineteenth Century America," *Journal of Interdisciplinary History*, 4(1973), 25–52; Smith-Rosenberg, "The Hysterical Woman"; Ilza Weith, *Hysteria: The History of a Disease* (Chicago: University of Chicago Press, 1965); Maria Rarnas, "Freud's Dora, Dora's Hysteria: The Negation of a Woman's Rebellion," *Feminist Studies*, 6(1980), 472–510. Physicians who used the term "hysteria" to characterize chlorosis include: Bevill, "Cases of Neurasthenia or Chlorosis"; Hammond, "On Mental Therapeutics"; McShane, "Chlorosis"; Thompson, "Chlorosis"; Neftel, "Some Recent Researches in Pathology."

60. While this new feminine ideology can be considered a "positive" step in that suffering was no longer the core of femininity, historians have pointed out the drawbacks of late-nineteenth-century feminine ideals. See Rosalind Rosenberg, "In Search of Woman's Nature, 1850–1920," *Feminist Studies*, 3(1975), 141–154; Jill Conway, "Women Reformers and American Culture, 1870–1930," *Journal of Social History*, 5(1971–1972), 164–177.

CHAPTER 9

The *Caddie Woodlawn* Syndrome

American Girlhood in the Nineteenth Century

Anne Scott MacLeod

CADDIE WOODLAWN, a historical novel for children written by
Carol Brink in 1935, held for many years the status of a minor classic of children's literature. Its portrayal of a girl growing up on a pioneer farm in Wisconsin in the mid-1860s was presumed to be faithful both factually and in spirit
to the realities of children's lives in the United States of the period. Briefly, the
narrative centers on a young girl who has been allowed to grow up side-by-
side with her brothers, running free as they run free (and as her two sisters
do not) because her father hoped that such an outdoor life would improve
her fragile health. At the time of the story, Caddie is twelve and approaching
puberty; her mother is becoming less and less tolerant of her untrammeled
ways. The climax of the novel comes about when Caddie and her brothers
conspire in some minor meanness to a visiting girl cousin, but only Caddie
is punished for it by their mother. As Caddie smarts under this injustice, her
father comes and talks to her, letting her know that the time has come when
her life must begin to change, describing the special, separate, and, in his

description, exalted role that women play in the adult world. It is women, he tells her, "who keep the world sweet and beautiful. Women's task is to teach men and boys gentleness and courtesy and love and kindness. It's a big task, too, Caddie—harder than cutting trees or building mills or damming rivers. . . . A woman's work is something fine and noble to grow up to, and it is just as important as a man's. . . . No man could ever do it so well."

But women's work, Mr. Woodlawn makes clear without saying so, requires skills and a discipline impossible to acquire in the free life his daughter had led so far. The real burden of her father's talk is to tell Caddie that her childhood, and with it her freedom, is about to end: "How about it, Caddie," he asks, "Have we run with the colts long enough?"[1] Mr. Woodlawn's lecture on womanly responsibilities is quite in line with the mid-nineteenth-century conception of what was called "woman's sphere."[2] The idea of woman's place as separate and different from the rest of the universe was central to nineteenth-century society, and there is no lack of evidence on the point. Magazines, journals, newspapers, novels, advice books of every kind expounded endlessly on the subject, and most of these expositions, barring those by rebellious women, described the duties and dimensions of women's work very much as Mr. Woodlawn did. His was indeed the bargain offered nineteenth-century women: influence in exchange for freedom; a role as "inspiration" in place of real power; gratitude and affection from family rather than worldly reward or renown. General consensus in America held that woman's sphere was moral rather than intellectual, domestic rather than worldly; her power was indirect; her contribution to the world was through husband and children, her reward their love and respect. What Caddie heard was the lesson every nineteenth-century American girl learned at some time before she embarked on her adult life. So far the novel is on sound historical ground.

But the premise of the novel as a whole is that Caddie's childhood freedom was highly unusual in the United States of 1875. Her two sisters, whose lives are shown as housebound and mother-modeled, are clearly meant to represent a more standard nineteenth-century upbringing for girls. The notion that family discipline divided along sex lines is central to the story: "We expect more of girls than of boys," Caddie's father tells her. When she accepts her girlhood (as opposed to an asexual childhood), the author of the novel makes it clear that Caddie is accepting both greater restrictions on her freedom and higher standards for her behavior.

I suspect that most Americans share these assumptions about nineteenth-century childhood, and particularly about the difference between girls' and boys' experience in that era. Reading backward from the restrictions imposed on adult women, it is perhaps natural to assume that strict limits were also put on girls from the beginning. We tend to believe that the lives of young girls were like the lives of adult women, bounded by the household and its duties.

But was it true? Are we right to assume that because nineteenth-century womanhood was confined within narrow limits, a nineteenth-century girlhood was no more than an apprenticeship to the same limitations? Is it a fact that girls were more restricted than boys, that they were less physically active and less enterprising, that they were confined to the household and its "womanly" duties while their brothers roamed more freely, learned more eclectically, tested themselves and their skills more thoroughly?

Having asked this much, we come to the next question: how do we find out? If historical evidence for the conventional view of woman's place is voluminous, the same cannot be said for the realities of children's lives in a past time. Few children leave documented accounts of their lives; even journals and diaries were more likely to be kept by adolescents than by children younger than, say, thirteen or fourteen. Whatever the evidence that allows us to describe how children lived in the past, it is almost always at some remove from the children themselves.

Fortunately, one source, while removed, is still reasonably direct. Autobiography written by women who grew up in the United States during the nineteenth century before about 1875 is rich with information about how girls lived before their adolescent years. Many American women wrote such memoirs in their later years, to preserve for their children and grandchildren, if not for a wider audience, some account of lives lived in a rapidly changing country. The authors were a diverse lot, from the daughters of pioneers, whose schooling was at best sketchy, to women who had enjoyed the most comfortable homes and the best education the country had to offer girls at the time, as well as many more whose circumstances fell somewhere in between extremes. All but a handful can be called "middle class" as that term applies to the fluid and flexible social structure of nineteenth-century America. In these autobiographies where women recorded their childhood memories, often in considerable detail, we may catch a glimpse of the ordinary lives of middle-class American girls, remembered, it is true, by adults, but remembered by the adults who had themselves experienced the childhood they described.

Many autobiographies of childhood lived before 1875 suggest that Carol Brink's assumptions about an American girlhood, however logical they may seem in the light of adult social-sexual arrangements in the nineteenth century, must not be accepted uncritically. Far from being unique, what I think of as the *Caddie Woodlawn* Syndrome seems to have been common in America during that period. In a surprising number of memoirs is an account of just such an experience of childhood freedom followed by just the same closing of the doors as the girl neared puberty. If autobiography can be accepted as any kind of sample of common practice, then it would seem that in a good many households the sharp differentiation between appropriate behavior and activity for prepubescent boys and girls was not as firmly applied as we often suppose. Many American women could and did look back to their childhood years as a period of physical and psychic freedom unmatched by anything in their later life.

They recorded that freedom with a joy that rings down through the years and out of the pages of their autobiographies. Instead of being confined to house and hearth, many girls, like Caddie, "lived as much as possible in the open" and thrived on it. Carolyn Briggs, growing up in Northampton, Massachusetts, had her freedom as a gift from the family doctor, who thought her threatened by consumption and decreed that she live "out of doors as much as possible, without regard to weather, always being well wrapped up with flannel underclothing . . . and . . . long sleeves. . . . How I blessed the dear man for giving me my freedom," she added fervently.[3]

For many others, doctors' orders were not necessary; many American families allowed their little girls to live nearly as unfettered and vigorous an outdoor life as their brothers. Country children in particular roamed their world without much restriction. "Our family discipline was not more rigid than it was in other families, and I was not under special supervision," wrote Caroline Creevey of her Connecticut childhood. And Elizabeth Allan echoed in her memoirs of a Virginia childhood: "I suppose someone must have had an eye on me, but I was conscious of no surveillance, and I roamed at large until the boys got out of 'school,' when I attached myself resolutely to them, doubtless becoming a great nuisance." Once a week, Caroline Briggs lost her accustomed freedom to Sunday strictures. Her description of that privation emphasizes her usual liberty: "At sunset Saturday night, the straightjacket was put on . . . [and] all the joy of life was laid aside." Fortunately, Caroline's mother was not overly doctrinaire. Once Sunday dinner was over, "wisely and well, my mother let me run like a young calf in the meadow back of the house. So the nice clothes were all taken off, and I was given my freedom. I thank God for that every year of my life."[4]

What these girls did with their freedom was what children have always done; there would be nothing remarkable in their remembered activities had they been girls of a later period or boys of any time. It is only because they were nineteenth-century girls that we are surprised to read that they dammed streams, fished and trapped, swam in ponds and rivers in summer, sledded and skated in winter. "For fair weather," wrote Creevey, "there were the orchard, the garden, the groves of chestnut and other trees, . . . the field and woods. . . . In winter our own hill afforded fine coasting, and big sleds with bright, smooth runners were cherished by girls as well as boys."[5]

Any image of prim and proper little girls who imbibed with their mother's milk a deep concern for the state of their clothing dissolves before the autobiographical accounts. These American girls climbed trees, fell into rain barrels, fished in the horse troughs. "We played I Spy, mumblety-peg, stalked about on forked-stick stilts, skinned up the trees, bent limbs for a teeter, climbed on and jumped off the stable roof," recalled Sarah Bonebright. With the clarity of hindsight, they recorded years later how they had abused their clothes. "I often climbed trees and tore my clothes," wrote one, and Anna Clary told of climbing a tree with her skirt filled with grapes. After a while, she slid back down the tree trunk, to the considerable detriment of both grapes and dress.[6]

City children—a minority in nineteenth-century accounts, as they were in the population—obviously had less of the natural world available to them, but they were not necessarily housebound or sedentary for that reason. Una Hunt grew up in Cincinnati in the 1870s and 1880s, climbing "every tree and shed in the neighborhood." There is no reason to assume that the trees and sheds were low, easy ones, either, since she also recorded that "I was often badly hurt, but after each fall, when vinegar and brown papers had been applied, [my mother's] only comment was 'You must learn to climb better,' and I did."[7] She topped her career by climbing to the tip of the church belfry, where she panicked and had to be helped down. Her mother drew the line then, but only at belfries; and Una went back to slightly less exalted heights.

This girl, like some others, also invented some vigorous indoor sports, not always with family approval. She and the other children in her family liked best what they called "indoor coasting"—they used tea trays to slide down the stairs, but only, she confessed, when the family was all out. Elizabeth Allan stayed home from church one Sunday during a visit with some city cousins. Long afterward, she remembered the "wild hilarity" of the afternoon in the 1850s. "I initiated my city cousins in the fun of playing 'Wild Indian' . . . I amazed them by leaping from tops of high bureaus and tables, and boasting how many more spots in the carpet I could jump over than their prim little legs could encompass." Later, her "Presbyterian conscience pricked [her] sharply," not for the wildness of the games, however, but because they had been played on a Sunday, "which [she] should have spent on the stool of repentence."[8]

Nineteenth-century American families did differentiate in their treatment of girls and boys; most twentieth-century families do also. But the distinctions insisted upon in nineteenth-century America may have been fewer and less strict than we commonly suppose while children were preadolescent. Even the strictures against boys and girls playing together, familiar from novels and memoirs, seem to have been unevenly applied. Some girls were indeed forbidden to play with boys, unless perhaps with their brothers, but others chose boys as companions and met no objection from their parents.

Most nineteenth-century children knew work at least as well as play. In a woman's memoirs of childhood, we expect to read that domestic chores dominated her share of the work, and it is true that nearly every autobiography written by a woman records some housekeeping skills acquired young. Girls learned to knit, sew, and cook, to wash clothes, clean house, and preserve food. They gathered eggs and picked berries, washed dishes, and carried wood for the kitchen stove. They were expected to help care for younger children in the family, sometimes to the point where a woman referred to a younger brother or sister as "my child." Under normal circumstances, the tasks, though constant, were not overly arduous. When the mother of the family was ill or dead, however, the weight of domestic responsibility on a young girl might be considerably heavier. Several accounts tell of virtually full responsibility for housekeeping passed to girls at an early age.

The point about housework, however, was not whether girls were expected to do some of it, or even a good deal of it, as children; of course they were. Children's help was indispensable in most American homes where servants were few and chores were endless. The question is whether work was divided along strict sex lines, with some activities reserved strictly for one sex or another. And here the answer is less absolute. In some rural families, at least, autobiographies indicated that boys helped with domestic work before they were old enough to work beside their fathers in the fields. And while most girls learned housekeeping in the expectation that they would eventually have houses to keep, their autobiographies show that they also learned other, less domestic skills during their childhood years. Virginia-born Ellen Mordecai was brought up by her aunts after her mother's death. They were capable women, who could "do anything," according to Mordecai, and they taught her to fish and trap. Ellen was deft with wild things. She caught a woodpecker in her hand once, just to admire his feathers. Once, she climbed a tree to investigate a hole. She put her hand in, felt something soft, and ran back home for a large silver spoon. Up in the tree again, she put the spoon gently into the hole, to scoop up several baby flying squirrels. These, too, she admired without harming and put back in the tree. And Ellen, taught by her aunts, fished enthusiastically, as they did.[9]

The parents of Frances Willard (who ultimately became president of the Women's Christian Temperance Union) enforced no connection at all between sex and kinds of work.

Mother did not talk to us as girls, but simply as human beings, and it never occurred to me that I ought to "know house-work" and do it. Mary took to it kindly by nature; I did not, and each one had her way. Mother never said "you must cook, you must sweep, you must sew" but she studied what we liked to do and kept us at it with no trying at all. I knew all the carpenter's tools and handled them: made carts and sleds, cross-guns and whip handles. ... But a needle and a dishcloth I could not abide—chiefly, perhaps, because I was bound to live out-of-doors.[10]

Sunday dinner preparation in the Willard household rotated among mother, father, and Oliver, the latter two being, in Frances' words, "famous cooks." The Willards represented a thoroughly open-minded attitude toward child nurture, which cannot be considered typical of American households in general. Yet their approach, and that of others more conventional, suggests that American parents were often flexible and common-sensical, rather than rigidly doctrinaire in teaching skills or allocating tasks to children. Many parents seem to have been willing to consider convenience and children's tastes rather than some arbitrary view of what was "suitable" work for girls or boys.

This kind of pragmatic latitude is a key note in many American women's childhood memories. The early years of childhood offered a certain psychic as well as a physical freedom to most American children. "We were a neighborhood of large families," wrote Lucy Larcom in *A New England Girlhood*, "and most of us enjoyed the privilege of 'a little wholesome neglect.' Our tether was a long one, and when, grown a little older, we occasionally asked to have it lengthened, a maternal 'I don't care' amounted to almost unlimited liberty." Larcom, who read mostly English books as a child, contrasted the picture of an English childhood she found there with her own American experience: "We did not think those English children had so good a time as we did; they had to be so prim and methodical. It seemed to us that the little folks across the water never were allowed to romp and run wild; . . . [we had] a vague idea that this freedom of ours was the natural inheritance of republican children only."[11]

Though the children of pioneering families faced greater hazards than did those of long-settled places, their parents were no more inclined to hover over them, according to Sarah Bonebright, who grew up on a pioneer farm in Iowa. "We had received instructions and the warning admonition from our parents and were expected to circumvent the [wild] creatures or avoid the danger." Girls as well as boys were expected to cope. Bonebright told of being sent on an errand three-quarters of a mile away, across the river and deep in the woods. She lost her way, making three false starts before finding it again, and was home late. "I do not recall that I was questioned about the delay, or that anxiety was expressed at my unusually long absence. I had accomplished the mission. To be able to 'make a shift' for any contingency was expected of both young and old."[12]

In fact, in view of the common belief that a Victorian upbringing was strict and narrow, especially for girls, the record of parental attitudes which can be found in many memoirs is enlightening. The autobiographies rarely report physical punishment, and then only for serious or extremely exasperating behavior. Alice Kingsbury's laconic remark, "Our parents never cared much about punishing us," was echoed by other authors. Kingsbury, recalling that she was spanked only once, wrote: "Usually when I had a tantrum, my mother took me in her arms and sat in a rocking chair, rocking and singing to me." Ellen Mordecai called her home "happy and indulgent," and Una Hunt wrote that the children of her family were "never ordered to do anything or told arbitrarily that we must obey."[13]

This is not to say that children were undisciplined. Hunt's parents, like most others of these accounts, expected a good deal of their children in many ways, including a sensitive awareness of right and wrong. In fact, most autobiographies suggest that nineteenth-century children developed tender consciences early in life. But many parents seem to have tempered their expectations with a sympathetic tolerance and a feeling for child nature that we (rather arrogantly) think of as wholly modern. Rachel Butz, for example, was withdrawn from her first school because her teacher was overly stern. Her parents, she wrote, "had the good sense to let me remain [home] until I could have a teacher who . . . could understand the wants and needs of childhood." Later, when she went away to boarding school, she suffered acutely from homesickness. "I had lived such a free, joyous life that . . . restrictions were hard to bear." She returned home before the end of the first term, with her parents' consent. With the sensitive conscience trained into so many children of the time, she deplored her own "failure," but she was grateful for her parents' leniency. "They did what was right for my highest good . . . I am thankful for their sympathy." This is by no means an isolated story; many women recalled such sympathetic understanding. Laura Richards, daughter of Samuel Gridley and Julia Ward Howe, remembered herself at four or five, afraid of the dark. More than once, she went "into the lighted drawing room, among all the silks and satins, arrayed in . . . a 'leg-nightgown,' demanding her mother . . . and I remember that she always got her mother, too."[14]

But this "free, joyous life" described again and again in American women's autobiographies came to an end for them, as it did for Caddie Woodlawn, when they crossed the fateful line that marked the end of childhood and the beginning of young womanhood. Timing varied, but not the outcome. For some, the door closed at thirteen; for others not until fifteen or even later, but close it inevitably did once the claims and constraints of nineteenth-century womanhood were laid upon the growing girl.

Most authors say only a very little about the loss of their freedom, which is perhaps not surprising, since every girl was well aware of the dimensions of "woman's sphere" long before she reached puberty. Generally, the regrets must be read between the lines of these women's memoirs, in the passionately fond recollections of girlhood freedom. But those who recorded the moment of change and their feelings about it often gave a glimpse of the conflict they faced. Rachel Butz called her adolescence "that most trying and uncomfortable age, when physically I was almost a woman, but at heart, was still a child." Lucy Larcom was more specific: "The transition from childhood to girlhood, when a girl had an almost unlimited freedom of out-of-door life, is practically the toning down of a mild sort of barbarianism. . . . I clung to the child's inalienable privilege of running half wild; and when I found that I really was growing up, I felt quite rebellious." Even late in life, Ellen Mordecai spoke with fierce regret of the close of childhood. Her thirteenth year ended her "happy-go-lucky, carefree childhood," she wrote: "In memory's book, that leaf wears forever a margin of black."[15]

Of them all, it was Frances Willard who lodged the most heartfelt protest. She mourned not just the loss of childhood freedom, but what that loss meant to her as an adult human being:

> No girl went through a harder experience than I, when my free, out-of-door life had to cease, and the long skirts and clubbed-up hair spiked with hairpins had to be endured. The half of that down-heartedness has never been told and never can be. I always believed that if I had been left alone and allowed as a woman what I had as a girl, a free life in the country, where a human being might grow, body and soul, as a tree grows, I would have been ten times more of a person in every way.[16]

Not every woman's memoirs spoke so forcefully of their author's reaction to the profound alterations that adolescence brought. Many recorded without comment their authors' entirely conventional adult lives as wives and mothers, offering no hint of whether they resented or regretted a social system that gave and then abruptly retracted the gift of freedom. To understand the meaning of their loss—and it must have had meaning for every woman who experienced it—we must turn to less direct testimony.

One resource, oblique yet revealing, exists in the form of children's books. The latter half of the nineteenth century saw the beginnings of a great age of children's fiction, an outpouring of literature written by middle-class adults for middle-class children, much of it in the tradition of domestic realism, which was intended to be true to the common reality of daily life. As an index to reality in any period, children's fiction is admittedly problematical—indirect, allusive, edited, and perhaps idealized by its authors, often burdened with didactic intent. But it is also rich in emotional truth. In any period, authors writing realistic fiction for children tend to recreate the shape and feeling of their own childhood. Constructing literary childhood, adults often replay the patterns of their own early lives, sometimes romanticizing, sometimes justifying them, sometimes bringing them to a more satisfactory conclusion than they achieved in reality. Realistic children's fiction, then, is another avenue to an understanding of nineteenth-century women's feelings about their own childhood experiences. Women who wrote children's stories of everyday life in the latter half of the nineteenth century usually described childhood of a generation earlier, drawing upon the memories of their own young lives. Their stories of childhood and adolescence resonate with feeling; in them are clues to their authors' attitudes toward their early years, unconscious as well as conscious, which can hardly be reached by a straighter path.

It is surely significant that so many women who wrote "girls' stories" chose as their subject the transition from childhood to adolescence, or, more accurately, to young adulthood. The typical nineteenth-century girls' story was seldom about very young children, nor did it deal with a heroine who was wholly within young adulthood. Until about the turn of the century, when the earlier years of childhood gained favor with writers, the characteristic girls' novel centered on heroines of about twelve to sixteen years old, girls who stood just at the end of childhood and on the verge of young womanhood.

The stories were, typically, intensely domestic and interior. Where the boys' books increasingly revolved around a young man's encounter with the outside world—in the army, in the West, in the city—and around active, extroverted adventure, girls' novels focused on character and relationships, as, of course, girls' lives did as they approached womanhood. And within the context of character and relationships, nineteenth-century writers repeatedly identified the decisive moment in a girl's life as that time when she left behind the relatively undifferentiated personality of childhood to take on the required characteristics of an adult woman. They saw this transition as a dramatic event in a girl's life; certainly they saw it as the supremely fitting moment for a didactic message defining the obligations and the limitations of a woman's future.

Louisa May Alcott was one of the earliest and is doubtless the best known today of the nineteenth-century women who wrote such novels for children. Alcott's books were sufficiently entertaining so as to make readers, even today, tend to overlook how much preaching is in them. In fact, they were quite didactic; Alcott consistently pushed her convictions on upbringing, family life, womanly virtue, and other values in her writing for children. While in some respects her views were advanced, even feminist—she always endorsed the idea of independence for women and was always as interested in work for women as for men—in her children's books, at least, Alcott generally upheld the conventional tenets of nineteenth-century womanhood. The portraits of admirable women and children are immensely (and consciously) instructive as models of conventional ideals. Yet between the lines of these stories, it is often possible to catch signs of Alcott's less openly acknowledged responses to the limitations women faced in her era.

Her first and most enduringly popular story for girls is, of course, *Little Women*. As a quasi-autobiographical novel, it is both more revealing and more carefully hedged against revelation than her less autobiographical books. In *Little Women*, Alcott retraced and also reshaped the patterns of her own life; truth and wish were bound together.

Characterization is at the heart of the book's remarkable perennial appeal. As every reader recognizes, Jo March is the author, the author is Jo March, and so is every girl who reads the book. It is Jo—her roughness, her ambition, her earnest yearning to be good; and above all, her humanness, good, bad, and mistaken—to whom every reader responds. Meg is admirable, Amy exasperating, and Beth too perfect to be believed, but Jo is drawn from Alcott's own character and feelings; her character has a vivid reality still.

Without recapitulating the familiar story, one can note that *Little Women* is again the story of girls who stand just on the brink of young adulthood. Alcott conveys in some detail the texture of the March girls' childhood existence, and then carries her story forward to their young womanhood and their destinies as women. Through Jo's eyes we see the transition from childhood to adolescence and the meaning of that passage for Louisa May Alcott.

The dominant emotion is a passionate regret for the childhood about to be left behind, for the family unity about to be splintered as the girls move toward their separate futures. Meg's marriage signals the inevitable destruction of childhood, and Jo is frankly jealous, not of Meg as she assumes an adult role, but of John, who is taking Meg away.[17] Jo's reaction to her own growing up recalls several autobiographical accounts. Like Lucy Larcom, Frances Willard, Ellen Mordecai, and others, Jo resists and resents the approach of adulthood. Partly, of course, the resistance can be read as a shrinking from the greater responsibilities, both social and sexual, of adult life, but much of it is to the loss of freedom. Unlike the twentieth-century child who usually sees adult status as liberation, nineteenth-century women more often identified freedom with childhood and clung to it as long as they could. Generations of girls sympathized with Jo's plea to "let me be a little girl as long as I can," and with her wish that "wearing flatirons on our heads would keep us from growing up," because they knew, as she did, that adolescence was the beginning of limitations and restraints that would last the rest of their lives. Adolescence was the fork in the road where boys' and girls' paths diverged, as Jo ruefully acknowledged when Laurie proposed that they run away together. "If I was a boy, we'd run away together, and have a capital time; but as I'm a miserable girl, I must be proper, and stay at home. . . . 'Prunes and prisms' are my doom."[18]

Jo's rebellion against the restrictions of "woman's sphere" came directly from Alcott's own heart; Jo's emotions are usually an accurate record of her own adolescent feelings. Since she was writing fiction, however, she could extend to Jo the compromise between ambition and acceptance that she never found for herself, as she did in Jo's marriage to Professor Bhaer. For over a hundred years, romantic readers have groaned over Jo's rejection of handsome, devoted, wealthy Laurie, but Alcott knew her own mind. Marriage with Laurie would have made Jo a feminine success in conventional terms, certainly; she would have been beloved, no doubt, and comfortably well-off—but she would also have been idle. As Mrs. Laurence, she would have had no function in the world beyond the domestic doorstep. Marriage to the unromantic Professor, on the other hand, gave her domestic happiness in the form of affection and children, but with it, work. Jo acquires husband and vocation together, while Alcott, who found no such bargain in real life, remained unmarried.

Jack and Jill, a more purely fictional story by Alcott, offered little compromise and less hope to freedom-loving girls. This novel, one of Alcott's lesser-known books, concentrates on the process of transforming an untamed girl into a promising adolescent. In a sense, it is the second half of the Caddie Woodlawn story. Where Brink devoted most of her story to Caddie's experiences as a free and enterprising child, Alcott begins her tale only moments before the crisis that precipitates change, and spends the bulk of the book showing how and to what end Jill's character is reformed.

The story revolves mainly around Jill, secondarily around her two girl friends, Merry and Molly. Jack and a couple of other boys play a part as well, but their roles are subordinate to the girls.' The central, and certainly the most keenly felt theme is exactly the transition girls must make between childhood and young adulthood, precisely the changes adolescence must bring to the ways of a lively, spirited girl. In Jill's case, and to a lesser extent in Molly's as well, that transition reiterates the patterns so often laid out in autobiography. Both Jill and Molly are weaned from their childhood "wildness" in the course of the story, tamed and constrained into the beginnings of acceptable womanhood.

Alcott gives only the briefest glimpse of Jill before the sledding accident that brings about her transformation, but that glimpse is revealing. As Jack and Jill, inseparable friends, are sledding, Jill is challenged by a boy who says she "wouldn't dare" to attempt a difficult run. Jill responds vigorously: "I won't be told I don't dare by any boy in the world," she declares. She is "as brave and strong" as anyone, and she demands that Jack take her down that risky run.[19] Jack demurs, because the hill is dangerous, but willful Jill prevails, and down the hill they go, twice safely, but the third time to disaster. The sled hits a fence, goes over a steep bank and shatters. Jack suffers a broken leg, which will immobilize him for a time, but Jill injures her back and finds herself facing the certainty of months in bed and the possibility of permanent crippling.

Brief as it is—the whole action takes but a chapter to tell—the sledding scene establishes all the strong (and unsuitable) elements in Jill's character that will be corrected in the story to come. Jill is "headstrong," proud, willful, dominant, and competitive; one could hardly draw a better roster of unacceptable characteristics for a nineteenth-century woman.

The rest of the book recounts Jill's months of recuperation and her education in patience, obedience, resignation, and concern for others. The transformation is dramatic. To her mother, pre-accident Jill is "as wild a little savage as I'd like to see," while 200 pages later, Jill can see herself as "a sort of missionary" whose "constant well-doing" has made her "a joy and comfort to all who know and love her."[20] Moralistic it surely is, yet Alcott tells the story with a certain realism. She never minimizes the hardness of the lessons for a spirited girl. Jill suffers pain, fear, boredom, lapses of virtue, and bitter self-reproach; there is no sentimental suggestion that the damping down of a vigorous and willful personality is either swift or simple.

In the best nineteenth-century tradition, most of this education in womanliness takes place through the example of an ideal woman. Jack's mother, Mrs. Minot, leads Jill through her painful experience with precepts and kind encouragement. She also supplies a model for Jill to emulate by telling her of a woman she knew who had been crippled at fifteen, and yet was happy. "Why, how could she be? What did she do?" cried Jill.

> She was so patient, other people were ashamed to complain of their small worries; so cheerful, that her own great one grew lighter; so industrious, that she made both money and friends by pretty things she worked and sold to her many visitors. And, best of all, so wise and sweet that she seemed to get good out of everything, and make her poor room a sort of chapel where people went for comfort, counsel, and an example of a pious life.[21]

Here is the formula by which women "make the world sweet and beautiful," as Mr. Woodlawn had said. Here are the traits of patience, cheerfulness, industry, and the ability to "get good out of everything," which are the hallmark of womanhood and which are also, of course, diametrically opposed to Jill's childhood character.

Molly's and Merry's stories supply the other piece of Mr. Woodlawn's list of womanly duties, the gentling of men and boys, and the bringing of an order to their lives that they, according to one of the most cherished tenets of the nineteenth-century code, cannot manage on their own. Both girls turn themselves into "notable housewives," making home pleasant for their male relatives and reaping their reward in love. With Molly, Mrs. Minot succeeds in making "a tidy little girl out of . . . the greatest tomboy in town," while Merry learns to put limits on her aspirations, giving over dreams of being "a queen or a great lady" in favor of more modest goals: "Now I don't care for that sort of splendor. I like to make things pretty at home, and know they all depend on me, and love me very much. Queens are not happy, but I am."[22]

Again, it is the patterns that interest us, the parallels between Alcott's story and the autobiographies. Alcott assumes the openness of childhood as a familiar, acceptable phenomenon. For all her moralism, nowhere does she deplore childhood freedom, even if Molly and Jill are "wild" or "tomboyish" as a result of it. Indeed, she has one old woman observe to another that "them wild little tykes often turn out smart women."[23] It is all a matter of timing. At the time of the story, all three girls are fifteen—and fifteen is, in every Alcott book, the moment of transition from childhood to young adult status. What was acceptable in children is not tolerable in young women; it is time, this story says, just as *Caddie Woodlawn* did, for new directions.

Jack and Jill illustrates well the characteristic ambivalence of an author who remembered her own rebelliousness against the prevailing social code, but who had to accommodate it in some fashion. In Merry, Alcott shows the conventional training of a girl played out to its logical end of marriage and contentment within the bounds of conventional society. In Molly, who remained a "merry spinster all her days," she suggests an alternative way of life, not rejecting social convention, but evading the specific restrictions and demands of womanly subordination in marriage. Moreover, Alcott heartily asserts the possibility of the choice as a happy, fulfilling one, for Molly and for the community as well. In Jill, she equivocates. Jill is tamed, quenched, and pressed into the mold of a nineteenth-century woman who has learned to play her subordinate role and put the happiness of others above her own. For her efforts, the rehabilitated "savage" is rewarded with the natural companion of her life, Jack. But just when the picture seems complete, and Jill's enforced education in passivity an unqualified success, Alcott retrieves a small piece of the resistant independence that identified her with her creator in the first place. As she matured, Alcott tells us, Jill "was very ambitious in spite of the newly acquired meekness, which was all the more becoming because her natural liveliness often broke out like sunshine through a veil of light clouds." Still, the ambition apparently breaks no barriers: Alcott tells us only that Jill married Jack and became "a very happy and useful woman."[24]

But it is at the level of metaphor that Louisa May Alcott's less conscious or, at least, less consciously expressed, attitudes appear. The central metaphor of *Jack and Jill* is certainly striking: a crippled woman is held up as a model of womanhood, and Jill's education in feminine virtue is a direct result of her own crippling. Though she eventually recovers physically, the transformation of Jill's character is permanent and laudable, in the conventional terms in which Alcott is dealing. The message is unmistakable: the characteristics of a permanent invalid making the best of her lot are a useful example for all women.

A second image, used by Mrs. Minot, is equally arresting. "I'm not sure," says Mrs. Minot to Jill, toward the end of the novel, "that I won't put you in a pretty cage and send you to the Cattle Show, as a sample of what we can do in the way of taming a wild bird till it is nearly as meek as a dove." Whatever level of Alcott's being produced this thought, it is memorable, as is Alcott's telling remark that Jill "had learned to love her cage now."[25]

Oddly enough, Alcott's *Jack and Jill* parallels closely an earlier and very popular girls' story by Susan Coolidge (Sarah C. Woolsey). *What Katy Did*, which was published in 1872, eight years before Alcott's book, tells a remarkably similar story of a vigorous, tomboyish girl who learns her womanly role when she is invalided with an injured spine. Woolsey spends more time with her heroine before her accident than Alcott did, giving her readers an opportunity to know this lively personality before it is pressed into the standard mold. And a very engaging personality it is, too. Katy is a character straight out of many nineteenth-century autobiographies: she "tore her dress every day, hated sewing, and didn't care a button about being called 'good.'" Her mother is dead, and her father encourages his children's vigor: "He wished to have the children hardy and bold, and encouraged climbing and rough plays, in spite of the bumps and ragged clothes which resulted." Katy is the leader of the pack, and full of heady ambition. "There were always so many delightful schemes rioting in her brain, that all she wished for were ten pairs of hands to carry them out . . . she was fond of building castles in the air, and dreaming of the time when something she had done would make her famous. . . ." She means to "do something grand" with her life, perhaps "nursing in a hospital, like Miss Nightingale" or possibly she will "paint pictures, or sing, or scalp—sculp." She isn't sure what it will be, only that "it will be *something*."[26]

The story finds Katy at twelve, with obviously much to learn about womanly virtue. Her education begins, as Jill's did, as the result of an accident. Like Jill, Katy brings about her injury by her headstrong insistence on her own way. Like Jill again, she takes as her model a permanent cripple—"Cousin Helen"—who teaches, in person, in this case, the lessons of patience, cheerfulness, and care for the needs of others who make her the center of the household in spite of being bedridden. Under such tutelage, Katy's ambition is replaced by attention to others, a far better occupation for a woman, according to Cousin Helen, than "scurrying and bustling over [her] own affairs." Katy learns, as every nineteenth-century woman had to learn, that her "own affairs" were never of real consequence, that she must always be ready to put them aside to tend to other people, taking her reward in love. In a remarkable passage, Cousin Helen suggests that her own invalidism was more pleasing to her father than blooming health ever was: "He had been proud of his active, healthy girl, but I think she was never such a comfort to him as his sick one, lying there in her bed."[27]

Katy absorbs these lessons thoroughly, though it takes four years of invalidism to do it. By the time she is able to walk again, she has taken over the running of the Carr household, and becomes a substitute mother to her sisters and brothers. "To all the . . . children, Katy was . . . the centre and the sun. They all revolved about her, and trusted her for everything." Her description now, "the gentle expression of her eyes, the womanly look, the pleasant voice, the politeness, the tact in advising others, without seeming to advise," tells us that "The School of Pain," as Cousin Helen called it, has educated her well in the nineteenth-century ideal of womanhood.[28]

Louisa May Alcott and Sarah Woolsey were illuminating, if unwitting witnesses to women's reactions to the patterns their society imposed on them. How guilelessly and yet how plainly these authors drew the analogy between physical crippling and the limitations a girl faced as she approached womanhood! And how revealing was their chosen literary metaphor of their own ambivalence toward the code that governed women's lives. Writers of children's books rarely preach rebellion, nor did these two. They intended their stories to put forth the most conventional concept of women's special place and particular virtues; they meant to use fiction to guide the young into acceptable paths. Yet to the modern reader, if not to their contemporaries, their strong personalities transcended their intentions. No one today can read these two novels, so much alike, without hearing the piercing, if unconscious, cry of outrage beneath the smooth and proper surface.

A generation later, two books appeared within a few years of one another as curiously alike and as representative of their era as *Jack and Jill* and *What Katy Did*. Both were enormously popular girls' books, which announced some changes on the theme of spirited young girls verging toward womanhood and which accurately reflected some subtle but fundamental shifts in conventional attitudes toward children. Whether, in the end, either of them held out more hope to their heroines for an adult life with more options for their particular qualities is doubtful, I think, though both aspired to do so.

Rebecca of Sunnybrook Farm (1903) by Kate Douglas Wiggin and *Anne of Green Gables* (1908) by L. M. Montgomery are assembled of virtually identical elements. Both tell stories of little girls who leave rather straitened circumstances (Anne is an orphan, Rebecca comes from a family oversupplied with children and undersupplied with the means to raise and educate them) for a new home, which is by no means rich, but which can offer a chance for education. The locale in each case is a village, and the woman into whose care the child is delivered is, in both books, a crusty, exacting spinster whose heart has withered for lack of a woman's normal accoutrements: that is, husband, children, and the giving and receiving of human affection. The span of time covered is also similar in the two novels; each takes the heroine from about her eleventh to her seventeenth year, showing again the passage from childhood to young womanhood.

Both books are primarily character studies. Of the two, *Rebecca* is better written, more realistic, and less sentimental than *Anne*, but in all other respects the characterizations are practically interchangeable and belong firmly within the romantic tradition. Anne and Rebecca embody the idea of childhood that celebrated the child as child and saw a child as perfect in itself, in harmony with itself and with nature, innocent, spontaneous, imaginative, loving. Each eleven years old, highly verbal, poetic, and imaginative, the little girls make a vivid contrast to the cramped and colorless adults around them. Their stories show them touching and in some cases transforming the lives of others, bringing happiness to adults who have lost the innate joyousness of childhood, and, in fact, nearly lost the knack of being truly alive. Rebecca and Anne grow, learn, and of course, suffer mishaps and correction of their childish mistakes, but they are never really wrong or bad. They have no true "faults"; they only make mistakes on the way to learning the complicated rules of adult society, which is, often as not, more truly at fault than they are, since it is less simple and natural than childhood. They are William Blake's vision of children: "Innocence! Honest, open, seeking the vigorous joys of morning light."[29]

As romantic children, Rebecca and Anne are of a quite different order of being from the children of Alcott's books. Louisa May Alcott, born in 1833, was a full generation older than Kate Douglas Wiggin. The view of childhood in her writing for children belongs to the rationalistic, preromantic view that dominated children's books until the latter part of the nineteenth century. It is an attitude accepting of childhood and children, but it is not romantic. Alcott's opinion of her young heroines has none of the doting fondness of Wiggin's feeling for Rebecca or Montgomery's for Anne. Likeable as Jo March is, she cannot be mistaken for the author's idea of perfection.

The very title, *Little Women*, is indicative: to Alcott, as to most Americans of her time, children were adults-in-process, apprentices to the rigors and demands of adult life. It was not a matter of viewing children as "little adults"; that was not a nineteenth-century attitude. It is simply that Alcott, like many of her contemporaries, saw childhood primarily as a period of preparation; children were properly engaged in learning, becoming, forming a worthy character for the future; certainly they were not considered finished and wholly admirable as they were.

Alcott's attitude toward her characters' faults illustrates the point. Without suggesting that perfection was a likely human attainment, she nevertheless saw Meg's envy, Jo's temper, and Amy's selfishness and vanity as serious matters that it was absolutely necessary to correct. Even Beth's timidity had to be conquered in some degree. It was the responsibility of adults to help children overcome their character flaws, to guide them along the right paths to creditable adulthood, as Mrs. March and Mrs. Minot do; there was no suggestion that the children were naturally better than adults. In the nature of things, a child was pupil to an adult.

Once romantic attitudes had penetrated the literature, however, the picture children's books presented of adult responsibility toward children altered subtly but profoundly. The right sort of adult could still act as guide and mentor to a child, but the effort had changed from molding childish character into acceptable moral and social form to easing it toward adulthood without destroying the special virtues inherent in children. In the romantic view, the best (though the least likely) adult character was one which preserved most completely the qualities of childhood. Adam Ladd, obviously Rebecca's future husband, and Miss Maxwell, her devoted teacher, had many conversations about Rebecca as she neared young womanhood, all of which centered on how she should be educated without obliterating or dampening her special personality. Or, to be more exact, they regretfully conceded the reality of Rebecca's growing up, and tried to decide how they might help her negotiate her inevitable maturity while protecting the perfection of her childhood being.

Though Montgomery's sequels to *Anne of Green Gables* carry her protagonist into adult life, it is clear that she and Wiggin alike were most entranced with their heroines as children. It was childhood that gave full scope to Rebecca's and Anne's personalities. During those years, their dramatic and poetic imaginations were not unduly constrained by consciousness of conventional expectations. They prattled on, using extraordinary vocabularies gleaned from omnivorous reading, unconsciously amusing and charming those adults perceptive enough to appreciate them. They were strong-minded and full of enterprise and too innocent yet to know that leadership was not for females. They summarized in themselves all that their authors thought attractive and promising in a child.

The question, therefore, is what became of all this as these girls neared womanhood? In the answer to that question lies a volume of commentary, whether or not the authors intended it so, on how little had changed since Louisa May Alcott looked for a satisfactory, if fictional, niche for Jo's forceful character, and since she and Sarah Woolsey could draw a close parallel between womanly virtue and physical crippling.

By the time Wiggin and Montgomery wrote, enterprising or needy girls had a few more acceptable opportunities to consider than had their mothers and grandmothers. Anne and Rebecca both acquired the education that was accessible to girls by the end of the century, though it was clear in both books that scholarships or private benevolence were necessary if girls as poor as these were to go to school past the level of the local grammar school. And both girls looked forward to paid work as teachers; they did not have to choose from the limited and distasteful array of occupations the March girls faced: governess, seamstress, companion, or (possibly, with luck, talent, and determination) a writer.

Yet the narrowness of the future choices available to Rebecca and Anne is quite apparent when one considers what expectations a boy with their talents would have had without question. In childhood, the two girls demonstrate intelligence, energy, and a capacity for leadership that their companions concede without jealousy. Such qualities in a boy would all but assure an interesting, probably a public, career. Not so for these girls, as their creators tacitly concede in their descriptions of their heroines' adolescence. As the girls grow older, their personalities become less emphatic. Their colorful (and undeniably intrusive) qualities of mind and imagination dim to "dreaminess" in their mid-teens, while their ambition turns toward conventionally acceptable careers as teachers. They never rebel and never yearn for what they cannot have; indeed, they never even recognize that there is work in the world for which they are suited by nature but from which they are prevented by social convention.

Nor does their ambition in any way interfere with their acceptance of the traditional womanly possibility to care for others if the need arises. Anne and Rebecca were openly ambitious throughout their school years; they were even, though less openly, competitive. And each won by her efforts the offer of a choice teaching position as she left high school. But before she can collect the reward of her talent and hard work by moving into a paid employment, each girl is faced with a crisis in the form of a seriously ailing relative who needs care. In both cases, the girls respond without hesitation, cheerfully shelving previous plans and undertaking a sacrificial role as a matter of course. It is as though the authors wanted to demonstrate that neither ambition nor achievement had destroyed the selfless sense of duty that was the core of the nineteenth-century womanly model. It was, too, as though these authors saw a period of self-abnegation as a necessary stage in a girl's way to womanhood, just as Alcott and Woolsey had a generation before. Less overtly than their predecessors, but still clearly enough to be understood, Wiggin and Montgomery conveyed the message that the paths a woman trod were likely to be steep and stony for a girl just leaving the freer territory of childhood.

Perhaps for this reason, Kate Douglas Wiggin declined to deal at all with Rebecca's life as an adult. In the original *Rebecca* book, she rounded off her story with Rebecca's graduation from high school at seventeen. Adam Ladd's interest in Rebecca as a woman is plainly enough indicated, but Wiggin was not ready to go further. Though Adam finds Rebecca "all-beautiful and all-womanly," the time is not yet: "He had looked into her eyes and they were still those of a child; there was no knowledge of the world in their shining depths, no experience of men or women, no passion, nor comprehension of it." And so the book ends, with Rebecca still a child.[30]

New Chronicles of Rebecca does not, as readers might have expected, pick up where the first book left off. Instead, Wiggin dips back into Rebecca's young years for more anecdotes, as charming and amusing as those of the first book, of Rebecca's childhood. Once more, Wiggin brings Rebecca up to the age of seventeen, and this time also to the betrothal of her "bosom friend" of childhood. The story ends on a note of nostalgic sadness. Rebecca, watching Emma Jane and her fiancé walk away arm in arm, feels her childhood is slipping away "like a thing real and visible . . . slipping down the grassy riverbanks, . . . the summer night."[31]

The mood is wistful, rather than passionately regretful. It is much less clear here than in *Little Women* what is being lost as childhood "slips away." Jo March knew very well what she mourned: the intact family of her childhood and the freedom to behave according to her nature rather than to a prescribed code for her sex. And Jo, within the strictures of nineteenth-century behavior (and of nineteenth-century children's books) was rebellious and resentful at her loss. Anne and Rebecca are not rebellious; their passage into adult life is made to seem gradual and free of conflict. Though their strong personalities would seem to presage a struggle over the need to trim their sails to the prevailing nineteenth-century wind, Wiggin and Montgomery will not have it so. Anne and Rebecca are romantic children, whose inborn natures are beyond reproach; not they, then, but their creators, must accommodate convention. These girls must ease into adolescence and then into maturity without strife or storm; they must become the most desirable models of young womanhood without seeming to give up any of their childhood perfection, and so they do. For all their vibrancy as children, Anne and Rebecca sail into their womanly backwaters without a murmur.

If the pattern I have described was common in the lives of nineteenth-century American girls—as I think it was—it may seem strange that only a few adult women openly revolted against it. At first glance and from the distance of our own time, a system that allowed for so much freedom at one stage of life and so little at the next, would seem destined to produce resentment and rebellion.

Anne Scott MacLeod

But human reaction is rarely so simple or so linear in its logic. Like most people who live in a reasonably coherent and consistent culture, nineteenth-century American girls accepted the view of life their culture presented to them, and with it, the view of women's proper role. Not only accepted: they absorbed and internalized it and eventually passed it on to a new generation. The books they wrote for children suggest how the processes of adaptation and accommodation actually worked.

Little Women, for example, shows the process underway as the girls, including Jo, try to emulate the example of their model of womanly behavior, their mother. Jo's "boyishness" has been well tolerated, apparently, in her family; no shame or disapproval of it is ever expressed by her parents. But Meg, who at the time of the story is close to the ideal of adult womanhood herself, tries to cure Jo of her whistling and her "wildness," pointing out that she must relinquish such ways now that she is growing up. Though she resists, Jo does understand that the moment is approaching when it will no longer be excusable for her to be rough, abrupt, ill-kempt, bluntly tactless. Her bitter disappointment when Aunt Carroll chooses Amy for the European tour Jo had hoped to make, because of Jo's own outspoken and all-too-independent opinions, points up the high cost of nonconformity for a girl.

And if the price of nonconformity was high, so too was the cost of conscious resentment. Raised in a society largely united on the acceptable role for women, wooed by a social code that made a virtue of dependency and exalted the submissive and unselfish qualities of ideal womanhood, faced with the discomfort of putting themselves outside convention if they rebelled against their fate, many women must have chosen not to look too closely at the discrepancies between the expectations of their humanity, on the one hand, and their sex, on the other. The briefest pair of sentences in the diary of a young southern girl gives a telling glimpse of the decision many women made, consciously or unconsciously, to accept their social destiny for the sake of their own peace. In 1862, Lucy Breckinridge wrote, "I read some in Michelet's book on 'Woman.' I do not like that kind of reading. It scares me of myself, and makes me rebel against my lot." Lucy Breckinridge was not at all optimistic about the happiness of women's lives, as her diary makes abundantly clear ("Poor women! Why did God curse them so much harder than men?"). But she had few, very few, alternatives to choose from, and she knew it. No wonder a book that outlined women's disadvantages so complacently "scared her of herself."[32]

Yet to opt against an open rebellion against injustice was not quite to neutralize resentment. Pushed out of sight it might have been; obliterated, it probably was not. Women's resentment of their lot must have surfaced in dozens of ways we can only guess at. It surely emerged, as we have seen, in children's books, and often, paradoxically enough, in the very stories that were written with conscious intent to perpetuate the conventional ideal. Responses ranging from outrage to something like mourning run just under the surface of books utterly conventional in their openly asserted attitudes. At the very least, women's sense of loss fed the nostalgia for childhood that children's books often expressed. The child who read late-nineteenth-century books could hardly avoid the conclusion that the end of childhood was also the end of the best part of life. Certainly a girl was unlikely to miss the message that puberty would be for her the beginning of her imprisonment in a "woman's sphere." She would surely understand that for her the central task of adolescence as defined by her culture was to trim her qualities of mind and character, whatever they might be, to fit the model society had prepared for her.

It was 1777 when Hannah More delivered herself of some profoundly dampening comments on the upbringing of girls:

> That bold, enterprising spirit, which is so much admired in boys, should not, when it happens to discover itself in the other sex, be encouraged, but suppressed. Girls should be taught to give up their opinions betimes. . . . It is of the greatest importance to their future happiness, that they should acquire a submissive temper, and a forbearing spirit; for it is a lesson the world will not fail to make them frequently practice, when they come abroad into it, and they will not practice it the worse for having learnt it the sooner.[33]

More than a century later, Rebecca Randall acknowledged that More's prescription had by no means passed out of date. "All of us can have the ornament of a meek and lovely spirit," she observed, and added, with her customary accuracy, "especially girls, who have more use for it than boys."[34]

The evidence suggests that American girls often enjoyed a season of freedom before they had to face up altogether to what More and Rebecca agreed was the lot of their sex. But sooner or later, the most blithesome girl had to recognize the reality that awaited her. And whether she chose to rebel against or to accede to the demands of her culture, a nineteenth-century girl could not but realize, with all her sex, that after childhood, gender (to paraphrase Freud) was inexorably destiny.

Notes

1. Carol R. Brink, *Caddie Woodlawn* (New York: Macmillan and Company, 1935), 240.
2. See Barbara Welter, "The Cult of True Womanhood: 1820–1860," *American Quarterly* 18 (1966): 151–174, for a survey of the concept of womanhood in the period.
3. Caroline Briggs, *Reminiscences and Letters*, ed. G. S. Merriam (Boston: Houghton, Mifflin, and Company, 1897), 6.
4. Caroline A. Creevey, *A Daughter of the Puritans* (New York: G. P. Putnam and Company,

1916), 15; Elizabeth R. Allan, *A March Past*, ed. Janet Allan Bryan, (Richmond: Dietz Publishing Company, 1938), 60; Briggs, *Reminiscences and Letters*, 54.

5. Briggs, *Reminiscences and Letters*, 15, 16.

6. Sarah Bonebright, *Reminiscences of Newcastle, Iowa*, (Des Moines: Historical Department of Iowa, 1921), 180; Anna L. Clary, *Reminiscences* (Los Angeles: Bruce McCallister Publishing Company, 1937), 47.

7. Una Hunt, *Una May* (New York: Charles Scribner's Sons, 1914), 24.

8. Hunt, *Una May*, 23; Allan, *A March Past*, 70.

9. Ellen Mordecai, *Gleanings from Long Ago* (Savannah: Braid and Hutton, 1933), 4, 5, 10.

10. Frances E. Willard, *Glimpses of Fifty Years* (Chicago: Woman's Temperance Publishing Association, 1889), 25.

11. Lucy Larcom, *A New England Girlhood* (Boston: Houghton, Mifflin, and Company, 1889), 30, 104.

12. Bonebright, *Reminiscences of New Castle, Iowa*, 183, 162. Note her distinction by age, rather than by sex.

13. Alice Kingsbury, *In Old Waterbury* (Waterbury: Mattatuck Historical Society, 1942), n.p.; Mordecai, *Gleanings from Long Ago*, 39.

14. Rachel Butz, *A Hoosier Girlhood* (Boston: Gorham Press, 1924), 52, 83; Laura E. Richards, *When I Was Your Age* (Boston: Lauriat Publishing Company, 1894), 202.

15. Butz, *A Hoosier Girlhood*, 16; Larcom, *A New England Girlhood*, (Chevy Chase: Corinth Books, 1961), 166, 167; Mordecai, *Gleanings from Long Ago*, 140.

16. Willard, *Glimpses of Fifty Years*, 69.

17. For the direct parallel with Louisa's feelings about her sister Anna's marriage, see *Louisa May Alcott: Her Life, Letters and Journals*, ed. E. D. Cheney (Boston: Little, Brown, and Company, 1930 [1928]), 80.

18. Louisa May Alcott, *Little Women* (Boston: Little, Brown, and Company, 1915 [1868, 1869]), 164, 217, 226.

19. Alcott, *Jack and Jill* (Boston: Little, Brown, and Company, 1928 [1880]), 5.

20. Alcott, *Jack and Jill*, 41, 201.

21. Ibid., 85.

22. Ibid., 228, 321, 322.

23. Ibid., 220.

24. Ibid., 323.

25. Ibid., 310, 198.

26. Susan Coolidge [Sarah Woolsey], *What Katy Did* (New York: Garland Publishing, Inc., 1976 [1872]), 11, 12, 32.

27. Ibid., 185, 181.

28. Ibid., 272, 273.

29. William Blake, "Visions of the Daughters of Albion," in *The Prose and Poetry of William Blake*, ed. E. Erdman and H. Bloom (Garden City: Doubleday and Company, 1965), 48.

30. Kate Douglas Wiggin, *Rebecca of Sunnybrook Farm* (Boston: Houghton, Mifflin, and Company, 1904), 320.

31. Ibid., 227, 278.

32. Lucy Breckinridge, *Lucy Breckinridge of Grove Hill: The Journal of a Virginia Girl, 1862–1864* ed. M. D. Robertson (Kent, Ohio: Kent State University Press, 1979), 25, 31.

33. Quoted in P. M. Spacks, *The Adolescent Idea* (New York: Basic Books, 1981), 120.

34. Wiggin, *New Chronicles of Rebecca* (Boston: Houghton, Mifflin, and Company, 1907), 84.

CHAPTER 10

The Politics of Dollhood in Nineteenth-Century America

Miriam Forman-Brunell

"Of doll haters I have known quite a few," wrote a contributor to *Babyhood* magazine about the "hoydenish" little girls she had observed swatting their dolls.[1] The observations of this Gilded Age writer stand in sharp contrast to the more pervasive image of the angelic Victorian girl who was, in the words of one nineteenth-century poet, "sugar and spice and all things nice." In this essay, I challenge the widespread assumption that attributes minimal agency to girls assumed to have played in socially prescribed ways.

We begin in antebellum America, where the political ideology, class values, and cultural and economic forces of the young nation shaped new attitudes about dolls, play, and girlhood. Mothers, informed by the new domestic advisers, instructed their daughters to be "useful" within the matrix of the family. Dolls, of which there were few, served as training in everything *but* emotional development and expression. Daughters of the evolving middle class made cloth dolls to develop sewing skills that integrated leisure with instruction in domestic economy. Outdoor play, education, and a schedule of daily, weekly (punctuated by the Sabbath), and seasonal responsibilities limited the role that dolls played in girlhood.

In broad terms, utilitarian purposes of dolls and of girls became increasingly obsolete in the Gilded Age as simplicity yielded to splendor in urban middle-class families. Girls' lives, like those of their parents, were affected by the shift from household production to conspicuous consumption. Children's magazines, books, poems, songs, and stereographs revealed that girls were encouraged by adults to develop strong emotional bonds with their numerous dolls, to indulge in fantasy, and to display their elaborately dressed imported European dolls at such ritual occasions as tea parties and social calls.

Although adults, especially parents, perceived dolls as useful vehicles in feminine socialization, this rehearsal for adult womanhood met resistance as it had earlier in the century. At least some daughters with a different agenda from their parents used dolls for purposes other than training in the emotional and practical skills of mothering. Girls' funereal doll play, for example, revealed far more evidence of resistance than of accommodation to newly formulated prescriptions and proscriptions. Memoirs, autobiographies, biographies, oral histories, and the expressive "language" of play reveal that girls—and boys— challenged parental authority, restrictive social customs, and gender roles. Girls in the process of constructing their own notion of girlhood engaged their parents in a preconscious political struggle to define, decide, and determine the meaning of dolls in their own lives and as representations of their own girls' culture.

Domesticity and Dolls

Dolls and their clothing, argued Catharine Beecher and Harriet Beecher Stowe in *The American Woman's Home* (1869), provide girls with "another resource . . . to the exercise of mechanical skills." Girls should be "trained to be healthful and industrious." Earlier in the nineteenth century, advice books, "ladies'" magazines, and other printed sources similarly urged mothers to apply Christian principles to the regulation of the bourgeois family, which only recently had become the mothers' domain. Thus, they were to direct their children's play toward useful ends. Printed material that offered practical advice and philosophical explanations to middle-class mothers standardized methods of antebellum childrearing. In the prescriptive literature published starting in the 1820s, middle-class girls and their mothers were kept informed of genteel manners, bourgeois values, and domestic training.[2]

Girls were urged toward usefulness in their play as natural training in the republican values they would need as future wives and mothers of citizens.

New attitudes about girls' play were shaped in part by the political ideology of the young nation. Experts advised mothers to use "gentle nurture" to teach their children to be self-governing and to exercise "self-control" while at play. Eliza Leslie, author of the *Girls' Book*, suggested, as did other prescriptive writers, that making dolls rather than indulging a love of dress and finery would prevent degeneration into godless anarchy. In her moral tracts, Mary Sewell exhorted mothers to inculcate "habitual restraint" by structuring play periods with "habitual regularity."[3]

"In this land of precarious fortunes, every girl should know how to be 'useful,'" wrote Lydia Maria Child, one of the best-known writers of the period. A girl's vocation, to which dolls contributed, was to be a domestic one shaped in response to the world beyond the Victorian hearth. A canon of domesticity contrasted the safety of the home, where women presided, to the restlessness, competition, selfishness, and alienation of the masculine world beyond. Although the reality of slipping down the economic ladder was obscured by the mythology of the self-made man whose life of hard work, moderation, and temperance promised untold rewards, young ladies were nevertheless forewarned to make themselves useful should misfortune strike.[4] *Mothers' Monthly Journal*, one of the leading maternal association periodicals, advised its broad readership that dressing dolls provided "a semblance of the sober activities of business." Making dolls, nurturing the family, and taking care of household duties constituted a girl's informal apprenticeship for being a wife and mother. According to such experts as Maria Edgeworth, who "firmly believed in the utility of toys," sewing dolls and doll clothing stressed a pragmatic contribution to the domestic economy of the antebellum household. Popular "ladies'" magazines often included directions for making pen-wiper dolls (to clean nibs), sewing dolls (whose pockets held thimbles and other items), and pincushion dolls.[5]

It was from their mothers, who were newly endowed with both the capacity and the social responsibility to determine the fate of their children, that girls were to learn their lessons, both practical and moral. Although the widespread availability of cloth meant that women no longer had to weave the household's supply of fabric, family comfort still depended on skillful use of the needle. Catharine Beecher, who felt "blessed with the example of a most ingenious and industrious mother," suggested that "when a little girl begins to sew, her mother can promise her a small bed and pillow, as soon as she has sewed a patch quilt for them; and then a bedstead, as soon as she has sewed the sheets and cases for pillows; and then a large doll to dress, as soon as she has made the undergarments; and thus go on till the whole contents of the baby-house are earned by the needle and skill of its little owner. Thus, the task of learning to sew will become a pleasure; and every new toy will be earned by useful exertion."

In their treatise on household management, the nineteenth-century architects of domesticity boasted that they "had not only learned before the age of twelve to make dolls, of various sorts and sizes, but to cut and fit and sew every article that belongs to a doll's wardrobe."[6] In the absence of mothers, other female kin such as Lucy Larcom's "adopted aunt" provided instruction in how to knot thread and sew clothing for rag dolls. A doll character in one children's story recalled that "there were hours and hours when she [her owner] had to sit quietly beside grandmother, and sew her stint."[7] In addition to adult women, older sisters often helped younger ones create homemade dolls. "I once knew a little girl who had twelve dolls," wrote Lydia Maria Child. "Some of them were given her; but the greater part she herself made from rags, and her elder sister painted their lips and eyes." One of Lucy Larcom's older sisters outlined faces on her dolls with pen and ink."[8]

Despite the practical suggestions provided to mothers by experts and in turn passed along to girls, the hours during which toys were expected to absorb their attention were limited by genuine household responsibilities.[9] Few matched the ideal as represented in the numerous extant canvases—showing girls leisurely holding dolls—painted by itinerants for socially conscious, middle-class parents. Though the texture of girls' lives was changing, childhood was still neither as precisely demarcated nor as prolonged in the early 1800s as it would be by the end of the century. Instead, a mother of a large rural family was likely to be assisted by the elder children, especially her daughters, as soon as they were able, despite decreasing household productivity and the increasing availability of commercial goods. Thus, the number of hours a girl spent in play would have been circumscribed by immediate familial obligations. Though minding younger siblings combined amusement with training, it was a weighty responsibility nonetheless.

Time spent in doll play was also limited by school attendance, which required an increasing number of girls to spend a portion of their day in decidedly nonleisure activities, and by Sabbath observance. In a childrens' story from the 1850s, retribution was visited upon two girls who skipped school in order to play with their dolls. Similarly, on Sundays, which were "not like any other day," girls were expected to pray, not play. All middle-class Christian children were expected to observe the Sabbath like adults, even those who were not very religious. "We did not play games nor read the same books," on Sunday as on other days, recalled one girl from the 1850s, and church services and Sunday school seemed to last forever.[10] Consequently, girls were less likely to devote much of their time to doll play.

Though the number of toys had increased since the colonial period, there were still few dolls around in the average middle-class household in the 1850s, a fact of doll demography that would change dramatically only after the Civil

War. "Life for children was simple in the extreme [as] there were no array[s] of costly toys," recalled one New England woman in her autobiography. "[My sister and I] had the regulation rag doll with long curls and club feet, very ugly but dear to our hearts," and no others. Harriet Robinson, who grew up a New England mill girl, "had no toys, except a few homemade articles of our own. I had but a single doll, a wooden-jointed thing, with red cheeks and staring black eyes."[11]

Because of the scarcity and cost of dolls, parents and relatives tended to treasure those they purchased far more than did their daughters, grand-daughters, and nieces. One father in Petersburg, Virginia, included the two large dolls he had bought for his daughter in his will. With little regard for a doll's economic value, however, girls like Lucy Larcom rejected the "London doll that lay in waxen state in an upper drawer at home." To her, this "fine lady did not wish to be played with but only to be looked at and admired." Larcom, instead, preferred the "absurd creatures of her own invention." Antebellum writer Eliza Leslie similarly observed that cloth dolls "remain longer in favor with their young owners, and continue to give them more real satisfaction, than the handsomest wax doll that can be purchased."[12]

Yet many girls who lived in rural areas preferred to spend their time out-doors instead, largely forgoing the pleasures of even cloth dolls. Lucy Larcom played on farms and in fields, rivers, quarries, and cemeteries; Emily Wilson and Frances Willard (who later led the national temperance movement) pre-ferred skating, sledding, and running to playing with dolls. Carol Ryrie Brink's fictionalized stories about her great-grandmother depict Caddie Woodlawn as an active girl. According to the historian, Karin Calvert, girls were more likely to recall rolling hoops, tossing snowballs, and jumping rope to playing with dolls. Hiding in the attic, Harriet Robinson secretly played high-low-jack with the playing cards her brother had made. Little girls lived "as unfettered and vigorous an outdoor life as their brothers."[13]

Bourgeois Bébés

After the Civil War, doll play absorbed and channeled a number of interrelated changes in the lives of American girls: increased affluence, new consumer outlets, smaller family size, and greater emphasis on imitation of adult social rituals and the formalized play it encouraged. In the country but especially in cities, middle-class girls born in the postwar years amassed quantities of dolls unknown to the previous generation. In contrast to the four decades preceding the Civil War, dolls sold well and widely after 1865 as the traditional moral, utilitarian, and even political functions of dolls were gradually replaced with "needs" based on new middle-class notions.

A rising personal income meant that most middle-class Americans could become consumers of articles formerly available only to the rich whom they admired along with the Europeans that the rich emulated. Nevertheless, buying imported dolls still required a solid bank account. In 1890, when the annual income of an industrial worker was $486, a French jointed kid doll with a composition head cost between $3 and $30. As a result, the majority of dolls remained prohibitively expensive for working-class families. In one doll story, a poor seamstress was unable to purchase a wax doll because she "could not afford to spend her money that way." Her little girl asks, "Does she cost a great deal, mamma?" Her mother answers, "It would be a great deal for us—she costs $10, Lucy."[14]

A revolution in European doll production enabled jobbers, manufacturers' agents, importers, and distributors to channel European toys to American retail stores where mothers and fathers purchased great quantities of dolls made out of china or bisque with open mouths and little teeth or some with closed mouths.[15] Some of the most expensive French fashion dolls in the 1870s and 1880s arrived with fully packed trunks, often tripling the price of the doll alone. French and German dolls—with hourglass figures and *bébés*, idealized and romanticized representations of European bourgeois girlhood—flooded U.S. markets at a time when most Americans began to enjoy increasing affluence.

For those living far from urban centers with financial resources, mail-order catalogues brought the opportunity to shop at home and share in the consumer-goods market for dolls. Seven years after Richard Sears began advertising watches to the rural market, Sears, Roebuck broadened its wares to include dolls. Wholesale suppliers like Butler Brothers provided the small merchant of the rural Midwest with dolls and other items.[16]

Beginning in 1865, department stores including R. H. Macy, Jordan Marsh, and Marshall Field dazzled shoppers as spectacular "places of consumption." By 1875, Macy's stock featured dolls and other toys in addition to dry goods and home furnishings. While Macy's was the first to establish a toy department, others soon followed its lead. "Most of us adults can recall the time when the toy shop exhibited but a slim stock," commented one observer. But in the years after the Civil War, toy shops, some of which issued illustrated catalogues, increased in number and size. "Enter one of our big toy shops now and there is really an *embarrass de richesses*," noted one contemporary observer. In fact, "the first impression of the visitor to the big toy shop is . . . apt to be one of bewilderment."[17]

Toy stores also catered to a clientele of urban middle-class women, most of whom did not work outside the home and for whom shopping for self, friends, and family was becoming a central activity. According to an 1881 *Harper's Bazaar*, dolls and other toys were "chosen by mothers with a view to giving their girls correct ideas of symmetry and beauty." In stories from the late nineteenth century, nurturing female shopkeepers patiently assisted leisured female customers. In "A Doll's Story," a jointed bisque doll recalls seeing from inside her glass display case "mostly mothers and young children—sometimes nurses with small children."[18]

Women were the largest group of consumers, but fathers also purchased dolls—some of which said "Papa"—for their daughters at each birthday or homecoming. Bourgeois fathers began at midcentury giving gifts to their children at Christmas, instead of to their employees or to the poor as previously had been the case. One fortunate middle-class daughter of German immigrants recalled that she received gifts only on Christmas and for her birthday, typically in an abundance suitable for several children.[19]

In doll stories, "papas with weary heads" committed to a business ethos were frequently too preoccupied to notice a sick or a sad daughter. Fathers were increasingly separated from the family during the day, especially those who commuted from the sprouting suburbs. Sons might have been more acutely affected by their diminished opportunities to assist fathers, but the relationship of fathers to their daughters was influenced as well. Gift-giving could solace an alienated father and reinforce his belief that he was fulfilling his role as provider. As a result, "most fathers," observed a writer for *Doll's Dressmaker*, "are inclined to overindulge their daughters." In one story, Pearl's father "bought me a beautiful bedstead," narrated a doll character, "round which were hung some elegant blue silk curtains." In *A Doll's Journey*, a story written by Louisa May Alcott, one sister reassured another that "papa will give you a new doll."[20]

Generous gift giving, whether on Christmas or at other times of the year, had been a recent consequence of a number of factors, including the increasing emotional distance between parents and children. Busy parents with fewer children provided their daughters with the companionship of dolls, thereby lengthening childhood and prolonging their "dollhood." Middle-class women had become not only increasingly isolated from production but also from their children. Mothers' contact with their children became circumscribed shortly after birth. By the late 1890s, leading pediatrician Luther Emmett Holt observed that "at least three children out of every four born into the homes of the well-to-do-classes" were not fed at the breast. Instead, fashion and etiquette, shopping, and visiting dominated the life of the matron. Fashion magazines, as one indicator, far outnumbered mothers' magazines. Many children probably saw more of "nanny" than their mothers and fathers.[21]

Girls living in urban and newly created suburban areas were given far less productive work, fewer responsibilities, and fewer siblings to look after. Middle-class mothers had successfully limited their number of children, spaced them farther apart, and ceased child-bearing earlier than had previous generations. As a result, fewer brothers and sisters to watch increased the amount of time for play but decreased the number of friends and kin with whom to share it. Instead, girls were given many more toys, books, magazines, clothing, and furniture made especially for them. As a single child of well-to-do parents, Margaret Woodbury Strong adored the numerous dolls she received—now the foundation of the museum in Rochester, New York, that bears her name.[22]

In the decades that followed the Civil War, gradually dolls began to serve a more modern and symbolic function than a utilitarian one. Doll play in the postwar era emphasized the display of high fashion rather than the sewing skills emphasized earlier. In one story from the period, Pearl adores the doll she sees in Mrs. Lieb's toy shop though she hesitates to purchase it because it is undressed. "You know, dear mother," she says in a whisper, "how badly I sew." The emphasis on sewing for dolls had become obsolete by the 1880s. Instead, organized doll play developed rules that became nearly as formalized as those recently devised for baseball. Pastimes that had made previous generations of well-to-do Protestants uneasy now became increasingly accepted. As with production and consumption, amusement in general became a more structured activity.[23]

This organized amusement came to be located in the nursery, which for the middle class was the arena where (similar to organized sports), values, attitudes, and standards of behavior were imparted. Changes in the family, childhood, and new marital ideals had given rise to the middle-class nursery by the second half of the nineteenth century, differentiating households as well as the space between family members. The nursery—where the large numbers of dolls, their accoutrements, and other toys could be kept—became indispensable. Although Victorian houses were spacious, they were cluttered with possessions too precious to risk around children at play. In the autonomous space of the nursery described by J. M. Barrie in *Peter Pan*, children lived apart from parents and the rest of the household. A room of adorable miniature adult furniture became a standard feature especially of the spacious upper-middle-class Victorian home. Some chairs were stenciled with affectionate names like "My Pet," and miniature tea tables painted to represent marble imitated adult lavishness.[24]

Adults expected girls to imitate the new rituals of high society with their largely imported dolls in their nurseries. Elaborately dressed dolls were thought useful in the instruction of social conventions such as housewarmings. Far more common, however, were dolls' tea parties, frequently depicted in stereographs, tradecards, and books like *The Dolls' Tea Party*. Adults proudly noted that "the children's doll parties of to-day are counterparts of grown-up people's receptions."[25]

In addition to tea parties, girls were urged to imitate another adult social ritual of polite society in the Gilded Age, that of visiting. Dolls could be purchased wearing "a stylish visiting dress, and also accompanied by a trunkful of clothes ready for all the demands of fashionable occasions." Miniature calling cards, which were a measure of family standing to neighbors and friends, imitated their mothers' cards for girls who paid formal visits with their dolls. Now instead of singing, "Here we go round the mulberry bush," girls were encouraged to sing, "This is the way we carry them . . . when we go visiting." Popular magazines like *The Delineator* advertised instructions for making visiting dresses and even "a stately toilette for Miss Dolly to wear on the promenade." "With their companions or dolls you will hear them imitating the discussion [on fashion] . . . that they daily hear in the parlor or nursery from their mother," observed Mrs. H. W. Beecher in 1873.[26]

Not all the feelings and issues that doll play accommodated were superficial and sweet. Of all the newly constructed middle-class rituals girls were urged to imitate, doll funerals were by far the most common. In a change from sparse and somber colonial funeral customs, late-nineteenth-century Americans (following Queen Victoria's lead) romanticized grief and burial practices. Mourning was demarcated by shades of black dresses, stationery, and other mourning accoutrements. According to Harvey Green, "Visiting ill or dying relatives and friends was an expected and socially required part of women's sphere, part of the broad set of nurturing responsibilities with which she was charged." To middle-class parents in the second half of the nineteenth century, that children devised imaginary and miniaturized funerals was not seen as evidence of a morbid preoccupation with death. As a result, adults encouraged rather than discouraged the doll death ceremonies their daughters conducted. Mourning clothes were even packed in the trunks of French dolls in the 1870s and 1880s. Fathers constructed doll-sized coffins for their daughters' dolls instead of what we consider the more usual dollhouses.[27]

The process of learning about the meanings of grief began early in life, as the etiquette of mourning became an integral part of a girl's upbringing. Young students in private schools learning the decorative arts created countless embroidered mourning pieces filled with new iconographic symbols such as willow trees and morning glories. Even the fictional Rebecca of Sunnybrook Farm routinely staged deaths and funerals with her rural friends. As the ritualization of mourning increased during the course of the century—all maintained within the feminine sphere—it is no wonder that parents encouraged funeral ceremonies meant to properly sanctify the "bodies" and protect the "souls" of those poor, deceased dolls.[28]

Miriam Forman-Brunell

Short stories about dying dolls were included in the popular fiction for children and provided them with new ideas about how they should play with dolls. By contrast, earlier in the century so few stories about dolls had been written that one disappointed doll in a story from the 1840s remarked, "I never heard any stories about dolls, and what they thought, or what happened to them!" In the years after the Civil War, however, a conspicuous doll culture unfolded in widely available children's books and popular magazines. Beginning in the late 1860s, colorfully illustrated and miniature books were printed for girls (and their dolls). Nursery shelves were lined with books about dolls, books *for* them such as *The Dolls' Own Book*, which went through numerous editions, and even books *by* dolls. Stories such as "Dolly's Experience, Told by Herself" or doll memoirs were ostensibly written by doll authors.[29]

It was the fictional literature of "doll culture" that broached the more powerful feelings of love and violence. Doll fiction provided girls with both an outlet and a way of playing with their dolls so as to grapple with serious needs. Unlike the antebellum literature for children that stressed the development of skills and morals, doll fiction of the Gilded Age emphasized the exploration of self, interpersonal relationships, and fantasy. Despite the innumerable images of girls washing their dolls and doll clothing, grooming had not yet become a primary justification for doll play because most dolls made out of horsehair or wood shavings had little chance of surviving a good dunking. Instead, it was through her relationship to her female dolls—also portrayed as passive, pretty, enigmatic, domestic, dainty, mute, vain, and delicate—that a girl learned about the essence of "true love" and how to distinguish it from more superficial feelings. While the more elaborate dolls were often portrayed as shallow, one bisque sophisticate observed, "Oh, it's nice to be grand and all that, I suppose/But of late I'm beginning to reap/The knowledge that happiness isn't fine clothes/And that beauty is only skin deep."[30] Although hopelessly unfashionable, rag dolls were most likely to have insight about interpersonal relationships.

> Lillian Grace is a fine city girl
> I'm but a queer "country cousin,"
> I have one dress of coarse cotton stuff,
> She has silk gowns by the dozen.
> She is so pretty, and dainty and gay
> I am so homely and funny;
> I cost a trifle, I'm but a rag doll,
> She costs a whole heap of money,
> She came from France in a big handsome box,
> I, from a country bazaar,

Things are more precious I've often been told
That travel so long and so far.
Yet it is strange, but Oh! it is true
We belong to the same little mother
And though she loves Lillian Grace very much
It is queer, but somehow or other,
I have a spot in her dear loving heart
That Lillian Grace cannot enter;
She has a hold in the outermost rim,
But I have a place in the center . . .
And all the silk dresses and other fine things,
Though they do look so fair to the eye,
Are not worth a thought since they cannot win love.
O a happy rag dollie am I![31]

The portrayal of love between a doll and a girl, which often straddled the boundaries between maternal love and romantic love, was reciprocal, communicative, and passionate. By the early 1890s, the growing importance of mothering and child study had influenced popular ideas about doll play for girls. *Doll's Dressmaker* (a monthly magazine first published in New York City in 1891) reprinted images of girls with their bevies of dolls, which conveyed a new maternal fecundity out of step with actual demographic changes (families were getting smaller) but in step with more scientific notions about mothering. Thereafter, in numerous images girls cradled *bébés* with maternal sentimentality while contemporaries rhetorically asked, "Is it not the harmless, childish joy that develops and educates the young girl's maternal instinct, and in so doing helps to elevate her to the pinnacle of true womanhood?"[32]

Elsewhere, fictional characters encouraged the pursuit of feminine submission to masculine dominance. In fact, girls' dolls were often portrayed as hapless victims of mischievous boys who taunted girls and tortured dolls. The incorrigible boy was familiar in fiction, art, cartoons, advertisements, and the enormously popular stereographs of the period. One doll in a story recalled that her "little mistress" had a book entitled *Mischievous Tommy*, "about a troublesome, rude boy" who had disgusting manners. As Mary Lynn Stevens Heininger and others have noted, the mischief and manipulation by the boys in *Tom Sawyer* and *Peck's Bad Boy* fulfilled the expectation of stereotypical masculine behavior. Such was the case in another popular story in which a girl named Gladys is portrayed as defenseless against her scheming, scissors-wielding brother who cuts "a great patch of hair out of the poor doll's head."[33]

In addition to bad boys, other threats restricted the boundaries of safety for dolls and, hence, their owners. In numerous stories, birds, cows, and monkeys

Miriam Forman-Brunell

like "Naughty Jacko" stole, pecked, gnawed, and kicked defenseless dolls unable and unwilling to resist. In *The Dolls' Surprise Party*, a roving mother pig and her piglets attack a group of dolls enjoying their picnic. Although most stories attributed powerful emotional responses to dolls and thus to girls, in fiction both often sat helplessly with "wooden legs" while antagonists hounded them.[34]

Home provided little safety for two dolls in a Beatrix Potter tale in which "two bad mice" destroy their domestic security. In this 1904 children's story, two working-class mice (a foul-tempered husband and his thieving wife, Hunca Munca), ransack the house of two wooden dolls absent from the nursery. Returning from their stroll, the dolls are shocked into victimized passivity. One doll merely "sat upon the upset kitchen stove and stared," while the other "leant against the kitchen dresser and smiled—but neither of them made any remark." Doll policemen and nurses (brought into play by the girl whose doll house has been burglarized) set mouse traps. To make a short story even shorter, the repentant mouse husband pays for everything he broke and "very early every morning—before anybody is awake—Hunca Munca comes with her dust pan and her broom to sweep the Dollies' house!"[35]

Stories did not completely siphon off the underlying aggression. Dolls were not necessarily safer in the hands of little girls. In *Little Women* "one forlorn fragment of *dollanity* had belonged to Jo; and, having led a tempestuous life, was left a wreck in the rag-bag." The top of the doll's head was gone, as were her arms and legs. George Eliot's fictional heroine in *The Mill on the Floss*, nine-year-old Maggie Tulliver, expressed her rage by hammering nails into her wooden doll's head, beating it against a wall, and grinding it against a rough brick. In numerous American stereographic images that became a parlor staple by the turn of the century, girls used more typical domestic implements, cutting their dolls with scissors or forcing them through clothes wringers. Like other "Conduct Stereos," these pictures were probably intended to dramatize proper feminine manners and behavior through humor.[36]

Playing with Dolls

Although a juvenile mass culture was imposed from above by parents and other adults with their own intentions, what about the interactions of girls—and boys, for that matter—with dolls and other toys? Abuse of dolls at the hands of their owners alerts us that adult prescriptions for proper play were often not what girls had in mind. In the last decades of the century stereographs and other images suggest a middle-class ideal of girls, overflowing with metaphors of abundance, yet we know far more about adult expectations than we do about childhood reality. Prescriptive literature tells us little about how ordinary girls actually behaved. Did girls identify with the dolls they heard about in stories? Did they confide in the dolls they cradled in studio portraits? Did they actually prefer dolls to other toys and activities? Were girls who played with dolls more gentle and nurturing than boys or girls who preferred more active play?

There is no disputing that girls in late-nineteenth-century America liked dolls, but not just any doll. According to one study, girls preferred dolls made of wax, paper, rag, and china over those made of rubber, kid, wood, tin, or celluloid. Among the favorite dolls were those made of cloth. Emily Kimbrough disliked the fashionable doll her grandmother gave her but adored her Topsy-turvey rag doll. Adults were often at a loss to understand why their daughters preferred ragged and "countrified" dolls to brightly colored and elaborately dressed ones.[37]

Among rag dolls, black ones were a favorite among white children, observed one contemporary shopper. Both Mary Hunt and her friend favored black dolls over white ones. "My little girl has two such [rag] dolls," commented a mother, "one white and the other black, but her affections are centered on the colored woman . . . never going to bed without Dinah in her arms, and crying for 'di' if the nurse had forgotten to put it in her crib." African American women played an increasingly significant role in the rearing of middle-class children. Suggesting a relationship born of affection, one four-year-old girl fed everything that tasted good to her black rag doll.[38]

Despite their uniform fictional portrayal as adversaries, boys were also among doll lovers. One contributor to a mother's magazine reported that her son treated the doll he loved with "the greatest care and tenderness." Nor did boys like this one shed their dolls along with their diapers. G. Stanley Hall found that 76 percent of the boys he studied played with dolls to age 12. Not surprising, then, are the numerous examples of boys especially fond of doll play. A boy doll (c. 1875) named "Theodore" became a "chum" to a little boy for eight years. A man who participated in a 1987 doll oral history project recognized a painted cloth boy doll as one similar to his childhood toy.[39]

Boys, like girls, sang to and rocked the dolls they endowed with emotional, intellectual, physiological, moral, political ("democrat"), and religious qualities. They "fed" dolls milk, bread, buttons, or pickles when they were "hungry," occasionally breaking tiny teeth and heads in order to do so. Children succored dolls sick with measles or brain fever with remedies like tapioca and paper pills or dissolved candy. According to one ten-year-old girl, "My doll Liz had a headache, so I put on her micado and read her some of Longfellow's *Hiawatha*, as she wanted me to."[40]

Miriam Forman-Brunell

Girls and boys often played with their dolls in socially prescribed ways. While girls pretended to be little mothers to their dolls, boys often assumed authoritative public roles such as doctor, preacher, and undertaker to sick, dying, and dead dolls. One eight-year-old doll dentist used toothpicks as dental tools. Another boy shot his doll full of holes with a bow and arrow so that he could dress its wounds. Boys' play also included doll crucifixions and executions. Unlike the girl characters in doll stories, however, girls did not always mind. "When my brother proved my doll had no brains by slicing off her head, I felt I had been deluded; I watched him with stoicism and took no more interest in dolls."[41]

Examples of girls like this one—who either always or eventually preferred other activities to doll play—are also numerous. Present expectations that dolls are for girls and not for boys are confounded by the fact that less than one quarter of the girls in T. R. Croswell's study of 2,000 children in Massachusetts considered dolls to be their "favorite" toy. Eleanor Abbott (granddaughter of Jacob Abbott, author of the *Rollo* series) preferred paper dolls, toy soldiers, or fights with her brother to her dolls. As before the Civil War, school-aged girls still largely preferred sledding, jumping rope, or playing tag, hide-and-seek, or any other game to playing with dolls. "In my own immediate family," recalled an aunt, "a canvass through three generations of women shows only two doll-lovers out of fifteen little girls, the rest decidedly preferring rough and tumble, active play in the open air." Someone asked "Wouldn't you rather play with dolls?" of a girl playing horse and driver with her friend. "We'd rather run," replied the pair.[42]

Although Karin Calvert found few girls' diaries from the late nineteenth century that even mentioned dolls, they nevertheless played a prominent role in the lives of many. Surprisingly, however, girls' play behavior was not always submissive nor instinctively maternal; evidence reveals that doll players pushed at the margins of acceptable feminine and genteel behavior. A wide variety of sources suggests that in their doll play, numerous "hoydenish little girls" expressed anger and aggression nearly as frequently as love and affection. "Of doll-haters, I have known a few," wrote the contributor to *Boyhood* magazine in 1905. Punishments were often particularly brutal. One thirteen-year-old girl broke her doll by knocking it against a window for crying. A four-year-old girl disciplined her doll by forcing it to eat dirt, stones, and coal.[43]

Although parents believed doll funerals could be assimilated to proper forms of femininity, girls were often more interested in the unfeminine events that led to these solemn rituals. In the numerous doll funerals that appear with startling consistency in doll stories, memoirs, and questionnaires, it was not the passive grieving that provided doll players with pleasure. Doll funerals probably appealed to girls in part because the domestication of heaven (along with the beautification of cemeteries where families found rest and recreation) made the afterlife sound fun. For others, the staging of doll funerals was an expression of aggressive feelings and hostile fantasies. George Eliot remembered that she "only broke those [dolls] . . . that could not stand the test of being undressed, or that proclaimed their unfleshy substance by falling and breaking their noses."[44] According to an article in the *Pittsburgh Post*, a five-year-old girl purposely broke her doll, then declared with satisfaction, "it was dead." Girls like this one changed the emphasis from ritualized funerals to cathartic executions. Using available kitchen utensils she dug a grave in the backyard and then invited other little girls to do the same. "I have vivid memories of harrowing games with Mary Gordon," wrote Ethel Spencer in her turn-of-the-century memoir, "during which our children [dolls] became desperately ill and died." Though this gruesome scenario bordered on the unacceptable by the end of the nineteenth century, their fascination for girls was not at all unusual. "Funerals were especially popular, with Becky [doll] ever the willing victim," confided one doll player. "No day was too short for a funeral, just so they [my friends] all got home for supper."[45]

For some, a doll's worth was determined by its ability to subvert convention, mock materialism, and undermine restrictions. For example, doll parties, considered entirely too sedate by some girls, were transformed into invigorating activities unlikely to win the approval of adults. Some girls preferred exhilarating "indoor coastings"—sliding down the stairs while sitting on a tea tray—to dull tea parties. Zona Gale and a friend wreaked havoc on their tea party by smashing their unsuspecting dolls to bits. Gale, who became a writer and a feminist, had consciously determined to live life unencumbered by sex roles.[46]

Through their doll play, girls also seemed to enjoy the challenges they posed to patriarchal authority. One autobiographer recalled deliberately sewing clothes for her doll on Sundays, "quite as on other days," until finally sobered by the warning that "every stitch she sewed on Sunday, she would have to rip out with her teeth when she got to Purgatory." Undaunted, she decided to learn how to rip out the stitches that way before she got there. The task, however, proved to be such a difficult one that she gave up sewing on Sundays until her mother purchased a Wilcox and Gibbs chain-stitch sewing machine. "After that, I did all my Sunday sewing on the sewing machine, feeling it would only be an additional pleasure to rip it out [with her teeth] in Purgatory, and with a deep satisfaction at having gotten the best of the Devil."[47]

Girls who played with dolls in late-nineteenth-century America sometimes developed a sense of self that was anything but submissive. Sarah Bixby, who was raised in southern California, skinned, dressed, and boiled rabbit meat for her doll, Isabel. In one story, Lydia smacks a roving pig with her wooden doll, formerly an outcast among her doll peers but thereafter their heroine. Late-nineteenth-century autobiographies similarly reveal that, contrary to the prescribed version, girls whose dolls fell victim to aggressive animals or belligerent boys defended themselves and their dolls instead of seeking male protection. One young girl "burst out" and "flew at" her friend, Harry (who bullied and teased), after he bit a hole in her favorite doll. She "grabbed him by the shoulders . . . ready to fight to the death for [her] rights, [when] he burst into cries for help . . . I shall never forget my surprise and triumph as I realized that I conquered—conquered in spite of being small, with a strength I could always command. I only had to set [myself] free, to let her come, outside, and she could do anything."[48]

By the turn of the century, dolls with their own wardrobes, literature, and ideology had altered the nature of doll play. Girls born and raised in middle-class antebellum households had few dolls, and those they had were mostly of their own making as prescribed and instructed by a literature directed at mothers and daughters. Making dolls and playing with them had fostered skills useful to character development, self-government, and a domestic economy. In the years after the Civil War, as European imported dolls proliferated and became more splendid, the meaning of dolls in girls' lives changed. Doll stories provided companionship and the seed of fantasies, which brought girls beyond the confines of the material world. Girls were encouraged to display the store-bought dolls they received on holidays and from indulgent relatives. The productive and "useful" activities of their mothers' generation had left the dollhouse as it had the American household, gradually replaced by new values and skills revolving around status (and kin). Previous generations had learned useful household skills, but girls in the Gilded Age were encouraged to play with their china and bisque dolls in ways that increasingly aped the conspicuous display of consumer goods and social status epitomized by the European bourgeoisie their parents emulated.

Although postwar popular culture differed dramatically from the antebellum period, girls revealed obvious continuities over the course of the century. If they played with dolls at all, they rejected elaborate dolls for coarse ones, favored black rag dolls over white ones, resisted rote prescriptions of play rituals by substituting their own earthy versions, and often preferred active "physical culture" to passive doll culture. At times, boys also challenged sex-role stereotyping and at other times reinforced it. Those girls who resisted patriarchal prescriptions in their play displayed confidence, not conformity. Their play, like language, revealed girls' agency in the construction of their own identity, subculture, and upbringing.[49]

Notes

1. "The Natural Instincts of Boys and Girls," *Babyhood*, April 1905, 143.
2. Mary Lawrence, "Dolls: Logically Considered," *Babyhood*, Oct. 1895, 330–331. On conspicuous consumption, see Thorstein Veblen, *Theory of the Leisure Class: An Economic Study in the Evolution of Institutions* (New York: Macmillan, 1899).
3. Catherine E. Beecher and Harriet Beecher Stowe, *American Woman's Home* (1869); rpt. Watkins Glen, N.Y.: Library of Victorian Culture, 1879), 298. Literature about child rearing included Theodore Dwight, *The Father's Book* (1834); Dr. John Abbott, *The Mother's Book* (1844); and Catherine Beecher, *Treatise on Domestic Economy* (1847).
4. Beecher and Stowe, *American Woman's Home*, 299. Eliza Leslie, *The American Girl's Book or Occupations for Play Hours* (New York: C. S. Francis, 1831), intro. Mary Sewell quoted in Linda Pollock, *A Lasting Relationship: Parents and Children over Three Centuries* (Hanover, N.H.: University Press of New England, 1987), 103–104.
5. Lydia Maria Child, *Girl's Own Book* (New York: Clark Austin, 1833), iii, iv.
6. Mary Ryan, *Cradle of the Middle Class: The Family in Oneida County, New York, 1790–1865* (Cambridge: Cambridge University Press, 1981), 161; *Mother's Monthly Journal*, July 1837, 127; Richard Meckel, "Educating a Ministry of Mothers: Evangelical Maternal Associations, 1815–1860," *Journal of the Early Republic* 2, no. 4 (Winter 1982): 402–423); Nancy F. Cott, *Bonds of Womanhood: Woman's Sphere in New England, 1780–1835* (New Haven: Yale University Press, 1977), 43; Paula Petrik, "The Paraphernalia of Childhood: New Toys for Old and Selchow & Righter Co., 1830–1870," typescript, 5. "Pincushion," Work Department. *Godey's Lady's Book* 74, Aug. 1867; "Doll Pin-cushion," *Peterson's* 48, Sept. 1965, 209; "The Little Companion," *Peterson's* 47, Jan. 1865. "Fancy Pen Wiper," *Godey's Lady's Book* 60, July 1884, 66, cited in Beverly Gordon, "Victorian Fancywork in the American Home: Fantasy and Accommodation," in Marilyn Ferris Motz and Pat Browne, eds., *Making the American Home: Middle-Class Women and Domestic Material Culture, 1840–1940* (Bowling Green, Ohio: Bowling Green State University Popular Press, 1988), 63.
7. Cott, *Bonds of Womanhood*, 43; Susan Strasser, *Never Done: A History of American Housework* (New York: Pantheon, 1982); Ruth Schwartz Cowan, *More Work for Mother: The Ironies of Household Technology from the Open Hearth to the Microwave* (New York: Basic Books, 1983), 63, 66, 201. Beecher and Stowe, *American Woman's Home*, 298.
8. Lucy Larcom, *A New England Girlhood* (Boston: Northeastern University Press, 186), 29. Jean M. Thompson, "The Story of Rosamond," *Harper's Bazaar*, May 1906, 474. S. Anne Frost, *The Ladies' Guide to Needlework, Embroidery, Etc.* (New York: Adams and Bishop, 1877), 132–138; Child, *Girl's Own Book*, iii, iv.
9. Paintings in the National Gallery of Art, Smithsonian Institution, Washington, D.C., Inez McClintock, *Toys in America* (Washington, D.C.: Public Affairs Press, 1961), 68.
10. "Two Sisters," reprinted in *Children's Stories of the 1850s (Americana Review)*. Emily Wilson, *The Forgotten Girl* (New York: Alphabet Press, 1937), 7.
11. Wilson, *The Forgotten Girl*, 14–15; Harriet Robinson, *The Loom and the Spindle: or, Life among the Early Mill Girls* (1898; reprint, Kailua, Hawaii: Press Pacifica, 1976), 23.
12. Suzanne Lebsock, *The Free Women of Petersburg: Status and Culture in a Southern Town, 1794–1860* (New York: W. W. Norton, 1984), 64. Larcom, *New England Girlhood*, 29; Leslie, *American Girls' Book*, 287–288; see also Maria Edgeworth and Richard Lowell Edgeworth, *Practical Education* (New York: Harper, 1835), 16–17.

13. Larcom, *New England Girlhood*, ch. 1; Kathryn Kish Sklar, *Catherine Beecher: A Study of American Domesticity* (New York: W. W. Norton, 1973), 9; Wilson, *Forgotten Girl*, 14–15. In *The Mother's Assistant and Young Lady's Friend*, Sarah S. Ellis advocated "exercise in open air" as an antidote to "artificial habits" causing a "host of numerous maladies" in genteel daughters. Karin Lee Fishbeck Calvert, *Children in the House: The Material Culture of Early Childhood, 1600–1900* (Boston: Northeastern University Press, 1992); Bernard Mergen, *Play and Playthings: A Reference Guide* (Westport, Conn.: Greenwood Press, 1982), 25; Robinson, *Loom and the Spindle*, 23–24; Anne Scott MacLeod, "The Caddie Woodlawn Syndrome: American Girlhood in the Nineteenth Century," in Heininger et al., *A Century of Childhood*, 97–120.

14. *Ridley's Fashion Magazine*, cited in Jan Foulke, "Dolls of the 1880s," *Doll Reader*, Nov. 1988, 98. "A Doll's Story," *Doll's Dressmaker*, May 1893, 103.

15. *Ridley's Fashion Magazine*, cited in Foulke, "Dolls of the 1880s," *Doll Reader*, Nov. 1988, 103.

16. J. E. Jeuck, *Catalogues and Counters: A History of Sears, Roebuck & Co.* (Chicago: University of Chicago Press, 1950); Joseph J. Schroeder, Jr., ed., *The Wonderful World of Toys, Games, and Dolls* (Northfield, Ill.: DBI Books, 1971), intro.

17. Susan Porter Benson, *Counter Cultures* (Urbana: University of Illinois Press, 1988), 14; *Playthings* Oct. 1903, 6. Philip G. Hubert, Jr., "Some Notes as to Christmas Toys," *Babyhood*, Dec. 1893, 15–16.

18. William Leach, "Transformations in a Culture of Consumption: Women and Department Stores, 1890–1925," *Journal of American History* 71 (Sept. 1984): 319–342; Elaine S. Abelson, *When Ladies Go A-Thieving: Middle-Class Shoplifters in the Victorian Department Store* (New York: Oxford University Press, 1989). *Harper's Bazaar* (1881) cited in Foulke, "Dolls of the 1880s," 94. "A Doll's Story, Told by Herself," *Doll's Dressmaker*, Jan. 1891, 5. *Doll's Dressmaker*, May 1893, 101–102. Una Atherton Hunt, *Una Mary: The Inner Life of a Child* (New York: Scribner's, 1914); Meta Lilienthal, *Dear Remembered World: Childhood Memories of an Old New Yorker* (New York: R. R. Smith, 1947).

19. Elizabeth Seelye, "Suggestions Concerning Toys and Amusements," *Babyhood*, Dec. 1890, 17; "Toys for Children," *Doll's Dressmaker*, Nov. 1892, 283. Mary Hunt's uncle gave her a French bisque doll (Hunt, *Una Mary*, 161), Lilienthal, *Dear Remembered World*, 43.

20. H. Coyle, "Papa's Weary Head," *Doll's Dressmaker*, May, 1891, 98. Wishy, *Child and the Republic*, 16; Heininger, "Children, Childhood," 19–20. *Doll's Dressmaker*, May 1891, 100; *Babyhood*, Jan. 1891, 5. Louisa May Alcott, *A Doll's Journey* (Boston: Little, Brown, 1873), 5.

21. One author of a study of Polish children found that doll play ceased at age 10—earlier than among American children (Madam Anna Grudzinska, "A Study of Dolls Among Polish Children," *Pedagogical Seminary* 14, no. 6 [Sept. 1907]: 385–390). L. Emmett Holt, "Infant Feeding," part of an address given before the Cleveland Medical Society, Oct. 26, 1900, 10, and *The Diseases of Infancy and Childhood* (New York, 1897), 158, cited in Kathleen W. Jones, "Sentiment and Science: The Late Nineteenth-Century Pediatrician as Mother's Advisor," *Journal of Social History* (Fall 1983): 86; Janet Golden, "Trouble in the Nursery: Physicians, Families and Wet Nurses at the End of the Nineteenth Century," in Carol Groneman and Mary Beth Norton, eds., *"To Toil the Livelong Day": America's Women at Work, 1790–1980* (Ithaca, N.Y.: Cornell University Press, 1987), 126.

22. *Youth's Companion* was founded in 1827, *St. Nicholas* in 1873, *Children's Magazine* in 1879. Other children's magazines include *Harper's Young People* and *Frank Leslie's Chatterbox*. Mintz and Kellogg, *Domestic Revolutions*, xix; Daniel Scott Smith, "Family Limitation, Sexual Control and Domestic Feminism in Victorian America," *Feminist Studies* 1

(Winter-Spring 1973): 40–57. *A Tribute to Margaret Woodbury Strong*, Rochester, N.Y.: Margaret Woodbury Strong Museum, 1986), 7.

23. "A Doll's Story, Told by Herself," 5.

24. J. M. Barrie, *Peter Pan* (1911; reprint, Toronto: Bantam, 1985). The Division of Domestic Life of the National Museum of American History (Smithsonian Institution, Washington, D.C.) has an extensive collection of Victorian juvenile furniture.

25. My thanks to John Gillis for bringing out this point.

26. *Pretty Pursuits for Children* (London and New York: Butterick, 1897), 61; *The Doll's Tea Party* (Boston: Lothrop, 1895); "Dressing Dolls," *Doll Reader*, June 1892, 145.

27. "Dressing Dolls," *Doll Reader*, June 1892, 144; Evelyn Jane Coleman, *Carte de Visite; Doll Reader Album de la Poupée*, 1978 reproduction; *Pretty Pursuits*, 78; "Styles for Dolls," *Delineator*, Nov. 1897, 558; Mrs. H. W. Beecher, *Monthly Talks with Young Homemakers* (New York: J. B. Ford, 1873), 293.

28. Thomas J. Schlereth, *Victorian America: Transformations in Everyday Life, 1876–1915* (New York: Harper Collins, 1991), 290–293; Harvey Green, *The Light of the Home* (New York: Pantheon, 1983), 165; Karen Halttunen, *Confidence Men and Painted Ladies: A Study of Middle-Class Culture in America, 1830–1870* (New Haven: Yale University Press, 1982), ch. 5; Ann Douglas, *The Feminization of American Culture* (New York: Avon, 1978), ch. 5. McClintock, *Toys in America*, 78; Barbara Pickering, "In Loving Memory—Dolls and Death," *Doll Reader*, Nov. 1988, 132.

29. C. Kurt Dewhurst, Betty MacDowell, and Martha MacDowell, *Artists in Aprons* (New York: E. P. Dutton and the Museum of American Folk Art, 1979), 60–62, 66–70; Rozika Parker, *The Subversive Stitch: Embroidery and the Making of the Feminine* (New York: Routledge, 1989). Kate Douglas Wiggin, *Rebecca of Sunnybrook Farm* (1903; rev. ed., Middlesex, U.K.: Puffin, 1985), 63. Mary Alves Long, *High Time to Tell It* (Durham, N.C.: Duke University Press, 1950), 23. Slave children staged funerals as well, according to David K. Wiggins, "The Play of Slave Children in the Plantation Communities of the Old South, 1820–1860," in Hiner and Hawes, eds., *Growing Up in America*, 178.

30. Mrs. (Richard Henry Horne) Fairstair, *Memoirs of a London Doll, Written by Herself* (London: 1846; reprint, New York, 1967). R. Gordon Kelly, ed., *Children's Periodicals of the United States* (Westport, Conn.: Greenwood Press, 1984); R. Gordon Kelly, *Mother Was a Lady; Self and Society in Selected American Children's Periodicals* (Westport, Conn.: Greenwood Press, 1974). *The Doll's Own Book* (Ohio, n.p., 1882); many also had large print, such as *Twilight Stories* (New York, London, Manchester, Glasgow: n.d.). See issues of *Doll's Dressmaker* for other installments by the same author. Mrs. Jane M. Besset, *Memoirs of a Doll: by Itself* (Philadelphia: American Sunday School Union, 2nd. ed., 1856).

31. Reynale Smith Pickering, "Christmas in Song and Story," and "The New Christmas Doll Complains" (poems) *Ladies Home Journal*, Dec. 1908, 126. See also the poem by Laura Starr, *The Doll Book* (New York: Outing Co., 1908), 199.

32. S. K. Simons, "The Happy Doll," *Doll's Dressmaker*, April 1893, 90.

33. Gillis, "Ritualization," 15; Francesca Cancian, *Love in America: Gender and Self Development* (Cambridge: Cambridge University Press, 1987). "Dolls: Logically Considered," *Babyhood*, Oct. 1895, 330–331.

34. Thompson, "Rosamond," 474; Heininger, "Children, Childhood," 26–27; see also Anita Schorsch, *Images of Childhood: An Illustrated Social History* (Pittstown, N.J.: Main Street Press, 1985), ch. 6; "The Tragical-Comical Tale of Mrs. Kennedy and Punch," *Frank Leslie's Chatterbox*, 1885–1886, 10.

35. "Naughty Jacko," in *Dolly in Town* (New York: R. Tuck, 1912). In "The Little Doll," a poem by Charles Kingsley in *The Water Babies* (Philadelphia: J.B. Lippincott, 1917), a wooden doll's arms are "troddened off by cows." See "Kate Douglas Wiggin's Poetry for Children," *Ladies' Home Journal*, Oct. 1907, 50. Aunt Laura (pseud.), *The Dolls' Surprise Party* (Buffalo, N.Y.: Butler, 1863).

36. Beatrix Potter, *The Tale of Two Bad Mice* (New York: F. Warne, 1904), 46, 59.

37. Louisa May Alcott, *Little Women* (1868; reprint, New York: Penguin, 1989), 39. Schlereth, *Victorian America*, 197.

38. Hubert, "Some Notes as to Christmas Toys," *Babyhood*, Dec. 1893, 14. Emily Kimbrough, *How Dear to My Heart* (New York: Dodd, Mead, 1944), 76–77; Lilienthal, *Dear Remembered World*, 20–21.

39. "The Doll of the Colored Children," *Babyhood*, Oct. 1894, 351. Hunt, *Una Mary*, 20. A. C. Ellis and G. Stanley Hall, "Study of Dolls," *Pedagogical Seminary* 1, no. 2 (Dec. 1896): 134. "Home-Made Rag," *Babyhood*, Sept. 1908, 417. David Katzman, *Seven Days a Week* (Urbana: University of Illinois Press, 1981). Ellis and Hall, "Study of Dolls," 141.

40. M. H. Jones, "Dolls for Boys," *Babyhood*, June 1896, 216. "Of average city school children below 6 years, 82% of boys . . . played with dolls; between 6 and 12 yrs., 76% of boys" (Ellis and Hall, "Study of Dolls," 155); Calvert, "To Be a Child," 156; *Maiden America & Friends: Parade of Playthings*, Nov. 1984, 51; Dorothy Washburn, "Report: Preliminary Results, Doll Oral History Project," 2, Margaret Woodbury Strong Museum, Rochester, N.Y., doll 79.9962.

41. Ellis and Hall, "Study of Dolls," 145.

42. Ellis and Hall. "Study of Dolls," 145, 147, 149, 150–151; Jones, "Dolls for Boys," 216.

43. T. R. Croswell, "Amusements" (Worcester, Mass.: J. H. Orpha, 1899), 347. Eleanor Abbott, *Being Little in Cambridge When Everyone Else Was Big*, cited in Bernard Mergen, *Play and Playthings: A Reference Guide* (Westport, Conn.: Greenwood Press, 1982), 186–187. Croswell, "Amusements," 5; Brian Sutton-Smith, "The Play of Girls," in Clare B. Knapp and Martha Kirkpatrick, eds., *Becoming Female* (New York: Plenum, 1979), 229–230. "The Natural Instincts of Boys and Girls," *Babyhood*, April 1905, 143.

44. Ellis and Hall, "Study of Dolls," 146–147; "Young Mrs. Winket Scolds her Dolly," *Babyhood* 2, 1 (Boston: Lathrop, 1878), 10. Death and burial were the subjects of late-nineteenth-century schoolgirls' ring games; see Brian Sutton-Smith, "Play of Girls," in Knapp and Kirkpatrick, eds., *Becoming Female*, 232; Schlereth, *Victorian America*, 292; "Burying Baby Dolls," *Doll's Dressmaker*, Nov., 1891, 240; Ethel Spencer, *The Spencers of Amberson Avenue: A Turn-of-the-Century Memoir*, ed. Michael P. Weber and Peter N. Stearns (Pittsburgh: University of Pittsburgh Press, 1983), 65; Alice Kent Trimpey, *Becky My First Love* (Baraboo, Wis.: Remington House, 1946), 1–2; According to one nine-year-old, "doll broken, funeral just for fun" (Ellis and Hall, "Study of Dolls," 146).

45. Calvert, "To Be a Child," 153. Lawrence, "Dolls: Logically Considered," 330–331. "The Natural Instincts of Boys and Girls," *Babyhood*, April 1905, 143. Ellis and Hall, "Study of Dolls," 140, 141.

46. James Sully, *Children's Ways* (New York: Appleton, 1897), 492.

47. Hunt, *Una Mary*, 14. Zona Gale, *When I Was a Little Girl* (New York: Macmillan, 1913), 196.

48. Hunt, *Una Mary*, 163–165.

49. Aunt Laura (pseud.), *The Dolls' Surprise Party*. Victoria Bissell Brown, "Female Socialization among the Middle Class of Los Angeles," in Elliott West and Paula Petrik, eds., *Small Worlds: Children and Adolescents in America, 1850–1950* (Lawrence: University of Kansas Press, 1992), 246. Hunt, *Una Mary*, 20.

CHAPTER 11

Inscribing the Self in the Heart of the Family

Diaries and Girlhood in Late-Victorian America

Jane H. Hunter

Scholars have emphasized the discontinuity in the lives of such middle-class women as Jane Addams and M. Carey Thomas, who emerged from sheltered Victorian girlhoods into the social activism and committed vocation of New Women. In particular, they have stressed the role of college education in breaking the dependence of daughters on families. Without minimizing the significance of the collegiate experience for women, this essay suggests that the roots of turn-of-the-century change also extend back into the Victorian family itself. The practice of the diary, for one, contributed to the development of the "enhanced sense of self," which one scholar considers central to claims of New Women for a public role. It did so without requiring girls to reject the support or many of the familial principles of home.[1] This essay focuses on the function and the practice of the Victorian girl's diary, providing an analysis of the strategies by which girls used diaries both as technique and discipline in their formalization of one kind of self.

Even more than their parents, upper- and upper-middle-class Victorian girls lived through the written word. We know Victorian girls in the United States as avid readers—of romances, biographies, histories, and serials. A rich scholarly literature now debates the significance of their reading to their own aspirations, the publishing industry, and turn-of-the-century culture.[2] Victorian girls were also avid writers. They spent long hours at writing desks producing pages of letters, composing poetry, copying passages from literature, keeping all manner of diaries and journals. The historical literature has been less attentive to the cultural significance of girls' *writing*.

Like their reading, girls' writing emerged in the context of new leisure available when parents hired servants; like reading, its meaning was shaped by parental hopes for refinement and improvement. And like reading, parental expectations could not control the fantasy released in private literacy. Unlike reading, *writing* obliged girls to organize their daydreams or structure their self-scrutiny, to experiment with a voice that they could call their own.

The diary initiated a discourse about the self rather than establishing a definition of what the self was or ought to be. Diary-keepers and advice-givers alike often failed at first to distinguish girls' individualized needs and desires from familial roles. As Michel Foucault suggested about sexuality in the nineteenth century, the act of writing constrained individuals as much as it freed them. Parents and authorities promoted diary-writing among girls as an effort to contain selfishness and encourage conformity to social expectations. Like the Catholic confessionals described by Foucault, diary-writing was an internalized discipline of the self. But like the Greco-Roman rituals also described by Foucault, diary-writing became a constructive "technique of the self," adopted lovingly by girls.[3] As both discipline and technique, diary-keeping contributed to the process by which late-Victorian girls amassed fragments of experience into identity.

The exhortation to diary-keeping in part reflected the flowering of a romanticism that encouraged the recording of reveries as part of an exploration (or construction) of the secular self. Karen Lystra's work demonstrates how the experience of romantic love in nineteenth-century America fostered an "ideal of an essential self, what we today call a personality," which challenged a God-centered universe.[4] Yet religious moralism made an equally important contribution to the Victorian idea of the self. Richard Rabinowitz's history of religious experience notes the impact of an activist moralism in challenging Calvinist passivity. As orthodoxy crumbled, the characteristic narrative of the self changed from the conversion narrative to a daily diary that documented a route to salvation through good deeds and regular habits.[5]

The Victorian tension between the dictates of romanticism and moralism was nowhere more apparent than in adult relations with children or youth. Though adults claimed rights to privacy for themselves, and granted them to other adults, they generally did not extend these rights to their children. Although they often presented their daughters with diaries for self-exploration, they remained ambivalent about girls' rights to a self separate from family duties and responsibilities.

The conflict between romanticism and moralism especially in adults' relations with youth is apparent in the historiography of Victorianism. Thus, Peter Gay celebrates the nineteenth century as "the golden age of the diary," and argues that self-reflective diaries "became almost obligatory companions to a class endowed with a modicum of leisure."[6] At the same time, he notes that parents would "open children's letters, superintend their reading, chaperon their visitors, inspect their underwear." Gay asserts, "if parents exacted truthfulness from their children, this all too often served as a screen for the brutal assertion of adult power, as an arrogant, and at times prurient, invasion of young lives."[7] Unlike the romantic explorations of some Victorian adults, girls' diaries did not permit uninhibited freedom, but instead remained "working papers" filled with tension and controversy. In response to this tension, girls initiated demands for privacy against intrusive parents. They came to use their diaries not as an escape from the Victorian family, but as a way of discovering—or constructing—the self *within* it.

"Victorian" is a contested and complex term which in America has connotations of gender, class, and region. "Victorians"—those who participated in a trans-Atlantic culture of literacy and uplift—were disproportionately female, and clustered in the middle and upper classes and the Northeast. Yet the precepts and aspirations of Victorianism spread beyond those focal groups and influenced many of those on the frontiers and many second-generation immigrants in the cities. The thirty-odd girls whose diaries constitute the primary source for this paper reflect this pattern. They lived predominantly in the urban East, and were likely to be from comfortable, even elite, native-born families. Their diaries are primarily archived in New England. As Peter Gay suggests, a degree of leisure helped to define both their lives and their diaries and contributed to the formation of a "Victorian" sensibility. Although all Victorian girls had chores, those represented here were not "working," either at shops, in factories, or as mainstays of the domestic work force. Most were attending school. Thus, the journal of Lizzie Morrissey, second-generation Irish from East Boston and a schoolgirl, is included here along with the journals of members of the Boston elite. Although Lizzie Morrissey's family employed no servants, Lizzie herself wrote an extensive diary in which she described *watching* the toils of mother and grandmother, excused from helping them by her attendance at Girls' High School and by the family aspirations she embodied.[8] The Victorian ideal for girlhood—like Victorianism itself—cast its influence well beyond those whose prosperity originally occasioned it.[9]

This chapter is primarily a study of the role of the diary in the lives of Victorian girls; in its exploration of the interactions of romanticism and moralism, it is also a study of Victorianism itself. But it speculates about how diaries might have contributed to the evolution of a generation of Victorian girls into the New Women of the Progressive Era. The dense documentation left by one diarist, Annie Winsor, especially illuminates the role of the private diary in helping girls formulate separate selves in the context of close family relations. Sharing middle-class origins and a notion of women's special gifts with their mothers, New Women differed from their Victorian mothers in their access to higher education and in their willingness to consider a public career. This essay raises the possibility that their later lives of some autonomy outside the home were in part enabled by their earlier discovery of regions of autonomy within it.

Girls' diaries were the ideas of parents, who promoted diary-writing for their daughters as a means to good character and refinement. Parents had always encouraged virtuous conduct among their offspring, but in eighteenth-century New England, sustained good behavior was secondary to a conversion experience as the mark of a good Christian. The disestablishment of the church and the dislocations of urbanization and industrialization ushered in new standards rewarding internalized character and steady habits. During the nineteenth century, moral character became an everyday affair, and diaries assumed new importance as regulators and also demonstrations of sustained virtue. Parents promoted diaries as a valuable "discipline" useful in structuring time and character.

Parents and advice-givers suggested journals for girls and boys. But the conventional wisdom was that girls took to diary-keeping more naturally. Agnes Repplier, who wrote a piece on "The Deathless Diary" for an 1897 issue of the *Atlantic Monthly*, repeated this common assumption:

> Even little girls, as we have seen, have taken kindly enough to the daily task of translating themselves into pages of pen and ink; but little boys have been wont to consider this a lamentable waste of time. . . . As a rule, a lad commits himself to a diary, as to any other piece of work, only because it has been forced upon him by the voice of authority.[10]

There were structural reasons for the popularity of diary-keeping among girls. The affluence of middle-class urban families marginalized daughters' work within the household. When servants were hired, as they were in approximately 15–30 percent of the households in Northeastern cities,[11] girls usually had more spare time than boys. As advice-writer William Thayer put it in 1859, "Many who continue to reside with their parents, have several hours at their command each day. Some spend these hours in fancy work, music, and idleness. With not a few it may be almost a study *how to kill time.*" Thayer proposed an alternative. "What an opportunity for mental culture and religious improvement!" By this Thayer did not mean that girls should indulge in introspection. Instead, he encouraged the development of order, answering the "pert miss" who asked, "how can a girl like me be orderly, when I have nothing to order?" with the wisdom, "There are [your] own wardrobes to superintend, and [your] rooms to arrange."[12] Along the same lines, of course, there was one's own life to systematize. In 1878, the children's magazine *St. Nicholas* gave as the first reason to keep a journal that it taught habits of order and regularity.[13]

In addition to its moral purposes, the keeping of a diary joined other activities sanctioned by parents to fill the time of privileged daughters. Lessons, either in school or out,[14] were one such activity as were piano classes and exercise. Girls were urged to walk regularly, sometimes as much as two hours a day. Piano practice was even more regulated, with girls recording in their diaries their obedience to a demanding daily practice schedule. Writing in a diary, then, was a similar obligation, considered character-building, time-filling, and refining.

The general principles of diary-writing reflected these values. Ideally, a diarist wrote daily, and often copied her sometimes copious diary entries twice. The diary was to be a credit to a girl's accomplishments, and those included her hand.[15] Writing a diary, like a constitutional, was usually a ritualized part of the day, which often took place in the bedroom immediately prior to retiring. It was considered less stressful than schoolwork by both parents and daughters.[16]

Since the purpose of a journal was to train a girl in orderliness, clearly the entries themselves ought to *be* orderly and reflect an orderly life. The *St. Nicholas* adviser, W. S. Jerome, suggested a routine recording of the weather, letters received or written, money paid or received, the day of beginning or leaving school, visits, books read, all set down in the correct order of time. The end result would be a useful family history. As he wrote, "Perhaps, some evening when the family are sitting and talking together, some one will ask, 'What kind of weather did we have last winter?' or 'When was the picnic you were speaking of?' and the journal is referred to."[17] Clearly the journals Jerome had in mind were semi-public family records rather than personal confessions. They were also designed for self-grooming along prescribed lines rather than experimentation.

The advice literature acknowledged that diaries could fill different functions for girls, though, and it rushed to close off those possibilities. No diary at all was certainly better than a diary that encouraged fantasy and ambition and distracted a girl from her domestic priorities. Almost simultaneously with its publication of Jerome's 1878 article of advice "How to Keep a Journal," *St. Nicholas* published two stories which represented a direct attack on the practice of school girl diary-keeping. These stories especially focused on the expanded agenda of the schoolgirl diarist and ended with schoolgirls repudiating their diaries, their fantasies, and even themselves, and taking a place again within their mothers' domestic households. Unlike Jerome's hortatory piece on diary writing, which was addressed to both girls and boys, the protagonists of these didactic pieces were both girls.

The ultimate violence and finality of both these Victorian "children's" tales is striking. "Jottings Versus Doings" by Margaret Eckerson describes a twelve-year-old diarist who renounces and then burns her diary. The eldest of several sisters, the diarist Margy is constantly besieged by demands on her time and person—babysitting duty and loans of her new silk parasol, for example. She escapes to her journal, where she embroiders on the mundane details of domestic life with musings about love, kindness, and the beauty of death. A dangerous fall down the stairs forces Margy to realize that she does not actually want to die, and she turns on her journal: "I haven't written the real truth about anything," she concludes contemptuously, and then proceeds to make a bonfire of the offending book. While her mother regrets its loss, her father, a minister, concludes, "Margy's burnt journal is no loss to her, dear, . . . for sometimes there is a vast difference between jottings and doings."[18] Beneath this mild comment lies a polemical position—a denial of Margy's right to imaginative self-definition and a reductionist insistence on appropriate role behavior as the measure of a person.

Whereas Margy's problem is silly fantasy, vain ambition is the problem for Dora, the heroine of Kate Gannett Wells's tale about diaries. Published in 1879 and described in the subtitle as a "Story for Big Girls," it was ominously titled "She Couldn't."[19] Alienated from her mother and brothers, fourteen-year-old Dora was a "'funny girl' or a 'queer girl'" who "wrote in her journal and made up stories." What *she couldn't* do was to reach fame by the age of fifteen. She launched several schemes for greatness, but failed in each, and finally resolved "to give up all idea of doing anything except school work and being good"—in itself a momentous undertaking. To commemorate this decision, she locked her door and made one last entry in her journal. Her entry took the form of two columns labeled "Wants" and "Oughts."

> Under the first she wrote: Want 1, to be real good; 2, to write splendid novels; 3, to be beautiful and great. Under the "oughts" she wrote: 1, to love stupid people; 2, to make everybody happy when I can; 3, not to think about myself, but just keep going on; 4, to talk all the time to my mother; 5, never to write another word in this journal.

For Dora, writing her journal was an assertion of ambition and of self at the expense of duty to others. (Interestingly, even a desire to be "real good" seemed to be overstepping.) Following this listing, she blotted the ink, tied her journal in black ribbon, had a good cry, ate some candy,[20] and returned to her mother's side, saying

> "Mamma, I have given up all trying after what I can't be. I am just going to love you all at home with all my heart, and then you'll love me; and I wont [sic] feel badly because I can't write books or help in big ways."

Wells appropriately described Dora's ritual of renunciation as "a kind of funeral over herself." For it is clear that in destroying their diaries both Dora and Margy are destroying their dreams and their independent selves, and rejoining a domestic world of self-surrender.

So what do we make of Wells's and Eckerson's tales of adolescent renunciation, published in one of the major magazines for youth and children in the late nineteenth century? Together with Jerome's piece from the same decade, they set the parameters of the girl's diary. As Jerome explained, a diary should promote order and discipline, even record the writer's "progress as a thinker and writer." As Wells and Eckerson made clear, it should *not* indulge in fantasies, or entertain inappropriate ambitions. The advice-givers thus agreed on the goal of promoting dutiful daughters but differed on the costs and benefits of the diary to this campaign. Jerome advocated the diary as a tool for self-discipline; Wells and Eckerson feared it as a surrogate for "splendid novels" and self-absorption. The moral for all the advice-givers was the same, though (as Wells's Dora puts it), "if I try to make you all real happy in little bits of ways, I guess it will 'come out gloriously'"—a classic message of fulfillment through domestic subordination. The girl's diary was clearly not meant to participate in the introspective romanticism or the self-creation that encouraged some nineteenth-century journals. Rather, the writing promoted by *St. Nicholas* had earlier roots. In endorsing *writing* for self-improvement, but not for fantasizing, the latter-day Puritans who published *St. Nicholas* were reflecting a frequently voiced Puritan judgment on appropriate *reading*.[21]

From the outset, then, diary-writing was considered both, or alternately, dutiful and dangerous. Girls who received diaries from mothers and fathers on birthdays participated in the explorations of duty and pleasure anticipated and feared by adult pundits. Most began their diaries in the dogged spirit of accountants of the soul. But what began as parentally enforced "discipline" often evolved into a self-referential "technique." This evolution sometimes involved only minute adjustments of perspective and often consisted of the internalization of strategies of self-discipline. Nonetheless, the evolution was real, and also practical. Girls' diaries offered them a compromise—a way to release and contain rebellious impulses, however circumscribed, without breaking with families. Like their own rooms, they claimed their diaries for themselves, beyond the gaze, but within the bosom, of their families. In these protected spaces, girls charted a middle way between the fiery rebel and the good daughter of advice books and fiction. Diaries offered several routes of mediation. Sometimes they served as surrogate battlefields upon which girls struggled to blend family expectation with personal impulse. Sometimes they served as parental talismans—and as security blankets—in girls' developing relations with peers. Sometimes they served to compartmentalize desire and to forestall conflict. Each of these strategies enabled Victorian girls to entertain imaginative freedom while preserving the networks of affiliation at the center of their lives.

The key to both the appeal and the success of the practice of diary-keeping was a growing claim to privacy—a gradual appropriation by youth of a notion central to their parents. Privacy for adults was an important Victorian notion. As recent historians of the bourgeois family have shown us, the cloak of privacy allowed for illicit behavior, which was tolerated as long as it was veiled.[22] The same protections were not offered to children. In fact, adults' increasing rights to privacy within their homes meant greater parental obligation to monitor children. The result was the surreptitious surveillance that we associate with Victorianism. Although we think of the Victorians as inappropriately intrusive, their recourse to indirection was a sign of their deference to the *idea* of privacy. Earlier generations would have had fewer scruples about direct intervention.[23]

Motivated perhaps both by the greater actual autonomy of their daughters, who were no longer constantly at their mothers' elbows, and also by their own increasing responsibility for girls' upbringing, parents were often interested in the contents of daughters' diaries and journals. Earlier in the century, parents who had scrutinized their children's writings for signs of grace were not indulging idle curiosity; they were fulfilling their highest parental responsibility to see to the spiritual salvation of their children. The substitution of character-building for salvation-seeking as the goal of adolescent socialization was a change in vocabulary rather than a revolution in parent-child relations.[24]

The result was that Victorian parents pried. The practice of Bronson Alcott's family in the midcentury was only an extreme form of common parental participation in the diary-keeping of children. Both Bronson and his wife Abba provided written commentaries on the journals their four daughters kept and sometimes read aloud for them.[25] In the 1890s, Rose Nichols's mother requested a journal of her European travels for all the family to read. And Agnes Hamilton reported a tantrum from her young brother who "flew into a terrible passion because Mamma told him to write in his diary which he keeps for Papa."[26] For good reason, girls felt that they needed to declare and fight for the privacy of diaries.

In fact, the unviolated diary was rare. The best-documented culprits were friends and sisters, who often flaunted their violations. A (perhaps former) friend of Emily Eliot's cracked her diary and lingered to give herself away with a comment on Emily's bad handwriting and a prediction: "When this meets your eye You will cry O fie!" Marian Nichols's younger sister Margaret wrote directly in her sister's diary "to make Marian mad." Cassie Upson's outburst against an "ugly little snip" who peeped into her "sacred diary" suggests the likely response to provocateurs.[27]

The language used on the covers and the front pages of diaries to warn off snoops was similarly direct and unmuted, quite distinct from much of the Victorian language of circumspection which characterized *entries* in diaries. In invoking a claim to privacy, Victorian girls knew they were invoking a household God. Emily Eliot had attempted to warn off her critical friend in 1870 with a front page inscription:

> *Look not in this book* for fear of *hate.*
> *For except to the owner it is strictly private.*

Ella Lyman titled her notebook of scattered thoughts "Private pages," and then elaborated, "To read another's secret is a crime. Pause and reflect and dare not do so!" Mary Thomas declared that if anyone read her diary, "I should hate them forever after for it, that is unless I gave them permission."[28] Within these curses and ritual incantations girls unleashed a kind of vocabulary—including the harsh "hate"—which otherwise was outside of appropriate usage.

This harsh language was a necessary defense, for among the issues that girls broached in their diaries, tentatively and carefully, were their relations with parents and authority. For extremely good reasons, concerns for privacy accompanied challenges to authority. In 1882, when she was fifteen years old, Margaret Tileston made the following (for her) momentous entry in her journal: "In the a.m. after church, Papa told me not to read the Bible. Very well, I acquiesce. Perhaps he considers it a bad book for the young." After writing that covert criticism of her father, Tileston grew concerned and at the bottom of the page made a resolution: "That this diary be not perused by others." At some later reading she regretted both the implicit criticism and the resolution of privacy, and attempted to obliterate both. Mary Thomas was not as protective of her diary, nor as circumspect within it, but when she challenged her father's view of the world (and simultaneously advanced a plan for her own financial security), she imagined how it might strike him:

if I ever have to work for my living, I think I will give lessons in Calysthenics [*sic*]. . . . I wonder what Papa would say, if I was to read him this part of my Journal, he would feel like shaking me, he has so much pride, he could never bear to see his daughter teach & right there where he is so well known & everyone thinks he is so well off too.[29]

Mary Thomas made *her* secret a potential challenge to the great secret of her father's insolvency. Diaries allowed girls to at least experiment with (and sometimes even savor) the feeling of challenging parental authority.[30] Having done so, they transformed their energies into a defense of their privacy. As long as such challenges were still secret, they were safe.

And as such, secret diaries facilitated the development of a multi-faceted self. Claims for privacy allowed for girls' experiments in independence without subjecting them to the battles and isolation of earned autonomy. With private diaries, girls could have it both ways—retaining the protected status of obedient daughters at the same time that they carved out a measure of imaginative independence. With private diaries, they could compartmentalize their experiment.

Diary-keepers agreed initially that the goal of being good required the suppression of self and the subordination of girls to their mothers. In the antebellum period, thirteen-year-old Louisa Jane Trumbull expressed a series of motivations for diary-keeping that characterized later diarists as well: "In keeping a journal I at first did it because my sisters kept one—afterwards I wrote because it was the wish of my mother." Now, she wrote, "it is done not only to serve as means of being employed about something useful and proper but because it is a source of pleasure to me."[31] This sequencing suggested the role of family, including older siblings, in sponsoring diaries; when socialization was most successful, girls internalized familial standards and defined their pleasure in the same breath as doing something useful and proper.

A prototypical model for this journey to goodness was literary—the immensely popular *Stepping Heavenward* by Elizabeth Payson Prentiss, the daughter of a Congregational minister. *Stepping Heavenward* appeared first in 1869 in fictional diary form and over the years sold 100,000 copies. It documents the efforts of Kate, a willful daughter, to grow up and be good. As with many actual diaries, *Stepping Heavenward* begins on a birthday with a series of resolutions. Kate no sooner makes these resolutions (while lolling in bed before school) than she breaks them (she grows late, forgets her prayers, disobeys her mother, and storms out the door). Her mother knows best, however, for upon Kate's return home, she finds her mother smiling wisely and a new writing desk in her room. This writing desk will allow Kate to keep the first resolution she has made—to begin her journal.[32] It is clear that at the least, writing a journal, like her other resolutions, is a form of self-denial that will lead to self-improvement; at the most, it might even be the exemplary discipline that will set the pattern for other forms of self-control. Charting Kate's progress through the loss of her father and a disappointed love affair, *Stepping Heavenward* finally brings Kate to a love of God and a simultaneous reconciliation with her mother. Her minister responds to her desire for greatness with a gentle reminder that her first act of heroism should be in "gratifying her mother" by helping around the house.

The morality play and the plan for action embodied in *Stepping Heavenward* were clearly models for adolescent diarists. If some of its readers "felt that they had written *Stepping Heavenward* themselves" (as some were said to have),[33] others attempted to use it as a model for their own chronicles of improvement on the way to good character and to womanhood. Mother and daughter Georgia Mercer [Boit] and Mary Boit both read *Stepping Heavenward* repeatedly, identifying with its impetuous heroine and its hopeful message of the possibility of improvement. For young Georgia, writing at the age of eighteen in the post–Civil War South, moral improvement meant increased love for God. On her nineteenth birthday, she stayed up late to ask for spiritual aid in serving God in the coming year, and recorded it in her journal.[34]

Georgia Mercer married a Bostonian and died young, leaving behind two daughters to a privileged existence. In 1891 her eldest daughter Mary Boit, who had remained in extended mourning, read and reread *Stepping Heavenward*, unaware that she was replicating the experience of her mother years before. Like her mother, Mary Boit also identified with Kate, but she focused on her efforts to be good rather than on her efforts to believe. She especially identified with Kate's hot temper and her anger toward her mother, for Mary Boit had a troubled relationship with her new stepmother. "I think that Katherine in the book before she gets good is exactly like me," she wrote. "I feel the same ways. I love her & I love the book this is my third time reading it. On my birthday I am going to try to turn over a new leaf & be a better girl." Twenty years and half a continent apart, mother and daughter patterned their experience on the same template—using the occasion of a birthday to redouble their efforts for goodness, and to record these efforts in a moral account book.[35]

There has been much debate over the impact of Victorian propriety on Victorian behavior.[36] Schoolgirl diaries testify to the strength of norms of denial and repression for girls in that era. The resolutions sprinkled throughout diaries suggest that exhortations to self-denial and service were not simply the stuff of advice manuals, but made their way into girls' own self-expectations. At the age of sixteen, Charlotte Norris made the following plans for the year 1886: "Duty shall precede pleasure. Save ten dollars by June 1st. Bathe regularly every day. Use chest weights every day until June 1st." In 1892, at nineteen, Marian Nichols offered a graver list:

> Incipit hic Vita Nuova.
> Resolved. not to talk about myself or feelings. To think before speaking.
> To work seriously.
> To be self restrained in conversation and actions.
> Not to let my thoughts wander.
> To be dignified.
> Interest myself more in others.
> Repentance is good, but it should not distract one's thoughts.[37]

Marian Nichols's listing of resolutions all tended to a narrowing of her possibilities—of conversation, action, thought. Even the feelings of guilt and repentance themselves, those staples of the Victorian mental diet, should be spurned as indulgences, a digression from the dull business of being good.

Nichols's list of negations and self-denials recalls the adolescent negation of another member of the Boston elite of an earlier era, the self-renunciation of Alice James, the invalid sister of Henry and William James. At the age of fourteen, James wrote in a later account, she discovered "what Life meant for her." What it meant was a kind of smothering of impulse, desire, and expression.

> I had to peg away pretty hard between 12 and 24, "killing myself," as some one calls it—absorbing into the bone that the better part is to clothe oneself in neutral tints, walk by still waters, and possess one's soul in silence.

By nineteen, Alice James's struggles to suppress her spirit and negate desire had led to a breakdown, to "full-blown hysteria," according to her biographer Jean Strouse.[38]

Alice James's life story is a famous and extreme case of the impact of narrow parental expectations on girls' behavior and self-estimation. Her description of the mysterious moment of self-repression and negation that ended her autonomous life at the age of fourteen resembles the black-binding or the burning of diaries—the funerals over the selves—mentioned in *St. Nicholas* fiction. We know about her decision of denial only because of an adult autobiography. Other girls used their teenage diaries as battlegrounds in these psychic wars, exhorting their wills to ride herd on their rebellious spirits. Agnes Hamilton's remarkable diary of her life in the illustrious Hamilton family is primarily a prolonged account of her struggles to be better. Within the terms of the Hamilton family (not so different from those of the James family), this meant in part to be more accomplished. Agnes made plans not to loiter, to stop talking so much, not to speak unkindly about anyone, not to read so many novels, and "not to think of myself and how stupid I am but of other people and how bright and splendid they are."[39] Agnes Hamilton's girlhood diary is a document in self-discipline.

But it is also a confessional diary that reveals some growth in self-understanding. At the age of nineteen, after four years of making and breaking resolutions, Hamilton made an important New Year's resolution: not to make so many resolutions, "never to plan at night what I shall do the next day . . . never to plan in the summer what I shall do in the Winter or in one term what I shall do in the next." The purpose of this resolution was not to give up resolutions entirely (for it is a case in point), but to make them more realistic. Therein Agnes acquired greater tolerance of herself by virtue of a better understanding of her family. "All this planning and never carrying out," she recognized as a *family* characteristic. And she even went so far as to say that it might not even be a fault "for we would be pretty miserable if we had to come out of our air castles."[40] After pages of writing about herself in which she inveighed against egotism and self-preoccupation, Hamilton used her understanding of the dynamics of her family to forgive herself.

In the efforts of girls to be good and repress self, diaries seem to have had a moderating effect. Certainly keeping a diary that recorded successes and failures on the road to virtue was an additional incentive to be good. A success could be recorded and celebrated. ("I was good and did not do much of anything," Mary Boit recorded ambiguously at the age of ten.)[41] At the same time, an always-listening, never-judging diary was something of a tonic. Girls who talked enough about their efforts to be good availed themselves of a simplified version of the "talking cure," which would be used soon by Sigmund Freud and Josef Breuer with middle-class Viennese girls. (The disproportionate number of adolescent or late-adolescent females in Freud and Breuer's early work, and indeed the role of hysteria in their formulation of psychoanalysis, corroborates the special salience of language therapy for Victorian girls.[42]) Diarists *were* likely to talk themselves through some of their most censorious impulses and end up with a modicum of self-awareness. It is significant that Alice James, whose adolescent renunciation represented a victory for the dark side of genteel Victorianism, did not record her life and her thought in diary form until she was forty-one and only then did she declare and explore the renunciation of her youth years before. Had she embarked on this venture in younger years, the creative transcendence that Jean Strouse attributes to the articulation of a "voice of her own" might have modulated her earlier decision of denial.

Within their diaries, girls assiduously recorded their efforts to be better—echoing, internalizing, and ultimately softening parental imperatives. Just as diaries moderated parental dictates, they mediated parental identifications.

As Katherine Dalsimer suggests, they proved to be revisited "transitional objects" useful in the processes of adolescent separation.[43] No other metaphor quite captures the depth of attachment that girls sometimes demonstrated to their "darling" diaries than that analogy to the anthropomorphic blanket or teddy bear of early childhood. Literally within vessels chartered and christened by parents, Victorian girls embarked on imaginative journeys that did not threaten to take them too far from home.

The function of the diary as mother substitute emerges especially dramatically in the disproportionate number of full, emotive, conversational diaries kept by girls without mothers. Elaine Showalter has observed that many Victorian women writers had lost, or were alienated from, their mothers. Showalter concludes that the resulting male identification contributed to their careers. The diary evidence from the United States suggests that the loss of a mother in itself may have encouraged writing—a form of communication with an absent or imagined other that may initially have been a lost parent.[44] For bereaved adolescents, a diary might function to preserve the memory and the moral voice of a lost or absent parent and to retain some level of parental participation from beyond the grave.[45]

For girls whose parents were living, the role of the diary as a transitional object, not only "of," but "away from" parents, was more direct. Girls frequently resorted to diaries to experiment with and negotiate new allegiances. Diaries granted more freedom than parents; girls could take on new attachments without abandoning old reliances. Thus, when Margaret Tileston went away to boarding school and developed a crush on an older girl, she recorded it in her diary—as well as the news that she had just written a twelve-page letter to her mother, "the longest letter I ever wrote."[46] And when Helen Hart fell in love with her cousin, she confessed to her diary the prolonged anguish of one "who had never a thought, much less a sorrow" without sharing it with her mother.[47] Such confessions to diaries replaced those to parents—but with parents' informal acquiescence. The diary was thus a tool for legitimating the ongoing reorientation of girls from parents to peers.

Often the diary's role in this transition was not symbolic at all, but quite concrete. Like rolling hoops, diary-keeping was a late-Victorian recreation that girls sometimes shared with friends. The playful fabrication of different personas in diaries was an engrossing amusement within Victorian friendships. Girls described writing diaries together in their rooms, on New Year's Eve, at boarding school, and even in the park.[48]

Shared diary-keeping carried more possibilities for emotional experimentation than rolling hoops, and diaries often became actors in the friendships themselves. Girls who wrote diaries together frequently wrote about each other, producing provocative documents that became the stuff of suspicion and intimacy. Writing diaries became a way of confessing, protecting, or creating secrets too private for speech. Mary Boit spent a delightful vacation with her cousin Manny, "a witch and a gypsy," with whom she became infatuated. The two girls did not do much at Manny's summer house on Cape Cod, Mary explained, except "write in our js [journals], bathe, read, and draw." They had a tiff, however, over Manny's request (which Mary refused) to let her read her journal. "Poor little witch," Mary exclaimed, repenting all the while. "I really think she will have to as I like her so much." Manny's reading of Mary's journal, of course, would let her know, as it does us, of the depth of her cousin's secret admiration.[49] Writing both privileged and protected that secret.

Without the embarrassment of spoken avowals, writing could summon a world of high seriousness distant from casual schoolgirl banter. The exchange between schoolmates Mattie Walker and her friend Mary Thomas (recorded by Walker in Thomas's diary) is a case in point. Walker had seized Thomas's diary in playful protest at being denied permission to read it. After ribbing Thomas for her appetite for peaches and then her penchant for flirtation, Mattie Walker's thoughts became more serious, as she explored the possibilities of writing for confession.

> Mary Thomas if I tell you something you declare that you wont tell. Did you know that I am engaged to a fellow that I talked about so. You have been the only person that I have ever told. Dont never tell Lessie or Ida [roommates], for I would not have any bodie to know it for anything now please dont tell, I was ashamed to tell you with my mouth so I will tell you by writing it; you can judge yourself who he is, I cant tell you if I do I will have to tell a story for I promise him that I would not tell it; if you ever tell I never will forgive you. I never will speak to you. Well I must close. Please dont let any bodie see this. Good bye my *honest friend*. I remain yours until Death.

Despite her conversational writing style, Mattie expressed shame at the idea of "telling with my mouth," revealing another dimension to the dynamics of the diary. In a Victorian world which celebrated civility, the diary could function as a conduit around awkwardness—even for such blithe spirits as Mattie Walker and Mary Thomas. As Ellen Rothman discovered in her study of Victorian courtship, *writing* allowed for intimacy that direct conversation inhibited. Written expression of course need never be acknowledged.[50] For the same reasons that parents might encourage their daughters to write to them—as a way of communicating without the embarrassment of face-to-face expression—girls might use their diaries among themselves. Writing allowed for the keeping up of appearances.

And that seemed sometimes to be the point of girls' diaries. Self-governance was expected in feeling no less than conduct, and the diary could prove both a convenient receptacle for—and an incitement to—emotional spillover. In addition to moderating harsh norms and mediating new allegiances, the girl's diary could inspire and then compartmentalize confusing emotions. Almost all diaries contained at least one moment of a confessional nature— sometimes crossed out, sometimes written down the spine in minute handwriting, sometimes just left dangerously on the page. But there were some girls for whom the diary's primary purpose seemed to be to provide a safe ground for documenting, exploring, and disciplining nascent sexuality. Victorians strictly limited open expressions of sexuality, but as Foucault persuasively argues, they dramatically encouraged discourse *about* sexuality. Precocious sexuality was both most censured and most discussed—an adult secret imperfectly kept from adolescents themselves.

Harriet Burton's diary, written between the ages of thirteen and seventeen, is a document "saturated" with desire. Initially, when she embarked on her diary at the age of thirteen in 1887, she was reticent: "I find it rather hard to confide all my 'inmost soul' to a journal for my 'inmost soul' is—*very inmost!*" But before long, she had discovered the purpose for which she came to rely on her diary—what she would later call her *"de-praving—deep raving."* Though she felt her passion "cannot be natural" for anyone her age, and imagined "how anyone would laugh, how greatly amused they would be at the mere idea of a 'mere-child' of fourteen—*loving*," she found her feelings "sweet" and despaired at the difficulty of doing them justice—of keeping them from seeming "small and weak." Her self-descriptions are as one crazed—for instance in this passage after her arrival for a summer visit in Oneonta, New York.

> I am in a very hilarious frame of mind today, and can hardly curb my prancing spirits enough to "wright" as this scrawl bears witness. My silvery voice has been heard at all hours of the day rolling forth in diabolical waves of laughter, and striking terror into the souls of the inhabitants of the house. My mind is so filled with plans which wont come true that I'm nearly crazy. My emotions for other people . . . become so conflicting that they brake from the narrow bounds of my inner man and find vent in a mad race around the house.

Despite her descriptions elsewhere of complete freedom for outdoor escapades of all kinds, Harriet Burton described herself here as a *confined* hysteric, very much within the mode of the "mad woman in the attic," the mad woman of Gothic romances. Her confinement was clearly metaphoric, a fictive imprisonment of impulse within a fragile shell. As in much of women's Gothic literature, Burton saw herself as really two people—a passionate inner self and an outer mask, "a placid calm expression of contentment on my face." And she lamented "how dreadful has [providence] been in giving no times of solitude times which the soul may assert itself and the face throw off the mask, and break out and away from conformity and be *itself*." In her appropriation of the spiritual term "soul" to refer to her uninhibited impulse, Burton demonstrates a modern, romantic tendency to regard human desire rather than moral conduct as the core of the authentic self.

For Harriet Burton, the only place where this self could be confessed—with all its inadequacies—was in her diary. "It seems so ridiculous and sentimental to think of writing in a journal, and I would not for anything have *anyone* know that I keep one," she wrote. "But I will confess it to myself it *is* a sort of comfort to sit and write, although it is only talking to myself, and it is often putting down in black and white the things I most despise myself for." She explained the same day, when she was seventeen years old, what is evident from the diary itself, that her diary was for a special purpose. "I only keep this book to write in when I feel a sort of wild feeling like this." She was determined not to be "such a creature of emotions and strange passions," and looked upon her diary as an "outlet."[51]

Harriet Burton's description of her crazed state of mind and her need for writing as an outlet are echoed by Charlotte Perkins Gilman's fictional heroine in her 1892 story "The Yellow Wallpaper." In Gilman's tale, a physician-husband has forbidden his wife (the narrator) from writing, arguing that "with my imaginative power and habit of story-making, a nervous weakness like mine is sure to lead to all manner of excited fancies, and that I ought to use my will and good sense to check the tendency." The protagonist (a Gilman surrogate), demurs, though: "I think sometimes that if I were only well enough to write a little it would relieve the press of ideas and rest me," she remarks.[52]

Burton's experience bears out *both* physician and protagonist. As the physician-husband argues, Burton's "nervous weakness"—or perhaps simply normal libido—did lead to "all manner of excited fancies," which were initially fueled rather than dissipated by the act of writing. But as Gilman's alter ego points out (and Gilman knew as a writer herself), the writing eventually helped to play out the fantasy and relax the writer. After a many-paged reverie of unfocused fantasy, Harriet Burton checked herself with her *own* "will and good sense."

> The wisest thing that I can do is to go and duck my head into cold water, eat something then go downtown where I can see plenty of faces, *real* ones, then come home study my latin—*real* latin, then go to bed, a *real* bed,—to *real* sleep, get up in the morning eat a *real* breakfast, go to school make some *real* recitations, by that time I may be in the realms of *reality* and common sense!"[53]

In Gilman's story, the physician-husband was the censor of fantasy, but in Burton's diary, the writer had become her own censor; either rested or fatigued she had orchestrated her own return to reality. As in girls' efforts to be good, the impact of the diary was a moderating one. The diary could soften behavioral commands issued by internalized authority; and it could also give rein and then harness runaway fantasies. As such it offered a middle way, a way of integrating feelings of independence with social expectations for appropriate behavior.

The use of youthful diaries alone as the major evidence for understanding the function of diaries has something of a self-referential quality. We usually have few outer sources to suggest how they fit into the context of a full life. The extraordinary paper collection left by Annie Winsor [Allen], however, allows us to assess the relationship of her private "journal" as she called it, to other ways of writing about and formalizing her life. Her writings demonstrate the way that a girl's private diary might function as a "compartment" for exploration and release within the context of an overarching loyalty to familial values. In addition to her private journal, Winsor wrote numerous letters to various family members and kept a diary for her parents to read. Winsor's journal allowed her private space within the heart of her close and even intrusive family, while her diary was the work of a dutiful daughter. Together Winsor's writings allowed her to express her grievances and affirm her separate opinions without threatening her familial lifeline. The resulting compromise between parental domination and personal rebellion helped her to go on to a notable career as a Progressive educator, while she continued to be sustained by her natal family. Winsor's characteristic Victorian diary was an accomplice in her transformation into a New Woman of the turn of the century.

Winsor grew up in Winchester, Massachusetts, the daughter of a normal school graduate and a Harvard-educated physician. The former Ann Ware Winsor was a powerful presence, both inspiring and overbearing. She took seriously her responsibilities for supervising the moral development of her seven children, and to this end, she expected access to their thoughts. Annie kept a college diary "For My Mother dear, and because *it* is for her, For My beloved Father," and when another daughter mentioned a journal she was keeping, her mother requested to see it. Most of all, Ann Winsor insisted upon reading her daughters' letters to other family members. When Annie was traveling in England at the age of twenty, for instance, her mother confessed that her feelings were hurt at not being the recipient of confidences exchanged among the sisters.

> Mary does not show me your private letters to her; which makes me sorry. . . . I don't love to think that my children say things & feel things that they are absolutely unwilling that I should know, even though I can understand their not wanting to say them at first hand.

She had no choice but to conclude, somewhat contrary to the evidence, that "Still, I can trust my children, & I do trust them."[54]

Her daughters, for their part, despaired of ever pleasing her, and alternately retreated from and resisted her intrusiveness. At the age of twenty-one, Annie wrote a revealing letter to her mother.

> I know very well—and I know it much to my mortification that I seem sort of sneaking and evasive when I am with you (and indifferent too). I have worried about it and even cried over it, mother. The conclusion I've come to is this. I am so afraid of the criticism, correction or dissatisfaction that may be in your face and eyes that I do not dare to look up.

She concluded with insight, "You see I care more than anything else at home to be a daughter who shall repay all the worry and care that have been expended on her."[55]

Especially on the matter of reading personal letters, though, the eldest sisters attempted to take a stand in defense of their privacy. The elder, Mary, in a letter addressed to her fourteen-year-old sister, asked that her mother be instructed to wait her turn "and that meantime she must possess her soul in patience and not be fired with jealousy." It was easier when the sisters grew older and had left home, Mary thought, "so that my letters to you won't either be shown round or make the family jealous by being kept for yourself." Voicing incantations more often used to defend diaries, the younger Annie at age twenty began a personal letter to her sister with a series of warnings: "Pedlars and mothers ragmen and sisters warned off the premises. Private. No Admission Except on Business! All rights reserved." And the next year, she addressed a curt reprimand to her mother for her snooping: "How did it happen, I wonder, that the letter you forwarded was opened. Can you explain the principle if you please?"[56]

In the face of this intrusiveness, Winsor kept a private journal to help her think about the rights of young people. Begun when she was sixteen and continued through the age of twenty-one, her journal consisted of high-minded reflections on the appropriate relations between the generations, a forum that allowed her to vent her frustrations with her own upbringing obliquely. In contrast with the direct language she used in defending her privacy, the private journal itself used the language of high-Victorian rationalism and abstraction (and the obfuscation of either the third person "one" or the first person plural). Through these means, Annie Winsor began to express a rebellion against her mother that she could not admit to more personally. She started her journal with an epigraph: "What youth saw plainly manhood loses sight of," and went on to explain her goals: "to help me to remember my faults, and my convictions as relate to the behaviour of older people toward younger." (She later simply referred to "O.P.s" and "Y.P.s.") She also voiced her hopes that her journal would remind her in later years "to try to keep up with the fashions and with the new manners and customs which are continually coming and going, so that when I have young people in my charge I may be in sympathy with them, and not restrain them with my 'old fashioned ideas.'"[57]

She embarked on a program of reflection ("Must we girls never think of the questions of love and marriage?"), self-admonition ("I incline to be too heavy and serious"), and resolve ("Perfect goodness is the only thing worth aiming at"). Her journal tentatively voiced complaints about her censorious home environment. "I can't see why a person who is evidently trying to do right as hard as she can, should ever be blamed as harshly as though she meant to do wrong," she wrote, and then pondered "why any person should ever be blamed harshly at all." She explored her claims to privacy, a right she had declared on the cover of this "private" journal. "I have a hatred of showing letters which come to myself," she wrote. Certainly parents had a responsibility to make sure the letters were suitable, she agreed, and she even agreed that "in the case of letters of general interest this feeling should be overcome. . . ." But at eighteen she protested having "one's faults, failings or anything of that personal kind talked of before a whole family."[58]

Before she was done, Annie Winsor had offered the skeleton for a generational rebellion against parental authority. She observed that little children often expect "to love without liking" because adults make themselves so disagreeable. She defended peer culture, arguing that "the way for people to have a really delightful time is to be with their equals." She supported the custom of going out to commercial establishments—presumably soda fountains or fairs—with young men, "since young men have no way of returning the hospitalities shown them by ladies except by taking the ladies to places of amusement, etc." And she even defended, and participated in, sexual high jinks.

> To me, there is an exquisite thrilling pleasure in real, hand to hand, private "fooling" with a boy that I like. . . . And yet I can easily see that an older person ought not to openly countenance it. I don't think it does me harm, but—positive good—it sort of ennobles me.[59]

Her vocabulary was high-minded, but with it Annie Winsor was defending the "ennobling" qualities of sexual pleasure and the rights of youth to defy parental dictates.

Winsor's journal from her sixteenth year was written in 1881, when she was a student at coeducational Winchester High School. She went on to attend the Harvard Annex (later Radcliffe), to teach school and participate in social reform, and then to found her own school, the Progressive, coeducational Roger Ascham school. Under a pseudonym she wrote frequent columns of advice on women's subjects. Winsor became an archetypal New Woman, attending college, marrying late, developing a career, and campaigning for sex education—however euphemistically she delivered her advice.[60] Her private journal was an important part of that development. In the measured voice of a true Victorian, she used that protected space to chip away at the fetters of obligation and guilt that still constrained her. Her critique declared a generational revolt.

Winsor's bid for personal autonomy within her family was always muted by family claims, and it is for this reason that her journal needed to be private: she was in no way eager to *sever* family bonds, quite the contrary. "It is my duty to confide in my mother, even though it be most difficult for me," she wrote after a declaration of her need for privacy. And that same year, she observed in her journal that journal-writing did not always satisfy her, that it seemed a little abstract and remote. "I want something more substantial. So I write to my mother. I can put my love in as much as I like."[61] Winsor might rail in her journal against the way Old People misunderstood Young People, yet she remained too dependent on her parents' moral and emotional universe to break away from home completely. Ultimately Winsor wanted to be good, and depicted her life as an independent woman with the moral earnestness of a good daughter. In this she shared emotional bedrock with Dora, Kate Gannett Wells's heroine who finally set aside her ambitions, bound her journal in black and resolved "to talk all the time to my mother" and "to love you all at home so you'll love me."[62]

But unlike Wells's heroine, Winsor did not forswear her ambitions—or her journal. Rather she protected her conflicted self within its *private* pages. This claim for privacy allowed Victorian girls to assert new selves without rejecting their domestic identities. They thereby could maintain without being oppressed by the maternal bonds that many historians see as the heart of the nineteenth-century women's world.[63] For Victorian girls, a blend of private experiment with public loyalty made sense.

Diary-writing by itself did not turn Victorian girls into New Women, but it allowed them saving compromises. Private diaries allowed for the retention of familial ties without forcing girls to retain familial destinies. Of course, one could argue that this effect was primarily conservative—that diary-writing provided a safety-valve that released and contained rebellious impulses, preventing the telling break with family that might lead to "true" autonomy. Recent work in the social science of adolescence, however, has suggested the importance of familial connection to the formation of identity. Research on privileged girls from troubled families concludes that "even in difficult circumstances, young women may struggle to maintain connection in order to know themselves and to be known by their parents."[64] Both our understanding of domestic culture and recent work on adolescent maturation suggest the advantages of exercises in identity that allowed Victorian girls to have it both ways: to entertain imaginative freedom while preserving the networks of affiliation at the center of their lives. Sustained by rather than isolated from natal families, Victorian girls participated in the modest historical evolution of their era.

This evolution was not without conflict, as attacks on the entire practice of the diary made clear. The willingness of a figure such as Kate Gannett Wells to condone the black-binding of a diary as a funeral over the self suggests the strength of the opposition to girls' separate selves. A clubwoman and educational reformer, Wells was also a leading Boston "anti"—an opponent of the woman suffrage movement. Her rejection of secret diary and of secret vote reflected her support for an older notion of a domestic sphere where women set aside self for service.

Such diarists as Harriet Burton and Annie Winsor, who ignored Wells's moral admonitions (if they read them), used their diaries for explorations of themselves, including their own innermost "deep ravings." Victorian girls worried about egotism, but in writing a diary about themselves—of whatever sort—they affirmed their rights to a degree of autonomy. Like Winsor and a scattering of other Victorian girl diarists, Harriet Burton went on to marriage and to a significant public life, in her case, as a leading turn-of-the-century suffragist.[65] The disagreement between Kate Gannett Wells and Harriet Burton over the rights of women to the vote embodied a more fundamental difference between Victorian and Progressive ideology over the autonomous female self.[66]

Not necessarily "New Girls," Winsor and many other Victorian schoolgirl diarists nonetheless became New Women. Barbara Sicherman has argued the significance of reading in broadening the horizons of Victorian girls and stimulating their later accomplishments as Progressive women.[67] But writing provided an even more active exercise in mediating between parental authority and personal autonomy. The mediations diaries accomplished in the exploration of sexuality, the indulgence of fantasies, and the forsaking of mothers for peers represented small but enabling victories over the constraining force of domestic rectitude.

Girls continued to write diaries in the twentieth century, but under different parental dispensations—at once less demanding and less intrusive. In popular culture today, diaries are almost exclusively the domain of the preadolescent girl—often merchandised in pastel colors with lock and key already affixed. But without the authority of the parental mandate (and the moralist religious premises behind it), and without the intrigue of possible surveillance, the appeal of the girlhood diary has diminished—and with it, too, cultural validation for the containment, rather than the enactment, of adolescent strife.

Notes

1. Carroll Smith-Rosenberg states that New Women "repudiated their mother's world" (245). "College education thus functioned to draw young women out of their mothers' and grandmothers' domestic mindset" (253). "The New Woman as Androgyne: Social Disorder and Gender Crisis, 1870–1936," in *Disorderly Conduct: Visions of Gender in Victorian America* (New York, 1985). Sara M. Evans suggests that the first generation of New Women "had been formed in the intense world of women's colleges" and notes the "stark choice" they faced on graduation between "the traditional domesticity of marriage and a career of paid work" (147). *Born for Liberty: A History of Women in America* (New York, 1989). In contrast, Nancy Woloch describes how the New Woman of the turn-of-the-century "integrated Victorian virtues with an activist social role." She also refers to the "enhanced sense of self, gender, and mission" which characterized the New Woman's move outside of the family. *Women and the American Experience* (New York, 1984), 269.

2. Ann Douglas initially blamed the development of a popular (and debased) sentimental culture on the reading habits of women and girls. *The Feminization of American Culture* (New York, 1977). By contrast, Rachel Brownstein has argued that romantic Victorian literature encouraged girls to think of themselves as the central subjects, the "heroines," of their lives. *Becoming a Heroine: Reading about Women in Novels* (New York, 1982). See also Nina Baym, *Novels, Readers, and Reviewers: Responses to Fiction in Antebellum America* (Ithaca, N.Y., 1984), and Cathy N. Davidson, ed., *Reading in America: Literature and Social History* (Baltimore, 1989).

3. Foucault stresses the role of authority in shaping self-scrutiny: "The obligation to confess is now relayed through so many different points, is so deeply ingrained in us, that we no longer perceive it as the effect of a power that constrains us. . . ." *The History of Sexuality*, vol. 1, Introduction, trans. Robert Hurley (New York, 1978), 60. His second volume locates the original "techniques of the self" in Greco-Roman culture, where Foucault describes them "as those intentional and voluntary actions by which men not only set themselves rules of conduct, but also seek to transform themselves. . . ." Vol. 2, *The Use of Pleasure*, trans. Robert Hurley (New York, 1985), 10–11. Foucault's argument against the notion of nineteenth-century sexual repression states instead that the nineteenth century was "saturated" with discourse about sexuality, and indeed that discourse "constructed" sexuality as we know it.

4. Karen Lystra, *Searching the Heart: Women, Men, and Romantic Love in Nineteenth-Century America* (New York, 1989).

5. The diaries of the eighteenth and nineteenth century were kept as often by men as by women, and served a variety of purposes, both practical and religious. While some diaries provided useful chronicles of farm and family life, others documented an ongoing relationship between self and God. Rabinowitz's account describes the importance of diaries to devotionalism as well as to moralism. He describes devotionalism as private

and intimate, especially an urban phenomenon, and characterized by female parishioners. Rabinowitz concludes that many devotional diaries "were kept by urban middle-class women, for whom devotionalism offered a flowering of one's internal spirituality that compensated for a woman's declining role in social and economic spheres." Richard Rabinowitz, *The Spiritual Self in Everyday Life* (Boston, 1989), 39, 257, 164.

In noting the importance of separating spheres, Rabinowitz echoes the work of historians of the middle class, who emphasize the significance of the development of separate public and private spheres in generating a new kind of romantic self-consciousness, to which women were especially prone. Margo Culley, *A Day at a Time* (New York, 1985) underscores the significance of women's separate sphere to their diary-writing. "As the modern idea of the secular diary as a 'secret' record of an inner life evolved, that inner life—the life of personal reflection and emotion—became an important aspect of the 'private sphere' and women continued to turn to the diary as one place where they were permitted, indeed encouraged, to indulge 'self-centeredness'" (3). Culley's work, like the work of Rabinowitz, sees the diary as compensation for women, a world they turned to with increasing frequency because it offered them a freedom unavailable elsewhere.

6. Peter Gay, *The Bourgeois Experience, Victoria to Freud*, vol. 1, *Education of the Senses* (New York, 1984), 446–48.

7. Gay, *Education of the Senses*, 446.

8. Diary of Elizabeth Morrissey, 21 Mar. 1876, 18 July 1876, Boston Public Library.

9. Daniel Howe argues the "hegemony" of American Victorianism over other cultures and subcultures during the second half of the nineteenth century. "Victorian Culture in America," in Howe, ed., *Victorian America* (Philadelphia, 1976), 6.

10. Agnes Repplier, "The Deathless Diary," *Atlantic Monthly* 79 (May 1897): 475, 642. Ellen K. Rothman, *Hands and Hearts: A History of Courtship in America* (New York, 1984), 9; Gay, *Education of the Senses*, 448. The authors concur that diary-writing was more common among women than among men.

11. Faye Dudden makes this estimate of the proportion of households with live-in domestic servants in *Serving Women: Household Service in Nineteenth-Century America* (Middletown, Conn., 1983), 1.

12. William M. Thayer, *The Poor Girl and True Woman, Or Elements of Woman's Success, Drawn from the Life of Mary Lyon and Others; A Book for Girls* (Boston, 1859), 21, 264, 266.

13. W. S. Jerome, "How to Keep a Journal," *St. Nicholas* 5 (Oct. 1878): 789.

14. Joseph Kett argues that high schools "were the perfect institutional outlet for . . . teenage female children," both because of their superfluity in the domestic work unit and because of the "appropriation by women of control over cultural life." The movement of women into teaching and the low opportunity cost of forgoing the labor of girls also made high school education popular as a way of providing respectable occupation for middle-class girls. *Rites of Passage: Adolescence in America 1790 to the Present* (New York, 1977), 138. Girls outnumbered boys in the late-nineteenth-century high school by a proportion as high as two to one, leading by the twentieth century to a perceived "boy problem." See David Tyack and Elizabeth Hansot, *Learning Together: A History of Coeducation in American Schools* (New Haven, 1990), 145, 165–200 and John L. Rury, *Education and Women's Work: Female Schooling and the Division of Labor in Urban America, 1870–1930* (Albany, 1991), 11–48.

15. Diary of Kate Upson (Clark), 19 July 1864, Sophia Smith Collection, Smith College, Northampton, Mass.; Diary of Elizabeth E. Dana, 18 Dec. 1864, Dana Family Papers

(A 85), The Arthur and Elizabeth Schlesinger Library on the History of Women in America, Radcliffe College, Cambridge, Mass.

16. Diary of Emily Marshall Eliot, 15 Nov. 1870, 20 Aug. 1869, 10 Oct. 1869, 3 Dec. 1869, 14 Dec. 1869, (MC 205) Schlesinger Library; Diary of Margaret Harding Tileston (Edsall), 13 Dec. 1882, 7 June 1878, (MC 354) Schlesinger Library; Diary of Kate Upson (Clark), 6 June 1862.

17. Jerome, "How to Keep a Journal," 790–91.

18. Margaret H. Eckerson, "Jottings Versus Doings," *St. Nicholas* 6 (Feb. 1879): 282.

19. Kate Gannett Wells, "She Couldn't: A Story for Big Girls," *St. Nicholas* 6 (May 1879): 462–67.

20. Dora's self-soothing through eating is interesting here in terms of recent work on the association between eating disorders and female identity. See especially Joan Jacobs Brumberg, *Fasting Girls: The Emergence of Anorexia Nervosa as a Modern Disease* (Cambridge, Mass., 1988). Wells, "She Couldn't," 463, 468.

21. David D. Hall notes the imprecations of seventeenth-century moralists who warned "Let not your Children read these vain Books, profane Ballads, and filthy songs. Throwaway all fond and amorous Romances, and fabulous Histories of Giants . . . for these fill the Heads of Children with vain, silly and idle imaginations." "The Uses of Literacy in New York," William L. Joyce et al., eds., *Printing and Society in Early America* (Worcester, Mass., 1983), 17.

22. One such notable account is the long and adulterous affair of Mabel Dodd Loomis, from Amherst, Mass., who Gay argues was protected from censure by secrecy and by observance of the conventions. *Education of the Senses*, 107.

23. Norbert Elias, *The Civilizing Process: The History of Manners*, trans. Edmund Jephcott, (New York, 1978), 182–90. David H. Flaherty writes of colonial New England "The prevailing theory of family government, while beneficial for the maintenance of good order in a Puritan society was inimical to personal privacy. It charged the head of the household with the duty of surveillance over the behavior of everyone, of ruling the home with an iron hand and all-seeing eye." *Privacy in Colonial New England* (Charlottesville, 1972), 56.

24. Rabinowitz, *The Spiritual Self*, describes the evolution from an orthodox notion of the self as "soul," whose fate was influenced by divine mercy, to a self defined as "character," which could be improved by steady efforts and good deeds.

25. Elizabeth Palmer Peabody, *Record of a School: Exemplifying the General Principles of Spiritual Culture* (Boston, 1835), 98, 47. Madelon Bedell writes that "in the Alcott family (as in many other families of their circle), journals were not a private matter. They were written to record the daily progress of each person. Each member of the family was free to read—and sometimes to write as well—in any one of the others' journals." *The Alcotts: Biography of a Family* (New York, 1980), 248.

26. Diary of Agnes Hamilton, 30 Mar. 1886, Hamilton Family Papers (MC 278), Schlesinger Library; Rose Nichols to mother, 24 Dec. 1893, Nichols-Shurtleff Family Papers (MC 212), Schlesinger Library.

27. Diary of Emily Eliot, last page 1871; Diary of Marian Nichols, 26 Apr. 1885; Diary of Kate Upson (Clark), 22 Mar. 1866.

28. Diary of Emily Eliot, 12 Sept. 1870; Diary of Ella Lyman, c. 1880, Ella Lyman Cabot Papers (A 139), Schlesinger Library; Diary of Mary Thomas [Lumpkin], xerox, 24 June 1873, Joseph Henry Lumpkin Papers, Hargrett Rare Book and Manuscript Library, University of Georgia, Athens, Georgia.

29. Diary of Margrett Tileston, 17 Dec. 1882; Diary of Mary Thomas, 27 June 1873.

30. Foucault describes the dynamics of "pleasure and power" that characterize challenges to rulings on appropriate sexuality, but his analysis applies equally well to subterfuges of other kinds of authority: "The pleasure that comes of exercising a power that questions, monitors, watches, spies . . . and on the other hand, the pleasure that kindles at having to evade this power, flee from it. . . . Capture and seduction, confrontation and mutual reinforcement: parents and children, adults and adolescents . . . all have played this game continually since the nineteenth century." *History of Sexuality*, vol. 1, Introduction, 45.

31. Quoted in Rothman, *Hands and Hearts*, 8.

32. Elizabeth Payson Prentiss, *Stepping Heavenward* (New York, 1869), 7.

33. Ola Elizabeth Winslow, "Elizabeth Payson Prentiss," in *Notable American Women* (Cambridge, Mass., 1971), 96.

34. Diary of Georgia Mercer (Boit), 23 July 1871, 6 Sept. 1871, Cabot Family Papers (A 99), Schlesinger Library.

35. Diary of Mary Boit (Cabot), 30 Aug. 1891, 3 Dec. 1890, Cabot Family Papers (A 99), Schlesinger Library.

36. The prime focus of this debate has been on the expression of sexuality, with Carl Deglar leading the challenge in his article, "What Ought to Be and What Was: Women's Sexuality in the Nineteenth Century," *American Historical Review* 79 (Dec. 1974): 1479–90.

37. Diary of Charlotte Norris, 1886, Sophia Smith Collection; Diary of Marian Nichols, 27 Jan. 1892, Schlesinger Library.

38. Diary of Alice James, as quoted in Jean Strouse, *Alice James: A Biography* (Boston, 1982), 87.

39. Diary of Agnes Hamilton, 10 Aug. 1886, 12 Dec. 1886, 7 Jan. 1884, 31 July 1887, Schlesinger Library.

40. Diary of Agnes Hamilton, 1 Jan. 1888.

41. Diary of Mary Boit, 2 Aug 1888.

42. Sigmund Freud attributes the origins of psychoanalysis to Josef Breuer's work with hysteria. "The History of the Psychoanalytic Movement," in A. A. Brill, trans. and ed., *The Basic Writings of Sigmund Freud* (New York, 1938), 933. Elaine Showalter writes of patient Bertha Pappenheim [Anna O.] that "Anna O., in fact, was the inventor of the 'talking cure' of psychoanalysis, Breuer's partner in a remarkably shared and egalitarian therapeutic exchange." *The Female Malady: Women, Madness, and English Culture* (New York, 1985), 155. Pappenheim was a bright, young woman of the middle class, who upon leaving school had become bored with enforced domesticity. "Her monotonous family life and the absence of adequate intellectual occupation left her with an unemployed surplus of mental liveliness and energy, and this found an outlet in the constant activity of her imagination, a disease considered to affect young women." Freud and Breuer, *Studies on Hysteria 1895–1898*, *The Standard Edition of the Complete Psychological Works of Sigmund Freud*, vol. II, trans. and ed. James Strachey (London: The Hogarth Press, 1955), 41–42. Brumberg suggests that Victorian girls lacked "voice," and resorted to appetite as one way of "speaking." "Since emotional freedom was not a common prerogative of the Victorian adolescent girl, it seems reasonable to assert that unhappiness was likely to be expressed in nonverbal forms of behavior." *Fasting Girls*, 138. However, like therapy, the diary represented one solution to the problem of emotional restraint that Brumberg sees embodied in food refusal.

43. This term is introduced and explored in Dalsimer, *Female Adolescence: Psychoanalytic Reflections on Literature* (New Haven, 1986). Nancy Chodorow notes that adolescents "replay" early maternal separation, and that this conflict is more intense for girls, for whom maternal identification is less completely disrupted in early childhood. *The Reproduction of Mothering: Psychoanalysis and the Sociology of Gender* (Berkeley, 1978), 130 ff.

44. Elaine Showalter, *A Literature of Their Own: British Women Novelists from Brontë to Lessing* (Princeton, 1977), 61.

45. Diary of Mary Boit, 30 Aug. 1891; Diary of Mary Thomas, 16 June 1873, 29 June 1873, 5 July 1873. In fact parental loss complicates the process of adolescent development by blocking normal separation impulses. Instead the mourning adolescent seeks to *sustain* rather than to attenuate the maternal bond. Dalsimer, *Female Adolescence*, 124.

46. Diary of Margaret Tileston, 4 Jan. 1882, 7 Jan. 1882, 11 Jan. 1882.

47. Diary of Helen Marcia Hart, 9 Oct. 1862, (A/H 325), Schlesinger Library.

48. Diary of Georgia Mercer, 8 Apr. 1871; Diary of Agnes Hamilton, 31 Dec. 1885; Diary of Mary Thomas, 1 July 1873; Diary of Mabel Lancraft, 13 July 1877, New Haven Colony Historical Society, New Haven, Conn.

49. Diary of Mary Boit, 11 Aug. 1891, 10 Aug. 1891.

50. Diary of Mary Thomas, 1 July 1873; Rothman, *Hands and Hearts*, 224.

51. Diary of Harriet Burton, 20 Apr. 1887, 29 Feb. 1890, 1 Jan. 1888, 27 July 1888, 23 Sept. 1888, 29 Feb. 1890, Harriet Burton Laidlaw Papers (A 63), Schlesinger Library. See also correspondence between 15-year-olds Eleanor Hooper and Annie Winsor: "Perhaps but few girls have experienced this longing so soon as we, for as a rule, womanhood comes before such feelings can grow while we are but girls in our first teens. . . . There are few girls with such mature, intense natures as we have. In truth, as far as I can find out, we have the thoughts and feelings of women with the few years and inexperience of little more than children." Hooper to Winsor, 7 Sept. 1880, Annie Ware Winsor Allen Papers (MC 322), Schlesinger Library.

52. Charlotte Perkins Gilman, *The Yellow Wallpaper* (Boston, 1899).

53. Diary of Harriet Burton, 29 Feb. 1890, 10 Mar. 1890, n.d. 1890.

54. Diary of Annie Winsor, 1884; Ann Winsor to Jeannie Winsor, Dec. 1889; Ann Winsor to Annie Winsor, 28 Sept. 1885, Schlesinger Library.

55. Annie Winsor to Ann Winsor, 7 Aug. 1886.

56. Mary Winsor to Annie Winsor, 7 Aug. 1879, 29 June 1883; Annie Winsor to Elizabeth Winsor, 12 Sept. 1885; Annie Winsor to Ann Winsor, 7 Aug. 1886.

57. Journal of Annie Winsor, 1881, 20 Jul. 1882, 7 Oct. 1882, 25 Feb. 1882.

58. Journal of Annie Winsor, 13 Dec. 1883, 15 Apr. 1883, 30 June 1882, 10 June 1883, 7 Oct. 1882, 3 June 1883.

59. Journal of Annie Winsor, 2 Aug. 1883, 19 July 1882, 24 Mar. 1885, 1 Aug. 1882.

60. In a letter to Mrs. Eickhoff, dated 29 Oct. 1907, she explained that "the virginal delicacy of a girl's very nature, the instinctive shrinking that is part of our own rightful inheritance" makes it inappropriate to "speak graphically and explicitly to any girl." But she did feel that a girl should know "from the time she enters her teens, that children, like flowers and all young things, spring from the union of a life-giving essence with a seed of the race," Winsor papers, Schlesinger Library.

61. Journal of Annie Winsor, May 1885, [n.d. 1885?]

62. Wells, "She Couldn't," 462–67.

63. Carroll Smith-Rosenberg has emphasized the significance of mother-daughter bonds to nineteenth-century female identity. "The Female World of Love and Ritual," and "Hearing Women's Words," in *Disorderly Conduct*. Mary Ryan describes daughters and mothers "lolling [together] in placid domesticity." "As in Chodorow's typology," she writes, "the Victorian daughter enjoyed a privileged position in a feminine universe where with relatively little trauma and at an easy pace, she learned her adult gender role from her mother, the source of her first and most enduring emotional connection." *Cradle of the Middle Class: The Family in Oneida County, New York, 1790–1865* (Cambridge, 1981), 193–94. As Carol Dyhouse has observed, even Virginia Woolf, who wrote so famously about killing "the angel in the house" remained at heart divided. Her strong words represented "the rational, intellectual part of herself," while her portrait of Mrs. Ramsay in *To the Lighthouse* "the apotheosis of that Angel," represented the emotional bond, and was a tribute to the memory of her mother. *Girls Growing Up in Late Victorian and Edwardian England* (London, 1981), 38. Woolf's strong words were perhaps the part that less forthright predecessors might have secreted in diaries. Thus Woolf reversed the Victorian pattern, with her public words of rational discourse bolder than the private emotions which emerged in the loving portrait of Mrs. Ramsay.

64. Judith P. Salzman argues the significance of attachment to adolescent development. Referring to the inadequacy of Freudian theory in this area, she suggests that "orthodox assumptions regarding adolescent development have not fully recognized the continuing importance of family attachments." "Save the World, Save Myself: Responses to Problematic Attachment," in Carol Gilligan et al., eds., *Making Connections: The Relational Worlds of Adolescent Girls at Emma Willard School* (Cambridge, Mass., 1990), 111.

65. Harriet Burton Laidlaw was active in the New York Woman Suffrage Party, and after 1917 was one of the directors of the National American Woman Suffrage Association. Her husband, James Laidlaw, whom she married in 1905 at the age of 32, served prominently in the National Men's League for Woman Suffrage, "Laidlaw, Harriet Burton," *Notable American Women*.

66. New work suggests the importance of nineteenth-century women's culture to modem ideas of the self. Lystra, *Searching the Heart*, documents the role of romantic love in creating the modern idea of a unique "personality." Gilian Brown, *Domestic Individualism: Imagining Self in Nineteenth-Century America* (Berkeley, 1990), argues the role of domestic ideology "in updating and reshaping individualism within nineteenth-century American market society." My view contributes to this literature, but stresses the conflict between romanticism and moralism in setting the terms for female identity and for a domestic woman's sphere.

67. Barbara Sicherman, "Sense and Sensibility: A Case Study of Women's Reading in Late-Victorian America" in Cathy Davidson, ed., *Reading in America: Literature and Social History* (Baltimore, 1989), 202.

CHAPTER 12

Reading *Little Women*

The Many Lives of a Text

Barbara Sicherman

"I have read and reread *Little Women* and *it* never seems to grow old," fifteen-year-old Jane Addams confided to a friend.[1] Writing in 1876, Addams did not say why she liked *Little Women*. But her partiality was by no means unusual among women, and even some men, of her generation. Louisa May Alcott's tale of growing up female was an unexpected success when it appeared in the fall of 1868. Already a classic when Addams wrote, the book has been called "the most popular girls' story in American literature"; a century and a quarter after publication, there are twenty editions in print.[2]

The early history of this publishing phenomenon is full or ironies. Not the least of them is the author's expressed distaste for the project. When Thomas Niles Jr., literary editor of the respected Boston firm of Roberts Brothers, asked Alcott to write a *"girls' story,"* the author tartly observed in her journal: "I plod away, though I don't enjoy this sort of thing. Never liked girls or knew many, except my sisters, but our queer plays and experiences may prove interesting, though I doubt it."[3] After delivering twelve chapters in June 1868, she claimed that both she and her editor found them "*dull*."[4] Niles assured her that he was "pleased—I ought to be more emphatic & say delighted,—so *please* to consider 'judgement' as favorable"; the following month he predicted that the book would "'hit.'"[5] Influenced perhaps by the verdict of "some girls" who had pronounced the manuscript "'splendid!'" Alcott reconsidered while correcting proof: "It reads better than I expected. Not a bit sensational, but simple and true, for we really lived most of it." Of the youngsters who liked it, she observed: "As it is for them, they are the best critics, so I should be satisfied."[6]

The informal "readers' report" was right on target. Published in early October 1868, the first printing (2,000 copies) of *Little Women, or, Meg, Jo, Beth and Amy* sold out within the month. A sequel appeared the following April, with only the designation *Part Second* differentiating it from the original. By the end of the year some 38,000 copies (of both parts) were in print, with another 32,000 in 1870. Nearly 200,000 copies had been printed by Roberts Brothers by January 1888, two months before Alcott's death.[7] Like it or not, with this book Alcott established her niche in the expanding market for juvenile literature.

Perhaps even more remarkable than *Little Women*'s initial success has been its longevity. It topped a list of forty books compiled by the Federal Bureau of Education in 1925 that "all children should read before they are sixteen."[8] Two years later—in response to the question "What book has influenced you most?"—high school students ranked it first, ahead of the Bible and *Pilgrim's Progress*.[9] On a bicentennial list of the best eleven American children's books, *Little Women*, *The Adventures of Tom Sawyer*, and *The Adventures of Huckleberry Finn* were the only nineteenth-century titles. Like most iconic works, *Little Women* has been transmuted into other media, into song and opera, theater, radio, and film. A comic strip even surfaced briefly in 1988 in the revamped *Ms.*[10]

Polls and statistics do not begin to do justice to the *Little Women* phenomenon. Reading the book has been a rite of passage for generations of adolescent and preadolescent females of the comfortable classes. It still elicits powerful narratives of love and passion.[11] In a 1982 essay on how she became a writer, Cynthia Ozick declared: "I read 'Little Women' a thousand times. Ten thousand. I am no longer incognito, not even to myself. I am Jo in her 'vortex'; not Jo exactly, but some Jo-of-the-future. I am under an enchantment: Who I truly am must be deferred, waited for and waited for."[12] Ozick's avowal encapsulates recurrent themes in readers' accounts: the deep, almost inexplicable emotions engendered by the novel; the passionate identification with Jo March, the feisty tomboy heroine who publishes stories in her teens; and—allowing for exaggeration—a pattern of multiple readings. Numerous women who grew up in the 1940s and 1950s report that they read the book yearly or more during their teens or earlier; some confide that they continue to read it as adults, though less frequently. Presumably for them, as for Jane Addams, the story did not grow old.

One of many intriguing questions about *Little Women* is how and why the "dull" book, the girls' story by a woman who claimed she never liked girls, captivated so many readers. An added irony is that Alcott, the product of an unconventional upbringing, whose eccentric transcendentalist father self-consciously tested his child-rearing theories on his daughters, took them to live in a commune, and failed utterly as a breadwinner, should write what many contemporaries considered the definitive story of American family life.[13]

My concern here, however, is with *Little Women* as a cultural phenomenon and what it can tell us about the relationship between reading and female identity. A cultural profile of the book and its readers casts light on *Little Women*'s emergence as the classic story of American girlhood and why, in the words of a recent critic, it has remained "a kind of miracle of preservation" when most other works of its era have long since disappeared from the juvenile canon.[14] Building on recent work in cultural criticism and history, this study also examines the "cultural work" *Little Women* performed for diverse reading communities.[15] Such an approach challenges traditional assumptions about the universality of texts. It also demonstrates the importance of reading for the construction of female identity.

Little Women was commissioned because the publisher believed a market existed for a "girls' story," a relatively new genre still in the process of being defined. The book's success suggests that this assumption was correct, although there is also evidence that its readership extended beyond the targeted group. Two unusual features affected the book's production and early reception. First, its two-stage publication gave readers unusual influence in constructing the plot, an important element in its long-term appeal. Second, the book was marketed in ways that elicited reader identification with author as well as heroine, an author, moreover, who was not only astonishingly successful but whose connections with Ralph Waldo Emerson (her intellectual mentor) and Nathaniel Hawthorne (her neighbor) were widely known. Enjoying consider-able popularity from the outset, *Little Women* became part of the prescribed reading of an American girlhood, as did Alcott's own life.

Knowing how a book is promoted is not the same as knowing how it is read, however. *Little Women* has been interpreted in many ways, by ordinary readers as well as critics.[16] Initially praised by readers and reviewers as a realistic story of family life, by the time of its successful stage adaptation in 1912–14 it seemed "quaint" to some.[17] In the twentieth century, Jo, always the most admired sister, was for many the only one who mattered.

With its origin as a girls' story—by definition a domestic story—and a plot in which the sisters overcome their personal failings as they move from adolescence to womanhood, *Little Women* has been viewed by some recent critics as exacting discipline from its readers as well as its heroines.[18] This interpretative line recognizes only one way of reading the story—a conservative one. Feminist explications have for the most part focused on Jo, who has been variously read as "the one young woman in 19th-century fiction who maintains her individual independence, who gives up no part of her autonomy as payment for being born a woman—and who gets away with it" and as a character who is betrayed and even murdered by her creator, who allows her to be tamed and married.[19]

Whether they discern negative or positive messages, critics agree on the importance of the story. *Little Women* has been called "*the* American female myth," and Jo "the most influential figure of the independent and creative American woman."[20] To read the book in this way, even as a failed bildungsroman, as do critics who view Jo's marriage as a surrender of autonomy and a capitulation to traditional femininity, assumes an individualistic outlook on the part of readers, a belief that a woman could aspire to and even attain personal success outside the family claim.

The formulation of *Little Women* as "*the* American female myth" is a distinctly middle-class reading, one that assumes both a universality of female experience and a single mode of reading Alcott's text that transcends class, race, ethnicity, and historical era. While adolescents from diverse backgrounds *can* interpret *Little Women* as a search for personal autonomy—and have in fact done so—this is by no means a universal reading. The female quest plot is inflected by class and culture as well as gender. The story has appealed primarily to an audience that is white and middle class. Historical evidence from working-class sources is scarce and is often filtered through middle-class observers. What we have suggests that working-class women did not necessarily have access to "the simple, every-day classics that the school-boy and -girl are supposed to have read," among them *Little Women*, and that many had a penchant for less "realistic" fiction of the sort usually dismissed as "escapist."[21] For some Jewish working-class immigrant women early in the twentieth century, Alcott's story provided a model for becoming American and middle-class rather than for removing themselves from women's domestic lot, as was the case with the native-born writers and intellectuals to whom *Little Women*'s appeal is better known. In this reading, *Little Women* was still a success story—but of a different kind.

Dissimilar though they are, in both interpretations women readers found in *Little Women* a sense of future possibility. Gerda Lerner has demonstrated that access to learning has been central to the creation of feminist consciousness over the centuries.[22] I would add that literature in general and fiction in particular have been critically important in the construction of female identity, although not always a feminist one. The scarcity in life of models for nontraditional womanhood has prompted women more often than men to turn to fiction for self-authorization.[23]

Little Women's long-lived popularity permits examination of the ways in which adolescent girls of diverse class, culture, and historical era have read the text. Where critics have debated the meaning of the novel, in particular whether Jo is a symbol of independent or resigned womanhood, I hope to show that meaning resides in the social location, interpretive conventions, and perceived needs of disparate communities of readers.[24] But the story of *Little Women* is one of continuity as well as difference, particularly in the common interpretive stance of white, middle-class women readers for more than a century. This persistence can perhaps best be understood as a consequence of the snail-like pace of change for women and the dearth of models for such a quest—in fiction and in life. In this context, Jo March was unique.[25]

Early Publishing and Marketing History

Alcott claimed that she kept on with *Little Women* because "lively, simple books are very much needed for girls, and perhaps I can supply the need."[26] She subsequently redirected her energies as a writer away from adult fiction—some of it considered sensational and published anonymously or pseudonymously—to become not only a successful author of "juveniles," but one of the most popular writers of the era. Alcott may have regretted being channeled into one type of literature, but she was extremely well paid for her efforts, a source of considerable pride to a woman whose father was so feckless about money.[27]

Juvenile literature was entering a new phase in the 1860s at the very time Alcott was refashioning her career. This literature was more secular and on the whole less pietistic than its antebellum precursors, the characterizations more apt; children, even "bad boys," might be basically good, whatever mischievous stages they went through.[28] An expanding middle class, eager to provide its young with cultural as well as moral training, underwrote the new juvenile market that included genteel literary magazines paralleling those read by adults. So seriously was this literature taken that even journals that embraced "high culture" devoted as much space to reviewing children's as adult fiction; thus the seeming anomaly of a review of Alcott's *Eight Cousins* in the *Nation* by the young Henry James.[29]

In contrast to the overtly religious antebellum stories, in which both sexes were expected to be good and domesticated, the new juvenile market was becoming increasingly segmented by gender. An exciting new adventure literature for boys developed after 1850, featuring escape from domesticity and female authority. Seeking to tap into a new market, Niles asked Alcott to write a "girls' story" after he observed the hefty sales of boys' adventure stories by "Oliver Optic," pseudonym of William Taylor Adams.[30] Since prevailing gender ideology defined tales for girls as domestic, it is understandable why Alcott, who idolized her Concord mentor Emerson, adored Goethe, and loved to run with boys, would be disinclined to write one. The designation "girls' story" connoted classification by age as well as gender. Although people of all ages and both sexes read *Little Women*, the book evolved for the emerging female youth market, the "young adults" in the transitional period between childhood and adulthood that would soon be labeled adolescence.[31]

These readers had an unusual say in determining Jo's fate. Eager to capitalize on his experiment, Niles urged Alcott to add a chapter "in which allusions might be made to something in the future."[32] Employing a metaphor well suited to a writer who engaged in theatrical performances most of her life, the volume concludes: "So grouped the curtain falls upon Meg, Jo, Beth and Amy. Whether it ever rises again, depends upon the reception given to the first act of the domestic drama, called 'LITTLE WOMEN.'"[33] Reader response to Alcott's floater was positive but complicated her task. Reluctant to depart from autobiography, Alcott insisted that by rights Jo should remain a "literary spinster." But she felt pressured by readers to imagine a different fate for her heroine. The day she began work on the sequel, she observed: "Girls write to ask who the little women marry, as if that was the only end and aim of a woman's life. I *won't* marry Jo to Laurie to please anyone." To foil her readers, she created a "funny match" for Jo—the middle-aged, bumbling German professor, Friedrich Bhaer.[34]

The aspect of the book that has frustrated generations of readers—the foreclosing of marriage between Jo and Laurie—thus represents a compromise between Alcott and her initial audience. Paradoxically, this seeming misstep has probably been a major factor in the story's enduring success. If Jo had remained a spinster, as Alcott wished, or if she had married the attractive and wealthy hero, as readers hoped, it is unlikely that the book would have had such a wide appeal. Rather, the problematic ending contributed to *Little Women*'s popularity, the lack of satisfying closure helping to keep the story alive, something to ponder, return to, reread, perhaps with the hope of a different resolution. Alcott's refusal of the conventionally happy ending represented by a pairing of Jo and Laurie and her insistence on a "funny match" to the rumpled and much older professor effectively subvert adolescent romantic ideals. The absence of a compelling love plot has also made it easier for generations of readers to ignore the novel's ending when Jo becomes Mother Bhaer and to retain the image of Jo as the questing teenage tomboy.[35]

At the same time, an adolescent reader, struggling with her appearance and unruly impulses while contemplating the burdens of future womanhood, might find it reassuring that her fictional counterpart emerges happily, if not perhaps ideally, from similar circumstances. For Jo is loved. And she has choices. She turns down the charming but erratic hero, who consoles himself by marrying her pretty and vain younger sister, Amy. Professor Bhaer is no schoolgirl's hero, but Jo believes that he is better suited to her than Laurie. The crucial point is that the choice is hers, its quirkiness another sign of her much-prized individuality.[36] Jo gives up writing sensation stories because her prospective husband considers them unworthy, but she makes it clear that she intends to contribute to the support of their future family.

By marrying off the sisters in the second part, Alcott bowed to young women's interest in romance. The addition of the marriage to the quest plot enabled *Little Women* to touch the essential bases for middle-class female readers in the late nineteenth century. In this regard, it was unusual for its time. In adult fiction, marriage and quest plots were rarely combined; success in the former precluded attainment of the latter.[37] The inclusion of a marriage plot in a book for a nonadult audience was also unusual. Even though critics noted the need for literature for the in-between stage, variously designated as eight to eighteen and fourteen to twenty, *Harper's New Monthly Magazine* judged the sequel "a rather mature book for the little women, but a capital one for their elders."[38] The conjunction of quest and marriage plots helps to account for the book's staying power: it is difficult to imagine large numbers of adolescent female readers in the twentieth century gravitating to a book in which the heroine remained single.[39]

Little Women took off with the publication of the second part in April 1869. A Concord neighbor called it "the rage in '69 as 'Pinafore' was in '68."[40] A savvy judge of the market, Niles urged Alcott to "'Make hay while the Sunshines'" and did everything he could to keep her name before the public.[41] Shortly after the appearance of *Little Women, Part Second*, Roberts Brothers brought out an augmented edition of her first critical success under the title, *Hospital Sketches and Camp and Fireside Stories* and in succeeding years published *An Old-Fashioned Girl* (1870) and *Little Men* (1871), a sequel to *Little Women*. Niles encouraged publicity about books and author, whom he kept informed about her extensive press coverage while she traveled abroad. Alcott was then at the peak of her popularity; between October 1868 and July 1871. Roberts Brothers sold some 166,000 volumes of her juvenile fiction.[42]

The well-publicized autobiographical status of *Little Women*, together with Alcott's realistic subject matter and direct style, encouraged identification by middle-class readers.[43] Reviewers stressed the realism of her characters and scenes; readers recognized themselves in her work. Thirteen-year-old Annie

Adams of Fair Haven, Vermont, wrote *St. Nicholas*, the most prestigious of the new children's magazines, that she and her three sisters each resembled one of the March sisters (she was Jo): "So, you see, I was greatly interested in 'Little Women,' as I could appreciate it so well; and it seemed to me as if Miss Alcott must have seen us four girls before she wrote the story."[44] Girls not only read themselves into *Little Women*, they elaborated on it and incorporated the story into their lives. In 1872 the five Lukens sisters from Brinton, Pennsylvania, sent Alcott a copy of their home newspaper, "Little Things," which was modeled after "The Pickwick Portfolio" produced by the March sisters. Alcott responded with encouragement, asked for further details, and subscribed to the paper; subsequently she offered advice about reading, writing, and religion and even sent a story for publication. She took their aspirations seriously, providing frank, practical advice about magazines, publishers, and authors' fees to these budding literary women.[45]

There was, then, a reciprocal relationship between the characters and home life depicted in *Little Women* and the lives of middle-class American girls. An unusual feature of this identification was the perception that author and heroine were interchangeable. Alcott's work was marketed to encourage the illusion not only that Jo was Alcott but that Alcott was Jo. When Alcott traveled in Europe in 1870, Niles encouraged her to send for publication "'Jo's Letters from Abroad to the March's [*sic*] at Home'"; the following year he asked her to select "from the million or less letters" some that could be published in a volume entitled "Little Women and Little Men Letters or Letters to 'Jo' by 'Little Women' and 'Little Men.'"[46] Neither book materialized, but *Shawl-Straps*, a humorous account of Alcott's European trip, appeared in 1872 as the second volume in the *Aunt Jo's Scrap-Bag* series. Niles sometimes addressed his leading author as "Jo," "Jo March," or "Aunt Jo." Alcott often substituted the names of the March sisters for her own when she answered fans; on occasion, she inserted them into her journal. The equation of author and character continued after Alcott's death. When her sister Anna Pratt supervised publication of *Comic Tragedies* (1893), a volume of childhood plays, she wrote the foreword as "Meg," and the title page read "Written By 'Jo' and 'Meg' and Acted by the 'Little Women.'"

Readers responded in kind. An ad for *Little Women* quotes a letter written by "Nelly" addressed to "Dear Jo, or Miss Alcott": "We have all been reading 'Little Women,' and we liked it so much I could not help wanting to write to you. We think *you* are perfectly splendid; I like you better every time I read it. We were all so disappointed about your not marrying Laurie; I cried over that part,—I could not help it. We all liked Laurie ever so much, and almost killed ourselves laughing over the funny things you and he said." Blurring the lines between author and character, the writer also requested a picture, wished the recipient improved health, and invited her to visit.[47]

The illusion that she was the youthful and unconventional Jo made Alcott a more approachable author. But the conflation of author and character had its risks. Young readers who formed an image of the author as Jo, a teenager for most of the novel, were startled by Alcott's appearance. When the Lukens sisters informed her that some "friends" had been disappointed in her picture, Alcott replied that she could not understand why people insisted Jo was young "when she is said to be 30 at the end of the book . . . After seeing the photograph it is hardly necessary to say that Jo and L.M.A. are *not* one, & that the latter is a tired out old lady of 42."[48]

With the publication of *Little Women, Part Second*, Alcott became a celebrity. Correspondents demanded her photograph and autograph seekers descended on her home while she "dodge[d] into the woods *à la* Hawthorne."[49] Customarily shunning the limelight, she was mobbed by fans on her rare public appearances. After a meeting of the Woman's Congress in 1875, she reported, "the stage filled . . . with beaming girls all armed with Albums and cards and begging to speak to Miss A. . . . 'Do put up your veil so we can see how you really look' said one. 'Will you kiss me please,' said another. . . . I finally had to run for my life with more girls all along the way, and Ma's clawing me as I went." Things were somewhat more decorous at Vassar, but even college students insisted on kissing Alcott and obtaining her autograph.[50] She avenged herself with a devastating portrait of celebrity hounds in *Jo's Boys* (1886), the sequel to *Little Men*.[51]

Alcott also drew more serious admirers, some of whom, like the Lukens sisters, sought her literary advice. In the 1860s and 1870s authorship was the most respected female vocation—and the best paid. Before the consolidation of the American literary canon later in the century, women writers had an acknowledged, though not unchallenged, place in the world of letters. Feminist critics and historians have recently been documenting women's presence, but Alcott has been largely left out of this reassessment, in large part because of her status as a writer of "juvenile fiction."[52]

Alcott was a well-respected writer during her lifetime, an era of relatively inclusive and nonhierarchical definitions of literature. An American literature course taken by Jane Addams at Rockford Female Seminary in 1878–79 covered authors of domestic fiction, Alcott among them.[53] But her literary reputation transcended the category. A review of *Little Men* pronounced: "Even thus early in her brief history as a country and a nation, America can boast a long list of classics—Prescott, Irving, Hawthorne, Longfellow—and Time, the great sculptor will one day carve Miss Alcott's name among them."[54] Alcott received nearly a page to Hawthorne's page and a half in James S. Hart's *A Manual of American Literature: A Text-Book for Schools and Colleges* (1873); both were listed under the category "Novels and Tales." She was compared with her former neighbor on more than one occasion; a younger Concord resident proclaimed: "In American fiction 'Little Women' holds the next place to the 'Scarlet Letter' and 'Marble Faun.'" Since Hawthorne stood at the pinnacle of American literature, this was high praise.[55]

A teenage girl contemplating a literary career could dream of becoming a published author who, like Alcott, might produce a beloved and immortal work. At a time when young women were encouraged, even expected, to take part in the literary activities that suffused middle-class domestic life, such success was not beyond imagining. From Hart's manual a reader could learn that Alcott began writing for publication at sixteen and, by hard work and perseverance, became both famous and self-supporting by her pen in her late thirties.[56] The real female American success story was Alcott's, not Jo's.

There were, then, many reasons why a young woman seeking a literary career in the 1870s and early 1880s would look to Alcott as a model. Most important was the story that brought pleasure to so many. Despite claims that *Little Women* is a text about disciplining girls into proper womanhood, a comparison with other "girls' books" marks it as a text that opened up new avenues of experience for readers.[57] The contrast with Martha Finley's *Elsie Dinsmore* (1867), a story in which strict obedience is exacted from children—to the point of whipping—is striking. In this first of many volumes, the lachrymose and devoutly religious heroine is put upon by relatives and by her father, who punishes her for refusing to play the piano on the Sabbath. Elsie holds fast to her principles but is otherwise self-abnegating in the extreme: it is difficult to imagine her even trying to have fun.[58] *Faith Gartney's Girlhood* (1863) by Mrs. A. D. T. Whitney, a forgotten but once highly acclaimed writer with whom Alcott was often compared, was the story of a girl's emergence into serious and self-affirming womanhood. Written for a female audience between fourteen and twenty to show "what is noblest and truest," the book is more complex than *Elsie Dinsmore*, the tone less charged. But Whitney relies heavily on didactic narrative and fails to exploit the emotional potential of her plot: the authorial voice is moralistic and the religion conspicuous.[59]

The fictional world of *Little Women* is strikingly different. Despite the use of John Bunyan's *Pilgrim's Progress* as a framing device, an older Calvinist worldview that emphasized sin and obedience to the deity has been replaced by a moral outlook in which self-discipline and doing good to others come first.[60] Consonant with *Little Women*'s new moral tone, so congenial to an expanding middle class, are its informal style and rollicking escapades. Aided by her love of the theater and influenced as well by her youthful idol, Charles Dickens, Alcott was a wonderful painter of dramatic scenes; some were heartbreaking, but many were high-spirited depictions of frolics, games, and theatrical productions.[61] She also had an ear for young people's language: her substitution of dialogue for the long passages of moralizing narrative that characterized most girls' books gave her story a compelling sense of immediacy. So did her use of slang, for which critics often faulted her, but which must have endeared her to young readers. Finally, the beautifully realized portrait of Jo March as tomboy, one of the first of its kind, spoke to changing standards of girlhood. Beginning in the 1860s, tomboys were not only tolerated but even admired— up to a point, the point at which they were expected to become women.[62] Perhaps it was fitting after all that it was Alcott, writing of her idiosyncratic childhood in the 1840s, who identified a new type of American girlhood for the 1870s.[63]

Why Alcott? Why *Little Women*? The questions were asked during the author's lifetime and after. *Little Women* was strategically placed within the new market for secular juvenile books as well as the more specialized category of "girls' books." A fortuitous combination of author, heroine, subject, and style, along with shrewd marketing, helped propel the book to popularity and its author to celebrity. Alcott, neighbor and friend of writers who were increasingly enshrined in the nation's literary pantheon, partook of their glory. But she had a luster of her own. Although often considered a "New England writer," she was also praised as a quintessentially "American" writer, a sign both of New England's dominance in the American literary tradition and of Alcott's prominent place within it.[64]

Jo as a Literary and Intellectual Model

Reading Alcott became a necessary ritual for children of the comfortable classes. Growing up at a time and in a class that conferred leisure on its young, children devoted considerable time and energy to literary pursuits. *Little Women* was a way station en route to more adult books. But it was also a text that acquired its own cachet. Alcott was such an accepted part of childhood that even Theodore Roosevelt declared, "at the cost of being deemed effeminate," that he "worshiped" *Little Men, Little Women*, and *An Old-Fashioned Girl*.[65]

Readers' explanations of their fondness for Alcott constitute a trope for personal preferences. Not all of Alcott's early readers focused on Jo; some were taken with the saga of the entire March family, which invited comparisons with their own. Charlotte Perkins Gilman, for example, who grew up in genteel poverty after her father abandoned the family, liked the fact that in Alcott, as in Whitney, "the heroes and heroines were almost always poor, and good, while the rich people were generally bad."[66] S. Josephine Baker, for her part, considered Alcott "the unattainable ideal of a great woman." A tomboy who became a prominent physician and wore ties to downplay her gender,

"Jo" Baker not only claimed Jo March as her "favorite character in all fiction" but pointedly dissociated herself from Elsie Dinsmore.[67]

Jo March also fueled the literary aspirations of M. Carey Thomas, one of Alcott's early readers, during the critical years of early adolescence. In the fall of 1869, the year of *Little Women*'s great success, Thomas and her cousin Frank Smith adopted the personae of Jo and Laurie, although as Quakers they should not have been reading fiction at all. At the ages of twelve and fifteen, respectively, Thomas and Smith began addressing each other and signing their letters as Jo and Laurie; they meted out other roles to friends and relatives. When Bessie King, Thomas's closest female companion, made a bid to be Jo, Frank wrote his cousin that Bessie must choose another part "if she won't be Jo 2., or Meg, or Beth, or Amy; or Daisy, or anybody besides Jo 1. since *thou will* be the latter." Since Jo was the only acceptable heroine of *Little Women*, Bessie chose Polly, heroine of *An Old-Fashioned Girl*, Alcott's latest.[68]

When Thomas began a journal in 1870 at age thirteen, she did so in Jo's name. Declaring at the outset: "Ain't going to be sentimental / 'No no not for Jo' (not Joe)," she had much in common with Alcott's heroine.[69] Both were "bookworms" and tomboys; both desired independence. Like Jo, Thomas wished to do something "splendid." In early adolescence her ambitions were still diffuse, but they centered on becoming a famous writer, a famous *woman* writer—"Jo (not Joe)." Her life was suffused with literature, with writing as well as reading: in addition to keeping a journal, she wrote poetry, kept a commonplace book, and compiled lists of favorite books and poems, some of them annotated. As she gravitated to such champions of aestheticism as Algernon Charles Swinburne and Dante Gabriel Rossetti, by her early twenties she had outgrown Alcott and other writers who upheld morality in their art. But Bessie King acknowledged the importance of their childhood play in 1879, when Thomas took the audacious step of starting graduate study in Germany: "Somehow today I went back to those early days when our horizon was so limited yet so full of light & our path lay as plain before us. It all came of reading over Miss Alcott's books now the quintessence [*sic*] of Philistinism then a Bible. . . . Doesn't thee remember when to turn out a 'Jo' was the height of ambition?"[70]

At the time Thomas was so engaged with *Little Women*, she was already a feminist. Sensitive to any gender restriction or slight, whether from people she knew or from biblical or scientific sources, she resolved at fifteen to disprove female inferiority by advancing her own education.[71] Despite its inception as a domestic story, then, Thomas read *Little Women* as a female bildungsroman, as did many women after her. This has in many ways been the most important reading, the one that has made the book such a phenomenon for so many years.

With its secular recasting of *Pilgrim's Progress*, *Little Women* transforms Christian's allegorical search for the Celestial City into the quintessential female quest plot. In a chapter entitled "Castles in the Air," each of the March sisters reveals her deepest ambition. In its loving depictions of the sisters' struggles to attain their goals (Jo to be a famous writer, Amy an artist, and Meg mistress of a lovely house), *Little Women* succeeds in authorizing female vocation and individuality. Nor did Alcott rule out the possibility of future artistic creativity: although married and managing a large household and school, Jo has not entirely given up her literary dreams, nor Amy her artistic ones. Beth, who has no ambition other than "to stay at home safe with father and mother, and help take care of the family," dies because she can find no way of growing up; her mysterious illness may be read as a failure of imagination, her inability to build castles in the air.[72]

In Jo, Alcott creates a portrait of female creativity that was not traditionally available to women:

> Every few weeks she would shut herself up in her room, put on her scribbling suit, and "fall into a vortex," as she expressed it, writing away at her novel with all her heart and soul, for till that was finished she could find no peace. . . .
>
> She did not think herself a genius by any means; but when the writing fit came on, she gave herself up to it with entire abandon, and led a blissful life, unconscious of want, care, or bad weather, while she sat safe and happy in an imaginary world, full of friends almost as real and dear to her as any in the flesh. Sleep forsook her eyes, meals stood untasted, day and night were all too short to enjoy the happiness which blessed her only at such times, and made these hours worth living, even if they bore no other fruit. The divine afflatus usually lasted a week or two, and then she emerged from her "vortex" hungry, sleepy, cross, or despondent.[73]

Alcott's portrait of concentrated purpose—which describes her own creative practice—is as far removed as it could be from the ordinary lot of women, at least any adult woman. Jo not only has a room of her own; she also has the leisure—and the license—to remove herself from all obligation to others. Jo was important to young women like Thomas because there were so few of her—in literature or in life. One need only recall the example of Margaret Fuller, a generation older than Alcott, who suffered nightmares and delirium from her hothouse education and often felt isolated as the exceptional woman. By contrast, Jo is enmeshed in a family that constitutes a sustaining community of women.[74]

More conventional readers of Thomas's era could find in *Little Women* practical advice on two subjects of growing concern to women: economic opportunities and marriage. Alcott was well qualified to advise on the former because of her long years of struggle in the marketplace. Though portrayed more starkly in *Work* (1873), an autobiographical novel for the adult market, middle-class women's need to be able to earn a living is a central motif in *Little Women*, as it was in Alcott's life. The novel can be read as a defining text on this subject, at a time when even conservative critics were beginning to concede the point. Mr. March's economic setback, like Bronson Alcott's, forces his daughters into the labor market. Their jobs (as governess and companion) are depicted as mainly unrewarding, although Jo's literary career is described with loving particularity. As we have seen, to please her readers, Alcott compromised her belief that "liberty [was] a better husband." But although the March sisters marry, Marmee March, who wishes no greater joy for her daughters than a happy marriage, declares that it is better to remain single than to marry without love. Opportunities for self-respecting singlehood and women's employment went hand in hand, as Alcott knew.[75]

If Alcott articulated issues highly pertinent to young women of her era, Jo's continued appeal suggests not only the dearth of fictional heroines to foster dreams of glory but the continued absence of real-life models. Perhaps that is why Simone de Beauvoir was so attracted to *Little Women*, in which she thought she "caught a glimpse of my future self":

> I identified passionately with Jo, the intellectual. . . . She wrote: in order to imitate her more completely, I composed two or three short stories. . . . [T]he relationship between Jo and Laurie touched me to the heart. Later, I had no doubt, they would marry one another; so it was possible for maturity to bring the promises made in childhood to fruition instead of denying them: this thought filled me with renewed hope. But the thing that delighted me most of all was the marked partiality which Louisa Alcott manifested for Jo. . . . [I]n *Little Women* Jo was superior to her sisters, who were either more virtuous or more beautiful than she, because of her passion for knowledge and the vigor of her thinking; her superiority was as outstanding as that of certain adults, and guaranteed that she would have an unusual life: she was marked by fate. I, too, felt I was entitled to consider my taste in reading and my scholastic success as tokens of a personal superiority which would be borne out by the future. I became in my own eyes a character out of a novel.[76]

De Beauvoir found in Jo a model of authentic selfhood, someone she could emulate in the present and through whom she could read—and invent—her own destiny. It was a future full of possibility, open rather than closed, intellectual and literary rather than domestic. By fictionalizing her own life, de Beauvoir could more readily contemplate a career as a writer and an intellectual, no matter how improbable such an outcome seemed to her family. She could also rationalize her sense of superiority to her environment and to her own sister. Although de Beauvoir later claimed that she first learned from *Little Women* that "marriage was not necessary," she responded to the romance as well as the quest plot.[77] Far from interfering with her enjoyment, her disappointment that Jo did not marry Laurie prompted her to rework the story to her own satisfaction. Her conviction that Jo and Laurie would marry some day and the "renewed hope" this belief gave her suggest the power of wish fulfillment and the reader's capacity to create her own text. There is no textual basis for this belief: Jo and Laurie each marry someone else; each is a parent by the end of the story. De Beauvoir's reading is therefore not just a matter of filling in gaps but of rewriting the text. Her powerful commentary suggests the creativity of the reading experience and the permeability of boundaries between life and art: lives can be fictionalized, texts can be rewritten, art can become life and life art.

Not all women read with the intensity of Thomas or de Beauvoir. But there is considerable evidence that, from the time of her creation until the recent past, Jo March provided for young women of the comfortable classes a model of female independence and of intellectual and literary achievement. This is not the only way of reading *Little Women*, but it constitutes a major interpretive strand, particularly in the twentieth century. Testimony on this point began as soon as the book was published and persists today among women who grew up in the 1940s and 1950s.[78] Thomas, whose love relations were with women, never mentions the marriage plot, but for de Beauvoir, writing in the twentieth century, it was both important and compatible with a quest plot.

Inflections of Class and Culture

Not everyone has access to the same cultural resources, wishes to engage the same texts, or interprets them in identical ways. Although class is by no means the sole determinant of what or how much is read, it is a critical variable in determining basic literacy and educational levels. These in turn, in conjunction with the aspirations of group, family, or individual, influence reading practices and preferences.[79]

For African American women, in the nineteenth century at least, class rather than race was probably the primary determinant of reading practices. Both Mary Church Terrell, a graduate of Oberlin College, and Ida B. Wells, the slave-born daughter of a carpenter and "a famous cook" who became a journalist and reformer, read Alcott. Terrell claimed that her books "were received with an acclaim among the young people of this country which has rarely if ever been equaled and never surpassed," while Wells observed: "I had formed my ideals on the best of Dickens's stories, Louisa May Alcott's, Mrs.

A.D.T. Whitney's, and Charlotte Brontë's books, and Oliver Optic's stories for boys." Neither singled out *Little Women*; both seem to have read Alcott as part of the standard fare of an American middle-class childhood.[80]

For African American writer Ann Petry, now in her eighties, *Little Women* was much more than that. On the occasion of her induction into the Connecticut Women's Hall of Fame, she noted her admiration for women writers who had preceded and set the stage for her—"'Think of Louisa May Alcott.'" *Little Women* was the first book Petry "read on her own as a child." Her comments are reminiscent of those of de Beauvoir and other writers: "I couldn't stop reading because I had encountered Jo March. I felt as though I was part of Jo and she was part of me. I, too, was a tomboy and a misfit and kept a secret diary. . . . She said things like 'I wish I was a horse, then I could run for miles in this splendid air and not lose my breath.' I found myself wishing the same thing whenever I ran for the sheer joy of running. She was a would-be writer and so was I."[81]

Two contrasting responses to *Little Women* from up and down the class ladder suggest the essentially middle-class and perhaps also middlebrow nature of the book's appeal. Edith Wharton, who drops the names of famous books and authors in an autobiography dominated by upper-class and high-culture values, noted that her mother would not let her read popular American children's books because "the children spoke bad English *without the author's knowing it.*" She claimed that when she was finally permitted to read *Little Women* and *Little Men* because everyone else did, "[M]y ears, trained to the fresh racy English of 'Alice in Wonderland,' 'The Water Babies' and 'The Princess and the Goblin,' were exasperated by the laxities of the great Louisa."[82]

Like Wharton, though for different reasons, some working-class women also found *Little Women* too banal. Dorothy Richardson, a journalist, suggests as much in *The Long Day*, an account of her life among the working class. In an arresting episode, Richardson ridicules the reading preferences of her fellow workers in a paper box factory. The plot of a favorite novel, Laura Jean Libbey's *Little Rosebud's Lovers; or, A Cruel Revenge*, is recounted by one of the workers as a tale of a woman's triumph over all sorts of adversity, including abductions and a false marriage to one of the villains. When Richardson summarizes *Little Women*, a coworker dismisses it: "'[T]hat's no story—that's just everyday happenings. I don't see what's the use of putting things like that in books. I'll bet any money that lady what wrote it knew all them boys and girls. They just sound like real, live people; and when you was telling about them I could just see them as plain as plain could be. . . . I suppose farmer folks likes them kind of stories. . . . They ain't used to the same styles of anything that us city folks are.'"[83]

The box makers found the characters in *Little Women* "real"—an interesting point in itself—but did not care to enter its narrative framework. Though they were not class conscious in a political sense, their awareness of their class position may account at least in part for their disinterest in a story whose heroines, despite economic reverses, had the leisure to pursue their interests in art, music, and literature and could expect to live in suburban cottages, conditions out of reach for most working-class women. Since *their* "everyday happenings" were poverty and exhausting work, the attraction of fictions about working girls who preserved their virtue and came into great wealth, either through marriage or disclosure of their middle- or upper-class origins, is understandable. Such denouements would have seemed just as likely—or unlikely—as a future in a suburban cottage. In the absence, in story or in life, of a female success tradition of moving up the occupational ladder, the "Cinderella tale" of marrying up was the nearest thing to a Horatio Alger story for working-class women.[84]

Reading practices depend on cultural as well as class location. It is a telling commentary on class in America that some Jewish immigrant women, who would be defined as working class on the basis of family income and occupation, not only enjoyed *Little Women* but also found in it a vehicle for envisioning a new and higher status.[85] For them, Alcott's classic provided a model for transcending their status as ethnic outsiders and for gaining access to American life and culture. It was a first step into the kind of middle-class family life rejected by Thomas and de Beauvoir. These immigrants found the book liberating and read it as a success story—but of a different kind.

In *My Mother and I*, Elizabeth G. Stern (1889–1954) charts the cultural distance a Jewish immigrant woman traveled from Russia and a midwestern urban ghetto to the American mainstream: she graduates from college, studies social work, marries a professional man, and becomes a social worker and writer.[86] *Little Women* occupies a crucial place in the story. After the narrator comes across it in a stack of newspapers in a rag shop, the book utterly engrosses her: "I sat in the dim light of the rag shop and read the browned pages of that ragged copy of 'Little Women.' . . . [N]o book I have opened has meant as much to me as did that small volume telling in simple words such as I myself spoke, the story of an American childhood in New England. I had found a new literature, the literature of childhood." She had also found the literature of America: "I no longer read the little paper-hound Yiddish novelettes which father then sold. In the old rag shop loft I devoured the English magazines and newspapers." Of the books her teachers brought her from the public library, she writes:

> Far more marvellous than the fairy stories were to me in the ghetto street the stories of American child life, all the Alcott and the Pepper books. The pretty mothers, the childish ideals, the open gardens, the homes of many

rooms were as unreal to me as the fairy stories. But reading of them made my aspirations beautiful.

My books were doors that gave me entrance into another world. Often I think that I did not grow up in the ghetto but in the books I read as a child in the ghetto. The life in Soho passed me by and did not touch me, once I began to read.[87]

Stern's testimony to the importance of reading in reconfiguring aspiration is not unlike de Beauvoir's, although the context is entirely different, as is the nature of the desire elicited by her reading. In American books, the ghetto fell away and the protagonist discovered both childhood and beauty. Far from being realistic, *Little Women* was an American fairy tale. Indeed, some of the narrator's "precocious" thirteen-year-old school friends "scoffingly averred that there were 'no such peoples like Jo and Beth.'" As she climbs the educational ladder, she discovers that such people do exist and that a life of beauty is possible, even for those of humble origin. With its emphasis on middle-class domesticity, *My Mother and I* is a story of Americanization with a female twist.[88]

Stern was not unique in reading *Little Women* as a vehicle for assimilation into American middle-class life or in conflating "American" and "middle class." More than half a century later, a Jewish male writer explored the novel's appeal as an "American" book:

[T]o me, a first generation American, raised in an Orthodox Jewish household where more Yiddish was spoken than English, everything about *Little Women* was exotic. It was all so American, so full of a life I did not know but desperately hoped to be part of, an America full of promises, hopes, optimisms, an America where everyone had a chance to become somebody wonderful like Jo March—Louisa May Alcott who (I had discovered that the Marches and the Alcotts were almost identical) did become, with this story book that I adored, world famous. [89]

What had been realistic to the early middle- and upper-middle-class WASP readers of *Little Women* was "exotic" to Jewish immigrants a generation or two later. Could there be a better illustration of the importance of historical location in determining meaning?

Teachers, librarians, and other cultural mediators encouraged Jewish immigrant women to read what many viewed as the archetypal American female story. Book and author became enshrined in popular legend, especially after publication of *Louisa May Alcott: Her Life, Letters, and Journals* (1889), the year after the author's death, by her friend Ednah Dow Cheney. Interest in Alcott remained high in the early twentieth century. There was a 1909 biography by

Belle Moses and a dramatization in 1912 that received rave reviews and toured the country. Alcott's books were sometimes assigned in public schools.[90] Jews themselves often served as cultural intermediaries between native and immigrant communities. When Rose Cohen, an immigrant affiliated with the Nurses' (later Henry Street) Settlement, found *Julius Caesar* too difficult, she asked the librarian at the Educational Alliance, a Jewish agency that assisted recent Eastern European immigrants, for a book "any book—like for a child. She brought me 'Little Women.'"[91]

Cohen was offered *Little Women* as a less taxing vehicle for learning English than Shakespeare. But Alcott was often prescribed as a safe and even salutary writer. Librarians had long debated the effects of reading on those who were young, female, and impressionable. They were echoed by some members of the working class, including Rose Pastor Stokes, an immigrant from Eastern Europe via England. Contending that "*all* girls are what they read," Stokes, writing as "Zelda" for the English page of the *Yiddishes Tageblatt*, admonished her readers to avoid "crazy phantasies from the imbecile brains" of writers like Laura Jean Libbey. She urged those sixteen and under to read Alcott, a writer known for her "excellent teachings" and one from whom "discriminating or indiscriminating" readers alike derived pleasure. Zelda also recommended Cheney, claiming that "the biographies of some writers are far more interesting, even, than the stories they have written."[92]

One of the Jewish immigrants for whom Alcott's success proved inspiring was Mary Antin, a fervent advocate of assimilation into American life. Alcott's were the children's books she "remember[ed] with the greatest delight" (followed by boys' adventure books, especially Alger's). Antin, who published poems in English in her teens and contemplated a literary career, lingered over the biographical entries she found in an encyclopedia. She "could not resist the temptation to study out the exact place . . . where my name would belong. I saw that it would come not far from 'Alcott, Louisa M.'; and I covered my face with my hands, to hide the silly, baseless joy in it."[93] We have come full circle. Eager to assimilate, Antin responded in ways reminiscent of Alcott's early native-born and middle-class readers who admired her success as an author. Antin, too, could imagine a successful American career for herself, a career for which Alcott was still the model.

Conclusion

Not all readers of *Little Women* read the same text. This is literally the case, since the story went through many editions. Not until 1880 did it appear in one volume, illustrated in this case and purged of some of its slang.[94] Since

Barbara Sicherman

then there have been numerous editions and many publishers. I have been concerned here with the changing meaning of the story for different audiences and with historical continuities as well. For many middle-class readers, early and later, *Little Women* provided a model of womanhood that deviated from conventional gender norms, a continuity that suggests how little these norms changed in their essentials from the late 1860s to the 1960s. Reading individualistically, they viewed Jo as an intellectual and a writer, the liberated woman they sought to become. No matter that Jo marries and raises a family; such readers remember the young Jo, the teenager who is far from beautiful, struggles with her temper, is both a bookworm and the center of action, and dreams of literary glory while helping to support her family with her pen. These readers for the most part took for granted their right to a long and privileged childhood, largely exempt from the labor market. Jewish women who immigrated to the United States in their youth could not assume such a childhood. Nor were those raised in Orthodox Jewish households brought up on an individualistic philosophy. Their school experiences and reading—American books like *Little Women*—made them aware of different standards of decorum and material life that we tend to associate with class, but that are cultural as well. For some of these readers, *Little Women* offered a fascinating glimpse into an American world. Of course we know, as they did not, that the world Alcott depicted was vanishing, even as she wrote. Nevertheless, that fictional world, along with their school encounters, provided a vision of what life, American life, could be.

Can readers do whatever they like with texts? Yes and no. As we have seen, *Little Women* has been read in many ways, depending not only on when and by whom it was read but also on readers' experiences and aspirations. It has been read as a romance or as a quest, or both. It has been read as a family drama that validates virtue over wealth. It has been read as a how-to manual by immigrants who wanted to assimilate into American, middle-class life and as a means of escaping that life by women who knew its gender constraints too well. For many, especially in the early years, *Little Women* was read through the life of the author, whose literary success exceeded that of her fictional persona.

At the same time, both the passion *Little Women* has engendered in diverse readers and its ability to survive its era and transcend its genre point to a text of unusual permeability. The compromise Alcott effected with her readers in constructing a more problematic plot than is usual in fiction for the young has enhanced the story's appeal. If *Little Women* is not exactly a "problem novel," it is a work that lingers in readers' minds in ways that allow for imaginative elaboration. The frequent rereadings reported by women in their fifties also hint at nostalgia for lost youth and for a past that seems more secure than the present, perhaps even an imagined re-creation of idealized love between mothers and daughters.[95] Most important, readers' testimony in the nineteenth and twentieth centuries points to *Little Women* as a text that opens up possibilities rather than foreclosing them. With its multiple reference points and voices (four sisters, each distinct and recognizable), its depictions of joy as well as sorrow, its fresh and unlabored speech, Alcott's classic has something for almost everyone. For readers on the threshold of adulthood, the text's authorizing of female ambition has been a significant counterweight to more habitual gender prescriptions.

Little Women is such a harbinger of modern life, of consumer culture and new freedom for middle-class children, it is easy to forget that it was written just a few years after the Civil War, in the midst of Reconstruction and at a time of economic dislocation. For the most part, Alcott left such contemporary markers out of her story, another sign of the text's openness. The Civil War provides an important backdrop and a spur to heroism at home as well as on the battlefield, but it is primarily a plot device to remove Mr. March from the scene. Despite her family's support of John Brown, Alcott does not press a particular interpretation of the war. A final reason *Little Women* has survived so well, despite the chasm that separates Alcott's era from ours, is the virtual absence of references to outside events that would date her story and make it grow old.[96] That way each generation can invent it anew.

Notes

1. Addams to Vallie Beck, March 16, 1876, *The Jane Addams Papers*, edited by Mary Lynn McCree Bryan (Ann Arbor: University Microfilms International, 1984) (hereafter cited as *Addams Papers*), reel 1.
2. Frank Luther Mott, *Golden Multitudes: The Story of Best Sellers in the United States* (New York: Macmillan, 1947), p. 102; *Books in Print, 1992–1993*.
3. May 1868, *The Journals of Louisa May Alcott*, edited by Joel Myerson and Daniel Shealy, associate ed. Madeleine B. Stern (Boston: Little, Brown, 1989), pp. 165–66 (hereafter cited as *Journals*). On rereading this entry in later years, Alcott quipped: "Good joke." Niles first requested a girls' book in 1867; Alcott says she "[b]egan at once . . . but didn't like" it September [1867], *Journals*, p. 158.
4. June [1868] *Journals*, p. 166.
5. Niles to Alcott, June 16, 1868 (#1) and July 25, 1868 (#2), bMS Am 1130.8, Alcott Family Papers, Houghton Library, Harvard University (all citations from Niles's letters are from this collection). On Alcott's publishing history, see Raymond L. Kilgour, *Messrs. Roberts Brothers Publishers* (Ann Arbor: University of Michigan Press, 1952), and Daniel Lester Shealy, "The Author-Publisher Relationships of Louisa May Alcott" (Ph.D. diss., University of South Carolina, 1985). I am grateful to Michael Winship for the last reference.
6. August 26 [1868], *Journals*, p. 166. According to most sources, Niles tested the manuscript on his niece, whose age is variously given.

7. For an account of Alcott's sales through 1909, by which time nearly 598,000 copies of *Little Women* had been printed by Roberts Brothers, see Joel Myerson and Daniel Shealy, "The Sales of Louisa May Alcott's Books," *Harvard Library Bulletin*, n.s., 1 (Spring 1990), esp. pp. 69–71, 86. I am grateful to Michael Winship for this reference. See also Roberts Brothers Cost Book D, [i], *87M-113, Little, Brown and Co. Papers, Houghton Library, Harvard University (hereafter cited as Little, Brown Papers). These figures do not include foreign sales. Although *Little Women* was not published in a single volume until 1880, I will refer to it in the singular except when one volume is specifically intended.

   Sales figures are unreliable for the twentieth century, in part because of foreign sales and the proliferation of editions after the expiration of copyright. Dorothea Lawrence Mann, "When the Alcott Books Were New," *Publishers' Weekly* 116 (September 28, 1929): 1619, claimed sales of nearly three million. According to an account published three years later, Little, Brown and Co., which had absorbed Roberts Brothers, reported that over 1.5 million copies of *Little Women* had been sold in the United States. "Louisa M. Alcott Centenary Year," *Publishers' Weekly* 122 (July 2, 1932): 23–24. Charles A. Madison, *Book Publishing in America* (New York: McGraw-Hill, 1966), p. 134, cites sales of 3 million but gives no sources.

   Sales, of course, are only part of the story: library use was high at the outset and remained so. Niles to Alcott (#18), undated fragment [1870? but probably about August 1869] and "Popularity of 'Little Women,'" December 22, 1912, "Press [illegible] Albany," in bMS Am 800.23 (newspaper clippings, reviews, and articles about Louisa May Alcott and her family), Alcott Family Papers.

8. Mann, "When the Alcott Books Were New."

9. "'Little Women' Leads Poll," *New York Times*, March 22, 1927, p. 7, reprinted in Madeleine B. Stern, ed., *Critical Essays on Louisa May Alcott* (Boston: G. K. Hall, 1984), p. 84.

10. See Gloria T. Delamar, *Louisa May Alcott and 'Little Women': Biography, Critique, Publications, Poems, Songs, and Contemporary Relevance* (Jefferson, N.C.: McFarland and Co., 1990), p. 167 and passim. I am grateful to Joan Jacobs Brumberg for this reference.

11. For an intriguing analysis of well-loved texts that takes *Little Women* as a point of departure, see Catharine R. Stimpson, "Reading for Love: Canons, Paracanons, and Whistling Jo March," *New Literary History* 21 (Autumn 1990): 957–76.

12. "Spells, Wishes, Goldfish, Old School Hurts," *New York Times Book Review*, January 31, 1982, p. 24.

13. The classic biography is still Madeleine B. Stern, *Louisa May Alcott* (Norman: University of Oklahoma Press, 1950), which should be supplemented by Stern's extensive criticism on Alcott. See also Sarah Elbert, *A Hunger for Home: Louisa May Alcott and "Little Women"* (Philadelphia: Temple University Press, 1984), and Martha Saxton, *Louisa May: A Modern Biography of Louisa May Alcott* (New York: Avon Books, 1978).

14. Richard H. Brodhead, "Starting Out in the 1860s: Alcott, Authorship, and the Post-bellum Literary Field," chap. 3 in *Cultures of Letters: Scenes of Reading and Writing in Nineteenth-Century America* (Chicago: University of Chicago Press, 1993), p. 89.

15. On cultural work, see Jane Tompkins, *Sensational Designs: The Cultural Work of American Fiction, 1790–1860* (New York: Oxford University Press, 1985). Two theoretically sophisticated, historically based studies of readers are Janice A. Radway, *Reading the Romance: Women, Patriarchy, and Popular Literature* (1984; reprint, with a new introduction by the author, Chapel Hill: University of North Carolina Press 1991), and Roger

Chartier, "Texts, Printing, Readings," in *The New Cultural History*, edited by Lynn Hunt (Berkeley: University of California Press, 1989), pp. 154–75.

16. Some excellent examples of critical literature include Stern, *Critical Essays*; Alma J. Payne, *Louisa May Alcott: A Reference Guide* (Boston: G. K. Hall, 1980); Judith C. Ullom, *Louisa May Alcott: A Centennial for Little Women: An Annotated Selected Bibliography* (Washington, D.C.: Library of Congress, 1969).

17. For nineteenth- and early-twentieth-century reviews, mainly in newspapers, see bMS Am 800.23, Alcott Family Papers, and Janet S. Zehr, "The Response of Nineteenth-Century Audiences to Louisa May Alcott's Fiction," *American Transcendental Quarterly*, n.s., I (December 1987): 323–42, which draws on this mostly undated collection.

18. For Foucaultian approaches, see Steven Mailloux, "The Rhetorical Use and Abuse of Fiction: Eating Books in Late Nineteenth-Century America," *boundary 2* 17 (Spring 1990): 133–57, and Brodhead, "Starting Out in the 1860s," pp. 69–106.

19. Elizabeth Janeway, "Meg, Jo, Beth, Amy and Louisa," *New York Times Book Review*, September 29, 1968, p. 42; Angela M. Estes and Kathleen Margaret Lant, "Dismembering the Text: The Horror of Louisa May Alcott's *Little Women*," *Children's Literature* 17 (1989): 98–123. See also Judith Fetterley, "*Little Women*: Alcott's Civil War" *Feminist Studies* 5 (Summer 1979): 369–83, and Linda K. Kerber, "Can a Woman Be an Individual?: The Limits of Puritan Tradition in the Early Republic," *Texas Studies in Literature and Language* 25 (Spring 1983): 165–78. ·

20. Madelon Bedell, "Introduction," *Little Women* (New York: Modern Library, 1983), p. xi, and Elaine Showalter, "*Little Women*: The American Female Myth, chap. 3 in *Sister's Choice: Tradition and Change in Women's Writing* (Oxford: Clarendon Press, 1991), p. 42. All quotations from *Little Women* are from the Modern Library edition, which is taken from 1869 printings of parts one and two.

21. Dorothy Richardson, *The Long Day: The Story of a New York Working Girl as Told by Herself* (1905; reprint, New York: Quadrangle Books, 1972), pp. 84–85. Alcott's juvenile fiction did not appear in the story papers most likely to be found in working-class homes; nor was it available in the Sunday school libraries to which some poor children had access. The latter might encounter Alcott in middle-class sites. In the late 1880s, for example, she was one of the three most popular authors at the reading room for "deprived" girls run by the United Workers and Woman's Exchange in Hartford; the others were Mrs. A. D. T. Whitney and Edgar Allen Poe. *Annual Report* 1 (1888): 8.

22. Lerner, *The Creation of Feminist Consciousness: From the Middle Ages to Eighteen-seventy* (New York: Oxford University Press, 1993).

23. Lewis M. Terman and Margaret Lima, *Children's Reading: A Guide for Parents and Teachers*, 2d ed. (New York: Appleton, 1931), pp. 68–84, found that "at every age girls read more than boys" (p. 68) and read more fiction. Half the adult female respondents in one study named *Little Women* as one of ten books read in childhood that they could recall most easily. Men's choices were far more varied.

24. By reading communities, I adopt the definition proposed by Janice Radway for those who, without necessarily constituting a formal group, "share certain assumptions about reading as well as preferences for reading material" based on their social location or, I would add, the position to which they aspired. "Interpretive Communities and Variable Literacies: The Functions of Romance Reading," *Daedalus* 113 (Summer 1984): 54. This essay builds on my earlier work on the interpretive conventions of specific reading communities in "Sense and Sensibility: A Case Study of Women's Reading in

Late-Victorian America," in *Reading in America: Literature and Social History*, edited by Cathy N. Davidson (Baltimore: Johns Hopkins University Press, 1989), pp. 201–25, and "Reading and Ambition: M. Carey Thomas and Female Heroism," *American Quarterly* 45 (March 1993): 73–103.

25. Carolyn G. Heilbrun emphasizes the lack of autonomous female models in literature and the exceptional nature of Jo in *Reinventing Womanhood* (New York: Norton, 1979), pp. 190–91, 212. See also Heilbrun, *Writing a Woman's Life* (New York: Norton, 1988).

26. June [1868], *Journals*, p. 166.

27. Niles told Alcott that her royalties were higher than any other Roberts Brothers author, including Harriet Beecher Stowe, whom he considered the American writer who could command the highest fees (Alcott possibly excepted). Niles to Alcott, June 7, 1871 (#25), February 17, 1873 (#39). Whether or not this was the case, Alcott was the firm's best-selling author, an awareness registered in a poem she wrote and sent Niles entitled "The Lay of a Golden Goose." Myerson and Shealy, "The Sales of Louisa May Alcott's Books," p. 67, settle on $103,375 as the most accurate estimate of Alcott's earnings with Roberts Brothers between 1868 and 1886; this figure does not include foreign sales or magazine earnings.

28. Other "juvenile" classics that appeared about the same time were *Hans Brinker; or, The Silver Skates* (1865) by Mary Mapes Dodge and *The Story of A Bad Boy* (1869) by Thomas Bailey Aldrich. A 1947 source claims that these titles, along with Little Women, "initiated the modern juvenile." *One Hundred Influential American Books Printed before 1900: Catalogue and Addresses: Exhibition at The Grolier Club* (New York: The Grolier Club, 1947), p. 106. Also of the period, though less highly esteemed, were *Elsie Dinsmore* (1867) by Martha Finley and Horatio Alger Jr.'s *Ragged Dick* (1868).

29. See Richard L. Darling, *The Rise of Children's Book Reviewing in America, 1865–1881* (New York: Bowker, 1968). Though he compared Alcott as a satirist to William Makepeace Thackeray and Anthony Trollope and thought her "extremely clever," James took her to task for her "rather vulgar prose" and her "private understanding with the youngsters she depicts, at the expense of their pastors and masters." *Nation*, October 14, 1875, pp. 250–51, reprinted in Stern, *Critical Essays*, pp. 165–66.

30. Elizabeth Segel, "'As the Twig Is Bent . . . ': Gender and Childhood Reading," in *Gender and Reading: Essays on Readers, Texts, and Contexts*, edited by Elizabeth A. Flynn and Patrocinio P. Schweickart (Baltimore: The Johns Hopkins University Press, 1986), pp. 165–86, is a useful brief analysis. See also Daniel T. Rodgers, *The Work Ethic in Industrial America, 1850–1920* (Chicago: University of Chicago Press, 1978), pp. 125–52, and R. Gordon Kelly, ed., *Children's Periodicals of the United States* (Westport, Conn.: Greenwood Press, 1984).

31. See Edward G. Salmon, "What Girls Read," *Nineteenth Century* 20 (October 1886): 515–29, and the ad for a series of "Books for Girls" whose intended audience was those "between eight and eighteen. . . . for growing-up girls, the mothers of the next generation." *American Literary Gazette and Publishers' Circular (ALG)* 17 (June 1, 1871): 88.

32. Niles to Alcott, July 25, 1868 (#2).

33. *Little Women*, p. 290.

34. November 1, [1868] *Journals*, p. 167; Alcott to Elizabeth Powell, March 20, [1869], in *The Selected Letters of Louisa May Alcott*, edited by Joel Myerson and Daniel Shealy, associate ed. Madeleine B. Stern (Boston: Little, Brown, 1987), p. 125 (hereafter cited as *SL*). Erin Graham, "Books That Girls Have Loved," *Lippincott's Monthly Magazine*,

September 1897, pp. 428–32, makes much of Bhaer's foreignness and ungainliness. The author recalls reading Alcott after the age of thirteen, when more "lachrymose" heroines had "palled" and she and her friends "did not take kindly to the romantic passion."

35. Jo's standing as a tomboy was recognized—and even respected; an ad for *Little Men* noted that "when a girl, [Jo] was half a boy herself." *ALG* 17 (May 15, 1871): 49. For girls in early adolescence and/or for lesbian readers, the young Jo may have been the primary romantic interest.

36. A conversation with Dolores Kreisman contributed to this analysis.

37. See Rachel Blau DuPlessis, *Writing beyond the Ending: Narrative Strategies of Twentieth-Century Women Writers* (Bloomington: Indiana University Press, 1985).

38. *Harper's New Monthly Magazine*, August 1869, pp. 455–56, reprinted in Stern, *Critical Essays*, p. 83.

39. For an analysis of changes in girls' stories as the heterosexual imperative became stronger, see Martha Vicinus, "What Makes a Heroine?: Nineteenth-Century Girls' Biographies," *Genre* 20 (Summer 1987): 171–87.

40. Frank Preston Stearns, *Sketches from Concord and Appledore* (New York: Putnam, 1895), p. 82.

41. Niles to Alcott, April 14, 1869 (#4). On advertising techniques of the era, see Susan Geary, "The Domestic Novel as a Commercial Commodity: "Making a Best Seller in the 1850s," *Papers of the Bibliographical Society of America* 70 (1976): 365–93.

42. "Roberts Brothers, Boston," *ALG* 17 (July 1, 1871): 118. Led by *Little Women, An Old-Fashioned Girl*, and *Little Men*, Alcott's fiction for younger readers continued to sell. Her adult books, including *Hospital Sketches*, which received excellent reviews, did not do as well. In general, sales fell off in the late 1870s but picked up again in the 1880s with the repackaging of *Little Women* as a single volume and publication of eight titles in a "'Little Women' Series." Roberts Brothers Cost Books, including summary in Cost Book D [i], *87M-113, Little, Brown Papers, and Myerson and Shealy, "The Sales of Louisa May Alcott's Books."

43. An early ad called *Little Women* a "history of actual life" (*Boston Evening Transcript*, September 30, 1868, p. 3), while an undated source claimed: "It was known to friends and acknowledged by Miss Alcott herself that 'Little Women' is the transcript, more or less literal, of her own and her sisters['] girlhood" (torn clipping, probably an obituary, bMS Am 800.23, Alcott Family Papers). See also [Franklin B. Sanborn], "The Author of 'Little Women,'" *Hearth and Home*, July 16, 1870.

44. Letter in *St. Nicholas*, February 1878, p. 300.

45. "Little Things," at first handwritten, then typeset on a small press, was part of a national phenomenon. See Paula Petrik, "The Youngest Fourth Estate: The Novelty Toy Printing Press and Adolescence, 1870–1886," in *Small Worlds: Children and Adolescents in America, 1850–1950*, edited by Elliott West and Paula Petrik (Lawrence: University Press of Kansas, 1992), pp. 125–42. Alcott's correspondence with the Lukens sisters, which extended over fourteen years, is reprinted in *SL*; it was published earlier in the *Ladies' Home Journal*, 1896, pp. 1–2. The Alcott sisters had their own Pickwick Club in 1849.

46. Niles to Alcott, August 30, 1870 (#16), August 14, 1871 (#29). Unfortunately, only a few letters from Alcott's fans survive.

47. Letter from "Nelly," dated March 12, 1870, reproduced in Delamar, *Louisa May Alcott*, p. 146.

48. Alcott to the Lukens Sisters, October 2, 1874, *SL*, pp.185–86. Readers' disappointment with her appearance is a recurrent subject in Alcott's letters. Alice Stone Blackwell, who

knew the writer, found her "positively unpleasant looking." See Marlene Deahl Merrill, ed., *Growing Up in Boston's Gilded Age: The Journal of Alice Stone Blackwell, 1872–1874* (New Haven: Yale University Press, 1990), p. 174.

49. April [1869], *Journals*, p. 171.

50. Louisa May Alcott to Amos Bronson Alcott, [October 18, 1875], *SL*, p. 198; see also September-October 1875, *Journals*, pp. 196–97. It is an interesting commentary on changing sex and gender expectations that Alcott had the kind of fan appeal for teenage girls that in the twentieth century has been reserved for male pop singers.

51. "Jo's Last Scrape," pp. 45–65.

52. See, however, Richard H. Brodhead's stimulating discussion of Alcott's professional options in "Starting Out in the 1860s." An earlier, more amateur mode of "starting out" is analyzed by Joan D. Hedrick, "Parlor Literature: Harriet Beecher Stowe and the Question of 'Great Women Artists,'" *Signs* 17 (Winter 1992): 275–303. For an analysis of efforts to make "high culture" a safe space for men, see Hedrick, *Harriet Beecher Stowe: A Life* (New York: Oxford University Press, 1994); on the literary marketplace, see Susan Coultrap-McQuin, *Doing Literary Business: American Women Writers in the Nineteenth Century* (Chapel Hill: University of North Carolina Press, 1990).

53. "American Literature," [1878–79] *Addams Papers*, reel 27, frames 239–95.

54. Undated review of *Little Men* ("Capital" penciled in), bMS Am 800.23, Alcott Family Papers.

55. Stearns, *Sketches from Concord and Appledore*, p. 84. Nina Baym claims that Alcott and Stowe were the only women included in the American literary canon at the end of the century. Baym, *Women's Fiction: A Guide to Novels by and about Women in America, 1820–1870* (Ithaca: Cornell University Press, 1978), p. 23.

56. See, e.g., Louise Chandler Moulton, "Louisa May Alcott," *Our Famous Women* (1883; reprint, Hartford: A. D. Worthington, 1884), pp. 29–52, which was prepared with Alcott's assistance. Reports of Alcott's financial success appeared frequently in the press. An obituary estimated her earnings for *Little Women* alone at $200,000. "Death of Miss Alcott," *Ladies' Home Journal* May 1888, p. 3. The figure is high, but it attests to belief in her success.

57. In this sense, *Little Women* may be considered a book that extends readers' "horizons of expectations," to use Hans Robert Jauss's term. Jauss, "Literary History as a Challenge to Literary Theory," *New Directions in Literary History*, edited by Ralph Cohen (Baltimore: Johns Hopkins University Press), pp. 11–41.

58. It is a sign of the changing times that the Elsie books were banned from some libraries on the grounds that they were commonplace and not true to life. Esther Jane Carrier, *Fiction in Public Libraries, 1876–1900* (New York: Scarecrow Press, 1965), pp. 356–60.

59. For comparisons of the two authors, see the review of *An Old-Fashioned Girl* in *Nation*, July 14, 1870, p. 30, and Niles to Alcott, January 13, 1871 (#20). Niles reported that Stowe wanted to know why Alcott's books were "so much more popular" than Mrs. Whitney's, which she considered "equally as good." *Faith Gartney's Girlhood* had a long run in the Sunday school libraries.

60. *The Ladies' Repository* ([December 1868], p, 472), while finding *Little Women* "very readable," pointedly observed that it was "not a Christian book. It is religion without spirituality, and salvation without Christ."

61. Alcott's depiction of home theatricals drew the wrath of some evangelicals. Niles to Alcott, October 26, 1868 (#3). *The Christian Union*, edited by Henry Ward Beecher, evidently did not include her books on its Sunday School list, to Niles's great irritation.

Lawrence F. Abbott to Roberts Brothers, June 6, 1882, with appended note by Niles to Alcott (#128).

62. On tomboys, see Sharon O'Brien, "Tomboyism and Adolescent Conflict: Three Nineteenth Century Case Studies," in *Woman's Being, Woman's Place: Female Identity and Vocation in American History*, edited by Mary Kelley (Boston: G. K. Hall, 1979), pp. 35–172, which includes a section on Alcott, and Alfred Habegger, "Funny Tomboys," in *Gender, Fantasy, and Realism in American Literature* (New York: Columbia University Press, 1982), pp. 172–83. Habegger claims that although remembered today only in the figure of Jo March, the tomboy became a major literary type in the 1860s (pp. 172–73).

63. The Katy books of "Susan Coolidge," pen name of Sarah Chauncey Woolsey, another Roberts Brothers author, are perhaps closest to Alcott's. But even Katy Carr, who begins as another Jo, an ambitious, harum-scarum, and fun-loving girl, is severely punished for disobedience; only after suffering a broken back and several years of invalidism does she emerge as a thoughtful girl who will grow into "true womanhood."

64. By the early twentieth century Franklin B. Sanborn, a New England writer and reformer, claimed that Alcott was more widely read than any other of the "'Concord Authors,' so-called." Sanborn, *Recollections of Seventy Years* (Boston: Richard G. Badger, 1909), 2:342, 338. He had earlier deemed her very American in "her humor, her tastes, her aspirations, her piety." [Sanborn], "The Author of 'Little Women.'" English reviews emphasized Alcott's Americanness.

65. Roosevelt, *An Autobiography* (1913; reprint, New York: De Capo Press, 1985), p. 17.

66. Gilman, *The Living of Charlotte Perkins Gilman* (1935; reprint, New York: Harper and Row, 1975), p. 35.

67. Baker, *Fighting for Life* (New York: Macmillan, 1939), pp. 17, 9.

68. Franklin Whitall Smith to Thomas, February 20, 1870, *The Papers of M. Carey Thomas in the Bryn Mawr College Archives*, edited by Lucy Fisher West (Woodbridge, Conn.: Research Publications, 1982) (hereafter cited as MCTP), reel 58. Thomas's reading is analyzed more fully in Sicherman, "Reading and Ambition"; on *Little Women*, see pp. 80–83.

69. M. Carey Thomas Journal, June 20, 1870, MCTP, reel 1.

70. Elizabeth King Ellicott to Thomas, November 23 [1879], MCTP, reel 39.

71. See Marjorie Housepian Dobkin, ed., *The Making of a Feminist: Early Journals and Letters of M. Carey Thomas* (n.p.: Kent State University Press, 1979), pp. 66–67 and passim.

72. These remarks draw on Sicherman, "Reading and Ambition," pp. 82–83.

73. *Little Women*, pp. 328–29.

74. See Nina Auerbach, *Communities of Women: An Idea in Fiction* (Cambridge: Harvard University Press, 1978), pp. 55–73.

75. On this subject, see Lee Virginia Chambers-Schiller, *Liberty, a Better Husband: Single Women in America: The Generation of 1780–1840* (New Haven: Yale University Press, 1984). In her next book, *An Old-Fashioned Girl*, Alcott ventures much further in envisioning a life of singlehood and lovingly depicts a community of self-supporting women artists.

76. Simone de Beauvoir, *Memoirs of a Dutiful Daughter*, translated by James Kirkup (1949; reprint, Cleveland: World Publishing Co., 1959), pp. 94–95. Despite differences in culture and religion, de Beauvoir found many parallels between the March family and her own, in particular the belief "that a cultivated mind and moral righteousness were

better than money" (p. 94). According to Deirdre Bair, de Beauvoir had read *Little Women* by the time she was ten. Bair, *Simone de Beauvoir: A Biography* (New York: Summit Books, 1990), pp. 68–71.

77. Bair, *Simone de Beauvoir*, p. 69. Shirley Abbott, who grew up in Arkansas in the 1940s and 1950s, was also dismayed by Jo's rejection of Laurie: "I took a page in my notebook and began: / JO AND LAURIE / by Louisa May Abbott"; she literally rewrote the ending to suit herself. Shirley Abbott, *The Bookmaker's Daughter: A Memory Unbound* (New York: Ticknor and Fields, 1991), pp. 133–34.

78. These conclusions emerge from my reading and from discussions of *Little Women* with more than a dozen women. They were highly educated for the most part and mainly over fifty, but some women under thirty also felt passionately about the book. Most of my informants were white, but see n. 81 below.

79. On the relation of class and education to cultural preferences, see Pierre Bourdieu, *Distinction: A Social Critique of the Judgment of Taste*, translated by Richard Nice (Cambridge: Harvard University Press, 1984). There was greater overlap in cultural tastes in the nineteenth-century United States than Bourdieu's analysis of late-twentieth-century France allows.

80. Mary Church Terrell, *A Colored Woman in a White World* (1940; reprint, New York: Arno Press, 1980), p. 26. Alfreda M. Duster, ed., *Crusade for Justice: The Autobiography of Ida B. Wells* (Chicago: University of Chicago Press, 1970), pp. 7, 21–22. Wells observed that in her early years, she "never read a Negro book or anything about Negroes."

81. *The Middletown Press*, June 1, 1994, p. B1, and Ann Petry to author, letter postmarked July 23, 1994; I am grateful to Farah Jasmine Griffin for the *Middletown Press* reference. *Little Women* continues to play an important role in the lives of some young black women. A high school student in Jamaica, for example, rewrote the story to fit a local setting. And a young, African American academic felt so strongly about *Little Women* that, on learning about my project, she contended with some heat that Aunt March was unfair in taking Amy rather than Jo to Europe; she seemed to be picking up a conversation she had just left off. Comments like these and Petry's suggest the need for research on the interaction between race and class in African American women's reading practices. A conversation with James A. Miller was helpful on this point.

82. Edith Wharton, *A Backward Glance* (New York: Appleton-Century, 1934), p. 51. Annie Nathan Meyer, a member of New York's German-Jewish elite who describes the authors in the family library as "impeccable," claims that Alcott was the only writer of children's books she could "endure." Meyer, *It's Been Fun: An Autobiography* (New York: Henry Schuman, 1951), pp. 32–33.

83. Richardson, *The Long Day*, pp. 75–86 (quotation, p. 86); I am grateful to Michael Denning for pointing out this episode. *The Long Day*, which purports to be the story of an educated woman forced by circumstances to do manual labor, must be used with caution. It was initially published anonymously, and many scenes read like sensational fiction. Leonora O'Reilly, a feminist trade unionist, was so outraged at the book's condescension and its insinuations that working-class women were immoral that she drafted a blazing indictment. Leonora O'Reilly Papers, edited by Edward T. James, *Papers of the Women's Trade Union League and Its Principal Leaders* (Woodbridge, Conn.: Research Publications, 1981), reel 9.

84. Michael Denning, *Mechanic Accents: Dime Novels and Working-Class Culture in America* (London: Verso, 1987), pp. 197–200, analyzes *Little Rosebud's Lovers* as a "Cinderella tale." He suggests that stories read by the middle class tended to depict working-class

women as victims (of seduction and poverty) rather than as triumphant. Joyce Shaw Peterson, "Working Girls and Millionaires: The Melodramatic Romances of Laura Jean Libbey," *American Studies* 24 (Spring 1983): 19–35, also views Libbey's stories as a "success myth for women." There were other sorts of female working-class traditions than the one suggested here, particularly among the politically aware. These included reading circles, some with a particular political or philosophical slant, and various efforts at "self-improvement." See, e.g., n. 83.

85. I have discussed Jewish immigrants at some length because of the abundance of evidence, not because I view them as the only model for an alternative reading of *Little Women*.

86. *My Mother and I* (New York: Macmillan, 1917) is a problematic book. Some contemporaries reviewed it as autobiographical fiction, but recent critics have tended to view it as autobiography. Theodore Roosevelt must have considered it the latter when he lauded it as a "really noteworthy story" of Americanization in the foreword. (A shorter version appeared in the *Ladies' Home Journal*, October 1916, as "My Mother and I: The Story of How I Became an American Woman, with an Appreciation by Theodore Roosevelt, to Whom the Manuscript Was Sent.") Moreover, the facts Stern gave out about her early life—including her status as an Eastern European Jewish immigrant—correspond with the narrator's history. Stern's older son, however, maintains that his mother was native born and Protestant and claimed her Jewish foster parents as her biological parents to hide her out-of-wedlock birth. T[homas] Noel Stern, *Secret Family* (South Dartmouth, Mass.: T. Noel Stern, 1988). Ellen. M. Umansky, who generously shared her research materials with me, concludes in "Representations of Jewish Women in the Works and Life of Elizabeth Stern," *Modern Judaism* 13 (1993): 165–76: "[I]t may be difficult if not impossible to ever determine which of Stern's literary self representations reflected her own experiences" (p. 174). Sources that appear to substantiate Elizabeth Stern's foreign and Jewish birth are the U.S. Census for 1900 and for 1910, which both list her birthplace as Russia; the certificate of her marriage, which was performed by a prominent Orthodox rabbi in Pittsburgh; and Aaron Levin's will, which lists Stern as his oldest child.

Despite its contested status, I have drawn on *My Mother and I* because Stern's choice of *Little Women* as a critical marker of American aspirations is consistent with other evidence. The narrative's emphasis on the differences between immigrant and American culture comports with representations in less problematic works by Jewish immigrant writers. Moreover, whatever the facts of Stern's birth, she lived with the Jewish Levin family for many years.

87. *My Mother and I*, pp. 69–71.

88. Ibid., pp. 71–72.

89. Leo Lerman, "Little Women: Who's in Love with Miss Louisa May Alcott? I Am," *Mademoiselle*, December 1973, reprinted in Stern, *Critical Essays*, p. 113. See also Stephan F. Brumberg, *Going to America, Going to School: The Jewish Immigrant Public School Encounter in Turn-of-the-Century New York City* (New York: Praeger, 1986), pp. 121–22, 141.

90. See, e.g., *The Louisa Alcott Reader: A Supplementary Reader for the Fourth Year of School* (1885; reprint, Boston: Little, Brown, 1910) and Fanny E. Coe, ed., *The Louisa Alcott Story Book* (Boston: Little, Brown, 1910). The former included fairy tales, the latter, more realistic stories, with the moral printed beneath the title in the table of contents, e.g., "Kindness to horses" and "Wilfulness is punished." In Philadelphia in the 1930s, *Little Women* was on a list from which seventh graders could choose books for reports.

91. Rose Cohen, *Out of the Shadow* (New York: Doran, 1918), p. 253.
92. "'Zelda' on Books," English Department, *Jewish Daily News* (New York), August 4, 1903; see also "Just Between Ourselves, Girls," ibid., July 12, 1903. Stokes also recommended the novels of Charles Dickens, George Eliot, Charlotte Brontë, and Grace Aguilar, an English Jewish writer, as well as Jewish and general history. I am grateful to Harriet Sigerman for the references.
93. Mary Antin, *The Promised Land* (Boston: Houghton Mifflin, 1912), pp. 257, 258–59.
94. Showalter, "*Little Women*," pp. 55–56; Madeleine B. Stern to author, July 31, 1993. The English edition continued to be published in two volumes, the second under the title *Good Wives*.
95. Paradoxically, in view of the sanctity of Victorian motherhood, *Little Women* is one of the few books of its era (adult or juvenile) that depicts a strong maternal figure; mothers are often dead, ill, or powerless. See Baym, *Women's Fiction*. The female-dominated March household and the figure of Marmee may, in consequence, have had a special appeal to Alcott's early readers.
96. Elizabeth Young, "Embodied Politics: Fictions of the American Civil War" (Ph.D. diss., University of California, Berkeley, 1993), reading *Little Women* in conjunction with *Hospital Sketches*, views it as a "war novel" (p. 108).

Contributors

Carol Devens (Green-Ramirez) was professor of history at Central Michigan University from 1992 until her passing in 1997. Devens also served as editor of the *Michigan Historical Review* and was the author of *Countering Colonization: Native American Women and Great Lakes Missions, 1630–1900* (1992). "Separate Confrontations: Gender as a Factor in Indian Adaptation to European Colonization in New France" appeared in *American Quarterly* (1986), and "'If We Get the Girls, We Get the Race': Missionary Education of Native American Girls" was published in the *Journal of World History* (1992).

Miriam Forman-Brunell is professor of history and the coordinator of the Girls' Studies Certificate at the University of Missouri-Kansas City. She is the author of *Babysitter: An American History* (2009) and *Made to Play House: Dolls and the Commercialization of American Girlhood* (1993; 1998). Forman-Brunell is coeditor of *The Girls' History and Culture Reader: The Twentieth Century* (2011), editor of *Girlhood in America: An Encyclopedia* (2002) and *The Story of Rose O'Neill: An Autobiography* (1997), and the series book editor of *Children and Youth: History and Culture*. She is also the codirector of *Children & Youth in History* http://chnm.gmu.edu/cyh/. Forman-Brunell has received fellowships from the National Endowment for the Humanities, National Woodrow Wilson Foundation, Smithsonian Institution, Andrew W. Mellon Foundation, and the Schlesinger Library.

Jane H. Hunter is professor of history and associate dean of the college at Lewis & Clark in Portland, Oregon. She is the author of *How Young Ladies*

Became Girls: The Victorian Origins of American Girlhood (2002) and *The Gospel of Gentility: American Women Missionaries in Turn-of-the-Century China* (1984). Her books have won the outstanding book prize from the History of Education Society and the Governors' Award of Yale University Press. Hunter has received funding from the National Endowment for the Humanities, the Schlesinger Library, and the Tanner Humanities Center at the University of Utah. Her current research interest is gender and Peace Corps/Philippines in the 1960s.

Anya Jabour is professor of history at the University of Montana. She is the author of *Marriage in the Early Republic* (1998) and *Scarlett's Sisters* (2007); the editor of *Major Problems in the History of American Families and Children* (2005); and coeditor, with Craig Thompson Friend, of *Family Values in the Old South* (2010). Her history of children in the Civil War South, *Topsy Turvy*, is forthcoming from Ivan R. Dee. Jabour's current research project is a biography of educator and reformer Sophonisba Preston Breckinridge. Jabour also is the recipient of the Helen and Winston Cox Award for Excellence in Teaching.

Anne Scott MacLeod is professor emerita at the University of Maryland. She is the author of *A Moral Tale: Children's Fiction and American Culture, 1820–1860* (1975), *American Childhood: Essays on Children's Literature of the Nineteenth and Twentieth Centuries (1996)*, and numerous articles on children's literature and American culture. MacLeod is also fellow and past president of the International Research Society for Children's Literature, and Distinguished Teacher-Scholar, University of Maryland.

Susan McCully is a lecturer in the department of theatre at the University of Maryland, Baltimore County. She is a scholar of feminist theatre and a dramaturg, as well as a playwright and performer. She has performed her one-woman show "Cyber Becomes Electra," at colleges and universities across the country, University of Toronto, University of Exeter and the Kolibri Pince in Budapest. At UMBC, she teaches a range of courses in theatre history, dramatic literature and works on the departmental productions in the role of dramaturg. She is a specialist in cross-gender casting and gender performance; she also teaches courses in queer theory and feminist representation for the Women's Studies Program.

Mary Niall Mitchell is associate professor of history at the University of New Orleans. She is the author of *Raising Freedom's Child: Black Children and Visions of the Future after Slavery* (2008). She has received fellowships and awards from the American Council of Learned Societies, the Harry Frank

Guggenheim Foundation, the Gilder Lehrman Institute of American History, the American Historical Association, the History of Education Society, and the Massachusetts Historical Society. The article reprinted here won the 2003 Constance Rourke Prize from the American Studies Association and the Anita S. Goodstein Junior Scholar's Award for Women's History from the University of the South, Sewanee.

Leslie Paris is an associate professor of history at the University of British Columbia. She is the author of *Children's Nature: The Rise of the American Summer Camp* (2008), coauthor of *A Paradise for Boys and Girls: Adirondack Summer Camps* (2006), coeditor of *Lost Kids: Vulnerable Children and Youth in Twentieth-Century Canada and the United States* (2009), and coeditor of *The Girls' History and Culture Reader: The Twentieth Century* (2011). Paris has published in the *Journal of Women's History*, the *Journal of the History of Childhood and Youth*, and several edited collections on children and youth. She is currently writing a history of American childhood between 1965 and 1980.

Barbara Sicherman is William R. Kenan Jr., Professor Emerita, Trinity College (Hartford), where she taught History, American Studies, and Women's Studies. Her publications include *Well-Read Lives: How Books Inspired a Generation of American Women* (2010), *Alice Hamilton: A Life in Letters* (1984), *Notable American Women: The Modern Period* (1980), and *The Quest for Mental Health in America, 1880–1917* (1980). She has received fellowships from the Guggenheim Foundation, the National Endowment for the Humanities, the Bellagio Study and Conference Center, and the Radcliffe Institute.

Carroll Smith-Rosenberg is Mary Frances Berry Collegiate Professor Emerita of History at the University of Michigan. She is the author of *Religion and the Rise of the American City* (1971) and *Disorderly Conduct: Visions of Gender in Victorian America* (1985), and the coeditor of *Women in Culture and Politics: A Century of Change* (1986). Smith-Rosenberg is also the author of numerous articles on gender and class, sexuality and culture in nineteenth-century America.

Christine Stansell is Stein-Freiler Distinguished Service Professor of American History and the College at the University of Chicago. Her books include *City of Women: Sex and Class in New York, 1789–1860* (1986); *American Moderns: Bohemian New York and the Creation of a New Century* (2000); and, most recently, *The Feminist Promise 1792 to the Present* (2010). Stansell has been a fellow of the Guggenheim Foundation and the Mary Bunting Fellow at the Radcliffe Institute.

Nancy M. Theriot is professor and chairperson of the Women's and Gender Studies Department at the University of Louisville. She is author of *Mothers and Daughters in Nineteenth-Century America: The Biosocial Construction of Femininity* (1996), "Childhood, Health and the Family in Nineteenth- and Early Twentieth-Century America"; *Everyday Life & Women in America, 1800–1920* (Adam Matthew Publications, 2006) http://www.amdigital.co.uk/collections/ Everyday-Life; and articles on the history of women and medicine.

Deborah Gray White is a Board of Governors Professor of History at Rutgers University. She is the author of *Ar'n't I A Woman? Female Slaves in the Plantation South* (1985, 1999), *Too Heavy A Load: Black Women in Defense of Themselves, 1894–1994* (1999), and *Let My People Go: African American 1800–1865* (1999), and the editor of *Telling Histories: Black Women Historians in the Ivory Tower* (2008). Professor White has received fellowships from the Guggenheim Foundation, the Woodrow Wilson International Center for Scholars, the ACLS, the American Association of University Women, and the National Research Council/Ford Foundation.

Index

Fictional character names are printed within 'single quotes.'
A *t* next to a page number indicates a table on that page.

anthropology, 137

Antin, Mary, 288

antislavery ideas. *See* abolitionist movement

Asian American girls, 11

Atlantic Monthly, 245

Aunt Jo's Scrap Bag (Alcott), 277

Avery, Cornelia, 98

Baker, S. Josephine, 280–81

Banks, N. P., 120–21

Barrie, J. M., 229

Barthes, Roland, 122

Beauvoir, Simone de, 283–84, 286–87n76

Beecher, Catharine, 59, 223

Beecher, Henry Ward, 130–31, 134–35

Bellows, Barbara L., 56

'Bhaer, Friedrich,' 275, 276

Bibb, Henry, 20–21, 23

Bibb, Malinda, 20–21

Birdson, Nelson, 16

birth control, 94

Bishop, Rufius, 76

Bixby, Sarah, 236–37

black girls. *See* African American girls

Boit, Mary, 252, 254, 256

Bonebright, Sarah, 203, 204

Bonnin, Gertrude, 104–5, 106, 111, 113, 114–15

books. *See* children's books; reading; specific books

Bordley, Elizabeth, 163, 164, 165

Boutwell, William, 107

Brace, Charles Loring, 92, 99–100

Breckinridge, Lucy, 219

Brent, Linda, 17

Breuer, Josef, 254

Briggs, Carolyn, 202

Brink, Carol, 199, 201, 226. *See also Caddie Woodlawn*

Brontë, Charlotte, 284–85

brothels, 83–84. *See also* prostitution

Brown, William Wells, 23

Brumberg, Joan Jacobs, 4, 193–94n6

Buffalo Ceremony, 114

Bulson, Susannah, 97

Bunyan, John, 279, 282

Burleigh, Margaret, 167

Burton, Harriet, 257–58, 263

Butler, Parke Lewis, 157

Butz, Rachel, 206, 207

Cabell, William. *See* "Grown Girls, Highly Cultivated" (Jabour), 31–32, 37

Caddie Woodlawn (Brink), 199–200

"The *Caddie Woodlawn* Syndrome: American Girlhood in the Nineteenth Century" (Scott), 8, 199–221

Callender, Eunice, 165

Calvert, Karen, 4–5, 226, 235

Carey, Matthew, 81

Carroll, Lewis, 90, 133

Censer, Jane Turner, 37

Charles, 121–22, 129–30, 139

Cheney, Ednah Dow, 287–88

Cherry Ripe (Millais), 133

Chesnut, Mary Boykin, 19

Child, Lydia Maria, 224, 225

childbearing, 19–20, 21–26

childbirth, 164, 177n66

childhood: assumptions of nineteenth century, 200–201; celebration of child as child, 215–16; child as adult-in-process, 215–16; child as agent of reform, 126–27; child as political tool, 142n12; freedom, 204–7, 209, 212; gender strictness relationship, 203–4; idealization of white little girls, 146n56; literature, 231–33; magazines, 239n22; parental attitudes and discipline, 206; pioneering families, 204; as racially shaped, 122–23; romantic attitudes, 215–16; sentimentalization by white people, 125–27; slave girls, 15–17; symptoms, 181; urban and town, 203; as vantage point for study of history, 5–6; work relationship, 203–4

child molestation, 90–93

child prostitution, 89–94. *See also* prostitution

children as agents of reform, 145n34

children's books: character studies, 215–16; girls' novels, 208; independence, 218–19; limitations for women, 217–20; loss of childhood, 209–10, 216; metaphors, 212–13, 216; middle class character, 207–8; moral values, 213–14, 216–17; romantic attitudes, 214. *See also* specific authors; specific books

children's history, 5–6. *See also* girls' history

Chinn, Nelson, 138

chlorosis: adolescence-adulthood transition,

185; alternatives, 192–93; child-rearing pattern, 185; controlling aspect, 189; education impact, 186–87; as exaggerated normality, 183–84; family structure, 185–88; as "family system" dysfunction, 184–85; feminine suffering and self-denial, 186–90; history, 180–81; ignorance and misunderstanding, 188, 197–98n46; mental state accompanying, 189–90; middle class character, 185; mother-daughter relationship, 185, 187, 191–92; as nervous disorder, 182; overview, 10, 180–81; psychoanalytic interpretation, 184; puberty, 189, 197–98n46; as rejection of female physical maturity, 187–90; romantic femininity relationship, 183–84; sexual abuse factor, 184–85, 195–96n30; social and cultural response explanation, 184

Chodorow, Nancy, 4

chores, 16, 156, 204, 244. *See also* housekeeping

Civil War. *See* abolitionist movement; whiteness (racial)

Clary, Anna, 203

Clay, Berry, 22

Clinton, Catherine, 32, 56

clothing, 21, 46, 56–57, 109, 132, 202–3, 223–25, 229, 231

Cody, Cheryll, 24

Cohen, Rose, 288

Comic Tragedies (Alcott), 277

consumer culture/commercial culture, 6, 11, 84, 100, 225, 261, 290

Coolidge, Susan, 213–14, 286n63

Corbin, Richard, 21

Couper, Mary Black, 166

courtship, 3, 19, 20, 24–26, 38–39, 41, 47, 49, 95, 97–98, 162, 256

Creevey, Caroline, 202–3

crippling metaphor, 212–13, 214, 216

Croswell, T. R., 235

Custis, Nelly Parke, 163, 165

Dally, Sarah, 96–97

Dalsimer, Katherine, 255

dancing, 34, 52, 71–75, 77, 83–84, 86

daughters: anxieties about, 131, 135n34; autonomy, 223, 234, 249, 251, 256, 260; different experiences and expectations of elder and younger, 31–32, 34–35, 37, 39–41, 50; incest, 14n12, 127; parents' socialization of, 2, 9–10, 20, 31–33, 35–38, 40–44, 46–48, 49, 51–57, 59, 61, 200, 222, 225–26, 228, 230, 239n13, 242, 244–46, 248, 251, 272, 283; relationships to mothers, 4, 9–10, 12n5, 18–19, 24–26, 31, 37–39, 41, 48, 50, 104, 108, 112–15, 155, 157–59, 160–61, 174n45, 179–80, 185–89, 191, 193, 194n6, 197n37, 197n44, 252, 269n63, 290, 296n76; working-class, 81, 87- 89, 92, 95–96, 98, 100. *See also* diaries; education; friendship; mother/daughter tension; Native American girls

Davis, Glenn, 185

death and dying, 164–65, 177–78n71

"The Deathless Diary" (Repplier), 245

DeCamp, William H., 125

DeKay, Helena, 152–54, 156, 158, 161, 170n13

The Delineator, 230

Deloria, Ella, 113

demographics and general information, 6–12, 200–201

Deutsch, Helena, 167

Devens, Carol, 9, 104

diaries: adolescent separation from home, 255; advice literature, 246–47; communication, 256; as confessional, 254, 256; courtship, 256; economic and social changes, 243, 246; emotional spillover, 256–59; as female phenomenon, 245–46, 264–65n5; hysteria, 254; identity formation, 243; infatuations and romantic ties, 255–58; literary portrayal, 247–48, 251–53; middle and upper class character, 243; mother-daughter relations, 255, 260–61, 267n63, 267n64; overviews, 242–46; parental authority challenges, 250, 251–52, 261–62; parental prying, 249–50; personality formation, 243, 269n66; privacy issue, 249, 250; pros and cons, 248–49; psychoanalysis relationship, 254; resolutions and character-building, 251–52, 254; romanticism, 243, 269n66; self-discipline, 243, 246, 253–54; self-improvement, 252; sexuality, 255, 257; as tool for identification within family and social structures, 248–49, 251; Victorianism, 252–53

Dickens, Charles, 90, 279, 284–85

discipline, 200, 206, 228

Divine Book of Holy and Eternal Wisdom, 75

dolls: apprenticeship for domesticity role, 224–25; black v. white, 234; boys', 234–35; domestic apprenticeship, 237; domesticity relationship, 223–26; funerals, 230, 235–36, 240n29, 241n44; limitations on play time, 225–26; literature and culture, 231–33; in *Little Women*, 233; mail-order catalogues, 227; overview, 222–23; play varieties, 233–37; popularity v. other childhood pursuits, 235; post-Civil War prosperity and middle-class consumption, 237; pre-Civil War limitation and simplicity, 225–26, 237; retail suppliers, 227–28; rituals, 230; romanticization, 230; simple v. elaborate, 226, 231–21; socialization, 229–30, 231–33, 237; sources, 227–28; stereotypes, 232; thematic continuity, 237

Doll's Dressmaker, 228, 232

A Doll's Journey (Alcott), 228

The Dolls' Surprise Party, 233

The Dolls' Tea Party, 229–30

domesticity, 45, 53–54, 60, 107, 109, 126, 160, 162, 174–175n47, 179, 224, 225, 269, 287; girls resistance to, 186, 267n42, 275, training with dolls, 223

'Dora,' 247–48

Dougherty, Peter, 107

Downs, Rosina ("Rosa"), 120, 121–22, 127, 129, 133, 139

DuPont, Eleuthera, 161, 162

DuPont, Sophie, 162, 164–65, 166–67

Dyer, Mary Marshall, 71–72

Eckerson, Margaret, 247, 248

Edgeworth, Maria, 224

education: benevolence and good works, 55–57; character formation, 46; classical scholarship, 34–38, 44–46; "crises" of classically educated girls, 39–40, 49–51; curriculum changes, 9; high schools, 265n14; home instruction v. academies, 51–53; intellect v. marriageability, 39–44; liberal arts curriculum, 34–38, 44–46; lyceum system, 58–59; marriageability v. intellect, 39–44; mission schools for Native Americans, 104–15; Native American girls' traditional, 111–12, 113–14; new opportunities, 8–9; New Women, 242, 245; nineteenth century overview, 32–33; northeastern overview, 33; orientation toward practical social and economic reality, 46, 50–55; overviews, 8–9; parental responsibility redistribution, 40–42, 46, 48–49, 57–58; personal quality development, 37; practical orientation, 41–45, 49–52; religion and morality, 9, 55–57; republican womanhood, 34; self-improvement, 8–9, 58–59; shift from school to home at adolescence, 38–39; socialization, 53–55; social reform movements, 57–58; southern regional development, 40, 43–45, 59–60; southern regional overview, 32–33

Eight Cousins (Alcott), 274

Eliot, Emily, 250

Eliot, George, 233, 236

'Eliza,' 129

Elmwood, 44–46

Elsie Dinsmore (Finley), 279

Ely, Edmund, 113

Emerson, Mary, 166

Emlen, Peggy, 165–66

escape from family, 94–97. *See also* independence; prostitution

'Eva,' 127–28

Faith Gartney's Girlhood (Whitney), 279

Farnham, Christie Anne, 43, 45

Feaster, Gus, 18

Feinstein, Howard, 180

Female Moral Reform Society, 99

female power, 69–70, 76–78. *See also* trance possession phenomena

female world: acceptance of limitations and restrictions, 219–20; apprenticeship system, 159–60; emotional functions, 158; evidence, 155–56; geographical mobility, 157; kinship, 157; as ongoing across centuries, 156–57; overview, 179–80; rituals, 163–65, 177–78n71, 177n66; rural, 156; separation from male world, 155, 157–58, 162, 169n3, 171n21, 176n57; social institutionalization, 155–56; social patterns, 175n48; transitional roles, 160–63, 175n48; urban and town, 156; vacation patterns, 156. *See also* specific children's books

"The Female World of Love and Ritual: Relations Between Women in Nineteenth-Century America" (Smith-Rosenberg), 8, 149–78

feminine suffering and self-denial, 212–13, 214

feminism, 70, 78–79n3

Finley, Martha, 279

Fluker, Frances, 19

Foote, Mary Hallock, 152–54, 156, 158, 161, 170n13

Forman-Brunell, Miriam, 5, 11, 222

foster mothers, 160–63

Foucault, Michael, 74, 77, 243, 257, 264n3, 267n30

freedpeople, 121

Freud, Sigmund, 168, 254, 267n42

Friedman, Jean, 56

friendship: adolescence, 160–63, 175n48; cultural norms, 150–51; duration, 166–67; education, 175n48; emotional functions, 158; factors supporting, 155; geographical mobility, 172n28; middle class perspective, 151; mother-daughter relations, 159–60, 174n45; ongoing continuum as social institution, 169n2; psychosexual perspective, 150, 155, 167, 168–69; romantic rhetoric, 163, 165, 167, 170n13, 171n17; sensuality, 151–52, 153–55, 163, 165, 167; social acceptance and encouragement, 167–68

Fulkes, Minnie, 19

Fuller, Margaret, 282

Fuller family. See education; "Grown Girls, Highly Cultivated" (Jabour)

Gale, Zona, 236

Galloway, Mary, 96

Garnett family, 44

Gay, Peter, 244

Gibson, Elizabeth Bordley, 161, 166

Gilded Age, 223, 226, 228–29

Gilder, Helena DeKay, 152–54, 156, 158, 161, 170n13

Gilligan, Carol, 4

Gilman, Charlotte Perkins, 258–59, 280

girlhood: age differences, 8; assumptions about, 200–201, 224; changing notions of, 222, 280; comparisons between, 7; as cultural construction (idealizations, ideologies, ideas), 2–4, 11, 200, 222, 227, 245, 272;

education, 36; freedom, 8, 11, 113, 200–202, 207, 244, 249, 257, 290; girls' construction of, 223; interdisciplinary approaches to, 6; lengthening of, 8; meanings, 3, 5; race and, 122, 126, 130, 132–33; requirements of, 272; stages, 7–8; transitions, 7, 40, 44, 48, 163, 167, 180, 187, 207; varieties of historical experience, 1, 11, 186, 205, 223

the Girls' Book, 224

girls' history: broader historical movements, 5–6; demographic overrepresentation, 7, 11–12; feminist scholarship, 4; nineteenth century overview, 1–4; physical and sensual experience, 9–10; physical labor, 9; sources, 6; stages of girlhood, 7–8; themes and overviews, 7–11; women's history scholarship, 4

girls' spirit possession. See sexuality; Shakers; trance possession phenomena

girls' studies. See girls' history

Goldsmith, Amelia, 95

Goodman, Felicitas, 69

Gordon, Ann D., 4

Grayson, Charles, 124

The Greek Slave (Powers), 131–33

Greeley, Horace, 81

Green, Rayna, 106

Green, W. M., 18

"green sickness." See chlorosis

Grew, Mary, 167

Groesbeck, Jane, 90

"Grown Girls, Highly Cultivated" (Jabour), 8–9

Gutman, Herbert, 24

Guy, Seymour Smith, 133

Hall, Charles, 106, 108, 109, 114

Hall, G. Stanley, 234

Hall, Sherman, 112

Hallock, Molly, 152–54, 156, 158, 161, 170n13

Hamilton, Agnes, 249–50, 253–54

Hamilton, J. G., 107–8

Hampton, Fanny, 157

Hanks, George, 120–21

Harper's Bazaar, 228

Harper's New Monthly Magazine, 276

Harper's Weekly, 121, 129

Hart, Helen, 255

Hart, James S., 278

Heininger, Mary Lynn Stevens, 232
History of Prostitution (Sanger), 80
The History of Sexuality (Foucault), 74
Hodes, Martha, 125
Holmes, Joseph, 16
Holt, Luther Emmett, 228
homoerotic ritual practice. *See* trance possession phenomena
homosocial networks. *See* female world
housekeeping, 16, 39–42, 44, 109–11, 204. *See also* chores
House of Refuge, 90, 93, 95, 96, 102n30
Hubbard, Marian, 98–99
Hunt, Mary, 234
Hunt, Una, 203, 206
Hunter, Jane, 5, 9, 242
hysteria, 180, 257–58, 267n42

idealization, 126–27, 145n34, 146n56
"'If We Get the Girls, We Get the Race': Missionary Education of Native American Girls" (Devens), 9, 104–19
immigrant girls, 1, 228, 244, 273, 288
incest, 126–27
independence: children's books, 218–19; diaries, 248–49, 251; 'Jo March,' 284; metaphors, 212–13, 216; prostitution, 98–99
industrialism, 245
Inness, Sherrie, 5
"Inscribing the Self in the Heart of the Family: Diaries and Girlhood in Late-Victorian America" (Hunter), 9, 242–69
Inskeep, Maria, 157

Jabour, Anya, 8–9, 21
Jack and Jill (Alcott), 210–13
James, Alice, 253, 254
James, Henry, 253, 274
James, William, 253
Jefferis, Edith, 158
Jefferis, Martha, 157–58
Jerome, W. S., 246–47, 248
'Jill,' 210–11, 212–13
'Jo.' *See* 'March, Jo'
Johnson, Mary, 138
Jo's Boys (Alcott), 278
"Jottings vs. Doings" (Eckerson), 247
juvenile prostitution, 89–94. *See also* prostitution

Kasson, Joy, 132
'Kate,' 251–52
'Katy,' 213–14
Kelly, Bridget, 95
Kemble, Frances, 16, 21
Kerber, Linda K., 32
Kilbride, Dan, 52
King, Bessie, 281
Kingsbury, Alice, 206
Kinney, Constance, 163

labor. *See* childbearing; work
Lacy, William, 41
Ladies' Industrial Association, 81
Larcom, Lucy, 1, 2, 4, 204–5, 207, 209, 225, 226
Lasch, Christopher, 180
Latina girls, 11
'Laurie (Theodore Laurence),' 275, 276
Lawrence, Catherine, 134
Lawrence, Fanny, 121, 134–35, 137
Lebsock, Suzanne, 56
Lee, Mother Ann, 70, 71, 73
Leslie, Eliza, 224, 226
Lewis, Eleanor ("Nelly") Parke Custis, 161, 164, 166
Lewis, Jan, 44
Libbey, Laura Jean, 285
Liberian Society, 45
Liddell, Alice, 133
"The Life Cycle of the Female Slave" (White), 8, 15–26
literacy. *See* education; reading
'Little Eva,' 127–28
Little Men (Alcott), 278, 280
Little Rosebud's Lovers; or, A Cruel Revenge (Libbey), 285
Little Women (Alcott): acceptance of limitations and restrictions, 219; as American in nature, 286–88, 286n64, 298n86; as bildungsroman, 281–84; black women, 297n81; competitors, 293n28; contrast to other contemporary girls' books, 279–80; cultural norms reflected, 284–88; dolls, 233; early success, 271; fans, 280–84; history, 274–80; importance, 292n23; Jewish immigrant women, 286–88; middle class character, 284–88, 292n21; overviews, 270–74, 280, 288–90; as quasi-autobiographical, 209–10, 276–77, 294n43; reader

245; Victorian era roots, 242–43, 244–45, 262–63, 264n1; work aspirations, 245

New York Missionary Society, 105

New York Times, 137–38

New York *Tribune*, 123, 123–24

Nichols, Marian, 250

Nichols, Rose, 249

Niles, Thomas Jr., 270, 271

nineteenth century general information and demographics, 6–12, 200–201

Norris, Charlotte, 252–53

nursery, 229–30

O'Connor, Michael, 91

octoroons, 136

"'Oh I Love Mother, I Love Her Power': Shaker Spirit Possession and the Performance of Desire," 9–10, 69–79

An Old-Fashioned Girl (Alcott), 280

"On the Condition of Women" (Wirt), 34

Optic, Oliver, 275, 284–85

Palmer, Erastus Dow, 132

patriarchy, 76–78, 99. *See also* powerlessness

Pattee, Asa, 72

Patterson, Daniel, 70, 71

Paulen, Mary, 161

Peck's Bad Boy (Peck), 232

peer culture, 5–6, 88, 93, 113, 249, 255, 263

Peter Pan (Barrie), 229

Petry, Ann, 285

photography, 10, 120–22, 135–40, 144n28, 144n29, 147n76

Pilgrim's Progress (Bunyan), 279, 282

Pittsburgh Post, 236

Plantation Manual (Weston), 21

play, 1, 6, 11, 16–17, 92, 113, 222–23, 225, 229, 239n21; boys, 234–35; changing attitudes about, 222, 224, 229, 231–32, 236; with dolls, 223, 229, 231, 233; and emotions, 230–31, 235; exploitation disguised as, 61, 91; formalization of, 226; forms of, 34, 45, 203–4, 213, 226, 235, 270, 277, 279, 281; as language, 223, 237; material culture of, 11; preferences, 226; prescriptions, 233–34, 237; as resistance, 6, 11, 235–36. *See also* dolls; tomboy

"The Politics of Dollhood in Nineteenth-Century America" (Forman-Brunell), 11, 222–241

power, 69–70, 76–78. *See also* trance possession phenomena

powerlessness, 69–70, 76–78

Powers, Hiram, 131

Pratt, Richard H., 108

Prentiss, Elizabeth Payson, 251–52

Presbyterian Board of Foreign Missions (BFM), 105

Progressivism, 263. *See also* New Women

propaganda, 10, 121–24. *See also* abolitionist movement

prostitution: brothels, 83–84; contradictions, 99–100; demographics, 87–89; economic reality v. social choice, 88–89; imagery, 99–100; inclination, 86–87; judgments based on class, 84–85; overview, 10; pedophilia relationship, 90–93; rape trials, 91–92, 103n32, 103n33; related problems, 89–98; roots, 86–87; "ruin" association, 85; social outcry against, 80–81; sophistication and masculine urbanity link, 84–85; statistics, 81–83, 82t; temporary, 83; urban v. rural environment appeal, 97; working class v. middle class, 84–85, 102n31; work reality for young women v., 85–87

psychosomatic illness. *See also* chlorosis

"Psychosomatic Illness in History: The 'Green Sickness' among Nineteenth-Century Adolescent Girls" (Theriot), 10, 179–98

puberty: childhood freedom v., 202, cultural norms surrounding, 188–90; ignorance and misunderstanding, 188, 197–98n46; Native American girls, 114; overviews, 7–8. *See also* adolescence

Rabinowitz, Richard, 243, 264–65n5

Randall, Rebecca, 220

rape trials, 91–92, 103n32, 103n33

reading, 243, 264n2

"Reading *Little Women*: The Many Lives of a Text" (Sicherman), 11, 270–299

Reardon, Rosanna, 91

'Rebecca,' 214, 215, 217, 218, 230

Rebecca (little slave girl), 121–22, 129, 133, 136, 139

Rebecca of Sunnybrook Farm (Wiggin), 214–18

Repplier, Agnes, 245

republican womanhood, 34, 223–24

Reynolds, Mary, 22
Richards, Laura, 206
Richardson, Dorothy, 285
Richmond Female Academy, 34
Ripley, Sarah Alden, 157, 159–60, 162, 163–64, 165, 166
The Rise and Progress of the Serpent from the Garden of Eden to the Present Day with a Disclosure of Shakerism Exhibiting a General View of Their Real Character and Conduct from the First Appearance of Ann Lee (Dyer), 71–72
rituals, 163–65
Robinson, Harriet, 226
romanticism, 183–84, 215–16, 218
romanticism-moralism tension, 243–46
Roosevelt, Theodore, 280
"'Rosebloom and Pure White,' Or So It Seemed" (Mitchell), 10, 120–148. *See also* abolitionist movement; idealization; photography; romanticism
Rothman, Ellen, 256
Rush, Benjamin, 34, 35–36

Sanger, William, 80, 81–82. *See also* prostitution
Schlatter, Eliza, 166–67
schooling. *See* education
Scott, Anne Firor, 32–33
"Scourged Black," 136
Second Great Awakening, 105
self-discipline. *See* diaries
sex trade. *See* prostitution
sexual exploitation, 10
sexuality: diaries, 255, 257; idealization of white little girls v., 146n56; little white girls, 133; miscegenation, 136–37; mulatto mistresses of white men, 147n82; Shaker girls' trance possession phenomena, 69–70, 73–78; slave girls, 19, 25, 133, 134–35
sexual maturation, 9–10, 17–20, 25. *See also* puberty
sexual repression, 74–78. *See also* powerlessness; Shakers
Shakers: beliefs and practices, 70; female power, 76–78; feminism, 78–79n3; homosexuality, 75; identification, 70; music and dance, 71–72, 73, 74, 77–78; patriarchy, 76–78; religious ritual, 79n5; rule codification, 75–76; sensuality, 75; songs, 71–72,

73, 74, 77–78; theatricality of ritual, 71–72; vilification by contemporary society, 72, 75; visionists, 73–74
Shawl-Straps (Alcott), 277
"She Couldn't: Story for Big Girls" (Wells), 247–48
Sheppard, Anne Jefferis, 157, 158, 161, 164
Sheppard, Moses, 158, 164
Showalter, Elaine, 255
Sicherman, Barbara, 5, 11, 263
Simon, Charles E., 183
sisters, 9, 16, 37, 47–49, 53–54, 56, 58–59, 62n21, 73, 77, 97, 114, 149–50, 157–58, 160–64, 189, 199–200, 204, 214, 221n17, 222–26, 228–29, 238n10, 247, 250–51, 253, 259–60, 270, 272, 276–78, 282–83, 290. *See also* female world
slave girls: as agents of reform, 126–27; childbearing statistics, 24, 28n31; childhood, 15–17; coercion by slave owners for childbearing, 22–24; family stability and significance, 24–25; life passages, 15; maidservant role limitations, 26; marriage and childbearing patterns, 19–21; matrilineal tradition, 25–26; mixed race, 125; motherchild relationship, 26; mothers' protective efforts, 18–19; photography and pornography, 136–37; preadolescence, 17; puberty, 17–18; sexual freedom, 19; stereotype, 25; valuation for procreation, 20–24; white appearance, 120–27; work and socialization, 17–18
Smith, Clementina, 166
Smith, Elizabeth McKie, 161
Smith, Frank, 281
Smith, Jerome, 183–84
Smith, Margaret, 41
Smith-Rosenberg, Carroll, 4, 8, 10, 57, 179–80, 186
socialization: diaries, 248–49, 251; doll play, 229–30, 237; Native American girls, 105–6, 111–13, 115; overview, 11; slave girls, 16–19, 23, 25–26. *See also* education; friendship
social purity movement, 57–58
spirit possession, 78n2. *See also* Shakers
spirituality, 113–14
Stansell, Christine, 7, 10
Steckel, Richard, 24
Steedman, Carolyn, 5
Stein, Stephen J., 75–76

245; slave girls, 15–17, 21, 25, 26; teaching, 265n14. *See also* chores; housekeeping; prostitution

Work (Alcott), 283

writing, 243. *See also* diaries; education

"The Yellow Wallpaper" (Gilman), 258–59

Yiddisches Tageblatt, 288

Zitkala-Sa, 104–5, 106, 111, 113, 114–15, 118n36

The University of Illinois Press
is a founding member of the
Association of American University Presses.

———————————————————————

Composed in 10.5/13.5 Adobe Minion Pro
with Archer display
by Jim Proefrock
at the University of Illinois Press
Manufactured by Sheridan Books, Inc.

University of Illinois Press
1325 South Oak Street
Champaign, IL 61820-6903
www.press.uillinois.edu